'God is working for the Liberal Pa
book arrives just in time to tell us hc
is the political territory that lies ne
radar of this country. *God Under Howard* breaks the codes and tracks the Bible Belt strategies John Howard has brought from the US to advance his cause. The result is an eye-opening exploration of the real politics of Australia.'

David Marr

'Marion Maddox rightly says, "We do Australia's soul no service by forcing religion out of visible public life into unanalysed undercurrents". She brings us a convincing and disturbing picture of the capacity of John Howard, and some of his friends, to co-opt God for their own political agenda. Perhaps the ultimate irony is that, when mainstream church leaders try to enter the discussion and reclaim the God they represent, Howard in effect tells them to "stop meddling" while at the same time taking advantage of what he sees as their capacity to deliver cheap welfare. This is an academically responsible but very readable book—one which should alert us all to significant dimensions of political cunning.'

Dorothy McRae-McMahon
Retired Uniting Church Minister and
Co-editor of the South Sydney Herald

'There is no doubt that your childhood religious instruction underwrites your attitudes and prejudices for much of the rest of your life, but I am staggered at how these values can easily get lost in public life. Marion Maddox has attempted to do the impossible in spelling out the complicated place of religion in Australian politics today.'

Professor John Hewson

By the same author

For God and Country: Religious dynamics in Australian federal politics (2001)

GOD UNDER HOWARD

THE RISE OF THE RELIGIOUS RIGHT IN AUSTRALIAN POLITICS

MARION MADDOX

First published in 2005

Allen & Unwin
83 Alexander Street
Crows Nest NSW 2065
Australia
Phone: (61 2) 8425 0100
Fax: (61 2) 9906 2218
Email: info@allenandunwin.com
Web: www.allenandunwin.com

National Library of Australia
Cataloguing-in-Publication entry:

Maddox, Marion.
God under Howard : the rise of the religious right in Australian politics.

1st ed.
Bibliography.
Includes index.
ISBN 1 74114 568 6.

1. Religion and politics - Australia. 2. Church and state - Australia. 3. Religious right - Australia. 4. Australia - Politics and government - Religious aspects. I. Title.

322.10994

Set in 10.5/13.74 pt Sabon by Bookhouse, Sydney
Printed by Griffin Press, Adelaide

10 9 8 7 6 5 4 3

To Shirley Maddox and Robert Maddox,
models of thoughtful faith and generous politics

Contents

Preface and acknowledgements

God Under Howard is the result of long cooking with contributions from many people. That there was an untold story in Australia's negotiations between religion and politics, and that our collective poor understanding of those negotiations was working against the interests of the most marginalised in Australia, first came home to me in 1995. Having grown up in Sydney, I moved to Adelaide in 1989, married, and came to feel partly like a South Australian. On leave in Sydney from my job as a religious studies academic, I became fascinated by the unfolding drama of Hindmarsh Island. Religious traditions were being dragged through first a scorching trial by media and, eventually, the full blaze of a Royal Commission. As the story progressed, it became increasingly obvious that among the many shortcomings the saga revealed was a woeful lack of understanding about religion on the part of media, lawyers and the public. As speculations about the supposed content of a secret-sacred tradition swirled through the stifling Adelaide media world and then were taken as fact and subjected to empirical tests in the Royal

Commission, I began to reflect on how secular Australia's inability to deal with religion on its own terms was producing, or at least making space for, substantial political consequences.

My husband Michael Symons, who is, among many things a former investigative journalist turned professional writer, had been growing increasingly aghast at the blatantly ideological coverage the issue was receiving in virtually all mainstream media. He suggested we collaborate on a book about the saga. The litigious atmosphere which was by then threatening any publication containing the words 'Hindmarsh Island' meant the book was never published; but the process of writing it stimulated the reflections on religion-politics intersections which has fed my academic work ever since. It also produced some still unreported dimensions of the way a minority religious tradition became an icon of the strange 'Us and Them' politics that eventually catapulted Howard to power. Some of those revelations are in chapter five of this book. My debt to Michael in the collaborative research that uncovered them is apparent in the footnotes which draw on interviews he conducted with key players.

Michael is also a visible presence in chapter four, which talks about our experiences of juggling work and family in a society increasingly remoulded in the image of Howard social conservatism. Less visible to the reader, but immeasurable to me, is Michael's contribution to the entire book through our ongoing conversation over a decade, through his thoughtful comments on the text (and tireless Googling of Dominionist websites), through his willingness to fit his own writing around the role of home-based carer for the past five years so that I could pursue my career, and through providing, along with our children Dorothy and Lawrence, my living reminder of 'family values' (if not always the ones often associated with that term).

After the Hindmarsh Island research, the next stage in the book's fermentation was a two-year stint at the University of Adelaide. By then, I was well into a PhD in political philosophy, and relished the opportunity to immerse myself in a more nuts-

and-bolts view of Australian politics than had been possible in religious studies. Nevertheless, it isn't every politics department that would hire a religious studies academic to fill a casual vacancy in Australian politics and, without the Adelaide department's interdisciplinary broadmindedness, I might never have had the opportunity to develop my gut feeling about religion's function as a mostly invisible but often powerful undercurrent in Australian politics. Conversations with colleagues there continued long after my contract wound up. I particularly thank Carol Bacchi, Carol Johnson and Jenny Stock for their ongoing friendship, encouragement and coaching on the finer points of Australian politics.

In 1999–2000, I was the fortunate recipient of the Australian Parliamentary Fellowship, based in Parliament House, Canberra. The unparalleled research resources of the Parliamentary Library, and the generous access I was given by present and past Members and Senators, resulted in my first book, *For God and Country: Religious dynamics in Australian federal politics,* published by the Department of the Parliamentary Library in 2001. In the process of writing it, I became interested in the increasingly organised efforts of an American-style religious right to gain a foothold in Australia's historically much more secular democratic institutions. *God Under Howard* develops that theme in new directions.

In mid-2000, my family and I moved to New Zealand so I could take up a position in religious studies at Victoria University, Wellington. I joined a department with a high profile in the developing understanding of religion-politics connections in Australasia, and a very supportive environment to continue my Australian research. My colleagues and students in religious studies and other departments provided valuable conversations, challenges and trans-Tasman comparisons which sharpened my view of what was happening back home. In addition, Victoria University provided financial support which enabled me to hire a research assistant to undertake archival searches in Australia, particularly helpful for chapter one. An earlier version of the archival findings appeared in *Journal of Australian Studies* 82, 2004.

That chapter also benefited from being presented as a conference paper to the Australasian Political Studies Association at its 2003 conference, and to seminars at the Parliamentary Library Information and Research Service, the University of New South Wales and the University of Sydney. Throughout the book's gradual fermentation, the opportunity to cross back and forth between religious studies and politics departments provided invaluable perspective. Also in 2003, I was awarded a Sabbatical Fellowship to the politics program in the Research School of Social Sciences at the Australian National University. The time, space, library resources and tea-room conversations there advanced the book considerably. I especially thank Marian Sawer for her encouragement and support.

Many other people provided indispensable source materials, shared reminiscences, commented on drafts, spotted Australian news items my New Zealand search engines were missing, checked details, and minded children. For reminiscences of Earlwood Methodist Church in the 1950s, I particularly thank Bob Howard, Peter Holden, Norma Hardy, Margaret Eyre, Tom Tregenza, Lauris Andrew, Brian Herbert and others who preferred not to be named. The Uniting Church archives in North Parramatta provided access to documents. Shirley Maddox co-ordinated research from the Sydney end, pored over back issues of the *Methodist,* scoured the minutes of church meetings and corrected my misunderstandings of 1950s Methodist language and protocol. Elizabeth Weiss and Rebecca Kaiser at Allen & Unwin provided encouragement and criticism as required. I am also indebted to Mike Mawson, Jonathan Nicholls, Irene Roberts, Rodney Smith, Lloyd Watson, Aliki Kalliabetsos, Jean O'Neill and anonymous referees. *God Under Howard* is an opinionated book, and the opinions, along with remaining errors, are my own.

Like John Howard, I was brought up in a family that was both unabashedly political and staunchly Methodist. Conversations about the relationship between religion and politics are among my earliest memories. But the politics that accompanied the Methodism of my childhood is unrecognisable compared with the religion and politics that have become part of Howard family folklore. This book is my attempt to trace how the God of Howard-style conservatism entered Australian politics, and what its influence has been.

M.M.
November 2004

A prince, therefore, need not necessarily have all the good qualities I mentioned above, but he should certainly appear to have them. I would even go so far as to say that if he has these qualities and always behaves accordingly he will find them harmful; if he only appears to have them they will render him service . . . To those seeing and hearing him, he should appear a man of compassion, a man of good faith, a man of integrity, a kind and a religious man. And there is nothing so important as to seem to have this last quality.

Niccolò Machiavelli, *The Prince* (1513), XVIII

CHAPTER ONE

Sunday morning at Earlwood Methodist

'Amen.' Reverend Cecil Collard folds his notes and steps down from the pulpit and the congregation rustles to life, ready for a hymn—probably one of the rollicking Methodist singalongs such as 'O For a Thousand Tongues to Sing', or a thunderer along the lines of 'Guide Me O Thou Great Jehovah'. They belt it out, a couple of hundred voices ringing the echoes of Welsh mining towns and Cornish chapels across the Sydney suburb of Earlwood. Then the morning service winds down: benediction, three-fold Amen and then—unless it is a communion Sunday—home for a hot midday dinner. For many, the day is already well underway: Christian Endeavour meetings had started at ten, and by 2.30 some two hundred young people and their teachers will be back for Sunday School. Then Fellowship Tea is in the church hall at five, followed by the evening service. In fact, church activities fill a good part of many people's week.

On this spring Sunday in 1961, the morning congregation would hear announcements about the Earlwood Methodist

Temperance Society and Mothers' Club, perhaps an update on mission projects and invitations to the social activities clustered around the church. Young people can punctuate their week with character-building Rays and Comrades (if girls) or Methodist Order of Knights (if boys), and physical culture class (girls) and cricket (boys). This particular Sunday, the church notices are evangelising on behalf of the C grade cricket team: 'Anyone among the young fellows interested in playing' is urged to contact John Howard.[1] He's keen to encourage new starters. The church's Quarterly Meeting minutes record that low enrolment in the previous year prevented the church team meeting its twelve pound ground fees, which John Howard covered out of his own pocket.[2]

Mona Howard and her four sons—twenty-one-year-old John is the youngest and her husband, Lyall, had died when John was fifteen—are familiar church faces. The Howard house is just across the road from the church. It is so handy that some congregation members recall the Howard boys taking up the back pew because the family's red setter dog insisted on coming.

Today's commentators almost automatically link John Howard's social conservatism and, therefore, his distinctive impact on governance, to his Methodist childhood. Methodism in the 1950s was credited with Howard's Indigenous affairs policies (what can you expect from the product of a missionary church?), reluctance to apologise to the stolen generations (who stole more children than missionaries?), reservations about reconciliation and multiculturalism (Methodists can't bear display and suspect difference), view of mutual obligation, industrial relations policies and belief in hard work as its own reward (that famous Protestant work ethic), emphasis on individual responsibility, support for censorship and retreat to picket-fence family values. The implication is that, while Howard's economics were a matter of considered political conviction developed through his career, his social policy was a kind of default mechanism, ingrained in childhood and never rethought (David Marr put it in a throwaway line: 'He's a good Methodist boy'.) Such attributions make it hard to remember that Howard has not been a Methodist boy for a long time. Neither, in Australia, has anyone else.[3]

Methodists became Uniting Church in 1977; by then Howard had already been long gone. In 1971 he married into Sydney Anglicanism and he identifies religiously as an Anglican. However, for many that carries nothing like the iconic weight of his childhood Methodism. As a rough indication of its explanatory force, a Google search found over twenty items describing the prime minister as a Methodist, nearly all linking his Methodism disapprovingly to some conservative policy position. (Throwaway references to Howard's Methodism are also relatively common outside any policy connection; for example, a letter to an editor asked, in connection with Howard's ability to withstand charges of dishonesty, 'Is this Methodist acting?')[4] By contrast, only three sites referred to his Anglicanism. Despite prominent events—notably the Hollingworth controversy—bringing the words 'John Howard' and 'Anglican' together in numerous news reports, opinion pieces and so on, writers eschew any temptation to connect the terms. All were straightforward biographical statements, innocent of policy overtones. The image of 'John Howard, Methodist' is evidently doing something in the public imagination beyond simple biography.

Howard himself has reinforced the impression of Methodism's special place in his political formation. In 1998, for example, he told ABC TV's *Compass* program that:

> Religion did play quite a role in my upbringing. I was brought up in a Methodist home, we went to a Methodist Sunday School and church . . . we talked about behaviour, but we didn't talk so much about theology and the more spiritual content . . . I still regard myself as having a strong Methodist deposit, I guess it's reflected in my attitude to some things like gambling. Though not drinking, I enjoy a drink . . .[5]

In contrast to early Methodists' association with labour politics and the genesis of the trade union movement,[6] Wesleyan egalitarianism in the Howard household translated into a 'distrust' of 'class division', with implications more aesthetic than political: 'We were brought up to—not to be hostile to what might be regarded as the upper classes, but there was a strong view in my family that people shouldn't be too pretentious. We were perhaps an understated people'.[7]

The explicitly political effect he attributed to his childhood Methodism was the idea of 'standing on your own two feet': 'They talk of the Protestant work ethic, and I was certainly brought up in the Protestant work ethic, very much . . . it's the idea of working and expecting some reward . . . And I regard that as part of the Protestant work ethic: that work has its own reward in return'.[8] Such reminiscences present a man forged in a quietly conservative denomination, where religion was a matter of private reflection and personal morality rather than public debate—let alone activism.

Finding the roots of Howard's social conservatism in his Methodist past carries a comforting subtext. To supporters, his social conservatism appears the product of a heartfelt commitment, contradicting any suggestion of political opportunism. To the Australian electorate, reared on larrikin anticlericalism, not liking its leaders to look religiously fanatical or excessive (we suspect fiery-eyed zealots), an association with an extinct denomination is particularly effective. What could be safer than a religion that no longer exists? 'John Howard, Methodist' also works its reassuring magic on those to whom Howard's social policy seems less benign. They might regret, even deplore, the consequences of his conservatism, but they should surely pardon what amounts to just a personal idiosyncrasy, an almost endearing reversion to childhood values. Moreover, since his opposition to gay marriages, suspicion of lesbian couples who want IVF babies, refusal to apologise to wronged peoples and so on are merely childhood throwbacks rather than conscious policy, they carry with them some assurance that, once the man finally vacates the Lodge, the policies will fade with him.

One often-noted feature of John Howard's prime ministership has been his rapid and unflinching roll-back of once-cherished liberal achievements. After the 1996 election, some long-term Howard-watchers predicted accelerated redistribution from poor to rich, systematic diversion of funds away from public health, schools and universities, anti-union activism and immediate cuts to Aboriginal programs. But who would have foreseen the children overboard affair, or prime ministerial conniving at the attempt to smear a High Court judge with a forged CommCar timesheet? Who'd have imagined a national distribution of fridge magnets urging citizens to suspect and betray one another, or Australian soldiers off to bomb a distant country to neutralise weapons that didn't exist? Meanwhile, those dismissed as the 'chattering classes', the 'politically correct' or 'the elites' watched the erosion or severe circumscribing of the Office of the Status of Women, the Affirmative Action Agency, the Human Rights and Equal Opportunity Commission, the *Race Discrimination Act*. Sex, race and greed got back in the news in ways many thought were gone for good. Fear became a permanent political subtext. Through years of Beazley–Crean dithering, the opposition, spooked by Howard's apparent invulnerability,[9] could not nerve itself against him. Voters accepted lies as political lingua franca and, even when not deceived, voted an increasingly notorious liar back and back.

This book is about faith, power and the assault which Australians' collective soul sustained over successive terms of Howard government. Given the explanatory—not to say, prognostic—burden which Howard's childhood churchgoing has so regularly been asked to bear, an inquiry into his corrosion of Australia's soul begins with 1950s Methodism, and the Earlwood congregation of which the four Howard boys were a part. What we find there upsets any easy association between Howard's childhood churchgoing and adult policies. Instead, it sets the stage for much more interesting questions about the relationship between religion and modern Australian politics.

•

At Earlwood Methodist Church, the Howard boys joined a Sunday School which declared itself 'one of the largest in the State'.[10] The 1943 seventieth anniversary commemorative publication shows a photo of some two hundred suited boys and beribboned girls (the three-year-old future prime minister, presumably just missing out). Five years later, an eight-year-old John Howard was among an even larger student body, cared for by forty-six staff, including thirty-four teachers, three pianists and various officials.[11] Another five years later, the church underwent substantial expansion and remodelling, topped off with a £7000 Sunday School hall incorporating 'a child's sanctuary'.[12] Sunday School staff received regular training, attended conferences and followed a centralised curriculum to prepare their pupils for annual external examinations.[13]

John appears on the congregation's Junior Roll in the archives of Earlwood Methodist Church (held in the Uniting Church NSW Synod Archives and Research Centre, North Parramatta). It is listed straight after his brother, Robert, along with their address, 25 William Street, Earlwood. Robert's name stands out clearly but John's has been neatly crossed off, the adjoining column noting his transfer to the Senior Roll. Sunday School exam results were printed in the church newspaper each year. In the columns for 1950, John Howard of Earlwood sat Division 7, for those aged ten on 1 January, and scored a solid 70. In 1952 he improved to 85—not exceptional by Earlwood standards, but creditable on a statewide basis—but he didn't stop there. In a leaner year for Earlwood generally, its 1953 showing was helped by 'John Howard 88'.

Not all the students took the Sunday School exams. Although the state's results took up several pages of the tabloid-sized *Methodist* weekly newspaper, Earlwood's 1952 field of 31 was only a fraction of its enrolment. Various incentive schemes tried to improve both the registrations and the results: Sunday Schools fielding the highest proportion of their students received 'Bannerettes', while those with the highest performing sitters gained 'Champion Shields'. Nevertheless, a notice in 1952 lamented, 'this year just on 3,500 scholars were examined,—not altogether a satisfactory' turnout from a potential 18,000.[14] In other words, Sunday School exams were for the most committed. For example, though Howard memories have churchgoing as a family ritual, none of John's older brothers appears in the results lists. John seems to have been the family's Sunday School enthusiast. Students could remain at Sunday School into their late teens, and even then, their association often continued. Many became teachers. Twenty-one-year-old 'Mr John Howard, LL.B.' became the Earlwood Sunday School's secretary, serving for two years until 1963.[15] (In the lead-up to the 2004 election, as religion was making headlines for the conservative side of politics, the prime ministerial website stated that he had been a Sunday school teacher, but the Earlwood archives say nothing about that.)

So what would someone at such close contact with the church during his formative years have encountered by way of social and political ideas?[16] The Methodist church of John Howard's youth was much more socially progressive than later commentators assume.

One obvious source of evidence is the Sunday School curriculum. Lesson materials included strictly theological themes ('Jesus the triumphant King', 'How can we know there is a personal God?') but also social concern ('Health for all', 'Food for all').[17] Regular lessons about the 'aborigines of our own land' reminded students that, 'Our "boomerang" children and we are bound together, one family with God our Father, and one in Jesus Christ our Lord'. A feeling of unity was not enough as students (presumed non-Indigenous) had to 'show them . . . that we shall do something, and not merely talk about it'. As a start,

Sunday Schools were advised to collect books about Aboriginal children and students to make scrapbooks of relevant newspaper clippings. Children who went to schools with Aboriginal students or lived in towns near a reserve were encouraged to make friends with their Aboriginal neighbours.[18]

Less directly pedagogical activities supplemented senior Sunday School, notably the annual (later biennial) National Christian Youth Convention (NCYC). The first NCYC was held 16–23 January 1955. Delegates came from across Australia, and from the USA, Tonga, Samoa and Fiji. More than a thousand full-time registrants spent a week in the Sydney Showground exploring the theme 'God Works' through small group sessions, tutorials and themed Bible studies ('God Works in Solving Personal Problems—Cattle Sale Ring'). Evening rallies swelled to six or seven thousand, with fifteen thousand turning out (in the pouring rain) for the closing 'Festival of Youth',[19] attended by NSW Labor Premier J.J. Cahill.[20] The Convention formed a significant part of Methodist self-understanding and fed substantially into Methodist thought at the time. For example, the Convention's concluding statement was reprinted in full in the *Methodist*, attracted approving coverage in the secular press and became prescribed curriculum for that year's senior division Sunday School exams. Whether he attended or not, the fifteen-year-old John Howard, firmly integrated into his local congregation, could hardly have remained unaware of this defining Methodist event. Its detailed records give us an intriguing insight into the political climate of 1950s teenage Methodism.

The visiting Los Angeles 'missioner', R.L. Smith, declared the sight of thousands of delegates kneeling 'in prayer on the sodden ground, with eyes upturned to a blazing cross imposed on a huge map of Australia' to be 'more moving and spectacular than anything of the kind produced in the New World'.[21] Such images evoke Billy Graham evangelicalism, but the rally was the culmination of a program whose social and political direction was markedly different from American models. Built on the premise that 'Australia is at the crossroads of its history', the Convention's program, speeches and press coverage indicate an overtly political interpretation. It concluded with a 'Parliament of Youth', which issued the Convention's closing message, 'the freely debated deliberately expressed point of view of young Australia' which through Christian youth speaks to the nation'.[22] Reproduced in full in the *Methodist*, the statement begins with declarations, 'Life has a purpose . . . The power of the crucified and risen Christ is the only power which can overcome the evil in the world'. The remaining roughly 500 words ennumerate the evils and how to overcome them.

The first 'evil' was that 'our nation is often ignorant and generally intolerant of other peoples'. The proper response was, firstly, the 'full status of citizenship' for 'our own aborigines' and, secondly, abandoning the White Australia policy: 'in our failure to befriend as equals the peoples of South East Asia and other coloured peoples, we violate the Christian principle that all men are equal'. The next 'evil' was world poverty. The convention demanded cuts to defence spending in favour of a boosted aid budget, and called on individual Christians to practise personal austerity and 'sacrificial giving'. It followed that Australians should avoid 'making money the goal of life'. Only then did the statement offer its single sentence on such personal failings as 'giving way to the power of alcohol, gambling and sexual indulgence', before affirming God's work in every sphere of life: 'God can work in the economic life of Australia by our seeking His will in industrial relations, trade unions and commerce'. The statement did not spell out what 'God's will' might encompass industrially, but it evidently included stronger church–union links. One of the many *Methodist* accounts of the Convention reported:

> [A] group of unionists came as full-time delegates, were impressed, asked ministers to address their meetings, and their wages and convention fees were paid by fellow workers . . . Surely there is a place in the Church of the

> Carpenter for carpenters. Continental Socialism came from rationalism: our Socialism in England came from the Church.[23]

The Convention grew out of the Mission to the Nation, an ambitious program undertaken by the Methodist church nationwide from 1953 until 1955. Over those years, the church experimented with various outreach techniques, including specially produced radio programs, booklets for mass distribution and home visiting programs. Its most visible feature was numerous local 'mission weeks' during which the 'National Missioner', Reverend (later Sir) Alan Walker, and his team descended upon a local congregation for a week-long festival of public meetings, rallies, special church services and 'processions of witness'.

To give an idea of the scale, the 1955 climax to the national mission, 'Sydney Week', included a street Procession of Witness of 5000, with another 7500 onlookers lining the route. Speeches at the Town Hall mass meetings were relayed to crowds in the Lyceum Theatre and Pitt Street Congregational Church and broadcast over church-owned radio station 2CH. One much-trumpeted innovation was 'Sydney's First "Drive-In" Service'. Friends in the City Council waived Prince Alfred Park's by-laws to let 1127 cars onto the grass, bringing 6000 passengers (who all heard perfectly, thanks to 'Mr Martin, the Methodist sound engineer').[24]

Earlwood circuit was in from the start. In 1952, its churches held a 'simultaneous mission', following what would become the Mission to the Nation's standard pattern of street processions, evening rallies, ladies', men's and youth meetings and worship.[25] In 1955, five visiting ministers joined the congregation's Reverend Albert Davis to conduct its own mini-mission week. That meant five days of special preparatory meetings, climaxing with the arrival of the National Missioner, Reverend Alan Walker, who took over with a weekend of rallies, a basket tea and special church services.

Though borrowing from the techniques Billy Graham was using in America, such as open-air preaching, Walker distanced himself from the American's biblical literalism and social disengagement.[26] Walker was at least as influenced by the British Methodist and socialist Donald Soper, though Walker never became a socialist. Where Graham found himself at home with the mood of cold war America, Walker's diary records a different motivation: 'What a hellish thing is capitalism. I am going . . . to fight it and fight it with the weapons of evangelism . . . What can I do? I see more clearly than ever that it must be a striking at the roots of capitalism'.[27]

Walker's Mission addresses regularly took up the causes of peace, disarmament and his plan for the Commonwealth to break 'the East–West deadlock' by heading 'a third group of powers' to stand between the superpowers.[28] Nor was his the only political voice. For example, during the Western Australian Mission, ALP Opposition Leader H.V. Evatt reminded the audience that Methodist local preachers helped found the labour movement.[29] One report assessed the Mission's impact on the eve of 1955:

> The Mission has certainly uncovered the 'sore points' of Australian life. It has constantly drawn to public attention the social evils and the sufferings of some of our forgotten people, such as aged pensioners and aborigine and half-cast people. From the beginning of the Mission the evil of war has been attacked and the things which make for peace have been upheld.[30]

A congregation's choices of where to put its money among the wider church's many charitable and mission-related efforts hint at its social and political commitments. Earlwood made regular donations to the Home Missions department, which supported country circuits with grants, building funds, the Methodist Nursing Service and emergency hospital visiting. Earlwood Quarterly Meeting minutes record an active Temperance Society campaigning to keep six o'clock closing. During the late 1940s, regular food parcels went to Methodists in rationing-afflicted England. During the late 1950s and early 1960s, Earlwood gave regularly to organisations with a strong tradition of progressive social service tradition and critique of government policy, including the Australian Council of Churches, World Council of Churches and Australian Student Christian Movement.

Earlwood also donated to Overseas Missions and to Sydney's Dalmar Children's Home, then branching out into a new venture. On 10 December 1955, the *Methodist* reported Dalmar Home's first Indigenous child removal. A central plank of the adult Howard's refusal to apologise to the Stolen Generations has been his insistence that the perpetrators of family separations believed they were doing the right thing at the time. He paints child removals as uncontested. His church's embrace of the policy, then, might be one point at which the explanatory icon of 'John Howard, Methodist' can be seriously invoked. Yet the church's own account of its new undertaking does not reflect carefree consensus.

Although the words were triumphalist, the front-page story announcing the new activity betrayed a nervous undercurrent. Most *Methodist* front pages of the era carried three or four staid, pictureless columns of fine print, with modest headlines crossing one or two columns. To announce the arrival of former Croker Island resident, 'Rosanna . . . rescued from almost unbelievable neglect and committed to our care by the Aboriginal Welfare Board', however, the *Methodist* broke out into inch-high letters across the entire page, amplified with white space above and below. In a tone approaching paranoia, the headline pronounces, 'YOU WILL APPROVE!' Rosanna's photo fills most of two columns. A tear-out donation slip reinforces the impression of a church trying to head off controversy: 'If you approve of this Service for these and all dependent children, please use the form provided when you send the concrete evidence of your goodwill', it asks, making the fund sound less important than the approval.[31]

The innovation was Rosanna's relocation to Sydney. The Methodist church had been removing Croker children from their families to a church-run 'settlement' on the island, 250 kilometres north-east of Darwin, for some time.[32] The church's Indigenous policies in general were, and remained into the next decade, a matter of considerable debate between different State conferences. The more conservative NSW church found itself regularly challenged by the Victorian Methodists' stronger push for Aboriginal self-determination.[33] It would have been difficult for those close to Methodist networks to miss divergent opinions.

Other church-sponsored Indigenous affairs initiatives sit less comfortably with the later Howard's position. To take one example, the Sunday nearest to Australia Day was designated National Aborigines' Sunday. Ministers received preparatory mail-outs from the National Missionary Council to help them and their congregations 'remember these original owners of our land in a very special way'.[34] Interpretations became more militant as the 1960s progressed: an article in 1960 described Indigenous peoples as 'the occupiers and owners of this whole continent for unnumbered centuries. They have never ceded to the white invaders their age-old title to the whole land'.[35] By 1963, the *Methodist* was declaring National Aborigines' Sunday to be about 'REPARATION . . . They don't need sympathy, they need our action to undo as far as possible what we have done'.[36] Perhaps the message did not get through very strongly in Earlwood: one member of the congregation would later thwart all attempts by a former Methodist minister, Australian Democrat Senator John Woodley, to have the word 'owners' included in the mention of Aborigines in the proposed new Preamble to the Australian Constitution.[37]

•

NSW Methodists' eponymous State newspaper was no lightweight throwaway: its weekly issues made the most of typically twelve or more tabloid-size pages. It attracted considerable advertising, not all obviously religious ('For the best navel oranges, write to . . .'), but that left plenty of room not just for accounts of church events but also for a remarkable breadth of social and political commentary. Indeed, historian Jennifer Clark has noted that: 'Of all the church newspapers, those of the Methodist Church are arguably the most generally and consistently reflective on wider social and political issues . . . Methodists were willing to debate at length topical issues of concern'.[38]

The NSW version offers a wealth of views a young Methodist might have encountered. Throughout the early 1950s, the paper worried about the traditional Methodist bêtes-noires of gambling and liquor. Those 'terrible twins' were responsible for 'a sharp rise in juvenile delinquency'.[39] NSW's proposed shift to ten o'clock closing became a rallying point in 1955: 'At one hotel in Queensland, about 9 o'clock one night, we saw a husband drinking at the bar, his wife drinking in the lounge of the same hotel, with their two small children running from one to the other. Hardly a scene of true domestic happiness!'[40] Half measures would not do: 'A nation, recognising the Christian ethic, will ruthlessly suppress this vice in the public interest of decent Australians'.[41] (Even the *Methodist* had to report, though, the 'gratifying' news that, once introduced, ten o'clock closing did not seem to have precipitated the feared increase of drunkenness.)[42]

The *Methodist* at one point endorsed Billy Graham's warning that juvenile delinquency 'almost equals communism in the problems we face today': youth gangs, juvenile delinquents, bodgies and widgies imperilled Australian life. Graham blamed parents, who neglect their children in favour of 'drinking and carousing'.[43] But, in contrast both to Graham and to the 'personal responsibility' mantra of the adult Howard, the *Methodist* thought the 'real delinquents' were media and advertisers who 'commercialise and dramatise evil, who prefer rape to love, criminals to heroes, and gangsters' molls to decent mothers'. Herod 'slaughtered the innocent . . . But Herod was an amateur compared to what the moguls of press, commercial radio, film industry, horror comics . . . are doing to our children'.[44] These capitalist delinquents were symptoms of 'a delinquent State',[45] ready to put private corporations' profits ahead of the public good.

Divorce was one cause of juvenile delinquency but here, again, the *Methodist* resisted punitive 'personal responsibility' solutions. Rejecting calls for more restrictive divorce law, the *Methodist* advocated 'divorce by consent' and uniform divorce law across Australia. Rather than deplore 'the processes for obtaining divorce', it was more important to consider 'ways and means of preventing marriages from breaking down'. Given that they do, the *Methodist* felt, 'if the idea [of divorce law reform] does no more than to get some speed into processes for tidying up divorce laws in general, it will be a good thing'.[46] At times, it deplored 'the emancipation of women' as opening the floodgates to communism[47] and fostering juvenile delinquency, but at others endorsed the feminist Women's Commission of the World Council of Churches and argued for women's ordination.[48] It determinedly opposed state aid to non-government schools, both on grounds of church–state separation and as undermining free and universal public education.[49]

Beyond child- and family-oriented topics, the *Methodist* explored a wide canvas of national and world affairs. It was concerned about the communist menace, but its proffered solutions can seem quite at odds with the adult Howard's positions. The *Methodist* feared 'organised business' as much as 'organised authoritarianism'.[50] In February 1955, it carried a piece by Neville Smith on behalf of the Committees in Support of A Call to the People of Australia, arguing that Australia should stop understanding itself in European terms:

> Our . . . destiny will lie with Asia rather than with Europe. But they are still teaching French and Latin in schools and the educational authorities report that there is little interest in learning Asian languages . . . What does the average person

> know about Asian races or legends or wars that have affected the fate of more than half the world's population? . . . Asia is very near to us, and events are moving fast there . . . For us, Europe is a culture and a tradition. For us, Asia represents the future.[51]

Although regularly denouncing communism,[52] the *Methodist* also devoted entire front pages to optimistic articles on 'Religion in the Soviet Union'[53] and 'Religion in China',[54] while letters and editorials advocated friendship across the iron curtain.[55] The *Methodist* nervously monitored McCarthyism, noting that many Australian and British Methodists feared 'a new totalitarianism' had 'seriously weakened' American democratic liberties. It detailed US Methodist Bishop Bromley Oxnam's dramatic appearance before the House Un-American Activities Committee, and his critique of the Committee's aggressive character-assassination techniques and use of unsubstantiated evidence often cited as a significant step towards its eventual discrediting.[56]

The *Methodist* also opposed Catholic anticommunism, finding it counterproductive.[57] In September 1955 a half-page space advertised a 'dramatic broadcast' on Sydney church-run radio station 2CH, 'Can Christianity Co-Exist With Communism', with a panel of three 'fearless' speakers: Dr R. Davidson of the Glebe Methodist Mission, Dr P. Ryan of the Sacred Heart Monastery, Kensington, and Sydney City Council Alderman T. Wright: 'These men will give no quarter'.[58] Fearless all may have been, but the following week's *Methodist* carried: 'Congratulations to Dr Reg. Davidson on a piece of great broadcasting . . . in between two speakers whose speeches and replies sounded like the stale play-back of gramophone records, Dr Reg. Davidson . . . hammered home the truth that neither Rome nor Moscow has the answers, but that Jesus Christ has the answer we need'.[59]

A series of front-page articles in 1953 urged continued action for peace, even though recognising the tendency for 'peace' in an organisation's title to imply 'a favourable attitude to the

Soviet Union'[60] or communist infiltration.[61] Through the 1950s, editorials campaigned against the atomic bomb and in favour of disarmament, urging support for the UN Disarmament Commission. It spent two columns in May 1955 exhorting Methodists to see *Children of Hiroshima*, a film made by the Japanese Teachers' Union and imported by the Australian Peace Convention Bureau and the Peace Council. The film would prove 'a greater answer to the atomic bomb than all the anti-aircraft guns and guided missiles in the world'. Another 'surer way to peace than an exploded hydrogen bomb' was 'a full bread basket', so the sincerity of Australia's commitment to peace would be judged by its efforts at more equal distribution of wealth.[62]

With South Africa as a frequent example,[63] the paper inveighed against racism, declaring 'the claim to racial superiority' a 'peculiarly vicious form of sin. It is idolatry'.[64] By 1961, it warned Menzies:

> We are not surprised that the Prime Minister is afraid that once Africa's attitude to race is opened up, other countries including Australia are bound to be questioned . . . it is obvious from his remarks that his judgments on South Africa were coloured by the situation for which he is responsible in Australia.[65]

The *Methodist* also campaigned for refugees, pointing out that 'Despite wire fences and observation posts, pitfalls, ramparts, wire-traps and alarm devices, refugees somehow get across borders, leading to freedom'. It applauded government resettlement efforts and urged churches, and individual members, to find additional funding and sponsors for new arrivals.[66]

At home, the paper explicitly advocated political involvement. Although the church 'as such' professed reluctance to become involved in politics, it also had a duty 'at times' to 'speak fearlessly and frankly . . . to give prophetic leadership to the nation'. Individual Methodists were to lobby politicians and also consider joining their ranks: 'Churchmen must be active in the political parties of their own choice', where their 'services are sorely needed'.[67]

In April 1955, the *Methodist* applauded that: 'Politics and ethics should go together, and we have some ethical voices in parliaments, fine Christian men who speak plainly'.[68] One already well established was Gill Duthie, Labor Member for Wilmot (subsequently Lyons), who in 1947 had resigned from the Methodist ministry in order to stand (and stand: he eventually held the seat for 29 years). The 1955 federal election only improved the situation. That December the *Methodist* announced:

> [T]here are good Methodists on both sides of the new Federal House. Mr Richard Cleaver, the new [Liberal] Member for Swan (WA), is one of the brilliant young men of our Church. A member of the Mission Board and General Conference, he is one of the finest and sanest Christian Endeavour leaders we have had for many years. Parliament should be all the better for his presence.[69]

The church resisted efforts to align it with either party. The president felt regular pressure:

> 'Why doesn't the Church come straight out for Dr Evatt!' and 'Why don't you tell Methodist people to vote for Mr Menzies!' . . . The writer of Ecclesiastes knew his business when he said: 'There is a time to keep silence and a time to speak!' I cast my vote for him.[70]

The *Methodist* through the 1950s reveals a church sensitive to criticisms of partisanship, with divergent opinion on key social and political questions. However, the general political orientation is considerably removed from the attitudes regularly associated with the icon of 'John Howard, Methodist'. NSW Methodists in the 1950s encountered regular advocacy of an open door to refugees, engagement with Asia, full citizenship and other rights for Aborigines, a strong trade union movement and government action against poverty, and suspicion of big business and opposition to nuclear weapons. Although the *Methodist* upheld conservative concerns about the 'moral panic' topics of the 1950s—family breakdown, juvenile delinquency, alcohol and gambling—it was more likely to put the blame on corporate greed, timid government and unduly punitive divorce law than on unrestrained individuals. The icon of 'John Howard, Methodist' only works as a smokescreen.

•

Judith Brett has observed that Howard's rhetorical style includes frequent 'references to his personal experiences . . . to his own beliefs and feelings'. She argues that 'the real meaning of his references to his childhood in the 1950s' is 'not that he wants to go back, but that he legitimates his beliefs, both to himself and to others, in terms of his own experience rather than in terms of more abstract systems of cultural and social knowledge'.[71] But it is more complicated than that.

Howard could not take us back, even if he wanted to, because the 1950s childhood he evokes is, in important respects, a fiction. Even then, the world was less simple than nostalgia supposes; the very church from which his values are said to have emanated was more politically complicated. Having transmuted into another (also often politically confrontational) form since 1977, the Methodist church of Howard's childhood exists now as an image from the past, available to stand rhetorically for a set of commitments which have little to do with its actual history. And it is not only the church that has been substantially fictionalised.

John Howard's brother Bob recalls their regular attendance at Earlwood Methodist, but disputes that the denomination left much of a deposit: 'Our parents weren't into the Alan Walker aspect of Methodism at all—in fact, they were strongly against it'.[72] Their politics had more to do with small business. The garage, which had been in the family since the 1930s, was coming into its own as family cars became the 1950s emblem of a secure, prosperous future. The 1949 promise to end petrol rationing was surely not the only bond between Menzies and this nuclear unit of his 'forgotten people'—rather, it stood for a range of shared commitments: hard work, family pulling together, suspicion of those who want 'something for nothing'. Wal, the oldest Howard son, became a draftsman, but ended up maintaining the family small business tradition, running a Burwood bookshop and stationers. Stan moved up the scale from NSW legal bureaucracy to become a senior partner in Malleson's, one of Australia's biggest law firms. Bob, the second-youngest Howard brother, followed the others into the Liberal Party, but after becoming a teacher, a union member and a humanities student (in that order), he found the family certainties falling away. He is now a left-leaning political scientist in the University of Sydney's government department. That John's political values owe little to the church does not surprise Bob: 'In a way, we were a part of the church without really being a part of it. I went to church every Sunday but—it's a funny thing—I don't think I ever saw a copy of the *Methodist* in our house'.

The boys' mother, Mona, was the daughter of a Catholic mother, who died young, and an Anglican father, whose family raised Mona in the ways of Protestantism so effectively that she rejected her own early education to become determinedly anti-Catholic. Marrying Lyall Howard, she found herself in the heart of suburban Methodism, so she transferred her energies to the local Methodist church.[73] But church, to her family, meant 'attachment to an institution, decency and order', according to Bob. The family took a lot of note of how the church commemorated national events, such as Anzac Day—'Did this or that clergyman observe it properly?'—but discussion of theology, or the church's wider commitments, 'was just not part of it'. Instead:

> What we read was the *Reader's Digest* and the *Saturday Evening Post*. I remember the *Saturday Evening Post* arriving,

> every second Tuesday, a smorgasbord of American consumer goods. It went on for years—log-cabin-to-the-White House, kids selling lollies on the roadside—that sort of influence was more important than the church in shaping our family's values.[74]

If the *Methodist* seems unlikely soil for the adult John's social policy, the 1950s *Saturday Evening Post*, its very title now often invoked as shorthand for 'family values' conservatism, looks much more promising. Its Norman Rockwell cover paintings—wholesome milk-bar scenes, fireside Thanksgiving dinner-tables, mischievous schoolboys and doll-holding girls—celebrated post-war prosperity, nuclear families and suburban childhood innocence. The pictures posed the secure counterpoint to articles earnestly worrying about the assimilation potential of Japanese war brides (who 'think having their sleek black hair frizzled into dulled mops' and taking Red Cross housewifery courses will turn them into Americans[75]) and folksy reminiscences of Italian exchange students learning to appreciate 'stuffed pork chops and apple pie'.[76] Its fortnightly delivery from America to the lounge room of a suburban garage proprietor surely tells us something about the family's priorities.

John reflected the family ethos much more than that of the church; he stood out as conservative, even then. Earlwood old girls remember him as the boy it was wise to say 'no' to at church dances—not for the usual reason, but because, instead of dancing, he was likely to get you in a corner and harangue you about politics. Brian Herbert, still a stalwart, and organist, of Earlwood Uniting Church, remembers, 'We young people didn't talk much about politics, we talked about girls!' before adding, 'Except for John Howard, of course . . .'[77] Bob remembers one of the first Colombo Plan students joining the church, and John trying earnestly to argue the surprised newcomer from Southeast Asia into an appreciation of monarchy and empire.

According to Bob, neither parent was a great reader, though his father enjoyed Churchill's *Memoirs*, and other accounts of World War II. But, Bob recalls, there were always books around the house. 'I remember Schumpeter's *Capitalism, Socialism and Democracy*, E.H. Carr's *Nationalism and Beyond*, even Marx's *Capital*. I can't remember how they got there, but they were there'. Not that indiscriminate reading was encouraged: 'My mother was quite worried when I once brought home a book called *Science and Religion*. This raised questions you weren't meant to ask'. Universities were considered all right, as long as they stuck to vocational training, but the social sciences were suspect: 'The best-known humanities figure in those days was [Sydney University Professor of Philosophy] John Anderson, and he was regarded as dangerous, a threat to Christian morals'.

What Mona did read avidly was the newspaper. She was a formative political influence on the boys, especially John. 'She didn't go in for extended discussion, but you were never in any doubt what our mother thought.' Occasionally, John would dissent. 'One example was the *Communist Party Dissolution Bill*. John supported Menzies over that, but our mother disagreed.' She also took more liberal positions on abortion and on means-tested welfare. Generally, though, had Menzies listened in to the long political conversations around the Howard family dinner table, he wouldn't have heard much opposition.

The values of 'standing on your own two feet' and competing for limited goods were important themes in the family, according to Bob. The family had, he recalls, 'a real us-and-them thing. It was the climate we grew up in, not at all modified by the church. Even with other branches of the family, there was always a sense of competition, a constant undercurrent to the enquiries after cousins, "How is so-and-so going? What is he doing now?"'. Bob attributes John's exceptional Sunday School exam participation less to theological enthusiasm than to having found another avenue to compete. 'Competition served him well, and the fact that he did well in competitive environments of course reinforced the idea that it was the system in which real merit shows up, it brings out the best in people.' It is in that family culture that Bob finds sources for many of his brother's adult positions, citing the concept of mutual obligation, opposition to trade unions and a preference for selective schools.[78]

So has the adult John Howard simply transposed the values of his family and the *Saturday Evening Post* on to a church which the family attended but was largely deaf to, and with which the Bible of American consumerism had little in common? Other old Earlwood hands remember diverse political opinions in the church. 'Earlwood wasn't particularly well-to-do, so Alan Walker's ideas about social justice weren't a threat to the people there' is Norma Hardy's way of putting it. She was organist at Earlwood until she went to India as a missionary in 1945, but kept up her contacts. 'We learned a lot about social justice from the church', her younger sister, Margaret Eyre, recalls:

> But it didn't come particularly from Earlwood, it came from the wider church. We were exposed to it through Crusader camps. That was where we learned about poverty, religious freedom, tolerance—some Aboriginal children from Croker Island stayed at the Crusader camp site at Otford for a while, and we met them through the Crusader movement. All that was a big eye-opener to us.[79]

Margaret, a contemporary of the older Howard boys, does not recall John among the Earlwood Crusader campers, suggesting that he missed out on much of the broadening that the Methodist church offered to those who got involved beyond the local congregation. Some tried to carry that wider awareness back to Earlwood. Everyone I spoke to, for example, remembered reverentially Alex Kilham, a lay preacher and Sunday School superintendent who made no secret of his pacifism or community causes, from collecting clothes for inner city relief work to employing former psychiatric patients in his own business. The

Methodist church offered 1950s suburbia a window to a quite different set of values from the *Reader's Digest* and *Saturday Evening Post*—but you had to be willing to look through it.

We must seek other sources than church archives and newspaper back-issues for the Howard brand of social conservatism, especially for why it resonates now in an electorate far removed from 1950s Earlwood. Moreover, we can ask why the grown-up John Howard apparently sees political advantage in depicting his conservatism as religiously based, when the weight of evidence suggests his childhood religion tended in a quite different political direction.

•

If the God invoked Sunday by Sunday in William Street, Earlwood, is not the sponsor of Howard's policies, there is nevertheless plenty to be said about Howard's spiritual warfare. Theological battles have been fought throughout his prime ministership, even if often in subterranean ways, not immediately obvious to this highly secularised electorate. Capitalism, the 'hellish thing', has successfully co-opted many of Walker's 'weapons of evangelism' into its own crypto-religion. In the process, religiously inflected social conservatism has become firmly enmeshed with right wing economic thought, even as many churches continue to criticise from the left. Techniques honed by the American religious right have proved invaluable to Howard's sales pitch, while carefully avoiding the zealously religious language likely to alienate Australia's much more secular population.

This book explores Howard's spiritual assault on Australian values. In Part One, 'White Picket Fence', I examine the Howard government's version of American-style 'family values' rhetoric. Debates surrounding sexuality, parenthood and bioethical issues such as euthanasia have provided opportunities to talk up 'the family' and make oblique appeals to religious authority, while entrenching his position as the leader most likely to keep conservative issues on the policy front-burner. The Lyons Forum, a grouping of right wing Christian Coalition MPs which received some attention in the 1990s and then faded from view, steps out of the backroom to reveal a seldom-heard story about policy formation and the maintenance of power in the Howard Liberal Party.

Part Two, 'Race to the Top', explores Howard's unparalleled ability to play the 'race card', even while denying it. For a couple of years before the 1996 election, the Hindmarsh Island controversy was a morality play acted out across the nation's front pages which entrenched the message of greedy 'special interests' and dangerous 'sacred claims' imperilling Australian democracy. It was actively promoted by the then Opposition Leader Howard, helped by members of his front bench. Election strategists attributed a significant part of the 1996 swing to the Hindmarsh effect. Asylum seekers did a similar job during Howard's reign: a small group, little known to most voters, reduced to scary images and threatening slogans, helped keep him where the Hindmarsh controversy had helped to put him.

When Australia considered a new constitutional preamble, Howard decreed it begin 'With hope in God'. The constitutional convention debates leave readers wondering: which God? Part Three, 'Market Values', offers an answer. Under Howard, the market has taken on divine qualities. It requires sacrifices, promises rewards, has opinions and emotions (jittery one day, confident the next) but, demanding propitiation, is nevertheless beyond complete human control or prediction. This jealous God demands single-minded loyalty and resents rival deities. In its own name it sabotages family and community life and strangles democratic safeguards, such as government-sponsored welfare. In place of love, it makes competition the fundamental value. 'Family values' and 'individual responsibility' turn out to be pious appeals to the old God behind which the Market God disguises its chaotic theophanies. At its most extreme, this God undermines democratic traditions while justifying hatreds: vilification of homosexuals, punishing the unemployed, cruel border protection and illegal war. Howard and the Market God have served each other well. Understanding their relationship, and how Australia has fallen under their thrall, we can reject market idolatry and reclaim more inclusive, loving ways of life.

PART ONE

White Picket Fence

CHAPTER TWO
Bypassing Lazarus

In 1974, after twelve years in a Sydney solicitor's office, thirty-six-year-old John Howard was elected to the federal seat of Bennelong. He was its second incumbent, taking over from J.O. Cramer, who had held it for the Liberals since its proclamation in 1949. The timeline at the end of this book shows a political career that flowered early. Howard landed his first portfolio, Business and Consumer Affairs, when the Liberals took government the year after his election. Under Prime Minister Malcolm Fraser, he rose to Treasurer in 1977 and then Deputy Leader in 1982. In 1985 he took the leadership—which, by then, meant leader of the opposition—from Andrew Peacock, and held on to it for three and a half years before Peacock reclaimed it.

Howard was known to be economically on the 'dry' side of Fraser and Peacock, and also to their right on other matters. For example, Fraser's staunch opposition to South African apartheid contrasted with Howard's opposition to the sanctions aimed at ending it. His social conservatism on domestic issues drew a dividing line between him and Peacock but, with a public profile forged in financial portfolios, it was not Howard's defining feature. Indeed, to many inside and outside the party, what defined both him and Peacock was not ideology so much as the crippling power struggle between them, coupled with their mutual inability to break the ALP's run in government.

Howard's leadership was fatally marked by an early effort at wedge politics. In August 1988, attempting to capitalise on a perceived gap between a Labor government committed to multiculturalism and many of its traditional supporters said to be nervous about increasing cultural diversity, he began advocating 'slowing' Asian immigration.[1] His leadership limped along for another eight months, but party colleagues judged the comments decisive in his downfall.[2] One lesson he learned from his 1989 leadership loss became a strategy hallmark of the later Howard: letting others campaign on his behalf, putting risks at one remove.

Peacock returned to the leadership for less than a year before economics professor John Hewson took on the mantle of saviour. After four years of Hewson disappointments and the party's brief, disastrous flirtation with Alexander Downer, Howard won back the Liberal leadership which he had ignominiously lost—a resurrection he had once dismissed as 'Lazarus with a triple bypass'. One persistent, though suppressed, tradition casts Lazarus as Jesus' homosexual companion—ironic, then, that the Australian Lazarus owed his resuscitation to a campaign staked out most publicly on grounds of sexuality, particularly homophobia. His accession was the fruit of a careful program, going back at least to 1992, to win once and for all the internal party struggle between social liberals and 'family values' conservatives.

The successful family values crusade was waged by the Liberal Party's little-studied Lyons Forum. That crypto-Christian pressure group provides a key to Howard's 1995 leadership revival and continued ascendancy. Though Howard himself expresses only amorphous religious commitments, his position within the parliamentary party is shored up by his willingness to front, and exploit, a religious right social agenda. The campaign to bring that agenda to Liberal centre-stage began with a carefully orchestrated operation against the then leader John Hewson. Its trigger was Hewson's decision to send a message of support to the Sydney Gay and Lesbian Mardi Gras. From then on, the right's God had a central place in Liberal Party policy-making.

•

The Liberal Party of Australia was founded in 1945. Of its first 38 years, it governed for over thirty—less than five years of Chifley and less than three of Whitlam were the only stopovers on this express power trip. Then, in 1983, Bob Hawke preached a heady mix of 'national consensus', market liberalisation and multiculturalism, and stayed in power for eight years. The Whitlam-sired chattering classes were the new mainstream. As Hawke wore thin with voters and the increasingly bitter ALP leadership disputes broke through to the headlines more often, he was replaced mid-term by the self-styled 'Placido Domingo of Australian politics', Paul Keating.

Imagine you are a federal Liberal MP in the early 1990s. The party you joined is the supposed natural party of government, but it is stuck in opposition, drifting from one leadership debacle to the next. John Howard and Andrew Peacock's elaborate leadership quadrille has danced Peacock out of politics. The 1989 fallout has left Howard pronounced unrevivable. Saviour-designate John Hewson, yet to face his greatest political test (the 1993 'unlosable' election), is pursuing an economic line about which some in the party room are uncomfortable—even though the 1989 preselection purge of 'wets' and 'moderates' has left an almost uniformly desiccated front bench. What do the federal Liberals do?

In the ALP, disgruntled MPs might try to bring about changes through their faction. Liberals can't. Their party denies it has any. Often, representatives of minority 'tendencies' (as the informal, faction-like groupings are called) have resorted to 'clubs'—the William Pitt Club in the 1980s (by which Peter

Reith, Michael Wooldridge and Peter Shack proclaimed both their Young Turk self-perception and small-l liberal commitments), the Society of Modest Members (taking the newspaper nom-de-plume of Member for Wakefield Bert Kelly to invoke his then radical free market ideas) and the left-leaning Liberal Forum (scuttled by John Hewson's quick-drying 1989 preselections). All these 'dining clubs' enabled like-minded groups to share ideas, agitate from the backbench and at times lobby their seniors, while leaving the party, at least officially, faction-free.

It is one thing for club members to have a policy wish-list; making it happen is quite another. In the Liberal Party, the potential obstacles to change take a distinctive form. Despite moves in the 1990s towards a stronger 'policy partnership' involving the extra-parliamentary party, policy responsibility has remained substantially in the party room, indeed, mainly on a single chair.[3] The Liberal Party's structure gives its leader greater freedom than either the Labor or National Party counterparts. For example, Liberal leaders are not bound by organisational resolutions.[4] Consequently, as political scientist and former NSW Liberal Party Director Graeme Starr points out, 'Real power in the parliamentary Liberal Party rests with the leader', so that:

> The parliamentary party elects its leader and its deputy leader and, after that, the parliamentary organisation is whatever the leader wants it to be . . . The effect of this practice, of course, is that members of the parliamentary party are almost entirely dependent for their rise or fall to or from positions of power upon the patronage of the leader.[5]

On policy, too, as Dean Jaensch points out, 'the Liberal Party gives its leader authority beyond the platform and even the canvas'.[6] Consequently, as David Kemp put it (when he was a political scientist, before becoming one of the studied), 'The ultimate support of a leader's authority is his role as expounder of a philosophy or ideology which commands common consent and adherence in the party'.[7] The situation has changed little since Menzies's day when, 'The philosophy and platform of Liberalism and the authority of the Liberal leader of the opposition were closely linked'.[8] Political theorist Ian Cook interprets the leadership issue in philosophical terms. Borrowing categories from a classic account of the Liberal Party, Cook reads the history of Liberal policy formation as an ongoing contest between 'ameliorative' and 'individualistic' philosophies. The leader has the power to determine which will dominate, so the parliamentary party chooses a strand via its choice of leader. That sets up a philosophical direction, and also, potentially, grievances:

> In short, the adoption of one of the varieties of liberalism within the Liberal Party [through the choice of leader] will tend to marginalise certain potential office holders and power brokers, and to enhance the position of others.[9]

Moreover, as Randal Stewart and Ian Ward point out, the parliamentary leader's 'primary role in defining Liberal ideology' necessarily 'leaves him or her as the chief custodian of the party's electoral fortunes'. When those fail, or when ideological disagreement surfaces, there is little for it but 'for those who want to change policy direction to change leaders'.[10]

That much any Australian politics textbook will tell you. The Liberals' leader-dominated structure had particular ramifications for the party in the early 1990s. The exigencies of leadership manoeuvring, especially the need to develop a power base that looked as little as possible like a faction, opened the way for a kind of religious politics which most observers had assumed died with the DLP. Since no one expected to see it, we took a long time to notice it, and even longer to understand what we were seeing. The unusal prominence of religion in the 2004 election campaign, which many commentators saw as a novelty, was actually just the lastest act of a drama that had been unfolding on the conservative side of politics for over a decade. It owed a lot to the ascendancy of a politician who, though not himself particularly religious, proved exceptionally adept at playing to the passions of a nascent Australian religious right.

Howard had to play the game to the top twice: once in 1985 and again a decade later. His first effort came unstuck through lack of subtlety. He already had the technique of playing down scary hard right economic policy behind a mask of what would later be known (ultimately ironically) as 'comfortable and relaxed' social policy, but he and his backers had not yet prepared Australia for explicitly voiced anti-Asian racism or his overtly back-to-the-fifties vision. The path back involved re-educating fellow citizens to see race as a legitimate part of political debate (a course we chart in Part Two). It involved tying social conservatism to the 'inevitable' economic agenda (discussed in Part Three), seeing a particular brand of social cohesion as the counterbalance to the insecurities fostered by globalisation. It involved skilfully fostering the impression of 'mainstream' support for his views.

To sell his brand of policy to the wider public Howard had first to get majority support within his party. To help this agenda along, his supporters drafted a sponsor with strong appeal to long-untapped strata of political consciousness: God.

Discussion of tendencies in the modern Liberal Party typically focuses on 'wet' and 'dry'. The categories are overwhelmingly to do with economics. Each plausibly appeals to the party's Menzian heritage. 'Wets' emphasise the need for some state intervention to protect the weak, against 'dries', who want smaller government and freer markets. In these terms, the early 1990s in the parliamentary party was a time of fast philosophical homogenisation. As Dean Jaensch notes, by 1993 the tendencies' historical coexistence had suffered:

> The Liberal Party's leadership, since 1990, has sought *not* to provide representation for tendencies, especially at policy-

> making levels. Rather, the parliamentary party leadership has sought, by the various means available to it, to *exclude* from authority, power and input the wets and the pragmatists.[11]

Ultimately, Liberal wets were mostly excluded not just from authority and power, but from parliament. Names like Chris Puplick, Roger Shipton and Ian Macphee dropped off the ballot papers; Liberal voters in 1990 faced lists of textbook dries such as Peter Costello, David Kemp and Ian McLachlan. Senator Peter Baume, philosophical leader of the wets, saw what had happened and chose to jump before the push.[12] The few former wets who remained, such as Philip Ruddock and Senator Richard Alston, underwent rapid conversions. So thorough was the shift that, over the following decade, the Howard government regularly faced its most vigorous criticism not across the chamber but from its own elders, such as Malcolm Fraser, Fred Chaney, John Hewson and John Valder.

Selling the dry agenda is challenging. To voters, even by the early 1990s, it had come to mean relentless pressure and increasing insecurity. Terms like 'change', 'reform' and 'efficiency' suddenly took on new meanings, all seemingly euphemisms for fewer permanent jobs, more contract work, longer hours and the threat of unemployment if you didn't play along. Yet, even when internal party dissent on economic questions had been silenced, framing the party's philosophy purely in wet/dry terms overlooked another big division. If the Liberal Party members expressed little dissent about the agenda itself, divisions emerged over how to inoculate the people against its effects.

Hewson's answer was to combine dry economic policy, spelled out in his *Fightback!* program, with explicitly inclusive social policies. After losing the 'unlosable' 1993 election, he strengthened his public commitment to social liberalism. He was all over the papers advocating increased breast cancer research funding, championing working mothers and warning that government could not tell people how to structure their families. Describing himself as 'to the right of centre in economic matters and to the left of centre in social policy', he explained his philosophy, adopting terms from the political tradition that in Australia is quaintly called 'small-l' liberalism, to distinguish it from the policies of the party which carries its name but often not much else. Hewson's interpretation implicitly attacked the kind of authoritarian social conservatism where government tries to engineer social outcomes, such as by favouring one family form over others or trying to control sexual behaviour and impose private morals through public means. Instead, he harked back to the nineteenth century view of liberalism as enhancing individual rights, whose sources and impact in Australia have since been traced in detail by ANU political scientist Marian Sawer in *The Ethical State: Social liberalism in Australia* (though many of those dead reformers might have felt a subterranean shudder at the more *laissez-faire* aspects of Hewson's economic policy).[13] As he summed up his social vision:

> The individual . . . is supreme. The government is subservient except, of course, when individuals collectively choose otherwise . . . So I do not have any problem myself with issues that relate to women's rights or gay rights as they are called, to seeing abortion as a matter of choice for a woman in conjunction with her family and her doctor, to supporting legislation in relation to privacy or anti-racial vilification.[14]

By contrast, Howard's antidote to globalised insecurity was a retreat to the lounge room. In the Keating days, Howard was often accused of lacking a 'big picture'. With hindsight, it wasn't that Howard didn't have a big picture, but that he excelled in projecting it onto a very small screen. Framed by the sideboard, the sofa and the kids' sporting trophies, his vision for the nation merged unobtrusively into his imagined 1950s home.

While Howard was absent from the leadership—but not from the headlines—he still had a significant block of supporters who either identified personally with his conservative family image, or saw it as electorally saleable. They did not sit back and grumble. They did what disaffected Liberals often do: they formed a club. Called the Lyons Forum, the new club rallied in 1992 under a slogan borrowed from the maiden speech of one-time United Australia Party Member for the Tasmanian federal seat of Darwin, Dame Enid Lyons (who borrowed it from King George V): 'The foundation of a nation's greatness is in the homes of its people'. There from the beginning was Queensland Senator John Herron (subsequently Minister for Aboriginal Affairs, then ambassador to Ireland and the Holy See). A practising Catholic, he recalled:

> Religion wasn't a reason for my entering Parliament, but [preparing for] the maiden speech makes you think, 'What will be the basis of my actions while I'm here?'[15]

In his first speech, Herron set out his concerns about access to healthcare and falling private health insurance, tying them to questions about bioethical matters such as in vitro fertilisation and organ transplants. After health, his second big topic was what he saw as the then Labor government's 'apparently deliberate attempt . . . to denigrate the importance of the family unit in Australian society'. Specifically, he worried about the falling birthrate, rising divorce levels and increasing numbers of mothers in the paid workforce. He deplored the fact that having children had become 'an economic decision' for families, and linked falling fertility to the fact that 'too many children who might be born are not. We are losing one in four unborn members of our population'. He added, 'I am not so naive to believe that an appeal to moral values or adherence to the Ten Commandments will be successful', but instead argued it was up to government to implement policies 'which actively and positively discriminate in favour of the family'.[16]

Having set out his agenda, 'the processes of Parliament overwhelmed me for eighteen months', so much that Herron felt he made little headway in promoting it.

> Then Kevin Andrews came in [as Member for Menzies in May 1991] and said virtually the same thing. I'd never met him, but I walked over to him and said, 'Great speech, what are you going to do about it? We had a meeting, got together with five or six including Chris Miles. We sent a note around to the Coalition side—and got 60 people along![17]

According to Herron, after that initial meeting, 'Kevin [Andrews] and Chris Miles made the running. Chris was the inaugural chair'. While accounts of the Lyons Forum's origins differ about who actually called the first meeting (others nominated Miles as the source of the idea), they consistently name as co-founders senators Herron and Tierney and members of the House of Representatives Alan Cadman, John Bradford, Chris Miles, Kevin Andrews and John Forrest. Whether the Forum was founded to promote a specifically Christian agenda depends on whom you ask. Newspapers habitually employed, without challenge or retraction, such descriptions as 'the Coalition's ultra-conservative Christian faction',[18] 'the Howard-backed fundamentalist Christian faction',[19] 'the conservative Christian faction—Australia's answer to America's religious right'[20] or 'a group of right wing Christian MPs'.[21]

The Forum's statements and the comments by its spokespeople are rich in language long identified with the American religious right, whose generalisations about 'the family' encode a quite specific constellation of policy prescriptions, all directed at entrenching a model of two-heterosexual-parents nuclear families at the expense of other family models, and opposing abortion.[22] Yet the Lyons Forum differs from the various American religious right organisations in some significant ways. The Forum's religious motivation is more often asserted by its critics than its members. On one hand, its promotional brochure has occasional references to God and its founders have well-known religious commitments: Herron has never been reticent about his Catholicism;[23] Tierney describes himself as an active lay Anglican;[24] Cadman has been a member of the Parliamentary Christian Fellowship since 1980 and is a prominent member of Sydney's Hillsong Church;[25] until his 1998 defeat, Bradford served on the Parliamentary Christian Fellowship executive, making headlines when he left the Liberal Party to become the only Christian Democrat in the federal parliament; Andrews is an active lay Catholic;[26] Forrest chaired the Parliamentary Christian Fellowship until the duties of National Party Chief Whip made the workload impossible.[27] On the other hand, its members, almost to a person, deny any 'religious' identity for the group, spokesperson Eric Abetz going so far as to call it 'straight-out secular'.[28] He attributed the common perception of the Forum as a religious group to media 'demonisation'.[29] Both Miles and Herron concurred. Journalists dislike the Forum, they suggested, because journalists, in Herron's words, 'are dysfunctional in their personal lives'. In Miles's view, that made the Forum 'a threat to them personally'.[30]

The use of language closely associated with the American religious right enables the Forum to appeal to the minority of conservative Christian voters, who recognise the language of 'family' and correctly decode the associated policy agenda. At the same time, the ambiguity about the Forum's religious identity and the avoidance of much explicitly religious language helps its spokespeople avoid alienating a potentially wider secular constituency. And reticence in naming its drafted sponsor helps evade challenge from those who have trouble seeing where a loving God fits the intolerant message.[31] The right's God is most powerful just below the surface.

With or without divine help, this was one supper club whose influence was to prove momentous for the party, its leader and the nation. The Forum's sixty members included Howard's eventual deputy Peter Costello, as well as many who went on to experience rapid rises under Howard's prime ministership, including Tony Abbott, Nick Minchin and Kevin Andrews. Howard himself was a regular during its formative period.[32] The group had a clear policy picture from the start, and Liberal Party structure and policy processes made clear what their first step had to be. Miles hinted as much on ABC radio in one of the very few media notices of the Lyons Forum in its early years:

> Matthew Abraham: Is it fair to say, though, that members of the group would tend to support the very strong traditional family focus taken by John Howard, when he was leader?
>
> Chris Miles: Well, fine, if they were the things—and I think to a certain extent they were, the things which John Howard was talking about—then certainly the Lyons Forum is interested.[33]

It took a couple of years to bring the Howard agenda back from the policy fringe. Jaensch cited a defining moment for Liberal Party philosophy in the 1993 leadership ballot which reaffirmed (for the time being) Hewson's already faltering leadership. Concentrating on the economic 'wet' and 'dry' classifications, Jaensch argued that by 1993 'dry' homogenisation had advanced so far that all the leadership contenders were 'of one ideological persuasion'. Jaensch listed Hewson, Howard, Costello, Bronwyn Bishop, Ian McLachlan, Wilson Tuckey and Alexander Downer, adding, 'the reason why there were no wets or moderates available is that the leading members of these tendencies had either resigned from the parliamentary party, or had been purged'.[34] Jaensch's account left the impression of a contest reduced to personality, electoral appeal or leadership skills, rather than policy. True, the potential contenders were all economic dries, but social policy was another matter.

Jaensch himself, in another context, provided a matrix from which we can derive a more informed reading of the 1993 leadership contest and its aftermath. He took the various tendencies' view on the proper role of government as his philosophical divining rod. Asking whether Liberals want government to intervene on economic, social or moral questions produced eight broad groupings within the officially faction-free party.

		Economic	**Social**	**Moral**
I	Conservative	Yes	Yes	Yes
II	Cold Conservative	Yes	No	Yes
III	Social Liberal	Yes	Yes	No
IV	(no label fits)	Yes	No	No
V	Libertarian Dry	No	No	No
VI	Dry Warm Libertarian	No	Yes	No
VII	Dry Cold Conservative	No	No	Yes
VIII	Dry Warm Conservative	No	Yes	Yes

Jaensch traced the Liberal Party's origins to Menzies's 'type I Conservative' orientation, but argued that, by the mid-1980s, the party had developed 'tendencies and proto-factions . . . across almost all of the possibilities' in the table.[35] But some were stronger than others: Jaensch, writing in 1994, argued that the social conservative position (broadly, the table's positions VII and VIII) 'was, and remains, a tendency' within the Liberal Party, but had never developed 'proto-faction characteristics'.[36]

Jaensch's study was published two years after the Lyons Forum's formation, well before it became a household name. The social conservatives were in the process of quietly developing arguably the strongest 'proto-faction characteristics' of any Liberal Party grouping since the South Australian New Liberal Movement split from the party in the 1970s. In the 1993 contest, Hewson, in Jaensch's terms a 'Libertarian Dry' (or possibly 'Dry, Warm Libertarian'),[37] retained the leadership. By the time he lost it on 23 May 1994, the considerable distance between Libertarian and Conservative Dry stances had been thrown into relief by a series of carefully engineered controversies, which brought the social conservative agenda to prominence.

•

The wedge that brought the tensions to a head was Hewson's decision to send a message of support to the 1994 Sydney Gay and Lesbian Mardi Gras. According to news reports, a number of Liberal backbenchers objected to the message on the grounds that 'the event was not one Dr Hewson should have supported'. They thought the leader's endorsement implied 'that Liberals generally supported it', and responded with 'anger'.[38] It was an anger they had successfully contained when he had sent the same message in previous years, but it ignited Hewson's final leadership crisis.

The next day, senators and members from all parties were invited to sign a 'petition' to the Australian Broadcasting Corporation, objecting to the station's scheduled broadcast of the Mardi Gras at 8.30 p.m. the following Sunday. Credit for the petition idea was claimed by Lyons Forum co-founders Miles and Cadman. Chris Miles is a Baptist lay preacher, who was then opposition spokesperson on Schools, Vocational Education and Training, now remembered mainly for sponsoring events such as a 1994 'Say No To Sodomy' rally and using the Parliament House internal mail system to distribute vehemently homophobic literature from the anti-gay law reform group Tas-Alert. Miles and Alan Cadman approached Labor Member for Lowe Mary Easson to garner support on her side of the house. To her, and to many who signed the petition, the issue was simply a matter of the broadcast's timing in what they deemed 'family' viewing time. To others, including Miles, it stood for broader issues:

> Miles: The ABC rejected the view of 94 members of parliament. And I think that was a reflection of really how arrogant the ABC were in regard to their promotion of homosexu-

> ality in society . . . I think that does show a particular agenda which the ABC have had, and . . . I think they continue to have it.
> MM: Of promoting homosexuality?
> Miles: Of course. Homosexual practices—let's get that straight. Homosexuality and homosexual practices are different issues.[39]

The text sent to the ABC, worded as an open letter to then Managing Director David Hill, describes the signatories as 'Senators and Members of the Australian Parliament', and as 'representatives of millions of Australians'.[40] It won some seventy Coalition and twenty ALP signatures, as well as some notable refusals. One was Kathy Sullivan, then Liberal Member for Moncrieff.

No one could call Sullivan an advocate of homosexual practices. True, she believed in the rights of consenting adults to conduct their sex lives without state interference, but she worried that some material aimed at teenagers amounted to gay proselytising. She refused to sign the petition to the ABC not out of any special affection for the Mardi Gras, but because 'it is inappropriate for us to dictate to the ABC'. Moreover, when the petition was circulated in the chamber that Wednesday, her impression was that it was presented to signatories as an initiative of the Parliamentary Christian Fellowship, a bipartisan prayer and discussion group. She recalled, 'I was at the Parliamentary Christian Fellowship that morning, and nothing was said' about the petition.[41] The Fellowship, in her view, 'was never designed for networking', and associating it with the petition amounted to co-opting its bipartisan standing for party political purposes—in fact, for one sectional interest within one party. The petition's real message, according to Sullivan, had less to do with the Mardi Gras than with Hewson's leadership.

> The petition never reached the central table, so Hewson didn't get a chance to sign it. The next day, [Parliamentary

> Christian Fellowship President and Lyons Forum Vice-President John] Bradford phoned every Liberal who hadn't signed, to ask them to reconsider—with two exceptions. He didn't phone me, because he knew I wouldn't sign—we had neighbouring electorates and we've clashed too often. And he didn't phone Hewson. So Hewson was being criticised for not supporting it, even though he never had an opportunity to sign.[42]

As it happened, Hewson agreed that the Mardi Gras would be better not shown in 'family' viewing time, and he later said he would have signed if invited:

> You could argue that a handful of people might be trying to set me up because they didn't ask me to sign the petition. They feared, I think, that I might sign the petition and that would weaken their argument.[43]

Hewson's comments at the time suggest that he, like Sullivan, detected a religious undercurrent in the campaign against him. The petition's Liberal promoters—Miles, Cadman and Bradford—were all longstanding Parliamentary Christian Fellowship members and none was shy about airing their faith. The feeling of religious pressure prompted Hewson to offer (in the *Sydney Morning Herald*) a theological rejoinder:

> There is also a Christian streak to this debate . . . God didn't say, 'God so loved the world excluding homosexuals', or, 'God so loved the world excluding two-income families', or whatever.[44]

The petition's effect was to throw into further relief the differences between Hewson and the social conservatives. It lived in media reporting less as an attempt to influence the ABC than as an indication of widening Liberal rifts.

The political role which the petition came to play surprised some of those who had signed from the Labor side. Mary Easson recalled:

> What they [Miles and Cadman] raised when they talked to me, and what it was all about as far as I was concerned, was the issue of [the broadcast's] timing. That was how they sold it to me, and that was how I sold it on my side . . . But it blew out of all proportion, because there was another agenda running, to do with Hewson and the Liberal leadership . . . Then David Hill released [the letter] on TV, and it all blew up and it became clear that the Liberals were using it against Hewson.[45]

John Howard's was one of the Liberal signatures, but his name was not raised publicly in connection with the letter's genesis. Yet it effectively ended the leadership career of his then arch-rival, Hewson. That part of the destabilisation campaign was substantially run by avowed Howard supporter Miles. Once the Liberals finally attained power in 1996, Howard appointed Miles his Parliamentary Secretary to Cabinet. He retained that position until he lost his seat in 1998 (when Howard replaced him with Senator Bill Heffernan, whose similarly dauntless commitment to scouring public life of any taint of homosexual practices is discussed in chapter four).

At stake in the fight over the Mardi Gras was more than the right of men to be seen on television in flamboyant frocks or dykes to flaunt their bikes in prime time. The real issue for the Liberals was what it means to 'govern for all Australians'. To Hewson, it meant that 'if you want to be a party for all Australians, you have to . . . start out by recognising all Australians', including those of minority sexual orientation or who live in non-nuclear families.[46] Moreover, recognising minority groups was being true to Liberal tradition, which Hewson saw as giving 'the individual . . . control over their lives and choice'.[47]

Otherwise, he feared the party was trying to 'go back to some sort of traditional basic something . . . I mean narrow the party back and have nothing to do with this group or that group'. Any such attempt would have dire consequences even beyond the issue of sexuality: 'It leads people to say, "Oh well, I prefer White Australians to others"'.[48] It would also, he guessed, prove electorally damaging. In fact, it would leave the Liberal Party 'irrelevant in about six months flat'. The Labor Party, on the other hand, would 'laugh themselves stupid' at the Liberal Party's 'incredible misunderstanding of the nature and basic values of the people of Australia'.[49]

One year after the 'unlosable' election, few observers would have thought that Hewson, then already walking in a perpetual mist of leadership speculation, would need any hastening towards his valedictory address. Before the Mardi Gras story surfaced, Liberal politicians were repeatedly in the news using words like 'despairing', 'appalled' and 'had a gutful' about the leadership struggle.[50] The Mardi Gras controversy did not create his downfall, yet it did supplement news bulletins' concentration on the then continuing differences between Hewson and Howard over immigration, family policy and income splitting.

Rather than an attempt to undermine an already terminally shaky leader, it is more helpful to see the Mardi Gras petition as a pre-emptive move in the inevitable contest for his successor. It entrenched the conservative social agenda as a benchmark. Significantly, the petition surfaced just as Hewson was intensifying his bid for the socially progressive ground and support for 'minority groups' in an attempt to reclaim 'small-l' liberals whom he felt the party had lost to the ALP. That helps explain an otherwise perplexing aspect of the story. Asked whether the Labor signatories on the petition had been used as part of the Liberal campaign against Hewson, Mary Easson reflected:

> I don't think I was set up. I don't know whether the Hewson leadership agenda was there all the time, whether the petition

> was always part of a strategy, or whether it just grew out of it afterwards . . . I thought about it at the time, once the story was running, and people were putting all these Machiavellian theories about Chris Miles. But, if the theories were right, I couldn't see how our signatures helped. If it was an agenda to do with Hewson, they only needed the signatures from their side, they didn't need ours.[51]

If, on the other hand, the agenda was less about getting rid of Hewson (he was on the way out anyway) than establishing the social conservative agenda as a benchmark in the inevitable ballot for his successor, then the ALP signatures were very useful. From early on, the Lyons Forum emphasised social conservatism's popular appeal, identifying it with a 'mainstream' which flows beyond 'special interests'.[52] As with the proposals about family policy and tax (and as shall be confirmed in the next two chapters) the Forum has always proved chary of batting for its own policy positions, preferring to lay them at the door of 'public opinion'. Similarly, the petition's implied association with the non-partisan Parliamentary Christian Fellowship and the bipartisan collection of signatures it gained might have indicated to the party room that voting in a 'family values' leader would not automatically damn the party to a conservative electoral ghetto, as Hewson suggested.[53]

Interviewed several years later, and with the benefit of hindsight, Hewson shared Sullivan's interpretation of the events surrounding the Mardi Gras petition. Himself a practising Anglican, he recalled:

> I knew the Parliamentary Christian Fellowship was being used for political ends. I don't think they knew it at the time . . . That's been Howard's history. He uses groups like the Modest Members and the Pitt Club. People set these things up for the right reasons, but then they get manipulated.[54]

Hewson himself did not attribute his electoral career's collapse solely to his party's social conservatives. Left wing critique, including from the Christian churches, had successfully targeted his *Fightback!* package's potential to increase social inequality. However, under Howard:

> Now we've got a GST *and* the social conservatism. And Howard's GST is a much less fair, less socially responsible package than *Fightback!* I didn't just give compensation, I wanted to overcome discrimination, against the aged, for example . . . We had a focus on children, whether they were in one- or two-parent families—we weren't saying mum has to be at home with the kids. The present Liberal Party's socially conservative policy leads to a less fair society.[55]

•

In May 1994, Hewson lost a party ballot, and was replaced by Alexander Downer, Member for Mayo (SA). At the time, Downer was widely seen as a compromise candidate, filling in the gap for a party not yet ready for Peter Costello's overt New Right alignment, and still scarred from its last fling with Howard. Such analyses usually relate to Downer's position in the Liberal Party's economic spectrum. However, a similar claim could be made about his stance on the social issues dear to the Lyons Forum.

Downer was never a Lyons Forum member; however, he was a well-established critic of 'minority special interest groups'. His first speech, in 1985, attacked a Labor government held 'hostage' to the 'squeals and cries' of 'selfish and sectional interests'.[56] He railed against 'deals with . . . privileged interest groups', by which he seemed at the time to have in mind the traditional Liberal enemy, trade unions; but, in the party turmoil of the early 1990s, it translated readily into social policy. The Mardi Gras was a case in point. The man once photographed in fishnet stockings explained: 'What do I think about the Gay Mardi Gras? If it's your scene, have a nice day. It doesn't affect me'. Nevertheless, true to his 1985 vision, he did not want to see the party soliciting minority interests. Also, there were pragmatic concerns: 'When the 1995 Mardi Gras came around, I didn't send a message of support, and I can remember exactly why I didn't. It was because I didn't want another break-out in the party on an issue like that'.[57]

Downer's leadership lasted less than a year. By the end of January 1995, the Liberal Party had a leader in tune with the—by then—longstanding aspirations of the Lyons Forum.

CHAPTER THREE

The politics of death

In 1995, the residents of the Northern Territory gained the right to active voluntary euthanasia. It was granted by the Country–Liberal Party dominated Northern Territory Parliament in a dramatic series of conscience votes, interspersed with equally dramatic legal challenges. Chief Minister Marshall Perron introduced the Bill in February 1995 and the *Rights of the Terminally Ill Act 1995* passed into law after intensive committee scrutiny that June.

Under the *Northern Territory (Self Government) Act 1978*, the Commonwealth government could have intervened any time during the next six months to disallow the Act, in what would have been the first such intervention in the seventeen years of Territory self-government. The prime minister of the day, Paul Keating, found the Act an acceptable use of the Territory government's law-making power and 'not a matter for disallowance'.[1] However, the Northern Territory Parliament itself amended the Act in February 1996 to take account of technical concerns and, in the accompanying debate, revisited the initial question.

A proposed amendment, which would have repealed the whole Act, was defeated. So was another, which would have added a sunset clause, ending the Act's operation after three years. In May, the Act came under fresh challenge in the Northern Territory Parliament, this time from a private member's Bill to repeal it. That, too, was defeated. In June, the Northern Territory Supreme Court heard a request for an injunction to prevent the Act being proclaimed, but the injunction was not granted and the matter was referred to the full court of the Supreme Court, which upheld the Act.

The Act came into operation on 1 July 1996, though the cloud of challenges meant it was more than two months until the first patient, Bob Dent, and his doctor were confident to use it. One further attempt to modify the Act came in August, that is, after the Act had come into force but before it was used. A Bill was introduced into the Northern Territory Parliament to make it illegal for hospitals or health clinics to offer assistance under the Act. Once again, the change was voted down and the *Rights of the Terminally Ill Act 1995* survived.

If the Act had been passed by a State parliament, that would almost certainly have been that, and terminally ill people would presumably still be taking advantage of it. But the Australian Constitution gives the Commonwealth power to make laws for its territories (as opposed to States),[2] and the Territory's transition to self-government did not take away that power. Consequently, although the six months in which the Commonwealth can disallow a Territory Act had expired, the Commonwealth Parliament could still consider a law overturning it. The Lyons Forum had got its man into power in 1995 and saw its party into office in 1996. Here was its first chance to have a hands-on effect on Australia's soul.

The Liberal Member for Menzies and a Lyons Forum co-founder and secretary, Kevin Andrews, is a lawyer who has co-authored five books, including one on bioethics and another on biomedical regulation. Before entering parliament in 1991 he was involved in marriage education programs, and has remained active in that area even amid the demands of a ministerial career—for example, as an adjunct Lecturer in Marriage Education at Melbourne's conservative John Paul Institute for Marriage and Family. His first speech to parliament set out bioethics as one of his priorities. Nevertheless, he swallowed his ire at the Northern Territory Bill through the period when the government could have directly overturned the law. His moment came in June 1996 when he asked John Howard, now the prime minister, a 'Dorothy Dixer' about the legal challenge scheduled to open in the Northern Territory Supreme Court that July, in which it would be argued the Act was unconstitutional and in which the Commonwealth was named as defendant. Howard replied that the Commonwealth would argue neither for nor against, and was seeking to be removed as defendant. Howard also gave a personal opinion—the only time he directly told the parliament his view on euthanasia: 'Speaking as an individual, I have the strongest possible reservations about the legislation passed by the Northern Territory Parliament'. And he issued an invitation:

> The view of the government is that, if this matter comes before the parliament for determination or vote, as far as the Coalition parties are concerned, any response to that will be determined on a conscience or individual basis . . . of course, it is open to any member of this parliament, if he or she feels strongly about this issue, to introduce a private member's Bill.[3]

Kevin Andrews introduced the Euthanasia Laws Bill, which rapidly became known as the Andrews Bill, as a private member on 9 September 1996. It passed the Senate on 24 March 1997.

When Federal Parliament debated his Bill, many saw the crucial issue as the Northern Territory's legislative autonomy. Even some longstanding opponents of euthanasia, such as Senator Bob Collins,[4] found their Territory loyalties outweighed their bioethical concerns. For others, the moral justifiability of euthanasia trumped other considerations, so that even ardent defenders of State rights, such as Federal Treasurer Peter Costello,[5] had to suppress their longstanding fear of centralism to oppose the greater evil of euthanasia.

Another widely canvassed issue these events raised was representation. Many observers pointed out that opinion polls consistently showed around seventy per cent of the population was in favour of active voluntary euthanasia (and, indeed, has been at least since the 1950s). That being so, some wondered about the propriety of politicians, most of whom had been elected without their opinions on euthanasia ever being raised in their electorates, overturning legislation which apparently reflected public feeling, not only in the Northern Territory but also in their own constituencies.

Added to that was a perception that the move to overturn the Territory's Act was the product of a well-organised but seldom acknowledged campaign by religious conservatives. Some commentary suggested that the religiously motivated, whose views did not reflect public opinion, had no business exerting such an influence on the law of a democratically elected parliament.[6]

•

Both parties in the Federal Parliament gave their members a free vote (often called a 'conscience' vote) on the Andrews Bill. From early on, though, there was an intimation that some members' votes might have been freer than others. Howard did not speak in the debate (other than seeking guidance, just before the vote, as to what time the division was likely to take place, as he had to fit it around hosting some 'very eminent sportspeople' at the Lodge). The 'strongest possible reservations' about the Northern Territory law, which he admitted when opening the way for a private member's Bill on the question, were all the bioethical philosophising the parliament would hear from him. Yet there was a clear understanding, on both sides of the chamber, that the Bill progressed with his endorsement. That perception led one dissenting Coalition member to claim that 'Howard coming out like that . . . put so many people under pressure to fall into line that it really wasn't a conscience vote'.[7] It wasn't just that Howard announced his 'reservations'. That the Bill came up for debate at all was widely seen as an evidence of his imprimatur.

The parliamentary schedule has a special timeslot called 'Private Members' Business' when private members' Bills can be introduced and debated: such Bills get an hour and a bit on sitting Mondays (of which there were twelve in 1996). Since a 1988 rule change, it has debated about eight or nine a year.[8] Only one other 1996 private member's Bill (to do with regulation of movement at Sydney Airport) progressed beyond its first reading.

The Andrews Bill was exceptional, not just for getting heard, but for the amount of time devoted to it. Eighty members—more than half the chamber—spoke during its second reading, with more contributions during grievance and adjournment debates. Most of the second reading speeches were limited to ten minutes, but even so that still meant a total of over thirteen hours devoted to the Bill. If the House had stuck to its usual procedure for private members' business the Bill would, on its own, have taken up more than the entire debate time for the whole year's 'Private Members' Mondays'. Instead, the government gave some of its own allocation, despite the heavy end-of-year legislative load.[9]

When the Bill went to the Senate's Legal and Constitutional Affairs Committee, Greens Senator Bob Brown (Tasmania) spelled out the implications of the government's de facto sponsorship:

> It may be that many Senators are currently asking themselves exactly what their obligations are when they cast their conscience vote on the Andrews Bill . . . They may be wondering whether there really are 'party lines' (or at least 'factional lines') on this issue, and how the public record of their vote on the Andrews Bill may influence their political future within their party or faction.[10]

His concerns may have been influenced by the Bill's course through the House of Representatives, comfortably dominated by the Coalition since the 1996 landslide, where it romped through 88 votes to 35. The yes vote netted 53 Liberal, 11 National and 22 Labor members, plus two independents, while only 11 Liberals and two Nationals joined 21 Labor members and one independent in the no camp. In other words, only about one in five government consciences supported the right to die, while the ALP members were almost evenly divided. By contrast, the Senate vote was a tight 38 to 34 with one abstention. The closeness is partly accounted for by the more even party numbers in the Senate (29 ALP and 37 Coalition, compared to 49 ALP and 94 Coalition in the House), plus the fact that both the Greens senators and all but one of the seven Australian Democrats voted no. Nonetheless, between the major parties the breakdown was closer in the Senate than in the other chamber. Though the Coalition still strongly supported Andrews, the majority was less pronounced. The Labor side, on the other hand, split more sharply than they had in the House: twice as many Labor senators opposed Andrews as supported him.

There was another major difference between the Senate and House debates. Given the common perception, particularly in the media, that the anti-euthanasia campaign was being waged in the name of God, we might expect theology to feature in the debates. In fact, God scarcely entered the House of Representatives debate, getting a mention in only eight of the eighty speeches. All but one of the members who referred to their faith in God did so against the right to die. Federal Treasurer Peter Costello was typical of those who invoked God, arguing that opposition to euthanasia:

> [I]s a religious belief . . . You either take that [religious] view or you do not, in my opinion. I do take it. People who do not take it I do not think will ever be persuaded. But it is fundamental, I think, to the beliefs that have guided our

> civilisation and our society from the days of the Ten Commandments.[11]

Similar views came, more or less expansively, from fellow Liberals Paul Zammit, Neil Andrew, Bob Baldwin and John Bradford (who two years later abandoned the Liberal Party to become—fleetingly—Federal Parliament's sole representative of Fred Nile's Christian Democrats) and from the Nationals' Noel Hicks. In addition, Liberal Ross Cameron supported his anti-euthanasia views with a passing reference to 'a Jewish carpenter in northern Palestine about twenty centuries ago'. The sole theological rejoinder came from Labor's Anthony Albanese, who listed several reasons why 'I oppose this Bill', including 'because my Christian upbringing taught me that compassion is important'.[12] But religious arguments on either side were a small minority.

By contrast, the Senate debate sounded positively devout, with twenty-one of the fifty-six speakers invoking religious arguments in their support. What they said, though, hardly fits the media picture.

•

After the 1996 election, the Senate suddenly became a much more obviously religious place, and if you got there for the start of proceedings you could hardly have helped noticing. Like the House of Representatives, the Senate opens each sitting day with prayers led by the presiding officer. On the new 1996 Senate's second day its incoming president, Senator Margaret Reid, reported:

> Some senators have asked if I would have any objection to their saying the Lord's Prayer with me. I have no objection, and, if any senator wishes to, he or she may do so.[13]

Victorian Labor Senator Kim Carr noticed the change:

> You just get a sense in which there is a growing body of opinion in the Senate that feels the need to mumble very loudly their religious convictions every morning . . . I get the feeling there are now more people attending prayers from the conservative side of politics than there were when I first started . . . And the volume—! They actually put their hearts into it. Under a Labor regime perhaps they were a little bit shyer.[14]

With a Senate eager to wear its faith on its sleeve, you would expect to find senators putting their theology into the euthanasia debate. Even Greens Senator Bob Brown, who had vigorously opposed the Bill, said the morning after the vote: 'On the eve of Easter, it is quite remarkable that so many people got up and said, "I am a Christian. I vote for this Bill"'.[15] With respect to the House of Representatives, he may have had a point (though their debate took place in the shadow of Christmas, not of Easter).

Senate Hansard tells a different story. It is true that much of the discussion had a highly theological flavour—senators laced their speeches with descriptions of God—but strikingly few came from those supporting the Bill; that is, broadly, from those speaking against euthanasia.[16] Of the thirty-eight senators who supported the Bill, only six mentioned religious arguments in their speeches; and only four of those spoke explicitly about their own religious commitments. By contrast, one third of those on the opposing side (eleven out of thirty-three senators) supported their pro-euthanasia stance with religious arguments.

Among the comparatively sparse speeches citing religious arguments against euthanasia, South Australian Liberal Senator Grant Chapman, a Lyons Forum and Parliamentary Christian Fellowship stalwart, declared, 'My Christian conviction demands my support for the sanctity of life . . .' and concluded that 'no person has the right to play God with anyone's life, including their own. Only God has that right'.[17] Tasmanian Liberal Senator

Paul Calvert quoted both the National Council of Churches and the Pope against euthanasia, and recalled his own father's painful but unhastened death: 'God's way was the only way'.[18]

Victorian National Party Senator Julian McGauran quoted the Australian Catholic Bishops Conference that 'euthanasia is a revolt against God', and declared 'many, me included, have reflected upon their own religious beliefs to help them come to a final decision on this matter'. However, Senator McGauran, like other senators against euthanasia who mentioned religious grounds (and in contrast, for example, to Peter Costello's 'either you accept it or you don't' position), qualified his approach: 'I stress that Christianity is not a necessary criterion nor was a criterion for some taking a position against euthanasia'.[19] In the Senate, euthanasia opponents seemed remarkably wary of laying themselves open to any charge of religious exclusivism. There were some parallels on the Labor side.

Victorian Labor Senator Barney Cooney drew a connection between the 'religious, cultural and social beliefs which reject euthanasia' that are held by 'a goodly proportion of Australian citizens including me', but built his argument not so much on directly theological grounds as on the idea of inclusive representation: 'A person's stance on a particular matter should not be labelled invalid simply because it is based on his or her faith'.[20] Tasmanian Labor Senator Nick Sherry similarly warned against excessive partitioning between personal beliefs and civic responsibilities: 'I do not see it as an issue of separating church and state. But I still think that in our Western society these Judeo-Christian principles are very important and should be preserved'.[21]

New South Wales Labor Senator Michael Forshaw raised religious arguments but only to move beyond them: 'the right to life is not just a religious principle. What is often called the "sanctity of life" extends beyond religious faith and belief in a God. It is fundamental, I believe, to human existence, whether one follows a religious faith or not'.[22]

These theological (or quasi-theological) comments were the exception on the anti-euthanasia side: the large majority of Andrews Bill supporters in the Senate, like their House of Representatives counterparts, appealed to pragmatic objections. They insisted that modern palliative care is well able to control pain at the end of life. They warned that unscrupulous relatives might pressure the sick or elderly to 'choose' euthanasia. They worried that euthanasia would jeopardise the doctor–patient relationship. When anti-euthanasia speakers left pragmatic concerns to invoke general philosophical principles, they were much more likely to be in the secular language of applied ethics than in the terms of moral theology: they peered down slippery slopes, pictured hypothetical dystopias and worried about potentially devaluing life.

The relative sparseness of religious argument sits awkwardly with the perception of religious dominance of the anti-euthanasia side, a perception which seemed strong not only on the part of the public but even among participants on the other side of the debate, like Senator Brown. Indeed, the Senate Legal and Constitutional Legislation Committee's report on the Bill goes so far as to list 'religious beliefs' under the general heading 'Arguments Against Euthanasia', without qualification (despite the fact that it had received at least one significant church submission which did not assume euthanasia received an automatic divine veto).

By contrast, eleven senators' speeches followed theological routes to support euthanasia. Seven couched parts of their argument directly in terms of their own faith. For some, the critical principle was refusal to impose beliefs on others. Then Democrat Deputy Leader (and active member of Adelaide's Pilgrim Uniting Church), South Australian Senator Meg Lees, declared, 'I am a practising Christian and I have heard arguments about the sanctity of life from other Christians in this place', but argued that 'parliament should not seek to impose . . . beliefs' on those who 'place the notion of quality of life ahead of the sanctity of life'.[23] Some who did not refer to their own beliefs shared similar concerns about the proper place of religion in public life. For example, Tasmanian Labor Senator Sue Mackay took issue 'with those honourable senators who would seek to impose their private faith on others with the force of law',[24] while the ACT's Senator Kate Lundy argued: 'Passing the Andrews Bill would mean that the Senate is more willing to uphold the values of certain religious groups in our society [who] have mounted a well-resourced, strategic and highly emotive lobbying campaign in support of the Andrews Bill'.[25]

More directly, the Northern Territory's Country Liberal Party Senator, Grant Tambling, took a stance in keeping with his theological traditions as a Uniting Church lay preacher[26] (and against the majority of his Federal political allies) when he reported that 'I have certainly searched my own soul throughout the past two years . . . and I cannot find any scriptural condemnation of anyone who chooses to take their own life'.[27] Labor Senator Bruce Childs offered one of Hansard's occasional moments of Biblical exegesis in noting that 'the sixth commandment is not "Thou shalt not kill" but "Thou shalt do no murder"'. He further invoked the mutability of theological tradition, pointing out that in the past: 'Many Christians considered that the pain of childbirth was woman's punishment for Eve's sin and was given by God as a reminder of this, [while today] the concept of denying a woman pain relief because it is God's will that she should suffer seems barbaric'.[28]

Others advanced positive theological arguments for personal autonomy. Liberal Senator Jocelyn Newman, then Minister for Social Security and Minister Assisting the Prime Minister for the Status of Women, publicly thanked God for her recovery from breast cancer, seeing no conflict between the idea of life as divine gift and a conviction that individuals should nevertheless retain 'the right to knowingly choose the time of [their] death and the circumstances in which [they] die'.[29]

Then Labor Senator Rosemary Crowley describes herself as a Christmas-and-Easter Catholic ('I certainly believe in a spiritual dimension, but whether that's the same as religious I'm not sure . . . I think by any definition they wouldn't still have me, but I'm not defining myself out').[30] She concluded her speech against the Bill: 'None of us can know what is between [a] person and his or her conscience, that person and his or her God'.[31] The then Minister for Employment, Education, Training and Youth Affairs, Liberal Senator Amanda Vanstone, attributes her commitments to individualism and personal freedom partly to her Anglican schooling.[32] She mirrored Senator Crowley's implied view that different people's Gods may lead them in different directions: 'Your life is not mine to take, but what I do with mine should be between me and my God and no-one else'. She spelled out her position 'in a colloquial way' by speculating that 'any God is looking for converts not conscripts'.[33]

Most elaborately, Tasmanian Greens Senator Bob Brown enunciated a personal faith underpinning his concern for respect for diversity, both in modes of bioethical decision-making and in modes of religious belief. His speech, adopting the form of a creed, produced the debate's nearest approach to a developed theology of life and death:

> I believe in a universal life force which gives us that relay of life, passing on from generation to generation, an essential factor being death. It also gives us intelligence, sensitivity, rights and responsibilities. That is my God. And so it is for me to choose about voluntary euthanasia when I am dying and life has been overtaken by the matter of how to die. My God says that is my choice. Others in this place may have a God who does not give them that choice. Well and good. Abide by your God, but do not force your God on me and I will not force my God on you.[34]

Brown's theme of seeing death, along with life, as divine gift was also developed by other speakers. In contrast to Chapman and

Calvert's assumption that following 'God's way' rules out human hastening of death, Labor Senator Brenda Gibbs asked:

> How do we know that death is not a beautiful thing? If life on this earth is so unbearable, death is sublime. I have always believed in God or a superior being and I believe that we all have a certain time in this life and then our spirit goes home.[35]

Sanctity of life principles were taken by some speakers to conflict with state secularism. Senator Childs challenged the consistency of the view that 'God gave life and only God can take it away' by recalling that:

> in my lifetime I have seen that as soon as the flag is raised and patriotic fervour is whipped up, respect for the sanctity of life goes out the window, [often propelled by] many of the same people who raise their voices against voluntary euthanasia . . . If euthanasia is condemned only for religious reasons, then the fact that we live in a secular state should be enough reason to exclude voluntary euthanasia from the criminal code.[36]

Labor Senator Kim Carr acknowledged 'that many senators support this Bill on genuinely held religious grounds' and affirmed 'the right of any Australian to declare or practise their religion'. But Parliament's job is to legislate within an established framework, even if that means some views cannot be directly represented: 'these are religious concepts', while 'Australia is a secular nation, and as its Parliament we have an obligation to make secular laws, not religious ones'.[37]

The most detailed argument for state secularism was put forward by Senator Vanstone, citing her recent reading of *The Godless Constitution: The case against religious correctness*[38] to invoke sources from Roger Williams through Alexis de Tocqueville and Thomas Jefferson to contemporary studies of the United States constitution. The book had obviously had an impact: when I asked her about it she lent me her copy, complete with senatorial underlinings, margin notes and sticky labels marking important spots.

The relatively sparse attention paid to constitutional questions of church–state separation in the euthanasia debate indicates something significant about Australian political culture. One can't imagine a similar debate taking place in America without extensive Jeffersonian soul-searching. Despite the fact that Australia's separation clause (section 116) was modelled on its American forerunner, the anxieties which pervade US church–state relationships had not translated to the Australian setting.

•

The evidence of Hansard goes against the impression shared by some participants, the overwhelming mass of media commentary and popular opinion. Far from the debate being dominated by religious anti-euthanasia talk, the bulk of religious testimony came from proponents of a right to die. Given the well-known Christian convictions of many of Andrews's supporters, it is hard to avoid the conclusion that most consciously played down their religious motivations.

Asked about the place of religious argument in public debate, Andrews denied there is anything improper about elected representatives drawing on their religious convictions but added that, strategically, 'I don't think it ultimately gets you anywhere or solves anything, because there [are] religious people on both sides of the debate'. On euthanasia, he had consciously avoided religious argument: 'In all the debates, I don't believe I ever used a religious argument in relation to the issue. It was always on the grounds of what were the consequences of what we were doing'. He had also consciously avoided drawing attention to his Lyons Forum affiliation because he feared too close an association with the Forum would damage the anti-euthanasia cause.[39] During the House of Representatives debate, Labor's Peter Morris, who opposed the Bill, commented, 'What is so extraordinary about this debate is what is not being said . . . so much is being said, but so much more is not being said'. He did not specify what he sensed was being suppressed, but his remarks could well have applied to the debate's theological tenor.

It is hard to make more than the proverbially risky argument from silence. Yet the speeches do suggest an explanation, namely, that speakers against the Andrews Bill felt a need to resort to the language of faith not only because of the issue's depth and sensitivity, but also because they sensed an unspoken theological agenda in at least some of their opponents. This is implied, for example, in Senator Kate Lundy's allusion to the 'well-resourced, strategic and highly emotive lobbying campaign' mounted by 'certain religious groups in our society'.[40] Journalists noted the importance of churches' lobbying campaigns in the lead-up to the vote, the *Sydney Morning Herald*'s Jodie Brough commenting that 'Territory rights disappeared as an issue as soon as the anti-euthanasia juggernaut of the Catholic Church, Right to Life and the Anglican Church rolled into Canberra'.[41]

The 'rolling into Canberra' metaphor implies that religious concerns came from 'outside' the conventional sites of political power, while members and senators toppled helplessly beneath its crushing wheels. Brough underscores the debate's apparently destabilising characteristics by noting the 'weird bipartisan caucus' of parliamentary anti-euthanasia campaigners 'which included Coalition senators Eric Abetz and Julian McGauran as well as Labor's Mark Bishop and Independent Senator Brian Harradine'. As the *Australian*'s political editor Michael Gordon explained after the vote, the anti-euthanasia campaign was the work of a highly organised bipartisan parliamentary network called 'Euthanasia No', specially formed for that one debate and then disbanded. It aimed to keep both its religious commitments and, indeed, its existence out of the headlines: 'having a profile so low as to be almost subterranean was an integral component of the strategy'.[42] The anti-Andrews side was marshalled by a similarly weird alliance between the Liberal Country Party's Grant Tambling and Northern Territory Labor Senator (and anti-euthanasia Catholic) Bob Collins. On such accounts, euthanasia and the campaign against it erupted into national public life as a chaotic intrusion, destabilising existing associations. Yet the view which interprets the debate of March 1997 as a response to external pressures offers little insight into why the bulk of religious argument should have come from those opposing the juggernaut.

Attuned to the campaign techniques which characterised the conservative Christian push to bring Howard to power, we can find a more convincing explanation for the disjunction between perceptions of the debate and what people actually said by considering the anti-euthanasia push not as the bearer of an alien deity swept to the centre by external forces, but as the staged unfolding of the next act in the right's carefully scripted culture war. In one clue, Senator Chris Schacht noted the politics of the Bill's path to the debate:

> When was the last time that a private member's Bill has had this number of hours provided by special arrangement by the government? Why? Because the government itself, under the influence of the Lyons Forum, has made this, in effect, a de facto government Bill.[43]

'Government' can mean several things, but here we are meant to understand the Liberal leader and those close to him. Howard must have perceived advantages in rewarding the Lyons Forum, while taking another opportunity to divide his opponents and chalking up another success against his socially liberal bêtes-noires.

•

Schacht was not the only one to see the Bill's passage as a victory for the Coalition's Lyons Forum. But an argument that its Lyons Forum association implies a religious agenda does not follow automatically. As we saw in the last chapter, its religious associations are ambiguous. The group's motto and self-descriptions emphasise family values, and avoid overtly religious identification. One exception is a printed promotional brochure. Two versions of the same brochure declare, respectively, 'we believe that the family is the fundamental unit of society' and 'we believe that the family is the God-ordained fundamental unit of society'.[44] Both versions omit God when it comes to government action: 'We believe that the government through its activities should promote the family as the fundamental unit of society'.

Tasmanian Liberal Senator Eric Abetz welcomed being asked about the Lyons Forum's religion as a chance to set the record straight:

> Senator Abetz: I'm glad you asked, because the Lyons Forum in fact is non-religious. The Lyons Forum has four core beliefs, none of which is religious in nature . . . It is, if you like, straight out secular. Having said that, I personally have religious beliefs . . .
> MM: Would most or all members of the Lyons Forum, as it happens, share those religious beliefs?
> Senator Abetz: Most, I think it would be fair to say, hold part of the spectrum of Christian beliefs . . . But there are some who are in the Lyons Forum who wouldn't go to the Parliamentary Christian Fellowship, for example.[45]

Although a number of Lyons Forum members mentioned non-Christian colleagues, they were unwilling to name any. That reticence contributes to the difficulty of evaluating the media characterisation of the Forum as—in practice even if not in intention—a Christian group. Some had trouble not just in naming non-Christian members, but in thinking of them. For example, when I asked Forum co-founder and former Liberal Member for Braddon Chris Miles whether he could think of any who were avowed atheists, he ruminated: 'Any who was an avowed atheist? Ah, well, there are not many of those in the

Liberal Party. There are very few in the Liberal Party, but most in the Liberal and National parties have religious convictions.'[46]

Not all self-professed members distanced themselves from the Christian characterisation. Co-founder Senator John Herron answered the question about the Forum's Christian identity with a simple, 'Yes'. He saw this reflected in some agreed positions: 'We believe in God, we believe in marriage'.

Non-members were more likely than members to see the group as Christian. Notably, that interpretation was shared by a number of former Forum members who had subsequently distanced themselves from it. Former Senator Baden Teague combines a commitment to 'family values' with 'small-l' liberalism: 'There would be few in the Liberal Party further to the left than me'. He was an early member of the Lyons Forum. As he saw it, the Forum began as a lobby for the family but, 'after not many meetings, it became what the public see it as: a hard-right think tank'.[47]

NSW Senator John Tierney shares Teague's Anglicanism and was also a Lyons Forum founder but, unusually, he combined that commitment with his founding involvement in another Liberal club formed in the early 1990s, the socially libertarian John Stuart Mill Society, widely interpreted as opposing the Lyons Forum. He left the Lyons Forum because 'It was too public: I didn't mind the issues, but objected to the publicity technique'. On his account, 'The Lyons Forum was established to examine legislation in the light of Christian values'.

> MM: Are all its members Christian?
> Senator Tierney: Yes—I don't think you'd bother if you weren't.[48]

Tim Fischer, former National Party leader and deputy prime minister, was never a member but declared himself in sympathy with the Forum's conservative 'family' stance. Himself a practising Catholic ('I haven't come suddenly to Christ, it's something that's been there all the time'), he gave an unequivocal 'Yes' to the question about the Forum's Christian identity. Like Senator Tierney, his disagreement was about tactics, although on contrasting grounds: 'I didn't like their behind-the-scenes way of operating, I thought it should be more out in the open'.[49] Since, as we saw in the previous chapter, the Lyons Forum is most usefully understood in terms of its role in Liberal Party structures and the selection of its leader, one might also speculate that the Lyons Forum has less immediate relevance to the National Party, whose members get no say on the Liberal leadership, and where conservative social policy is uncontroversial.

One of the Forum's most prolific Labor critics, Member for Grayndler Anthony Albanese, went further, comparing it to the American religious right: 'The Lyons Forum is a right wing, Buchanan-type of politics entering Australia. It is an organised right wing religious cell in the Liberal Party—it's old-fashioned vanguard politics'.[50]

Both the policies and strategy of the Lyons Forum are plainly indebted to those of the American New Christian Right, which developed a well-funded, intricately organised and think tank-supported power base for the Republican Party following arch-conservative Barry Goldwater's defeat in 1964. While its endeavours have included some expensive failures, such as the Presidential campaigns of populist Republican candidates Pat Buchanan and Pat Robertson, the American movement has contributed to numerous right wing successes including, crucially, the eventual election of one of its own, George W. Bush, as President of the United States. In her important study of the US religious right, Ann Burlein documents how 1980s Moral Majority-style pulpit-thumping gave way during the 1990s to a more strategic, neutral rhetoric. Successor organisations to the Moral Majority, such as Focus on the Family and the American Christian Coalition, began to advise their officers and members to avoid explicitly religious language as potentially alienating to secular voters.[51]

One key element in the Lyons Forum's success in 'mainstreaming' its social conservative agenda has been its ambiguous association with Christianity. The 'Christian' identification arguably eased the acceptance of a new (proto-)faction within a party traditionally wary of internal division. At the same time, support from religious groups outside the parliament, together with many of its key members' involvement in organisations such as the bipartisan Parliamentary Christian Fellowship, provided one means by which the Lyons Forum was able to garner allegiance for aspects of its agenda not only across the Liberal and National parties, but even among some ALP senators and members—with the Mardi Gras and euthanasia being two textbook examples. As we shall explore further in the next chapter, the 'family' emphasis, eschewing too much explicitly religious language, allowed the Lyons Forum to allay fears of an insurgent religious right and to extend their agenda's appeal beyond a narrowly confessional constituency.

In the last chapter, we saw how Howard's highway to the top was made straight, the second time around, by the support of a powerful pressure group. The emphasis on 'family', 'values' and 'social stability' played a key role in rebranding far-right social conservatism as 'mainstream', by eliciting bipartisan support for carefully selected key wedge issues. The technique is most striking when—as in the case of euthanasia—Howard's position was in direct opposition to the mainstream he so successfully seemed to represent. His stolid, Methodist persona (never mind, as we saw in chapter one, that this was substantially fabricated as far as Methodism's connection to his political ideology goes) helped mask any deviousness or deliberate divisiveness. Howard excelled at maintaining a Pilate-like distance from the messy political work, quarantined behind an imaginary white picket fence. Sexuality and euthanasia were two benchmark areas in which the right was able to raise enough support from social conservatives on the left to make the issue seem non-political. Now we see how the same techniques have worked in the culture war over women's roles, parenting and the nature of family.

CHAPTER FOUR

Mothers and fathers

Camilla Nelson's satirical novel, *Perverse Acts*,[1] set some time in the twenty-first century, hypothesises a Republic of Australia. The transition to a republic has left some aspects of the parliamentary structure unchanged: not only does the décor retain familiar hues (squashed-strawberry grey in the Senate, gum-leaf grey in the House), but the unnamed neo-liberal party, like so many crusading governments before it, faces obstruction in the Senate. The only hope the party has to implement its Freedom From Government Bill and the associated Get Rich Quick tax scheme is to secure the balance-of-power votes of a minor party called the Circle of Light. Here is how a cynical narrator, Venus, describes the Circle:

> The Circle of Light was a relatively new phenomenon but its antecedents stretched back a generation or two, back to the end of the 1990s. Some say it started with an independent on the crossbench in the Senate, others as a faction within the ruling Party. (Did I say faction? Excuse me, I meant *forum*.)

> It all began with prayer breakfasts, a lot more prayer breakfasts and a giant circle of praise. And then, a lot more giant circles of praise and a really fashionable fad: the Christian men's weekend for strategy planning.
>
> The strategies included tighter censorship, denying government benefits to women who had left their husbands, and a general division of the public into morally deserving and undeserving. Only the former would be able to benefit from government-subsidised services, or claim tax rebates. But it was not until the government of the day caved in completely and set up the Foundation for the Enforcement of Traditional Values that people really began to notice.[2]

Nelson's 'family values' dystopia, published in 1998, has some increasingly familiar elements. The Circle of Light is not the government, nor does it have a formal Coalition with it; it merely provides the numbers in the Senate after satisfactory horse-trading. For example, it supports the Freedom From Government Bill and the National Liquidation Program in return for the government supporting its Single Mothers Obliteration Bill. Some members of the government declare themselves in sympathy with the Circle of Light's 'traditional values' agenda. Others, such as Venus's co-narrator, an ambitious male backbencher known only as M who 'secretly aspired to be the first prime minister . . . sacked for fornication' and wants his political biography to be subtitled *The Man Who Slept with 240 Women*, give the Circle the family values it wants in the spirit of the purest electoral cynicism.

Since the resurgence of the religious right in the USA in the 1970s, fiction has shown us a number of right wing dystopias, not always readily transferable to an Australian setting. For example, it is hard to imagine the murderously theocratic government of Margaret Atwood's *The Handmaid's Tale*[3] bearing much resemblance to Australian realities. Nelson's picture of a religious fundamentalist tail wagging a secular right wing dog is much more credible in the immediate Australian setting.

Successive Howard governments produced substantial successes for proponents of 'traditional values'. Until the 2004 election gave a Senate seat to a version of Nelson's fictional minor party, the pressure has come overwhelmingly from a faction—excuse me, I mean *Forum*—within the government. Like the Circle of Light, its success is due partly to its ability to present its conservative policies as pragmatic responses to economic or social pressures, rather than as religiously motivated social engineering. Some of its successes, such as tightened censorship, moves to allow the States to make marital status a criterion for access to reproductive technologies and explicit prohibition of gay marriage, fall directly under the heading of social policy. Others, like the watering-down of affirmative action and changes to the tax structure in favour of families with a stay-at-home parent, have emerged at least partly as by-products of economic measures.

The unexpectedly strong showing of Family First in the 2004 election was widely interpreted as a novelty. On Channel 9's *Sunday* program the next morning, with the Senate result still in doubt, Laurie Oakes interviewed the ALP and Liberal campaign directors, along with Andrew Bartlett, leader of what remained of the Australian Democrats. Oakes taxed each interviewee with having authorised preference deals that allowed 'the arrival of the religious right in Australian politics'.[4] Similarly, the *Sunday Telegraph*'s Glen Milne warned a Coalition government contemplating a Family First-dependent Senate majority that 'Many will be suspicious of any legislative deals that come at the cost of allowing religion to intrude into Australian politics for the first time'.[5]

In fact, of course, none of Oakes's interviewees could claim any such achievement. Taking a long view, we might think of the DLP and the Queensland Nationals, both of whom had plenty of claim to having offered the religious right secure political footholds. Family First's most immediate genealogy, though, lies within the federal Liberal Party. The religious right upsurge within a major party is likely to prove more lastingly influential than any minor party it might have fostered, because of the way Australia's political system keeps minor parties marginal. Even a Senate balance of power only works if the minor party can persuade enough members of the major opposition party and any other small parties or independents to gang up into a majority. The Coalition's outright Senate majority after July 2005 relegates minor parties even further onto the margins. The significant point about Family First's rise is that it shows how much more acceptable religious politics has become after three terms of Howard government. The real story, which we need to understand if we are to make sense of the shifting political territory in which a Family First senator suddenly became a possibility, is the Howard government's increasingly overt embrace of the extreme end of conservative Christianity.

This chapter explores the relationship between religion and politics in the Howard government's 'family values' agenda.

•

The Lyons Forum first attracted significant media attention with its 1995 submission to the Liberal Party executive on tax. Their proposals included abandoning no-fault divorce, withholding benefits from dysfunctional families and single mothers and income splitting to give single-income two-parent families a tax edge, a proposal Howard pushed for heavily during his public confrontations with Hewson. It presented each of these as 'the opinions of the Australian people', gathered from 'hearings' around Australia in the two years before the submission, rather than as its own initiatives.[6] Since then, the Lyons Forum has achieved much.

Its earliest credits included a formative role in the 1996 Family Tax Package,[7] being the driving force behind the *Euthanasia Laws Act 1997*, which overturned the Northern Territory's *Rights of the Terminally Ill Act 1995* (as discussed in the previous chapter), the Coalition's 1996 election promise to tighten film and video censorship, and the ensuing April 1997 cabinet decision to tighten restrictions on pornographic videos by replacing the X-rating with NVE (non-violent erotica).[8] Another 1997 Lyons stamp on public policy was cabinet's rejection of then Health Minister Michael Wooldridge's nominee for chair of the National Health and Medical Research Council, Professor John Funder. A Catholic personally opposed to abortion but also opposed to its criminalisation, Funder found himself in the undignified position of answering a request from then Attorney-General Darryl Williams to assure him that 'Neither I nor to my knowledge the Baker [Institute, which he headed] have ever been engaged in experiments on embryos, or the use of RU486 in humans. I have never performed an abortion, assisted in the procedure or referred anyone for abortion', though he did add, 'I would question whether such a statement should be considered necessary for appointment to chair NHMRC'.[9]

At the time, media coverage universally attributed the intervention overturning Funder's appointment to independent Tasmanian Senator Brian Harradine. His influence at the time was at its zenith, as he and ex-Labor Queenslander Mal Colston held the balance of power in the Senate; not that the issue came before the Senate—it was said (and he never denied) that he traded the Funder non-appointment for support on unrelated government Bills. In the wash-up, then Lyons Forum secretary Kevin Andrews told the *Age*'s Nikki Savva that 'the forum did not play a role in the Funder issue and did not meet while the issue was raging'.[10] However, watchers of the rising moral repressiveness within the Howard cabinet, with its impressive Lyons roll call, would have to wonder whether any meeting was needed, and also whether tales of Harradine's influence had been carefully overstated. As Kenneth Davidson pointed out in 1997:

> The Lyons Forum appears to be far more influential within the ranks of the government than the Left faction of the ALP

> was at any time during the currency of the Hawke–Keating governments or is now that the ALP is in opposition. But so far the Lyons Forum has only had a fraction of the attention given to the factions of the ALP.[11]

Some of the more extreme 'family values' agenda was slow getting enacted under the Howard government, but the Forum's most significant achievement was surely not so much in specific policy outcomes as in changing the climate of public debate. It was making room for a host of incremental changes, all tending in the same conservative direction. During the leadership battles of early 1994, an *Age* article entitled 'The Shadow Boxers of Morality and Policy' characterised the protagonists as 'Howard (suburban man) and Hewson (product of social change)'. Howard, 'a dag', and Hewson, summed up by his 'flashy cars . . . faded jeans and beautifully tailored reefer jacket', were 'shadow boxing' because, during the Labor ascendancy in the 1980s and early 1990s, social conservatives had lost so much ground that:

> Apart from rednecks like [then National Party leader] Tim Fischer who is reflecting the views of his small and shrinking constituency, they are not prepared to articulate any sort of clear vision of just what it is they want for fear of being ridiculed . . . For all his intellectual robustness, John Howard has been afflicted with timidity when it has come to articulating just what it is about John Hewson's attitudes to social issues that he finds objectionable.[12]

Not any more. Ensuing years saw the Institute of Family Studies feeling the heat to remould itself in the 'family values' image,[13] the Office of Film and Literature classification supplied with a more conservative panel of censors,[14] drug users encountering 'zero tolerance' and legislation on the books to enable the States to deny lesbian and single women access to IVF, to name but a few more examples.[15] Not all these changes were publicly credited to the Lyons Forum, which, as we saw in the previous chapter, goes to considerable effort to maintain a low profile, preferring to project its policies on to a carefully constructed 'mainstream'. Yet the net result was exceptionally good for its agenda. As the twentieth century rolled into the twenty-first, social conservatives had recovered from their shyness at articulating a 'clear vision of just what it is they want'.

•

When John Howard led the Coalition to victory in 1996, he did so under the slogan 'For all of Us'. The idea behind that slogan was that the outgoing Labor government had been ruled by 'Them'—namely, the chattering chardonnay set and their gaggle of minority and special interest groups. Pamela Williams's study of the 1996 election campaign attributes to the Liberal federal campaign director Andrew Robb the strategy to:

> devise a campaign around the concept of 'We' and 'Them' . . . with 'them' representing the many special interest groups associated with [Labor Prime Minister Paul] Keating . . . Keating was about 'them', the noisy interest groups who made the majority feel left out.[16]

The campaign centred on the impression of a tide of public 'resentment', a term well-hammered in Howard's 1995 'Headland' speeches, for example. It ushered in a government riding on the image of an alienated 'mainstream', said to feel excluded from other groups' 'special privileges'. However, examining the Lyons Forum's role in the Liberal Party structure through the early 1990s, I suggest that the 'minorities versus mainstream' divide, rather than arising from the immediate political necessities of the 1996 campaign, is a longstanding flashpoint in Liberal Party policy debate. Indeed, Lyons Forum spokesperson Senator Eric Abetz cites that feeling as a major reason for the Forum's formation:

> See, the Lyons Forum started because Australian politics was going along a path of you had to be a special interest group to access the government's attention . . . there were certain mainstream issues and, if you like, a silent majority that were being forgotten.[17]

The concept of the mainstream relies on a magical geometry. Everyone can see themselves as part of 'Us', imagined in opposition to a threatening 'Them'. But 'Them' is a strangely shifting category. Sooner or later, almost everyone ends up as part of that mysterious, dangerous 'Them'. At different times, as we shall see in the following sections, Howard's 'Us' has excluded same-sex couples, mothers in the paid workforce, single parents, step parents, stay-at-home fathers, feminists, migrants, Aborigines, churches, Muslims, other non-Christians, unions, ABC listeners, the tertiary-educated and more. These miraculously shifting exclusions begin to look less like social categories than a prescription for national paranoia. Under Howard, the ambiguous religiosity of Lyons Forum social conservatism and the suspicion of 'Them' come together. Their intersections are particularly apparent in issues relating to women.

In *McBain vs Victoria* (2000), Melbourne gynecologist John McBain sought clarification in the Federal Court of whether the Victorian *Infertility Treatment Act 1995*, restricting IVF services to heterosexual married or de facto couples, was inconsistent with the *Sex Discrimination Act 1984*. The State of Victoria chose not to appear in the case. In those circumstances, Justice Sundberg allowed the Catholic Bishops' Conference to appear as *amicus curiae* (someone who is not a party to the case but allowed by the court to give advice), so that there would be a voice for the Victorian Act. The Bishops failed to convince Justice Sundberg, who found that, in view of the inconsistency with federal law, the Victorian restrictions were invalid.

The federal government responded with the Sex Discrimination Amendment Bill No. 2, 2000 to change the *Sex Discrimination*

Act so as to allow States and Territories to make heterosexual couples the only IVF beneficiaries. Howard's argument, reiterated on several occasions by Federal Attorney-General Daryl Williams, was that the changes were necessary to protect 'the right of children to have a reasonable expectation, other things being equal, of the care and affection of both a mother and a father'.[18] Meanwhile, the action continued in the courts.

The Bishops sought to appear before the High Court to have the Sundberg finding quashed. Not having been parties to the original case (despite having been given the opportunity by the Federal Court), the Bishops would normally have had to demonstrate 'standing' (a sufficient interest to justify their being allowed to bring the case) before the High Court. They were spared the necessity by the intervention of Attorney-General Daryl Williams, who granted them a fiat (permission to make part of their proposed case without having to persuade the court of their need to do so).[19] In the event, the High Court found that various circumstances, including the long period between the Sundberg finding and the Bishops' decision to appeal and the fact that they had refused the opportunity to become parties to the Federal Court case, told against any responsibility on the part of the High Court to grant them relief, so it effectively tossed out their concerns.

In the meantime, the nation had gone to the polls in November 2001, re-electing the Howard government. With the end of the Thirty-Ninth Parliament, the Sex Discrimination Amendment Bill lapsed. So, on 27 June 2002, the Attorney-General introduced a slightly amended version, the Sex Discrimination Amendment Bill 2002. The government again argued that it is worth restricting some women's rights in the cause of ensuring that children have access, other things being equal, to 'the care and affection of both a mother and a father'.

McBain vs Victoria had only been about single women's access to IVF, but the federal government had introduced a new concern. Their legislation's aim was, the government said, to target equally the evils of children being raised by single mothers and by same-sex couples. In the government's subsequent rhetoric, one of those evils took on a considerably more sinister overtone than the other. No sooner had the Bill been introduced than the Attorney-General was forced to issue an Explanatory Memorandum because careless drafting had made it possible for the States also to discriminate against heterosexual de facto couples. In the press release announcing the revisions, Williams also responded to another criticism of the Bill, namely, that it denigrated the child-rearing efforts of families other than the 'mother and father' model. Although reiterating the government's view that single-parent families were less than ideal, he nevertheless paid tribute to their efforts. Strikingly, he made no parallel recognition of those raising children in same-sex couple families. Although single parents and same-sex couples were equally targeted by the Bill, it is hard to avoid the impression, both from the Attorney-General's repeated statements and from the tenor of the government's contributions to the Senate Legal and Constitutional Affairs Committee which considered the Bill's 2000 version, that same-sex couples pose the greater danger to social stability.

Critics of the Bill, including some Liberal members of the Senate inquiry who demured from the official government line, shared scepticism about its ability to deliver on its claimed purpose of ensuring children receive a father's 'care and affection'. The majority report concluded that the most the Bill could hope to ensure was that a child conceived by assisted reproductive technologies in Victoria, South Australia, Western Australia or the Northern Territory had a mother and father at the moment of conception; it is hard to see this as a big advance in children's rights. The proposed legislation, the Committee concluded, would restrict the rights of some women without creating any real rights for children.

If women lose and children don't gain, whom would the Bill actually help? Like the Mardi Gras and euthanasia debates, the Sex Discrimination Amendment Bill seems to have more to do with image than policy. It provided another spruiking-point on the path towards ideological climate change, another chance for Howard and his senior ministers to present themselves as the champions of the imaginary mainstream 'Us'. In this case, we were invited to picture 'Us' as a 1950s nuclear family in its model kitchen, living the *Saturday Evening Post* world of the schoolboy Howard.

In the magical Howard 'Us' and 'Them' story, 'we' can all identify with the solid mainstream; but the note of fear sounding through the story makes 'Us' feel, paradoxically, like a beleaguered minority, threatened with imminent submersion in the rising tide of 'Them'. The sepia-toned traditional family, though making up the 'mainstream', is imagined as embattled, its way of life jeopardised by single mothers, lesbians and untamed, fatherless children. That imaginary family's hope was to wage a culture war, imported from the US religious right. The script was already provided by think tanks, such as the Heritage Foundation, the Institute for Religion and Democracy and the American Enterprise Institute, which actively campaigned against gay couples and waxed positively apocalyptic about single parenthood. For example, American Enterprise Institute scholar Charles Murray is most famous for his 1994 book, *The Bell Curve*, claiming that the IQ of black Americans is some fifteen per cent lower than that of whites. At around the same time, he was pushing a campaign to 'restigmatise' illegitimacy, which he considered 'the single most important social problem of our time—more important than crime, drugs, poverty, illiteracy, welfare, or homelessness'.[20] Australian public opinion has not yet moved far enough to accept Murray's preferred solution, to 'end all economic support for single mothers', so that families faced with shouldering their care will be driven to 'make an illegitimate birth the socially horrific act it used to be, and getting a girl pregnant something boys do at the risk of facing a shotgun'. However, that does not mean that the Australian Christian right is not interested: ending government support for single mothers was one plank of the Lyons Forum's 1995 submission on family tax, together with refusing benefits to other families that the Forum deemed dysfunctional. Such proposals might seem far-fetched, but we should not on that account dismiss them. Although the Sex Discrimination Amendment Bill saw the light of day only in the wake of *McBain vs Victoria*, that was not the first time such a move had been mooted.

In 1997, the Lyons Forum pushed a proposal to modify the *Sex Discrimination Act* to exclude single women and lesbians from access to fertility services.[21] The suggestion did not make it into legislation at the time, and it was scarcely taken seriously in media commentary, most of which dismissed it as unrealistic posturing. But when the proposal resurfaced in August 2000 as the Sex Discrimination Amendment Bill (No. 1), the Lyons Forum was not mentioned in connection with it. The Bill's parentage, like the victoriously quiescent Forum itself, had been largely forgotten. On its rocky path through the Senate Legal and Constitutional Affairs Committee, the Bill's most vocal supporters (apart from the ever-reliable Harradine) were not the signed-up Lyons Forum members on the committee such as senators Abetz, Calvert, Gibson, Ferguson and Chapman, but two socially conservative Labor senators, Jacinta Collins and John Hogg. The Lyons Forum's Mardi Gras campaign, with its conceit of a bipartisan 'petition' to the ABC, effectively portrayed the small Labor minority it managed to wedge into the anti-Mardi Gras broadcast camp as evidence of the far right's 'mainstream' appeal. In the euthanasia campaign, the 'Euthanasia No!' group made invisibility a hallmark of its own success while pushing Labor euthanasia opponents to the fore. On the Sex Discrimination Amendment Bill, the Lyons Forum members wisely kept quiet and let the ALP conservatives write the wish-list. They advocated not only much greater government intervention in reproductive technologies (their minority report raises the spectres of embryo cloning, male pregnancy and ectogenesis) but even a rethink of such comparatively long-established practices as legal abortion.

The Sex Discrimination Amendment Bill was one link in a growing chain of successes for the Coalition's social conservatives. It was achieved by introducing ideas that at the time seemed beyond the pale of serious attention, only to have them resurface with token bipartisan support from an insufficiently vigilant left after a few years' careful cultural spade work. Much of this was done by socially conservative think tanks, such as the Centre for Independent Studies (CIS), whose mixture of flattery, paper bombardment and colonisation of the media opinion slots proved remarkably successful at attracting ALP allegiance (witness, for example, eventual Labor leader Mark Latham's list of CIS-sponsored publications and regular espousal, before his leadership accession, of anti-feminist, 'family values' rhetoric)[22]. Legislation with the aim of painting single and gay parents as enemies of civilisation should not be dismissed as mere symbolism or as affecting only a few. Such seemingly limited acts are the culture war's ammunition.

•

Another immediate way in which the *Saturday Evening Post* family rose up to thwart large numbers of real families in twenty-first century Australia was in the 2002 debates about paid maternity leave. The issue gave rise to a public conversation about children and parenthood, which in many ways paralleled discussions taking place at the same time over the Sex Discrimination Amendment Bill. But, because the government assumed paid maternity leave to be a concern of families with two parents of opposite sexes, there were also some striking differences. Comparing the two conversations highlights further the Howard government's underlying assumptions about what makes a mainstream family.

In 2002, Federal Sex Discrimination Commissioner Pru Goward produced a discussion paper about universal paid maternity leave. This was followed by a concrete proposal she hoped to see incorporated in the next federal budget. The issue prompted considerable media discussion and government disputation about the best form of early childhood education. Should young children be cared for at home by their mothers, or can they gain comparable educational and social benefits from childcare? Curiously, paid maternity leave, though it frees mothers from the paid workforce when babies are small, came to be associated with the 'childcare' side of the equation. Real supporters of maternal care would not have been in paid work to begin with, the implication ran.

The conservative think tanks leapt to their battle stations in newspaper opinion pages, while the federal government sprouted yet another intra-party discussion group, the Family Policy Interest Group, to campaign against paid maternity leave. Father of three Tony Abbott (also Employment and Workplace Relations Minister), promised paid maternity leave 'over the government's dead body'. Nick Minchin, also a father of three (and Finance Minister) displayed a curious impression of workplace demographics by denouncing government-sponsored paid maternity leave as 'middle-class welfare'—in fact, middle-class mothers are more likely to be already covered by employer maternity leave schemes, with working-class mothers the most exposed.[23] As Lyons Forum spokesperson Tasmanian Senator Eric Abetz put the argument, parents make better carers of small children than 'a qualified person [because] blood runs thicker than water . . . No matter how good a paid childcare worker is, to them it's just a job. They're going to leave the kid behind at five o'clock or whenever the working day finishes'.[24]

Howard declared his preference for a 'mother's wage', to be paid to all women on giving birth, so as not to discriminate against those who choose to give up work. The social conservatives' consensus was that children are best cared for by their mothers. If they were not cared for by their mothers, conservative apologists agreed, the second-rung alternative was childcare. Where were those fathers whose 'care and affection' assumed the status of a basic human right when the issue was access to fertility treatment?

Reflecting on the mysterious vanishing fathers of Australian conservatism set me pondering my own experiences of childbearing. I would have welcomed paid maternity leave. In fact, both my children were born while I was employed on short contracts that denied me any paid maternity leave, but required me to take twelve weeks' unpaid maternity leave. I was the main breadwinner for our family, with my husband taking on the role of home-based carer while remaining free to follow me from contract to contract—including, in one memorable eighteen months, moving house nine times. Compulsory unpaid maternity leave left us, therefore, without income. When our first child was born this proved an irritation but, as we owned our own house, it was not too serious. Our second pregnancy, however, coincided with a one-year contract in a different city, where we were renting.

Facing weeks with no income, we resolved to go 'home' for the birth, one of the attractions being that we could then live in our own house. But that meant incurring the costs of a 1200-kilometre move, so we also decided to explore what social security options might supplement our income. The Department of Social Security (DSS) told us regretfully that there had once been a payment for just such situations, but it had recently been abolished. Because I was employed (even though forbidden either to work or to get paid), I could not apply for the dole. The obvious solution for us was for my husband to apply for unemployment benefits but, because he had not been dropped from any payroll, he would incur the six-week waiting period from the time of applying before he could receive any benefits. Our situation convinced my employer to bend the rules enough to reduce my official twelve weeks' unpaid maternity leave to six, but that meant that Michael would only qualify for the benefit just as we no longer needed it. Simple mathematics suggested he should therefore apply, and begin the waiting period, before I finished work, so the benefit could start as soon as my salary stopped. Not so fast. As it happened, the city in which I was employed at the time had one of the lowest unemployment rates in Australia, whereas our home was in an area of relatively higher unemployment. Moving from an area of low unemployment to an area of higher unemployment was, in DSS terms, a 'breachable' offence. In other words, we were told, the move would disqualify him from the dole.

As home owners, recently enjoying a professional salary and anticipating its resumption after the birth—for at least the remaining few months of my contract—we found these successive coils of red tape frustrating and the loss of income awkward, but they did not throw us over any irretrievable financial precipice. What they did do was bring home to me that, for all the talk of equal opportunity, the notion of mothers as breadwinners has not really penetrated far into the ways work is organised. Being cared for by your father may be delightful, and may even—if we believe the Howard government—be a fundamental right, but, as far as the day-to-day arrangements of work, leave and contracts are concerned, the desire to have one's children enjoy their father's hands-on care might better be described as an awkward idiosyncracy.

The issue goes far beyond a 'father's rights' agenda. Paid paternity leave did not even enter the public debate. Goward memorably pointed out that the envisaged period of paid release covered only a child's first three months, by which time 'your nipples are still cracked, you've just got over the caesarean . . . you don't do anything much. You just struggle around . . . feeding, bleeding . . .'[25] In our case—and still more for other families in similar situations but without our relative financial security—paid maternity leave for the period immediately before and after the births would have made more feasible our choice for an unpaid father to be at home while our children were small.

So when does a child need the care of a father? Apparently, only when requiring it offers a route to restrict the rights of single mothers and lesbian couples. Once ensconced in heterosexual couples, fathers vanish from the policy landscape as suddenly as they entered it. The 'care and affection of a father' turns out to be one more symbolic weapon in the right's culture war.

•

Throughout Howard's third stint in the prime minister's office, the 'work–family balance' was his domestic catchcry. Setting out his third-term agenda, he declared the issue of juggling work and domestic responsibilities a national 'barbecue stopper'. Other announced domestic priorities for that term (notable for attracting a low ratio of policy to speeches) included Treasurer Peter Costello's 'intergenerational report' on population aging, and much national soul searching about Australia's declining fertility rate.

One side effect of the engineered fertility panic that arose during Howard's third term was an increase in documentation about the extent to which the difficulties of combining work and motherhood scare women off reproduction, rather than luring them back into the home.[26] Consequently, Howard found himself forced to acknowledge that many women choose to return to work part time after having children, and then went so far as to say the government should support them in that choice. In a rare departure for a prime minister regularly said to be suspicious of academics, and of the social sciences in particular, he attributed his new insight to the work of a British sociologist, Catherine Hakim.

Hakim is best known for her 'preference theory', which tries to account for women's varying patterns of work after child-bearing. According to Hakim (and Howard), there are three kinds of women. A minority is 'work-centred': their identity, self-esteem and life plans revolve around paid employment, and that is where they choose to put their energy. They are likely to remain childless but, if they do have children, they want to return to full-time work as soon as possible after their children are born. To them, Hakim says, children are 'a hobby', and 'no special social or family policies are required for work-centred women . . . their needs and interests are much the same as for men'.[27] Another group is their mirror image: a 'home-centred' minority focused on motherhood. They either never enter the paid workforce or happily toss their paid employment aside during their first pregnancy. From then on, their identity, self-esteem and life plans are bound up with their role as childrearers. The largest group, around eighty per cent of all women, Hakim calls 'adaptive', undertaking a mixture of part-time and full-time paid work as family arrangements permit. They regard their income earning as a secondary part of their life, typically do not have career goals or long-term plans and don't set much store by their qualifications—they take whatever paid work they can which fits around their family's needs.

Hakim's typology is certainly not without controversy. A number of sociologists, for example, have criticised her designation of 'preference theory'. They question how far mothers' different patterns of paid and unpaid work can really be said to result from preference, pure and simple. The term ignores the financial, family and social pressures which also contribute to the different combinations of paid work and childrearing in which women find themselves.[28] Another criticism is that Hakim's theory assumes a very traditional kind of gender arrangement, out of keeping with the realities of many families. Hakim's threefold model depicts a world of paid work and a world of domestic work, with women having to find their way between them. Lurking beneath this model is the assumption that the world of paid work is really the world of men, and that women who enter it do so at the cost of behaving as men traditionally have—leaving childminding to someone else, regarding their children as a 'hobby' (a designation surely as offensive to many fathers as it is to career-holding mothers). Her categories could thus be described as: one group of women who want to behave just like (traditional) men, another who want to behave not at all like them, and a third who want to combine elements of men's and women's roles. There is one group, however, which doesn't exercise any 'preference': men.

A male main breadwinner is an assumed part of all her three family models. Women who work full time (because they 'choose' to) are assumed to be part of a two-income couple. Women who give up paid work altogether can make that choice because their man is not entertaining any comparable choice. Women who work part time are assumed to have a male full-income breadwinner at their side. That, too, is Howard's picture, as he told cabinet in February 2003 (releasing his PowerPoint tables to the media afterwards to make sure the message got through). A minority of Australian families with children had both parents working full time (17 per cent), and another minority had one parent working full time and one at home (23 per cent). A majority—but not a vast one—had one parent working full time and one part time (27 per cent).

In considering paid maternity leave, Howard said, the government had considered all families with dependent children, not just the minority with both parents employed full time. Yet, he added, 'You would imagine from some writings that that is the norm and everything else is the exception'.[29] The strong implication of his message was that paid maternity leave was a measure designed for the 17 per cent minority. In other words, he automatically assumed that a woman's full-time income must be the family's second, and that, in the other two categories, the full-time working parent was the father.

Admittedly, our family, with a full-time paid mother and stay-at-home father, falls into a very small minority. The prime minister may have been right to assume that, statistically, we were not worth worrying about. Yet, as Anne Summers points out:

> Mr Howard did not apparently question the extent to which these circumstances matched the aspirations of the parents concerned—in particular the . . . numbers of women who would take jobs if they could find childcare—but instead

> merely drew his own conclusion, adding that he had been strongly influenced by Hakim's research on 'adaptive' women.[30]

In fact, Summers finds a disturbing correlation between falls in childcare places in particular regions and drops in women's employment participation rates in the same areas. Her conclusion gains support from Michael Pusey's Middle Australia Survey. Pusey finds that many women who work part time would prefer to work full time. He points out that the period in which women have entered the paid workforce in substantial numbers is also the period in which almost all the employment growth has been in casual and part-time work, while the proportion of available work in full-time, permanent jobs has dropped markedly.[31]

Hakim herself acknowledges, 'all three family models involve full-time permanent income earning roles for men'.[32] That might be partly explained by the fact that her survey question for determining sex-role preferences asked respondents to choose between three family descriptions, all of which include a full-time male breadwinner.[33] In fact, much of the research from which Hakim derives her 'preference' models is limited to married women. She justifies that restriction because 'women's choices only become sharply defined, and can only be implemented, after marriage to a breadwinner spouse'.[34]

Even if families (like ours), in which a full-time male wage is not the preference, are rare, there are plenty of circumstances (male unemployment and single motherhood, for example) that might make reality different from a pregnant worker's 'preferences'. It seems remarkable to take a study whose three models assume partnerships with a male breadwinner and apply it to an issue such as paid maternity leave, for which the criterion (so far) is pregnancy, not marital status. Surely Howard could not have been thinking that a woman's destiny in twenty-first century Australia is limited to either married motherhood or celibate spinsterhood? It seems incredible but, as we shall see below when we examine his comments on the nature of marriage, that does seem to be the assumption underlying his paternalistic policy shifts. Whatever else it achieves, writing whole categories of employed women out of the picture is one way to help the stay-at-home minority look 'mainstream'.

In my family, our running against the tide did not stop once the children had been born and I returned to paid work. We found, and still find, that there are many ways in which we are not just a mirror image of a father-at-work-mother-at-home nuclear family. One is our children's bedtimes. We often hear other parents of young children complaining of 5 a.m. breakfasts and an end to evening socialising, but our children have always slept in till (at least) 8 a.m. and, until starting school, went to sleep when we did. As toddlers, they often accompanied us on the kind of evening outings for which we would otherwise have hired a babysitter. Not that our children were chronically sleep-deprived: right up to school age, both enjoyed a daily afternoon nap, often for two or three hours, regularly eliciting comments (varying in tone from envy to disdain) from other parents, whose children had given up daytime sleeps in their first or second year.

We did not set out to organise our family routines that way; it just evolved as the most logical pattern for our way of life. The main reason has always been that, like so many other bread-winners, I don't get home until between 6 and 7 p.m. If our children had adopted the 7 o'clock bedtimes of many of their friends, I would hardly see them. Traditionally, that was just what many fathers did: come home to fed, bathed and pyjamaed children waiting to be cuddled, read to and kissed goodnight before the parents settled down to an adult dinner. That did not appeal to us. Gradually, we have discovered other families where the children's adult bedtimes are a more-or-less guilty secret. A friend who raises her children alone while holding down a professional job recently observed, 'People who phone after nine and get a child's voice answering nearly always begin their conversations, "Why aren't you in bed yet?!"' Invariably, in our experience, the families which buck the bedtime conventions turn out to be ones where the main wage is the mother's.

Bedtime is one small example of how 'preference theory' obscures the ways real families organise themselves. I don't know who Hakim's 'work centred' women are—singlemindedly focused on their careers, mirroring the traditional role of male breadwinners, and with minimal caring responsibilities. The families we know are not like jigsaw puzzles where you simply take out the father piece from the 'wage earner' spot and replace him with the mother piece, without changing anything else in the picture. On the contrary, we have found, starting right back in pregnancy and continuing to the present, that women being more actively involved in paid work has meant doing all kinds of things differently. Even when working full time as primary breadwinners, based on the families we know, women do not act just like traditional men, or want to. Painting women's work-and-childcare patterns as entirely a matter of choice, and those choices as between acting just like traditional men, the opposite of traditional men or a bit like traditional men, is one way of discouraging women not to think of themselves as full participants in the paid workforce. It took me a long time to work out why all the newspaper stories about Howard's conversion to the Hakim model made me so upset—until one day I found myself almost shouting, 'Why do I always have to go in the heartless, hard-nosed bitch category?!'

A rhetorical strategy of painting mothers in full-time work as career-focused (read 'uncaring'), ambitious (read 'selfish') and unmaternal (their children a hobby, along with the topiary box hedge) is the ideological companion of the Howard government's childcare and tax initiatives, whose combined effect makes paid work financially disadvantageous for mothers. As Summers demonstrates, the highest government payments through much of the Howard era were available to mothers who stay at home with children—regardless of their partner's income; while all payments to double-income families were strenuously means-tested, with reductions cutting in at the very modest combined family income of $31 755.[35] This eased slightly in the 2004 budget, but the government's most-favoured family still limited the mother to bringing in less than twenty per cent of the family income. As Sydney University economist Elizabeth Hill pointed out, a family with a joint income of $100 000 would receive an additional $7.69 per week in benefits if they shared the earning equally, but a generous $42.21 per week on the 80:20 model. The pattern is reproduced for lower totals, so that a family with a total annual income of $60 000 is over $23 per week better off on the 80:20 model than if the parents split the earning and caring.[36]

In light of the Howard government's attempts to amend the *Sex Discrimination Act*, in the name of giving children more of their father's care and affection, this budget move reads rather oddly. Given that we know from his PowerPoint presentation to cabinet that Howard assumes the main wage earner to be male, what the 2004 budget amounts to is, in the case of Hill's $100 000 family, a $1795 annual bonus and, for the $60 000 family, a $1219 bonus, to keep their father out of the home.

•

One aspect of the Lyons Forum's success has been its ability to harness the language of 'mainstream' to its concerns. As the Mardi Gras and euthanasia instances showed, mustering support from the ALP right helped create an impression of bipartisanship for socially conservative policy shifts. Camilla Nelson's fictional religious right achieves similar effects through its revolutionary behind-the-scenes Poltergeist lobbying agency:

> The thing about Poltergeist was that you never knew who, or what, was lobbying you . . . They operated through the assiduous use of well-placed, high-level contacts. Your own mother could have been a conduit for Poltergeist and you

> wouldn't have known it. Poltergeist operated by virtue of its ability to move others to move you.

Its invisibility enabled it to mask the fact that what it called 'the mainstream' was made up, 'almost entirely, of right wing Christians and ultra Catholics'.[37] The Lyons Forum does still better, dispensing with the need for an agency. Instead, it has successfully changed the climate of public debate and harnessed the image of the 'mainstream' to the point where, on issue after issue, from the Mardi Gras 'petition' to euthanasia, from lesbian couples' IVF access to family benefit changes, its political opponents do much of its campaigning for it, helped along by right wing columnists and talk show hosts reinforcing its American think-tank derived slogans and policies. Its successes have arguably been greatest when it gains least credit. It excels at providing early 'agit-prop' style sponsorship of what, at the time, seem unthinkably way-out proposals. But, of course, there is nothing like naming the unthinkable (preferably from inside a nondescript grey-suit) to make it thinkable.

During his behind-the-scenes comeback campaign (discussed in chapter two), Howard championed what then seemed to many commentators an outrageously inequitable proposal: income splitting, so that single-income couples could, in effect, claim two tax-free thresholds, greatly reducing their tax bill as against either single people (with or without children) or couples with both partners in paid work. The Lyons Forum's 1995 family tax proposal made the same suggestion which, again, was scarcely taken seriously. In March 2003, Howard boasted that he had achieved by stealth, through taxation and benefit changes favouring single-income couples, what he could not do up-front: 'We've effectively introduced income splitting'.[38]

What next? Some other early Lyons Forum proposals also enjoyed a twenty-first century comeback. For a while, prime ministerial protégé Tony Abbott was the only government member holding fast to the pre-1996 Lyons Forum flag of ending automatic no-fault divorce. He favours couples having the option to relinquish their right to no-fault divorce in return for tax benefits. But, with increasing confidence, other social conservatives rallied to the cause. First there was then Member for Parramatta Ross Cameron, arguing that Australian women needed governmental support, in the form of harder divorce, to tame commitment-phobic Aussie men (though his mid-2004 adultery confession would eventually rob that campaign of much credibility).[39] Even one-time small-l liberal Malcolm Turnbull joined in. As Liberal Party federal treasurer he told a Sydney University audience that, although no-fault divorce is here to stay 'for good or ill', a society worried about its fertility and stability should contemplate ways of valuing marriage more.[40] He was back at it in November 2003, arguing that the answer to the fertility crisis was to 'promote the traditional married family with a view to increasing the number of marriages and decreasing the number of divorces'. One method he proposed was giving couples the option to 'contract to a higher standard of marital commitment', voluntarily agreeing 'to make divorce harder'.[41] While Turnbull was preparing to contest Sydney's blue-ribbon seat of Wentworth in the 2004 election, Howard produced his own contribution to the divorce debate, proposing a presumption of shared care after divorce—though not before it; during an intact marriage, fathers mysteriously vanished again.

Another religious right chestnut that has recurred through Howard's prime ministership is asserting the value of 'traditional' families as opposed to same-sex couples, which accompanies a general sense of unease about homosexuality. Recall that the Sex Discrimination Amendment Bill, originally designed to stop single women using IVF in the wake of *McBain vs Victoria*, took on, in Howard's hands, the additional concern that lesbian couples might be seeking fertility treatment; and that, as the government's explanatory statements proliferated, same-sex couple families rapidly outclassed single parents as the prime threat to Australian domestic life. Then, in 2003, Howard responded to no particular domestic issue but to clarion calls from Rome and Washington by declaring that 'marriage as we understand it is one of the bedrock institutions of our society'. Marriage 'as we understand it' meant between heterosexuals or, as loyal interpreter Tony Abbott glossed it, 'traditional Christian marriage'.[42] Howard's reasoning was that marriage is 'very much about the raising of children . . . and the continuation of our species'. He added—in case anyone had been wondering—'I certainly would not be initiating any moves to change the law' to give gay relationships the same status as marriage,[43] though by mid-2004 he did initiate a move to change the law to explicitly rule out gay marriage. It seemed to have escaped his notice that many people continue the species in a variety of family formations, to which marriage is often at most incidental. The prime minister who calculated who needs maternity leave by looking only at partnered women displayed quaintly puritanical fantasies about the circumstances in which the species continues.

Both the Sex Discrimination Amendment Bill and the statements on marriage, while alarming to defenders of equality, were hardly out of the blue for the Howard that voters had come to know so well since 1996. But those two fairly predictable expressions of homophobia framed a far weirder episode in early 2002, one which gives us further insight into Howard's skills at mobilising the concerns, but not the explicit language, of the religious right in Bush's America.

Just as the plans for the Senate's first 'children overboard' inquiry were starting to put real pressure on a government widely seen until then as untouchable, Howard's parliamentary secretary to cabinet, Senator Bill Heffernan (who had taken over the job from Lyons Forum co-founder, Baptist lay preacher and notorious homophobe Chris Miles, of 'Say No to Sodomy' fame), walked into a near-empty Senate late on 12 March. He accused openly gay High Court judge Michael Kirby of using a commonwealth car to trawl for 'rent boys' in Sydney's Darlinghurst. Heffernan is well known as Howard's close ally in NSW Liberal

Party internal politics, and also for his longstanding crusade against homosexuality and paedophilia, amounting, according to critics, to an 'obsession'. His evidence turned out to be a Comcar driver's time sheet, given to him in 1998 by John Howard's personal driver, and which subsequently proved to be a forgery. Howard's response came in stages.

The first was to tell the House of Representatives that he had had no warning of Heffernan's intentions, though he made clear 'I do not say this critically—I offer it by way of information'. Under questioning he revealed that he did, however, know that Heffernan had been planning some attack along those lines, and had 'counselled him against any improper use of parliamentary privilege'. Howard's famously tight party discipline, restraining his party colleagues from any whiff of dissent, much less open defiance, might have been expected, therefore, to earn Heffernan swift retribution. Instead, Howard told the House that he understood that Heffernan had acted because 'he holds the views he expresses . . . very deeply and very conscientiously'. The fact that he had disobeyed his leader's 'counsel' did not stop Heffernan retaining 'my affection and my friendship'. Although Heffernan temporarily stood aside from his position as parliamentary secretary, Howard was at pains to point out to the House that this had been on the senator's own initiative—no one could conclude that Heffernan had been sacked. In the same speech, Howard tabled, and read into *Hansard*, a letter from Senator Heffernan which expanded upon the previous day's under-age sex allegations.[44]

Over the coming days, the prime minister repeatedly refused opposition calls to sack Heffernan. Only once the timesheet was found to be forged, six days after the initial Senate speech, did Howard demand Heffernan's resignation. The prime minister's support could scarcely be missed by his colleagues. When the *Sydney Morning Herald* tried to find Liberal parliamentarians to comment on the affair, it found a number of on-the-record Heffernan supporters, such as Don Randall, Peter Slipper, Barry

Wakelin and Bob Baldwin. Although it also unearthed 'a number of Coalition MPs' who 'expressed outrage at Senator Heffernan's actions', they 'refused to be named for fear of retaliation by the Prime Minister's office'.[45]

Given Howard's formidable reputation for political acumen and parliamentary strategy, his behaviour on this issue could seem bizarre. Why not distance himself sooner from the maker of a dubious accusation under privilege, well known for a homophobic obsession? Why, instead, did Howard stand by him and even add to his allegations? Given the claims concerned matters which had already been investigated and dismissed by the NSW police, Howard could hardly have failed to see the way the allegation was going, even before the forgery was confirmed. His personal friendship and respect for Heffernan hardly amount to a convincing explanation of his actions. It seems more plausible to assume that Howard found political mileage in the issue which outweighed the inevitable damage.

One explanation raised in some media commentary at the time about Howard's reactions was that the affair opened an opportunity for him to mount a more general challenge to the judiciary. His initial speech in response to Heffernan's allegations was in answer to a question without notice from then Opposition Leader Simon Crean. Nearly half of Howard's reply relates to a broader question: 'How in the future . . . we as a parliament should deal with allegations which are made against senior judicial officers of the Commonwealth'. He was concerned that, 'You have a situation where . . . a federal judge holds office until he or she reaches the age of 70 and can only be removed by a finding of both houses of parliament that he or she has been guilty of proved misbehaviour'. His proposal, to establish a body to investigate allegations against judges, amounted, according to Melbourne University academic Jenny Hocking, to 'vesting unprecedented power in the Executive' in 'a recipe for control, which is unnecessary and dangerous'. She argued that 'any allegation, regardless of its veracity and no matter how politically motivated, would result in irreparable damage to a judicial contender'.[46]

In addition to looking for spin-off issues when analysing Howard's manoeuvres, it is usually instructive to understand his more extreme 'family values' outbursts by looking at what else is going on at the time. In this case, an issue guaranteed to draw the fire of liberal journalists flared just at the moment when the 'children overboard' inquiry was starting to threaten the supposedly invincible Howard machine. Given Howard's reliance on the endorsement of the ambiguously Christian family values party power base which Heffernan epitomises, we can read Howard's backing of Heffernan as a timely reminder to social conservatives that he supports their agenda and is willing to continue to front it. The challenge for Howard is to reassure a conservative fringe that their views have been heard and respected, while not giving his opponents the room for accusations of extremism. It is a political strategy well developed by the US religious right.

President George W. Bush has a well-honed version which includes dropping lines from hymns and Bible verses into his speeches so that, to those who recognise the allusions, they convey an additional body of information inaudible to other hearers. For various reasons, Howard can hardly borrow that one. Whether or not he (or any of his speech writers) has the vocabulary, he is addressing an electorate in which only around nine per cent of voters claim to attend church weekly (compared to the US's sixty or so per cent), so he cannot assume an audience attuned to sotto voce religious messages. Moreover, of those voters who do attend church often enough to be fluent in the vocabulary, many would not respond favourably to finding it translated into politics. For these reasons, we do not find either Howard or other Australian political leaders imitating the 'God Bless America' specificities of US civil religion. However, Howard can convey a similar set of concerns below the secular radar by using terms that carry a religious inflection, rather than precise chapter-and-verse citations. His references to family, values and marriage as the unalterably heterosexual 'bedrock institution' of society, with their targeted appeal to religious conservatives, all do a job comparable to Bush's Biblical and hymn allusions.

The belated backdown and vaguely worded retraction, such as Howard used when calling for Heffernan's resignation, are further strategies well developed by the US religious right to enable political leaders to send different messages to different constituencies at the same time. As one analyst, Cynthia Burack, points out, Christian right leaders 'practise small duplicities—such as apologies—in order to be misunderstood by the "major population"' while simultaneously signalling a more extreme position to a right wing fringe. Her example is televangelist Jerry Falwell's suggestion that the September 11 attacks were God's judgement on America for allowing sexual immorality to flourish. After allowing time for the inevitable outcry to reach a crescendo, he issued a muted retraction. The apology, Burack pointed out, becomes in those circumstances a kind of 'niche-marketing'. Indignant liberals can be quelled by the retraction, while the original statement is allowed to hang in the air long enough to be clearly heard by the conservative audience at whom it is aimed. They can mentally discount the apology as a reluctant concession to politically correct liberal elites.[47]

As in the euthanasia debate discussed in the last chapter, one indication of a perceived religious motivation on the conservative side is the response of those at whom it is directed. The fact that more euthanasia supporters than opponents in parliament couched their arguments in religious terms could not head off a widespread perception of the Andrews Bill as a religious push. A similar pattern emerged in the Heffernan–Kirby affair. Avoiding religious language does not take away the effectiveness of a religious right dog whistle. On the contrary, it may make it all the more potent. It is up to the Opposition, as in the euthanasia debate, to name and counter the implied theology. Justice Kirby, a practising Anglican, issued a statement at the close of the affair which, in part, implicitly invoked a loving and inclusive God against the mean-spirited, punitive God of the right's homophobic creed: 'I have been sustained by my innocence, by the love of my partner and family and by support and prayers from all sections of the community'.[48]

That Howard's 'family values' and anti-homosexual comments successfully convey a quasi-religious undertone is apparent in other ways, too. A *Sydney Morning Herald* report mentioning Opposition Leader Mark Latham's agnosticism is a case in point. The report, while relating both leaders' beliefs to a touchstone issue, frames the Labor leader's lack of religious convictions as a contrast to Howard:

> Mr Latham put himself at odds with the Prime Minster, John Howard, on the nexus between religion and politics in defining the family.
>
> Describing himself as an agnostic, he said: 'I don't think love in relationships is defined on religious grounds . . . Whether it is a same-sex or different-sex relationship—I don't draw a distinction.'[49]

Yet Howard's statements on marriage, though welcome to religious conservatives, were not couched in theological terms. His only explicit justifying framework was biological, seeing marriage as pivotal to 'the survival of the species'. While that view could relate to a theologically grounded view of natural law, Howard did not (at least publicly) make that connection. That both the *Herald* and, apparently, Latham, felt free to draw a link between Howard's social conservatism and religious beliefs says much about his political success.

Although the Australian electorate is famously much more secular than America's, we don't necessarily regard religion as a bad thing. As will be explored in following chapters, Australians who have no religious commitments are often very willing to see religion as desirable for other people—as a means of discipline, source of beneficial values or a safe reference point in an uncertain world. This helps explain the appeal of an apparently sincerely (but not too in-your-face) religiously committed prime minister to a highly secularised electorate. It explains the phenomenon we encountered in chapter one of Howard's churchgoing childhood casting an aura of vague religiosity over his adult policies, an aura quite independent of the political tenor of real-life 1950s Methodism. More, these warm, fuzzy feelings towards an only vaguely grasped version of Christianity help explain the attractiveness of social programs which carry a (particular, conservative kind of) religious overtone, such as keeping marriage and parenting heterosexual and encouraging partnered mothers of young children out of the paid workforce.

•

At first, the new millennium did not hear much from the Lyons Forum. In its early life, according to members, the Forum met at least once a month when parliament was sitting, about eight meetings a year. Sometimes meetings would be more frequent, even weekly, during sitting periods. It boasted a membership of around half of the Coalition's parliamentary parties, including some fifteen front benchers. Compared to those heady days, the Lyons Forum at the turn of the century went quiet. 'I think we might have met once or twice this year', members told me doubtfully in 2000. Reflecting on the Forum's achievements, co-founder John Herron summed up, 'We got our policy in—we've gone quiet since we won'.[50] His colleague Alan Ferguson was similarly candid:

> The Forum has served its purpose. It was formed in opposition to make sure that all policy was assessed for its impact on families. But once we're in government, the party doesn't have as much input into policy, the executive does. But we keep the structure alive, in case we ever need to revive it.[51]

Howard's personal conservatism of course made him well-disposed to the Lyons Forum agenda. But Herron and Ferguson imply a commitment even beyond personal affinity. As we saw in chapter two, Liberal backbenchers' main say in policy direction comes via their choice of leader. If Ferguson's promise to revive the forum if 'we ever need to' sounds like a veiled threat, Howard gives all the appearance of having heard it. When Howard needs to remind his parliamentary supporters 'I'm your man', family and sexuality issues do the trick. When the going gets tough in the parliamentary party, the tough line on families and sex comes out strong. In early 2004 headlines were announcing 'Costello Denies Leadership Push', and Howard's famous hold on his party was for the first time starting to quiver. 'Just watch,' I told friends over lunch. 'There will be another family values explosion any minute.' Sure enough, by teatime, the headlines proclaimed, 'Howard hits out at ACT gay adoption'. The fine print threatened an Andrews Bill-style commonwealth move to overturn another territory's law.

This pattern of reminding party conservatives who their champion is seems to be holding among the next generation. As increasingly vocal leadership speculation in March 2004 exacerbated the Coalition's Latham-induced insecurity, Howard protégé Tony Abbott told Channel 9's *Sunday* program that he would not be challenging Peter Costello when Howard eventually left.[52] Two days later, Abbott addressed a Catholic students' organisation at the University of Adelaide and did something that had not happened for twenty-five years: he put abortion, carefully quarantined from federal debate by both sides ever since the 1979 Lusher motion tried unsuccessfully to prevent Medicare being used for terminations, squarely back on the federal agenda. Despite the fact that teenagers make up only a minority of those seeking abortions in Australia (and that abortion rates among teenagers have remained stable since 1977 while their birthrate has declined), Abbott blamed teenage promiscuity for Australia's abortion rate. In the weeks that followed, he proposed raising the maximum age at which parents can see their children's medical records from 14 to 16, again with the stated aim of curbing teenage promiscuity (though a number of experts pointed out that the move would more likely make teenagers resort to amateur advice and dangerous backyard abortions).

Though Liberal colleagues leapt to reassure a startled public that Abbott was only putting his personal views, the fact that they happened to be the personal views of the federal health minister mean we should not lightly dismiss them. Indeed, Abbott's University of Adelaide speech seemed to court more restrictive policy:

> Oddly enough, no local Christian has ever asked me how, as a Catholic, I can preside over a Medicare system which funds 75 000 abortions a year. I fear there is no satisfactory answer to this question . . . as a measure of the moral health of our society, 100 000 terminated babies is a statistic which offers no comfort at all.[53]

Abbott's tearing away from established bipartisan avoidance of the abortion issue seems all the more extraordinary in the light of the public political dynamics when he made the statement. Just when the re-energised ALP was focusing attention on 'generational' issues, to Howard's detriment, there was his favoured offsider raising yet again the spectre of a Liberal Party dominated by back-to-the-fifties social policy. On the other hand, watching Howard's skilful use of headline grabbing conservative touchstones to reinforce his position as the social right's man, Abbott's colonisation of an issue long thought relegated to federal political wilderness looks a lot like an imitation of that strategy. Having done the decent thing on Sunday, formally setting aside his aspirations in the interest of party unity, his remarks the following Tuesday can be read as a well-targeted dog whistle to his party's Lyons Forum religious right: once Howard goes, I'm your man.

The challenge for someone wanting to distinguish himself from Peter Costello on the matter of socially conservative credentials is that Costello, despite his image as more socially liberal than Howard, has given no reason to suppose he stands anywhere to his left on 'family' issues. Costello's socially liberal reputation rests on his espousal of a republic and his defiance of Howard to take part in the 2000 reconciliation marches. On same-sex marriage, he echoed the Howard line. On other family topics, he has steered clear of public statements, though as treasurer he oversaw the implementation of the tax policies we've encountered in this chapter, so presumably he was not in there fighting for the rights of mothers in paid work. Since the Abbott speech, Costello has gone out of his way to align himself with the religious right, first exhorting a return to the Ten Commandments at a National Day of Thanksgiving service in May 2004, then reiterating the call at Sydney's Hillsong church that July. In fact, anyone wanting to build up a self-portrait as being to the right of Costello on family issues has to go a long way, to what was previously the political fringe. No wonder Abbott brought abortion back into the limelight.

That interpretation gains force from the news, reported in the *Financial Review* in January 2004, that the Lyons Forum had quietly reformed five months earlier, responding to 'a perceived need for a greater effort at influencing government policy in line with traditional Christian values . . . with religion the key subtext in its strong views against abortion, pornography and the recognition of gay relationships'.[54] By April 2004, as Abbott was making his anti-abortion pitch, papers reported the influx of conservative Catholic Opus Dei members into NSW Liberal branches. Also in the news was the fact that an employee of Sydney's ultraconservative (and entrepreneurial) Hillsong megachurch, Louise Markus, had gained Liberal preselection for the marginal federal seat of Greenway (adjoining that held by fellow Hillsong congregant and convenor of the resuscitated Lyons Forum, Alan Cadman).[55] Voters have good reason to expect that American-style, religiously inflected social conservatism will remain a part of Australia's political landscape well beyond Howard's departure.

Family hot-button issues were Howard's recourse when his party room dominance wavered. They had a powerful counterpart, which he drew upon when the pressure came from outside the party room. While the Lyons Forum's first incarnation waged its back-room campaign to ignite the family fear factor in what would become the Howard Liberal Party's winning 1996 'Us and Them' strategy, another script was being developed to foster mainstream discomfort about race. Again, religion played a crucial part. Where the 'family' campaigns associated 'Us' with threatened conservative Christian values, the race campaigns singled out minority, marginalised religions, little understood in the wider electorate, as emblems of a menacing, powerful 'Them'. Howard's mainstream persona—the cricket-loving, suburban Methodist—pictures him as the grey-suited paladin of an imagined, endangered ordinariness. In the next section, we shall see how race works for Howard, time and again, when he needs to whip up a storm in the electorate.

PART TWO

Race to the Top

CHAPTER FIVE

Secret politicians' business

One hallmark of the 'Us and Them' strategy in relation to family, sexuality and the terminally ill was to pick on a group too small to wield much electoral clout but which could be brought to symbolise an issue close enough to many hearts to induce fear. As any tent-preacher knows, the battle for souls is a war of symbols. The race mission's first unsuspecting podium was a sleepy, windswept holiday spot on the South Australian coast. Its political task was to construct a bogey of 'Them' that could galvanise a nervous 'Us' to sweep Howard and his cast to power in 1996.

•

In his 1995 book *A Howard Government?*, former Howard advisor Gerard Henderson claims to find a psychological disposition for Howard to take fright at cultural difference. In interviews, Howard's brothers regaled Henderson with a series of family anecdotes about the anti-Catholic feeling in their home. This seems to be one aspect of maternal influence against which the young John Howard rebelled. 'I just thought it was stupid that people who were professedly Christian should be fighting each other as to who was the superior Christian', Howard responded when Henderson asked him about his own lack of sectarian sentiment. In Henderson's view, this was not the product of ecumenical conviction so much as 'the psychological process of denial'. Howard could not bring himself to acknowledge that 'difference (as in Protestant–Catholic) was a fact of post-1788 Australian life', so Howard learnt that avoiding discussion 'was better than arguing with his friends and family about the meaning of (Christian) life'. Henderson decided that for Howard 'unity, however artificial, was preferable to plurality if the latter led to emphasis on difference'. This avoidance of the recognition of difference, according to Henderson, formed the 'basis of Howard's early opposition to multiculturalism'.[1]

Conflating equality and sameness has been an enduring Howard theme. He has recalled, wistfully, that at Earlwood Primary School:

> Everybody was about the same. You had a few kids who obviously came from fairly poor families. You had one or two whose fathers had been very successful in small business. And the rest were sort of in the middle . . . You had that feeling that everybody was about the same . . . Some homes didn't have telephones, although most did. Some didn't have cars, although most did. But they all seemed to have a house and a backyard that you went and played in. It's different now.[2]

For Howard, sameness was not a tyranny, but a virtue that should extend from Earlwood's backyards to the nation's politics. Consequently, for the grown-up Howard, the policy of multiculturalism gives up on 'a common Australian culture. So we have to pretend that we are a federation of cultures and that we've got a bit from every part of the world. I think that is hopeless'.[3] Howard wanted a return to suburban sameness, which meant Indigenous Australians and non-Anglo migrants were left out in the cold.

The psychological profile sketched by Gerard Henderson might help explain John Howard's commitment to 1950s integrationist politics. Posed as a universal invitation to play in the backyard in William Street, Earlwood, it sounds positively alluring. But the equation of equality with sameness also happened to match the 'equal rights' propaganda being promulgated through the 1980s and 1990s by the hard right. Once radical, equal rights has been reworked into the language of right wing reaction.

The radical tradition of rights language wants everyone to finish up with roughly equal shares of whatever social good is being discussed (or at least, in some versions, an equal opportunity for acquiring it). If some are starting from behind, equal rights means they should be given extra help to bring them up to a fair starting point. Right wing equality, as reinvented by the neo-conservative think tanks in the closing decades of the twentieth century, wants everyone treated identically, regardless of where they start. Any extra help to some groups, however disadvantaged, amounts to 'special privileges', which breeds 'resentment' among those who do not qualify. The government's duty under this vision is to restore equality by taking the help away. Instead of sounding like proponents of greed and competitiveness, the right appealed to the noble ideals of a fairer, more equal nation.

The central example of Howard's equality as sameness in this chapter is his response to Indigenous rights. According to the newfangled equality, Aborigines should not be able to claim special land or spiritual rights—especially not when they get in the way of economic interests, such as those of mining companies (never mind that mining acts give mining companies special rights over other people's property).

•

The Earlwood ethos—everyone culturally much the same—has been evident in successive Howard policies. During Howard's first stint as Opposition leader, in December 1988, the Coalition developed a joint policy statement called *Future Directions*. In a decisive rebuttal of Fraser's multiculturalism, the new slogan was 'One Australia'. Its watercolour cover, showing a pale nuclear family behind a picket fence, could have graced one of those *Saturday Evening Post* editions of Howard's childhood. In the statement, difference came to be synonymous with disadvantage, equality with sameness. Multicultural programs, for instance, 'ensnare individuals in ethnic communities, denying them the opportunity to fully participate in Australian society'. A treaty between Aboriginal and non-Aboriginal Australia, then a hot topic in Hawke's Labor government, 'would permanently recognise them [Aborigines] as citizens apart, unable to participate in the mainstream of Australian life, even where they wished to do so'. All in all, recognising difference meant 'communities are kept separate from Australian society', leaving them 'no equality of opportunity'. Here 'Australian society' is redefined as the Earlwood dream.

Future Directions may have offered help to those previously excluded from the backyards of Earlwood, but no one was to blame for their exclusion:

> Displays of guilt about the past treatment of Aborigines and proposals for a treaty do nothing to overcome genuine problems. While we all live with the consequences of misdirected or ill-informed policies of the past . . . Australians today . . . are not guilty of those actions and should not be made to feel they are. Guilt is not hereditary.[4]

The blueprint, carefully distilled at party headquarters, also proposed limiting immigration on the vague grounds of 'the community's capacity to absorb change'. Howard in the raw, however, had been laying groundwork that left no doubt what was meant. On the radio and on television, in doorstop interviews and in parliament, Asian immigration had become his clear target, echoing ideas put forward four years earlier, in a welter of public debate, by conservative historian Geoffrey Blainey.[5] As opinion poll expert Murray Goot showed at the time, Blainey's views had generated considerable popular support. Polls taken before Blainey made Asian immigration a headline topic had not shown any particularly high levels of public concern, but the controversy seemed to create its own combatants.[6]

At the end of July 1988 Howard flew into Perth fresh from an inspirational visit to Margaret Thatcher's Britain. At the WA Liberal Party's State Council he proclaimed 'One Australia'. On Monday 1 August, he told Sydney radio 2UE's John Laws and the ABC's Paul Murphy that social cohesion would be improved if Asian immigration 'were slowed down a little'. Asked by Laws about the influx of Asians, Howard explained that a reduction in family reunion immigration (in contrast to, say, economic and business migration) would lead to a smaller proportion of Asians. While going to convoluted lengths to avoid saying he *wanted* this to happen, he added:

> I do think it's legitimate for any government to worry about the capacity of the community to absorb change and there is some concern about the pace of change involved in the present level of Asian immigration.[7]

True to the Iron Lady's example, he refused to retract, despite public outcry at what many saw as overt racism.

Prime Minister Hawke exploited divisions among the Liberals on the issue by moving a motion affirming the parliament's 'unqualified' commitment to non-discriminatory immigration policy. Four Liberals—Steele Hall, Ian Macphee and Philip Ruddock in the House and Peter Baume in the Senate—crossed the floor to vote with the government and against Howard. Political commentator Paul Kelly later attributed Howard's 1989 leadership loss to his 'stubborn ambiguity over Asian immigration'.[8] Racial 'resentment' had not yet gained the respectability of commonplace, nor the Liberal Party enough ideological homogeneity, for a leader to survive such straightforward appeals to racism. Within half a year of the Liberal manifesto for picket fence conformity, Peacock was back in the leader's chair.

The rhetoric of 1988 cost Howard eight more years service in humbler capacities and some carefully constructed comments about having changed his views. Even so, the echoes of that year remained loud enough in 1995 to cause Howard's advisors serious concern and to put him through exhaustive coaching in how to respond off the cuff to comments from old press releases and back copies of Hansard.[9] But the carefully coached politician was still the kid from Earlwood who wanted everyone to be 'much the same'—if not in wealth and power, then in culture. The *Future Directions* of Howard's leadership 1995 resurrection was called *The Australia I Believe In*. While it contained motherhood statements about the importance of reconciliation and recognition for ethnic communities, difference was more dangerous than ever. Where in 1988 difference meant disadvantage, and a more equal society meant assimilating those who did not fit the mainstream, by 1995 difference had become privilege. The 'broad Australian mainstream' was now held hostage to '"insider" interest groups' or, two paragraphs later, 'powerful vested interests'.[10] The Earlwood ethos would now mean stripping migrant and Indigenous communities of their resentment-generating 'special privileges'.

•

The race component of the mid-1990s battle for Australia's soul took as its 'Them' a network of families and community groups centred around the mouth of the Murray River. In late 1993 and 1994, the Ngarrindjeri people had begun publicly raising objections to an already contentious and long-fought marina proposal.

Developers Tom and Wendy Chapman had persuaded the previous State Labor government, under John Bannon, to build a bridge to their Hindmarsh Island marina development. The proposal had been fought first by a coalition mainly made up of State Liberals scenting yet another Bannon financial fiasco and well-heeled Adelaide residents whose lavishly appointed beach-side 'shacks' risked losing the area's castaway aesthetic (what one Adelaide QC described at the time as 'North Adelaide-on-the-swamp'). But Bannon's scandal-ridden government crashed in December 1993. The Liberal Party, led by Dean Brown, took over and, less than two months later, it announced it was reneging on its promise to stop the bridge.

With the most powerful of the previous bridge opponents suddenly vowing to build it, a broader-based opposition movement developed, with Ngarrindjeri now prominent members. Ngarrindjeri involvement sealed Hindmarsh Island's destiny: not only would the bridge be built, but the area would be front-page news for a good part of the next decade. The Ngarrindjeri people became the resentment campaign's mascot.

A group of Ngarrindjeri women appealed first to State Aboriginal Affairs Minister Michael Armitage and, when that failed, to his Federal Labor counterpart Robert Tickner, asking that the bridge not be built because it would desecrate an area sacred to them for reasons which belonged to a body of secret knowledge. In July 1994, Tickner announced a twenty-five-year ban on building the bridge. His decision, the developers' commitment to proceed, and, eventually, the Howard Liberals' determination to make the bridge ban into a 'special privileges' totem produced a series of legal challenges, government inquiries, legislation and defamation suits, which only wound up in the Federal Court in 2001.

Many details have been meticulously documented in Margaret Simons's 2003 *The Meeting of the Waters*,[11] and the ethnographic evidence comprehensively discussed in Diane Bell's award-winning *Ngarrindjeri Wurruwarrin*.[12] Here, we concentrate on the role the controversy played in the Howard campaign. The story was early evidence of what were to become tried and true Howard election-winning techniques: plotting from a distance, while others did the cut and thrust; deliberately offending so as to draw outraged media fire, while leaving a firm public impression; and imparting a feeling of panic to a substantial part of the Australian electorate by seizing on a small group posing a token threat. To turn the phrases 'Hindmarsh Island' and 'secret women's business' into national incantations of fear and derision, Howard called on powerful allies and tapped a quiet community re-education campaign, mostly from behind the doors of mining companies and think tanks.

Godfather to the resentment crusade against Indigenous sacred claims was a formidable theological force, the then chief of Western Mining Corporation (WMC), Hugh Morgan. Morgan's political involvement can be traced back to the Whitlam generation's embrace of multiculturalism, environmentalism and Indigenous rights. Sensing danger to his industry, Morgan backed pro-mining publicity campaigns, opinion polling, think tanks, right wing conference groups and the Liberal Party, much of his advocacy with a highly theological flavour. At one point, he even sponsored a book of theology to argue the godliness of mining.[13] Morgan credited the theological theme in his crusade to a land rights leaflet produced by the Uniting and Catholic churches in 1982 which, in his view, portrayed miners as evil. Morgan, then president of the Australian Mining Industry Council (AMIC), got the leaflet withdrawn by threatening to sue. He said that the experience taught him 'the extent of politicisation in the churches', prompting him to launch a Biblical defence of mining as part of WMC's campaign against the proposed 1984 national land rights legislation.[14] A 1985 *Bulletin* article on 'Western Mining's Messiahs of the New Right' wondered whether the organisation 'is a mining company, a speech factory, a first-class public entertainment service—or, simply, a political party that got lost in the desert, began to dig for gold to pass the time and found uranium and God in that order'. The accompanying cartoon showed a Bible-brandishing Morgan preaching from an outdoor lectern atop a mound labelled 'WMC Sacred Site—Keep Off', while sermon notes beginning 'Smite the heathen' flutter in the breeze.[15]

Morgan's speeches were apocalyptic, his fears primal. As Hawke–Keating Labor embraced Indigenous rights and made noises about a treaty, Morgan's rhetoric only escalated. When Hawke announced in June 1991 that a proposed Coronation Hill mine would be stopped to protect a sacred site, Morgan declared the decision a national disaster, 'like the fall of Singapore in 1942'. Worst of all, according to Morgan, was that the ban 'was decided openly, aggressively, by the Prime Minister himself, invoking all the authority of his office, on religious grounds'.[16] The mining industry, Morgan said, was threatened by 'religious crazies and the green antinomians'. The 1992 *Mabo* decision posed a new danger. Morgan warned, in a 1993 speech to the RSL, that recognising Native Title would produce an 'upsurge of resentment' in non-Indigenous Australia.[17]

The March 1993 federal election was meant to be a walk-in for the federal Liberals. Anticipating victory, Hugh Morgan urged, 'One of the early Bills a Coalition government must put to the Parliament, and if necessary to a double-dissolution election, is either repeal of, or substantial amendment to, the *Racial Discrimination Act 1975*'.[18] Instead, voters handed Paul Keating his 'sweetest victory of all', putting the program back for three years. In any case, it is questionable whether a Hewson-led Liberal party would have so readily done Morgan's bidding.

In speeches and newspaper interviews, Morgan came across as a quaint reactionary, representing an oddball New Right. Yet his positions, like the Lyons Forum's views of family, today no longer look so outlandish. On the contrary, many of his pronouncements proved uncannily prescient, and not a few of his policies are now enshrined in law.

To bring about an Australia in which the theology of mining was safe from sacred site heresies, Morgan's contribution to political climate change went well beyond his own pronouncements. With his then political specialist, WMC's Executive Officer Ray Evans, Morgan founded the pro-market H.R. Nicholls Society and the constitutionally conservative Samuel Griffith Society. He provided crucial seeding money to turn the Centre for Independent Studies into a significant opinion-shaper. Among the Centre's free-market and 'family values' campaigns, it developed a 'Religion and the Free Society Program' dedicated to re-educating church leaders in New Right orthodoxy. Evans became a founding board member of a specifically theological counterpart, the Galatians Group, formed to counter the perceived left wing and pro-Aboriginal bias in Christian churches. The Tasman Institute, which had WMC representation on its board through the early 1990s, the Institute of Public Affairs (IPA) and numerous smaller magazines and clubs also received Morgan's and Evans's assistance.[19] Through the IPA, Morgan helped support Ron Brunton, who later became a significant Hindmarsh Island pamphleteer,[20] to build his reputation as the right's anthropological apologist by publishing on such topics as 'Aborigines and Environmental Myths: Apocalypse in Kakadu' (denouncing the Coronation Hill decision) and 'Black Suffering, White Guilt?' (attacking the Royal Commission into Aboriginal Deaths in Custody).

Howard kept some distance from the H.R. Nicholls network of business leaders and their intellectual collaborators; yet Morgan and his ideological helpers had immense input into his highly successful politics of 'racial resentment'. In particular, Morgan's campaign against Indigenous sacred sites was closely tied to the Hindmarsh Island controversy, which was to prove so seminal to Howard's eventual victory.

Margaret Simons shows that, as early as 1993, long before Hindmarsh Island became a national byword, Western Mining's group geographer, Stephen Davis, went to the United States to photocopy (in somewhat mysterious circumstances) the entire journals of recently deceased anthropologist Norman Tindale. The originals of those photocopies would eventually become key documents in the Howard-instigated South Australian Royal Commission into the Hindmarsh Island affair, and a number of witnesses whose evidence supported the Howard-endorsed line would display uncanny knowledge of pages whose only other known copies were by then lying, uncatalogued, in packing cases in the basement of the South Australian Museum.[21]

Morgan and his company also enjoyed previously unreported access to cabinet ministers and others making decisions that greatly affected the course of the Hindmarsh Island affair. Western Mining Corporation had particularly close links with Liberal Premier Dean Brown's South Australian cabinet. These followed partly from the miner's importance to the State, as the operator of the Olympic Dam uranium mine near the town of Roxby Downs. The Brown government pinned its economic hopes on further exploration and mining, including a massive Olympic Dam expansion with a projected expenditure of $1.25 billion. But the company-cabinet links went further.

Back in the Bannon days when the State Liberals opposed the Hindmarsh Island bridge, Liberal *eminence-gris* and former Legislative Councillor, Donald Laidlaw, put the bridge opponents in touch with powerful advocates: Dean Brown, the future premier, and Diana Laidlaw, Donald's own daughter, who became Brown's transport minister. Both of them spoke at anti-bridge rallies in 1993, promising support if elected. At one such rally, in October 1993, just a few weeks before the State election which delivered victory to Brown, Ngarrindjeri people on the Lower Murray Aboriginal Heritage Committee spoke out for the first time against the bridge. That, too, was when Ngarrindjeri representatives wrote to the then shadow Minister for Aboriginal Affairs, Michael Armitage, seeking support.[22] That October meeting would have been Brown's and Laidlaw's first intimation that the bridge, whose well-heeled opponents they had pledged to help, was also worrying the region's Indigenous community.

The ironies, looking back, are excruciating. Brown, Laidlaw and Armitage won government on 13 December, anticipating increased investment from Western Mining, whose managing director, Hugh Morgan, viewed Aboriginal heritage as a World War II-scale threat to Australian civilisation. By 15 February 1994 Diana Laidlaw, until recently the leading bridge opponent, announced that the bridge would proceed. At the time the Brown government came to power, Donald Laidlaw sat on the board of Western Mining. According to the corporation's annual report, he also had a shareholding of around $1 million. In fact, documents obtained from the Australian Securities Commission show that his three daughters had significant slices of this stakeholding, worth around $100 000 each. That is, when she took over as transport minister—with direct say over, for example, the construction of a new bridge—Diana Laidlaw had a personal stake in a company with an unrivalled record of opposing sacred site claims. Diana's father sat on the company's board, backed by a significant financial interest in the company. And one of her sisters, also with a $100 000 stake in the company, was married to the other member of Brown's cabinet whose portfolio most directly related to the Hindmarsh controversy, Aboriginal affairs minister Michael Armitage.

When Brown's Liberals took government, they inherited a State bureaucracy in which responsibility for Aboriginal heritage sites belonged not to the Aboriginal affairs minister but to the minister for the environment. A restructure changed that. Armitage gained responsibility for Aboriginal heritage on 14 April 1994. Before that date, anyone seeking approval to disturb a listed heritage site would have needed to apply to the environment minister. From that date forward, Armitage was the man with the say-so. Curiously, it was just then that Armitage's sister-in-law (and Western Mining beneficiary), transport minister Diana Laidlaw, sought approval to disturb sites and objects so that the bridge could proceed.

Advice from his department indicated to Armitage that, in fact, the bridge site had enormous heritage implications. He was told that the Ngarrindjeri had valid objections, based on both material sites and spiritual concerns. The department wanted more time to complete a proper survey. The Ngarrindjeri wanted to be consulted about both the survey and proposed development. Armitage made it clear from the start that, though the site could be surveyed, the bridge would go ahead.[23] On 3 May 1994, Armitage gave his approval and bulldozers rolled onto the bridge site.

With his wife holding a financial benefit and his father-in-law on the board of a company renowned for its crusade against Indigenous sacred sites and with a number of significant heritage controversies looming (most notably WMC's plan to run a vast pipeline across Aboriginal land to support expansion at Roxby Downs), the minister responsible for protecting Aboriginal heritage must surely have worried about potential conflicts of interest. Armitage ran a risk of being interpreted as trying to put a lid on Aboriginal claims, and Brown had every reason to avoid too much public attention on the Aboriginal affairs portfolio. But pressure to put Hindmarsh Island in the spotlight would mount, from a quarter they could not ignore.

•

Soon after Howard's re-emergence as Liberal leader in 1995, acolyte Tony Abbott, the member for Warringah, explained in his monthly column in the *Adelaide Review*:

> After twenty years in public life, Howard is much-the-same man now as when he started. He lives in the same house in Wollstonecraft, holidays with his family at the same hotel at Port Stephens at the same time every year, and is not too proud to play social cricket badly but with great enthusiasm.

Significantly, in the light of events then and later, Abbott also reported:

> His 'honest and decent' image (and the reality it represents) limits his ability to target the Prime Minister's [Keating's] personal failings. These long-overdue attacks must be mounted by others.[24]

Howard's leadership triple-bypass left him a canny politician, adept at presenting a face of bland decency while highly skilled at manipulating issues behind the scenes and fighting at arm's length. His 'small target' strategy for the 1996 election meant avoiding clearly stated policies. Instead, as Abbott implied, he worked through 'others'—media supporters, think tank opinion shapers, low-level pamphleteering and sympathetic State governments. The seeming multitude of voices only added to the impression that Howard represented an 'excluded' majority.

The 'Us and Them' manoeuvre would later be outlined in a talk to the Sydney Institute on 1 May 1996 by the victorious Liberal Party federal director Andrew Robb. To win, he said, they had needed a 'resolve and ruthlessness not normally associated with the Party'. According to Robb, by the time of the election Labor had lost much of its working-class support. His research showed that Labor's vote among blue-collar workers fell from nearly 50 per cent in 1993 to 39 per cent in 1996. The Coalition's support in the same group jumped to 47.5 per cent. Robb's view was that this shift 'owes much to Labor's attempts over 15 years or more to chase the votes of the socially progressive, often highly educated, affluent end of middle class Australia'—people who would seem to have favoured helping the worse off. Keating and his colleagues came to reflect this group's values and priorities. Robb found that: 'From where I sat, Labor finished up in a cocoon of political correctness, a cocoon spun tightly by vocal minority groups and a union movement sadly sidetracked'.[25]

But Labor 'neglect' alone could not produce the blue-collar switch to Howard. As Robb went on to say, in politics, you have to keep pushing. 'If you are not setting the agenda, your opponent progressively improves relative to you'. So what unusual 'ruthlessness' did Howard and his backers pull off? Robb's speech implied two clues: twin royal commissions in Western and South Australia had been 1995's 'newsworthy campaign initiatives'.

Both royal commissions, which Howard would seem to have foisted upon resistant State Liberal governments, built up the image of the Keating government as run by and for 'special interests'. In Perth, sceptical Royal Commissioner Kenneth Marks found himself heading a blatantly political investigation of whether federal Labor star and former Western Australian premier Carmen Lawrence did or did not know something prior to a cabinet meeting. His exasperation prompted this mid-hearing outburst:

> I think I have been put in a position which is probably irrecoverable . . . The fact is that I took on the task of being a royal commissioner without actually realising the storm that was likely to be unleashed . . . On reflection I realise that in my life in the law nearly every royal commission that I can think of has been the result of pressure from interests who have wanted to open up other issues than the ones in the terms of reference . . . The sooner this commission comes to an end the better. I think that the experience here has demonstrated that the usefulness of royal commissions is fast receding.[26]

Even the Western Australian Liberal government's deputy leader, Hendy Cowan, questioned a royal commission into matters that, to most outside observers, seemed of breathtaking inconsequence. He could think of better ways of spending a million dollars, he said, and 'would like to know just exactly what is going to be achieved by that particular inquiry'.[27]

If its justification was unclear, its effect was immediately plain: the political neutralisation of a successful and highly visible Labor feminist. As ALP Member for Chifley Roger Price put it, 'Carmen Lawrence, as a woman, had the temerity not only to be an outstanding minister for health but also to be amongst those considered for future leadership of this party. That seems to have caused offence'.[28] In the process, Keating's loyal defence of his front-bench star was painted as being tied to the apron strings of 'feminist special interests'. In the Western Australian parliament, Liberal Premier Richard Court was asked, soon after calling the inquiry, whether he had discussed it with John Howard. He responded that he 'may well have',[29] though the decision had been his own. Once it was underway, though, Howard joined the sport. For example, as the federal Opposition leader he moved a dramatic censure motion against the federal health and community services minister:

> One hand in pocket, Mr Howard . . . gave his best parliamentary performance since he became Liberal leader . . . Animated, theatrical and constantly pointing at Dr Lawrence . . . He went on and on. Twenty minutes of it . . . Dr Lawrence sat on the green front bench couch and could do little to stop the onslaught, often not even looking at the man who by this stage was standing on tippy-toes trying to extract from his body as much volume as possible.[30]

In South Australia's companion event, public attention, mainly stirred through a series of newspaper columns by *Adelaide Review* editor and future Howard speechwriter Christopher Pearson, fixated on mysterious 'secret envelopes' marked 'to be read by women only'. These contained the evidence said by the Ngarrindjeri women to make the proposed Hindmarsh Island bridge a desecration. They were a crucial part of the Ngarrindjeri people's application to federal Aboriginal and Torres Strait Islander affairs minister Robert Tickner. The envelopes' contents were known, at first, only to the anthropologist who wrote them and the elder who gave her the information. Then they were read by a ministerial advisor, in the process of the heritage protection application for which they were written. Assured that the secrets constituted grounds for a ban, Tickner issued a declaration preventing the bridge from being built for twenty-five years. Through a bizarre coincidence, the envelopes then turned up in the office of the Liberal federal Member for Barker Ian McLachlan, who was already planning to discredit the bridge's spiritual opposition. There, they were read by (at least) one white man.[31] McLachlan, forced to resign from Howard's shadow ministry on 10 March 1995 for misleading parliament about how he came by the documents, may have felt he was falling honourably on his sword. Howard, seeing him off with expressions of 'great regret'[32] and assurances of undiminished personal esteem[33] (eerily similar to the formula he would later use for Senator Heffernan's offence in the Kirby affair), could hardly have imagined a better way to keep the secret envelopes in the headlines.

Then, on the evening of Friday 19 May 1995, in a carefully planned media offensive, McLachlan furthered the campaign against Aboriginal objections with a small group of so-called 'dissident women'. These women denied any knowledge of the 'secret women's business'. McLachlan nurtured internal Ngarrindjeri community tensions (many of which were entirely unrelated to the Hindmarsh Island claims, as Margaret Simons showed in her book) onto the national stage. Helped along by three hand-picked journalists, he pushed the inference that the fact that some Ngarrindjeri people had not heard of the spiritual beliefs amounted to a charge of 'fabrication' against those who had.[34] As soon as this fabrication idea surfaced Howard led the clamour for an inquiry into the authenticity of the South Australian secrets.[35]

In all the speculation about those tantalising female secrets, plenty of other secrets went unnoticed. Why did the South Australian Liberals suddenly switch from bridge opponents to determined bridge builders? What role did the controversy then play in the lead-up to the 1996 election? Why did Western Mining Corporation, and the Australian Mining Industry Council, become so interested in Hindmarsh Island? Why did South

Australian Premier Dean Brown call a formally irrelevant, but publicity rich, State royal commission into a matter already being investigated federally? As long as the public imagination remained fixated on one set of secrets, it was easy to forget about the bigger game being played out through the many now severely bruised local, cultural and professional communities caught up in the fights.

Like his Western Australian counterpart, Brown did not rush into royal commission territory; he had to be pushed. Pressure from within the South Australian cabinet was applied by then mines and energy minister Dale Baker, who railed against Brown's 'piss-weak' indecision. Baker said he had seen faster than others that Tickner's ban was a 'national issue'. No federal minister should block development on what Baker felt sure were spurious grounds. 'If he [Tickner] got away with it here, then every development could be at risk.' Brown's cabinet had to be persuaded the allegations were of national significance. 'It is fair to say that it took three or four discussions before cabinet decided to endorse my view', Baker said. He might have felt like a lone voice in cabinet, but there were still more powerful voices ranged against the Ngarrindjeri grandmothers: 'I'm close to Ian [McLachlan] and I'm close to John Howard . . . They could see, like I could, that it was a national issue', Baker said. It had taken persuasion from the very top to persuade Brown to call the commission but, eventually, Baker received a phone call saying that Howard had just contacted Brown and that Brown was finally 'shifting ground'.[36]

At the same time as he was pushing the SA Liberals behind the scenes, Howard and his team were publicly demanding a royal commission into 'secret women's business'. Their calls repeatedly tied the controversy to Howard's campaign symbol of a 'mainstream' of forgotten white 'battlers', imperilled by selfish 'special interests'. On 6 June 1995 Howard delivered his first 'Headland' speech, written by South Australian journalist and editor of the maverick *Adelaide Review*, Christopher Pearson. A close long-time friend of Howard favourite Tony Abbott, and also in regular contact throughout the Hindmarsh affair with Member for Barker Ian McLachlan, Pearson landed the job of Howard's speechwriter after nearly a year of pushing hard on the Hindmarsh Island campaign. The *Adelaide Review* had been running regular stories questioning the validity of the 'secret women's business'. Pearson said he knew from the moment of Tickner's twenty-five-year ban that the 'women's business', whose content Pearson claimed to know from 'laughter and anthropological gossip' around Adelaide, was trumped up.

From the start, Pearson helped launch the royal commission clamour. On 29 May 1995, his regular opinion column in the *Australian* anticipated 'the inevitable judicial inquiry'. Indeed, he said he already expected one a year earlier. 'It was obvious to me that a Royal Commission would have to be called when the bridge was banned, because an enterprising lie had taken over.'[37] With hindsight, it is not hard to watch Pearson's circle, and others, transfiguring 'secret women's business' into a sacred artefact of Australian politics. Their 'laughter and anthropological gossip' and then their organising, public speaking and writing soon made particular women's spiritual concerns into a white male totem of mysterious powers.

On 6 June, as Howard was delivering his 'Headland' speech and Pearson and McLachlan's 'fabrication' claim was gaining momentum, Channel 10 broadcast a clearly inebriated Aboriginal man, Doug Milera, 'confessing' to being the fabricator. The full tape of the interview, filmed the previous evening, reveals Milera struggling with a theological problem: whether being a Christian meant giving up traditional beliefs, or whether faith in the Christian God could coexist with Njarringdjeri traditions. Between theological musings, the full recording shows Milera alternately prompted or, when he seemed to be disputing the 'Lies, Lies, Lies' campaign line, interrupted by the interviewing journalist, Pearson's protégé Chris Kenny.[38] In the end, although the majority of his comments in the raw footage seem rather to contradict the fabrication story, Milera produced the right eighty seconds in his hour-long interview to lead that evening's broadcasts. The Adelaide *Advertiser* responded with its notorious headline, 'The Great Lie of Hindmarsh Island'. The next day, at Howard's prompting, the premier called his royal commission.

Howard had lost the Liberal leadership by his too-explicit racism in 1989. For the 1995 rerun of the 'social cohesion' argument, Howard had a carefully crafted example to hand, and he brandished it at every opportunity. Howard's Pearson-authored 'Headland' speech, one of a series of general pre-election manifestos, might have been tailored to launch a scare campaign with Hindmarsh Island as its beachhead. Howard complained that 'For the past 12 years Labor has governed essentially by proxy through interest groups' who 'seem to have the ear completely of the government on major issues' and who had become 'the vehicle through which government largesse is delivered'. He contrasted the 'noisy, self-interested clamour of powerful vested interests' with 'a frustrated mainstream' who felt 'utterly powerless to compete with such groups'.[39] Such was the national attention Pearson and his circle, including columnists and radio talkback sages, had generated for the Hindmarsh Island affair, there was no danger of the speech's coded references being missed.

On a Queensland tour just after the speech, John Howard told an audience at the Caboolture Golf Club that politics was about two things. First, 'it is about having a set of values, a sense of purpose and a sense of vision'. But Howard, who had learnt in 1989 that a forceful vision is not everything, added, 'it is also about having the political skills, and the tactical sense, to win the support of the Australian people'. A middle-aged man in the audience said he was sick and tired of the republic, along with women's rights and 'blackfellas' rights'. He wanted the focus back on jobs and law and order. According to the *Australian*'s political editor, Michael Gordon, following the unofficial campaign trail, 'Howard concurred'. Remember, Howard's candidate for the seat of Oxley at the time was Pauline Hanson, the future

One Nation leader. Then, at a fundraising dinner at the Cairns International Hotel, Howard received rousing applause for condemning the Labor government's Racial Hatred Bill as an 'attack on free speech in Australia'. He also said: 'The way Robert Tickner has sent bankrupt a couple of businessmen in South Australia with his ridiculous prohibition on that Hindmarsh Bridge is an example of how the Government of this country is prepared to use the full armoury of the Commonwealth to push and to economically bash up ordinary, decent Australian citizens.' Over enthusiastic applause, one woman shouted: 'It's terrible.'

At a press conference after the Cairns speech, Howard repeated his line that 'increasing numbers of Australians believe that this Government is run for minority groups, for special interests groups, and for nobody else'. He added, 'That is breeding resentment quite unfairly against some of those groups'. As an example, he cited 'Tickner's handling of the Hindmarsh Island bridge' which, he speculated, had 'set back the whole cause of Aboriginal and Torres Strait Islander people enormously'. One journalist there asked Howard if he walked a fine line tapping into such racial resentment. 'Of course you have to walk a fine line and I intend to do that. But I also believe it.' True to his arm's length strategy, he emphasised again, 'I'm not running around attacking special interest groups. I'm attacking the government'.[40] He did not need to attack the Ngarrindjeri traditions personally; he had worked hard to make sure others were doing that for him.

•

The South Australian royal commission into the Hindmarsh Bridge affair was set up to do one thing. As we saw above, Dean Brown's State Liberals were hardly going to court more scrutiny of their Indigenous heritage handling than absolutely necessary. Keeping it from venturing too far into sensitive territory, the commission was given a restrictive budget and imminent deadline. Its terms of reference were to inquire into:

> Whether the 'women's business' or any aspect of the 'women's business' was a fabrication and if so:
>
> (a) the circumstances relating to such a fabrication;
> (b) the extent of such fabrication; and
> (c) the purpose of such fabrication.[41]

Its job was preposterous because it did not know, and could not be told, the content of the tradition it was meant to investigate. Its range of creative solutions to this dilemma included taking newspaper speculation, much of it from Pearson's 'laughter and gossip' compilations, as fact. It also promulgated some speculations of its own as to what the women's secrets were. Lacking any means to test the accuracy of the speculations, it took another innovative tack by treating the (hypothetical) religious beliefs as empirical statements and subjecting them to tests.

The South Australian public was repeatedly assured the royal commission would be an inquiry into 'whether the beliefs exist'. However, many critics argued that deciding on authenticity would mean, in practice, inquiring into the validity of Ngarrindjeri women's beliefs. That implied a threat to religious freedom. For example, the South Australian Synod of the Uniting Church in Australia warned:

> In our tradition there have been times when political leaders have sought to wield control over spiritual belief . . . We will stand against any government of any persuasion which seeks to do so. We believe that this State Government has stepped beyond its powers in calling a Royal Commission into Ngarrindjeri beliefs.[42]

The South Australian Council of Churches accused the royal commission of being an inquiry 'into Aboriginal Women's beliefs, past and present'.[43] Adelaide's Catholic Diocesan Justice and Peace Commission maintained that such an investigation 'cannot hope to fulfil its terms of reference . . . without setting itself up as the judge of the spiritual beliefs of the Ngarrindjeri people'.[44]

The South Australian government called the criticisms 'unfair and misguided':

> The criticism might be valid *if* the Royal Commission was required to examine the validity of the spiritual beliefs of the Ngarrindjeri or any other people . . . it is not a function of government to be an arbiter of religious beliefs. However, the terms of reference of the Royal Commission do not require it to examine the underlying truth or validity of the spiritual beliefs. The Commission is required to examine whether those beliefs were a fabrication, ie whether they were devised or concocted for a particular purpose.[45]

Yet the royal commission appeared to find that distinction extraordinarily difficult to maintain. One example is its interest in the system of barrages which regulates the flow of water behind the mouth of the Murray. The barrages form one connection between Hindmarsh Island and the mainland, and one of the commission's guesses about the content of the secret tradition included the speculation that the Ngarrindjeri bridge opponents feared a connection between island and coast would impair future generations' fertility. Being in no position to confirm or disprove its speculation, the commission slipped smoothly into submitting it, instead, to empirical test. The barrages preoccupy several pages of the commission's final report. They are described in detail, from the dates of their construction to the number of timber piles (4470 in the Goolwa barrage, if you were wondering), and the dimensions of each of the components. Readers are told the construction materials (timber piles, steel-sheet piling, concrete piers and reinforced concrete floor), what fuels the gantry crane (diesel) and the mechanics of water level control. There is even a scale drawing of a cross-section through the Goolwa barrage's sluices. What had all this to do with the terms of reference? The commissioner explained: 'Work commenced on construction of the barrage system in 1935 and was complete in 1940. Aboriginal people worked on construction without apparent harm'. The commissioner reports that there was no 'consequent injury to the reproductive capabilities of Ngarrindjeri people, and to the fertility of the cosmos generally, following the permanent link to the mainland effected by the barrage system'.[46]

The commission seems to have been suggesting that nobody would believe something which was not empirically verifiable. The royal commission's treatment of the barrages is one of many examples illustrating the difficulty, in practice, of inquiring into 'whether . . . beliefs [are] a fabrication, i.e. whether they were devised or concocted for a particular purpose' without slipping into an examination of 'the validity of . . . spiritual beliefs'.[47] The royal commission appears to have taken 'validity' of a belief as a necessary condition for 'genuineness', with 'validity' amounting to empirical or logical demonstrability. The report concludes that: 'The beliefs said to constitute the "women's business" . . . are not supported by any form of logic'.[48] The harder questions of which religious beliefs *are* supported by logic, and what kinds of logic it is reasonable to look for in support of religious truth, the commission left unexplored. As an investigation, it was deeply flawed. As an exercise in spin, it was a resounding success.

The Adelaide *Advertiser*'s headline 'Lies, Lies, Lies'[49] summed up the lasting impression: Aborigines gratuitously lie about their religion to block development. For good measure, the commission threw in the idea that, even if they hadn't, the alleged beliefs (as imagined by the commission) were 'not supported by any form of logic' and, consequently, were too silly for any self-respecting government to take seriously. The issue was eventually pinpointed in federal parliament by Labor Member for Grayndler Anthony Albanese:

> Over there [on the government benches] you have got a mob called the Lyons Forum who have a particular spiritual belief. You can imagine the reaction of people like the member for

Menzies (Mr Andrews) or the member for Mitchell (Mr Cadman) if we said, 'We're going to have a royal commission into your beliefs; into whether you can prove the Holy Trinity exists'. What if we said, 'We're going to have a royal commission into Islam,' or into any other religious or spiritual belief? It simply has not happened. There would be outrage if anyone suggested it. But, for the Indigenous people of this country, it is fair game, open slather.[50]

Not all MPs found the parallels so straightforward. South Australian and Howard's immediate predecessor as leader, Alexander Downer, had difficulty accepting that Indigenous peoples had anything that could be called religion at all:

Downer: I'm not sure that sacred sites are religious sites. You could have an argument about that, I suppose. Not sure of the answer to that. I don't really know. I think I'd have to hear a bit more of the evidence. What do you think?
Staffer: I think they're cultural sites.
Downer: Why aren't they religious sites?
Staffer: Why aren't they religious sites? Because, what is the religion?
Downer: Yes, what is the religion?
MM: Well, in traditional societies there's not usually something parcelled off and called 'religion', but—
Downer: Okay, so they don't have a religion.
MM: No, no, you could just as well say everything's religion.
Staffer: Dreamtime, spirits—
Downer: Is that religion? I mean, is it religion?
Staffer: It's more racial.
Downer: Racial? No, I don't think it's racial. I suppose I've never really contemplated that this was a matter . . . of religion.[51]

Tony Abbott, who, as we saw in Part One, never baulked from invoking religious reasons in defence of the 'traditional family' and 'Christian marriage' or in opposition to abortion, and reappears in Part Three defending Howard's shift of previously government welfare services into the church charity sector, found Indigenous sacred heritage one area where religion was not relevant. While maintaining that it is 'perfectly reasonable' for a government to legislate to protect sacred sites, he stressed that 'It's not being done for religious grounds, it's being done for sort of cultural artefact-type grounds, in the same way that we like to protect old houses'.[52]

•

Howard's 1996 campaign slogan, 'For all of Us', exploited resentment. Like any good slogan, it was promisingly vague; however, it contained a key ambiguity. Some might have read the slogan universalistically as 'For *All* of Us', taking the capital 'U' as a mere design feature. But that would be utopian. The real meaning, as Aboriginal leader Noel Pearson kept warning, was 'For all of *Us*'. It implied a 'Them', those whom 'we' resented. In Liberal campaign literature, the slogan was regularly accompanied by such headlines as 'HAVE YOU BEEN LEFT OUT?'

Ngarrindjeri beliefs were perfectly chosen as an icon of otherness. In a highly secular society such as Australia, religion can seem slightly uncanny, an unfamiliar reason for stopping development, but this was not just any religion, it was the secret traditions of Indigenous Australians. If anything else were needed to make the tradition more alien to Howard's imagined 'mainstream', the sacred stories were exclusive to women. Indeed, it is hard to imagine four words more arousing of prejudices than 'Aboriginal', 'women's', 'sacred' and 'secrets'.

Through pamphleteering from the Morgan think tank network, tireless media work by the Pearson circle and Howard's hustings double entendres, the campaign's ripples extended 'Them' from a small group of Ngarrindjeri women and the federal Labor government which had supported them, to take in all those who doubted the 'Lies, Lies, Lies' campaign. By the time the issue had rolled through a royal commission, two federal inquiries and numerous court cases, 'we' could feel our interests imperilled not just by a handful of Ngarrindjeri grandmothers, but also by environmentalists (whose conservation reasons for wanting the bridge stopped had put them among the Ngarrindjeri's earliest allies), the ABC (the only media outlet to remain consistently sceptical of the 'Lies, Lies, Lies' spin), churches (who argued that victimising the Ngarrindjeri threatened religious freedom), unions (who had joined in community boycotts), feminists (who supported the women) and academics (particularly the anthropologists and historians who weighed in behind Indigenous claims). It worked.

After a 'policy-free', small-target election campaign, Howard's political strategists attributed the landslide to the success of wedge issues, identifying Hindmarsh Island as a key. Victory not only handed Howard his long-sought prize, but finished the royal commission's job of entrenching Honest John's 'Lies, Lies, Lies' campaign. As Howard's election strategist Andrew Robb would say later:

> We rode it [Hindmarsh Island] very hard. It was a clear wedge issue for Labor. Tickner was obsessed with holding the socially progressive agenda and so he held onto it. But the more he held on, the more he alienated Labor's blue-collar base. They wedged themselves. And the more we pursued it, the more it divided them.[53]

The Hindmarsh Island and Carmen Lawrence inquiries together, Robb estimated, 'cost the Labor Government three to four critical months from August 1995. It reinforced negative perceptions of Labor while preventing effective attack on the Coalition' and 'blocked any opportunity Labor might have had to apply the political blowtorch to the Coalition, to build momentum especially on the issue of "where are your policies"'.[54]

Only days into office, almost the first act of the Howard government was to announce punitive probes into ATSIC's financial management, prompting Indigenous magistrate Pat O'Shane to explain to *Sydney Morning Herald* journalist Deborah Jopson 'Why Aborigines Now Fear the Worst'.[55] Then, in June, the Minister for Aboriginal and Torres Strait Islander Affairs, Senator John Herron, used Parliament House as the venue to launch a nostalgically assimilationist book by long-time Flinders University academic in education Geoffrey Partington. Herron assured the audience that the assimilation policies of the 1950s still had a part to play, hailing the coming years as the 'era of opportunity'.[56] The same month, Morgan's offsider, Ray Evans, told the H.R. Nicholls Society he was concerned that 'our political leaders still seem to feel no real sense of urgency' over Indigenous rights. But, he predicted, 'This may change in the next twelve months or so'. He foresaw events leading to a political crisis. Within days of his prediction, actions by the Howard government led to speculation about a double dissolution election based on race, just as Morgan had demanded back in 1993. Three weeks after Evans's speech, the *Australian* was running successive pages of stories (with headlines such as 'Howard Greets Assimilation Policy Supporter', 'Back to the Future' and 'PM's Words "Prejudiced, Unforgiveable"') under the collective heading 'Towards a Double Dissolution'.[57]

In the event it did not come to that, but not for want of two years' concerted trying by the Howard government. There was a threatened double dissolution trigger over the *Hindmarsh Island Bridge Act 1997*, which amended the *Racial Discrimination Act* to prevent the Ngarrindjeri women, whose case had been blocked successfully from ever being heard in a court or valid government inquiry, having any further legal recourse. Labor, fearing annihilation in a race-based election in the resentment-inflamed atmosphere of early Howard rule, let the Act pass. The Ngarrindjeri challenged it in the High Court. Counsel for the government put the Howard Liberals' view: the Constitution's 'race power', being 'absolutely rooted in prejudice', gave the commonwealth power to make laws 'against any persons by reason of their race alone'—and that was what the *Hindmarsh Island Bridge Act*, quite legitimately, did. The High Court declined to comment on the scope of the race power, instead finding that the rights enshrined in the *Aboriginal and Torres Strait Islander Heritage Protection Act* are bestowed by parliament, and what parliament has done it can undo. Far from enjoying 'special privileges', the Ngarrindjeri women were allowed to sustain special disadvantages imposed just on them.

The High Court's decision came as the Senate was preparing to consider the *Native Title Amendment Bill*, limiting the rights of Native Title holders whose land had been subject to pastoral leases. Again, there was talk of a double dissolution race election. This time Labor resisted, meaning that the Bill's fate fell into the hands of Tasmanian Independent Senator Brian Harradine, his power then at its peak. When Harradine danced on the Parliament House forecourt with representatives of the Wik people, who had come to Canberra to see their destiny determined, a Senate rejection seemed certain. When the Senate divided, though, Harradine decided he could not hand the government the means to send Australia to the polls over race. Howard never got his race double dissolution; but, with a precedent in place whereby the *Race Discrimination Act* could be rolled back at whim, and with the rights of Native Title holders substantially curtailed, Morgan had nothing to complain about.

'Lies, Lies, Lies' was not the end of the story. Two federal inquiries, a major ethnography and a federal court case later, South Australian Aboriginal Legal Rights Movement spokesperson Sandra Saunders said that the next headlines should read 'Sorry, Sorry, Sorry'. On any neutral reading of the various inquiry reports, court transcripts, judgments and academic analyses, the 'fabrication' story never looked terribly convincing and the passage of time has only made it shakier.

The 'Lies, Lies, Lies' campaign suffered its first unravelling as early as 1996, when Justice Jane Mathews, commissioned by the former Labor government to report on the Ngarrindjeri claims, painstakingly authenticated documents the royal commission had ruled recent fabrications and found a confidential gender-restricted tradition associated with Hindmarsh Island was highly likely. The 'Lies, Lies, Lies' campaign got around that by challenging her appointment in the High Court on the grounds it violated the separation of powers. The High Court found her position unconstitutional and so her potentially explosive report, though tabled, was buried.

Hard on Mathews's heels came Justice Elizabeth Evatt's review of the *Aboriginal and Torres Strait Islander Heritage Protection Act 1984*. Hindmarsh Island emerges from her list of submissions as a cause célèbre; right wing think tanks and mining industry representatives such as AMIC argued that any protection order would have enshrined a fabrication, setting a precedent which would jeopardise future development. Evatt concluded that, in fact, the problem was not fabrication but red tape: the legislation made getting a valid protection order (such as the Ngarrindjeri had sought) prohibitively difficult.

Next, eminent anthropologist and expert on Aboriginal women's religion Professor Diane Bell produced her award-winning *Ngarrindjeri Wurruwarrin*, a Ngarrindjeri ethnography which, without revealing more than her informants were willing to make public, placed the secret traditions in the context of a living culture. Proponents of the 'Lies, Lies, Lies' line dismissed Bell's work, throwing around terms like 'feminist' and 'weaver' (an allusion to her book's central metaphor for Ngarrindjeri culture) as though that amounted to a reasoned critique.

Then in 2001, the last of a string of defamation and malpractice actions wound up in the federal court. Justice Von Doussa, known for his strong line on disclosure, brought the envelopes back into the headlines by forcing those who had known what was in them to tell some of the contents, and some who had not read them (notably former Aboriginal affairs minister Robert Tickner) to consider the information they contained. Von Doussa was so critical of the royal commission and so persuasive in his argument that the claimed confidential women's tradition was at least plausible, that his finding was much harder to dismiss—but it didn't really matter. By then the mud had stuck, baked on in the heat of Howard 'resentment'. Public attention had long since moved on. The bridge was finished before his judgment, and it now spans the Goolwa channel, a concrete monument to the 'Lies, Lies, Lies' campaign and its associated message—that Aboriginal sacred site claims are likely to be 'fabrications' hatched to hold up development.

Ian McLachlan did not have to wear his disgrace long: after the 1996 election he returned to Howard's front bench as defence minister. With the theology of mining taken care of, Hugh Morgan had time for other pursuits, such as his Howard-sponsored return to the Reserve Bank board. Ray Evans left WMC in 2001, but remained a mover and shaker of lobby groups, such as the Bennelong Society, which campaigns for a return to assimilationism as the guiding principle in Indigenous affairs. Christopher Pearson managed to fit his *Adelaide Review* and and other journalistic commitments around his new positions, first as a community representative to the Australia Council for the Arts and then as a Howard government appointee to the National Museum Council and SBS board. His protégé, Chris Kenny, became media officer to foreign affairs minister Alexander Downer. IPA controversialist Ron Brunton brought ideological rigour to the board of the embattled ABC.

It takes an open, welcoming and cosmopolitan spirituality to make room for sacred sites above financial bottom lines. Instead, the 1996 election's 'Us and Them' campaign delivered power to the little god of Howard conservatism, building a climate where racist attitudes thrive and spiritual beliefs which threaten financial interests are automatically suspect.

CHAPTER SIX

Crossing the floor

In 1966, when John Howard was in his mid-twenties and coming to the end of his Methodist involvement, the sociologist of religion, Hans Mol, conducted a major study of the beliefs and practices of Australians. Mol found that, on most counts, regular churchgoing went with more conservative political and moral attitudes. The more frequently his respondents went to church, the more likely they were to oppose abortion and support capital punishment, to disapprove of gambling and to admire patriotism. But questions designed to detect racism broke that association. The more religiously active his respondents, the more likely they were to feel 'friendly and at ease' with members of what he calls 'outgroups'—those a suburban 'us' might have thought of as 'them'. Mol's 'outgroups' included Japanese, Italians, Catholics, Jews and alcoholics. Only communists and atheists risked meeting churchgoers' disapproval.

Mol also asked how respondents felt about someone who wanted to keep Asians out of Australia. The more regularly Mol's subjects went to church, the more likely they were to disapprove of such racism. The less regular the churchgoing, the more likely that respondents would either applaud or 'think it was all right' if someone wanted to keep Australia Asian-free. The difference held true across all denominations. Mol found regular churchgoers 'spearheading a more liberal attitude to Asian migration than those who do not attend'. Interestingly for our story, churchgoing had the biggest effect of all on Methodists.[1] As we saw in chapter one, the Methodist church to which Howard traces his roots has a long history of advocating greater engagement with Asia, supporting an open refugee policy and promoting 'reparations' for taking Aboriginal land from its original owners.

In a 1981 follow up study, Mol found the same relationship between churchgoing and racial tolerance, including sympathy for refugees. And he noted a further correlation: as well as regular churchgoers, the other group most accepting of people of different races and most in favour of helping refugees was people of no religion. 'Nominal' Christians, who professed adherence to one denomination or another but attended church irregularly or not at all, still had much more conservative attitudes on race. Mol pointed out that on many other issues, regular churchgoers and those of no religion were 'poles apart'—for example, single parenthood and beliefs about whether a woman should put her husband and children ahead of her own career. He accounted for the fact that race makes bedfellows of the devout and the religionless in two ways. First, ironically, both are 'outgroups' vis-à-vis the nominally Christian mainstream: 'Obviously the committed Christians feel more responsible for the disadvantaged, and those with no religion (similarly on the fringe of society) favour many enlightened causes.'[2] He found a further explanation in the two groups' connections to wider associations and sources of information:

> In Australia the Christians who, through church going, are regularly exposed to information disseminated by religious

> bodies, feel responsible for those suffering from injustice and persecution in other countries. One can therefore expect them to favour the intake of refugees more than others. The international awareness of the 'no religion' intelligentsia and their proclivity for worthwhile (sometimes even 'trendy') causes leads in the same direction. By contrast the non-church going, modal Australians tend to look less beyond their shores and more to what is of immediate advantage to them personally.[3]

Mol's point certainly held true for Earlwood Methodist. The church's hosting of Colombo Plan students was backed up by the *Methodist*'s front-page stories such as 'Meet the Asians and extend them the hand of friendship'.[4] With White Australia in force, church was one place where suburban Anglo-Australians might encounter Asian faces, not only via the Colombo Plan, but through the various church parallel programs, missionary links and international church ties. Mission connections and national events such as the National Christian Youth Convention also brought suburban churchgoers occasional visitors from remote Aboriginal communities, a kind of encounter their nonchurch-going neighbours would likely never experience.

A recurring theme in this book is that religion is still welcome in Australia's exceptionally secular culture, but mainly as something we approve of for others, rather than participate in ourselves. We like to think of ourselves as a nation founded on Christian 'values', and think of religion as a good thing for political leaders to have. Between two-thirds and three-quarters of us believe in God (depending on the survey), but only around nine per cent take that belief to church Sunday by Sunday. At the other extreme, only one in two thousand Australians wrote 'atheist' on their 2001 census forms, though around fifteen per cent were happy with the less confronting, and vaguer, 'no religion'. In other words, in relation to Mol's findings, we lack the churchgoers and atheists who might resist a particular kind of racist politics. Firm in our belief in our own reasonableness, benevolence and common sense, most of us may have few resources to resist frightening stereotypes. That is just the sentiment that Howard has so skilfully cultivated. We pay a political price for religious naivety.

On one hand, Howard has raised spectres of 'Them', about to seize your backyard in a massive continent-wide Native Title land grab (he even faced TV cameras in 1998 holding a map of Australia with an ominously shaded 79 per cent Aboriginal land) or flood our shores in leaky boats. On the other, he repeatedly reassures us of our tolerance, civility and maturity. Whatever it is he encourages us to feel, it can't possibly be racism, because (he reassures us) the relaxed and comfortable mainstream aren't that kind of people.

•

When the Howard government came to office it had to deal with an Aboriginal affairs portfolio suffused with Christian traces. As political philosopher Michael Phillips demonstrated, the term 'reconciliation' which, with its ten-year 'reconciliation process' and the associated Council for Aboriginal Reconciliation, was part of Howard's awkward legacy from Hawke and Keating, owes its origins to a church push. Hawke's 1988 motion of reconciliation was adopted verbatim from a text proposed by the heads of fourteen Christian churches in a booklet entitled 'Towards Reconciliation in Australian Society'.[5]

True to Mol's picture, Christian churches were among the more vocal of the Howard government's critics on social policy, and few issues galvanised them as consistently as race. From Hindmarsh Island to the Northern Territory's mandatory sentencing laws, church leaders and politicians exchanged anathemas. A telling early instance in government was the criticism by a number of Christian churches of Howard's 1997 'Ten Point Plan' to amend Native Title legislation. Church reaction was so widespread, with even such normally conservative bodies as the Sydney Anglican diocese joining the condemnation, that the

Anglican Bishop of Canberra and Goulburn, George Browning, observed:

> I can't remember any other issue in recent times which has gained such a broad consensus of opinion amongst church leaders. We're very difficult to get on with in many ways! We argue about . . . a host of other issues, but on this one the unanimity of mind is quite extraordinary.[6]

The Executive of the National Council of Churches called on the federal parliament 'to refrain from treating the rights of Native Title holders in a discriminatory way'.[7] New South Wales Council of Synod of the Uniting Church, into which the Methodist Church was absorbed in 1977, passed a resolution declaring 'that extinguishment or diminution of currently existing native title would be discriminatory and unacceptable on moral, legal and financial grounds'. It exhorted the government 'to abandon the amendments proposed' and 'to enter into negotiations in good faith with Aboriginal people and Torres Strait Islanders' to produce a replacement Bill.[8]

Responding to church critics is tricky for a government. Castigating them directly risks alienating church members and, for that matter, voters without church connections but who respect churches' role as independent watchdogs on behalf of the marginalised. Ignoring them might work, but not if the opposing party is adept at making the most of critical comments, as the Opposition (then led by committed Anglican Kim Beazley) was showing signs of doing with Native Title. For example, Labor frontbencher Laurie Brereton testified in the midst of the Native Title Amendment debate:

> I am a practising but far from perfect Christian. I must say this: when I go to church and I pray the prayer for justice for all Australians, it means just that. It is a prayer for justice and a fair go for all Australians, whether they be black or white.[9]

Another possibility is to try to drive a wedge between church leaders and their decent, mainstream flock. Coalition politicians accused churches of being 'political', and (paradoxically) urged political tactics on parishioners, such as church 'boycotts'. Queensland National Party Senator Ron Boswell argued that churches joining the Wik debate 'have alienated their flock . . . They are driving people away from Christ'.[10] Liberal Member for Leichhardt Warren Entsch urged rural parishioners to 'boycott' their churches until collection plate pressure forced a policy rethink:

> What I'm suggesting is that they go to their local churches and they ask them to state their position on this, to listen to their side of the argument, and also to represent their views as well. If they're not prepared to do that, then I would suggest that they not bother to attend their churches.[11]

Howard produced a charter, first in Hansard and then by media release, of rights and duties for church leaders in public debate. First, 'the right to speak freely on a broad range of issues carries with it the obligation to speak in an informed, objective and constructive manner'. Second, clerical agitators have a responsibility to submit to criticism from 'others in the community' if their comments 'do not accord with the facts, or display undue bias'. Third, they should not 'allow the impression to be created that they speak on behalf of all adherents to their particular church or denomination'.[12]

The controversy following Entsch's boycott proposal provides another textbook example of a Howard strategy tried and tested by the American Christian right: cultivating others with a more extreme view than your own, making yourself look moderate by comparison.[13] Howard has customarily allowed others to make extreme comments which he does not directly echo, instead chiming in 'I understand . . .'. An obvious instance of this was his belated, and muted, 1996 response to Pauline Hanson's first speech. He wasn't endorsing her views, just celebrating the lightened 'pall of censorship' previously imposed by the politically correct (though his former candidate would later accuse him of stealing her One Nation party's policies). Another was his 2003 invitation to State governments to bring capital punishment back on the agenda. It was not that he personally supported it, he insisted, but people close to him whom he respected did, and surely their views deserved a hearing.[14] Heffernan got a prime ministerial 'I understand' in the Kirby affair.

Howard's 'I understand . . .' formula makes room for statements he was politically unable to make. It signals to politicians of his own and other parties, to talkback hosts and columnists that, if they up the ante, they will get no rebuttal from him. It is an invitation to heat the political atmosphere a few more degrees, firing right wing passions that he presents as popular, commonsense reactions—although, as we saw in the Hindmarsh Island affair, they in fact relied substantially on business-funded think tanks helped along by right wing commentators. In 1997, Entsch's church 'boycott' proposal elicited the refrain:

> May I say of my colleague the member for Leichhardt that I understand his sense of frustration—and the sense of frustration of many people in rural Australia—about the way in which this debate is being conducted. I do not support a call for a boycott of church attendance, but I can understand the sense of frustration he feels.[15]

Asked by the leader of the Opposition to apologise to church leaders for criticising them during the Wik debate, then Deputy Prime Minister Tim Fischer (while Howard was overseas) set an Anglican vicar from rural Queensland against his superiors:

> The parish priest of the All Saints Anglican Church in Charleville had this to say about church leaders: 'There are three words that could describe the comments made by the Archbishops. The first word is ignorant; the second word is uncaring; and the third word is hypocritical'.

Fischer, a Catholic layman, offered his two bits worth on Anglican ecclesiology: 'That is the church leader I support in relation to Wik and Mabo'.[16]

Another version of the same strategy, also well used by the American religious right, is to brand opponents as 'extreme', again putting your own position in the moderate 'centre'.[17] The strategy provides a handy response to allegations of racism: no, this is just common sense; the real extremists are over there.

American religious right speakers have demonstrated this technique's capacity when campaigning against homosexuality, for example, to conjure quite intense feelings of hatred in their hearers, while still reassuring hearers that what they are feeling is just 'common sense', a benign, natural reaction.[18] Howard demonstrated a race-oriented version in a November 1997 doorstop in response to a question about the threat of a race-based election. With his government warning of a massive Aboriginal land grab, overturning of existing property law and apocalyptic outlooks for Australia's mining and pastoral industries, Howard soothed:

> I think the Australian people are—the people of Australia, as distinct from some people who grab the headlines from time-to-time—are a lot more tolerant and understanding and smart and sensible than they are given credit . . . Despite what we foolishly say about ourselves from time-to-time, and despite the fact that we needlessly from time-to-time apologise to the rest of the world for being less than 100 per cent . . . we are a very tolerant, understanding, inclusive people . . . And I think that if you did, at the end of the day have an election in which the Native Title legislation were a principal issue, that the Australian people would take no notice of extreme statements no matter what side they came from, they would not be deterred by or intimidated by those statements. They would look at the merits of the argument and they would make an appropriate decision. I think we allow

> ourselves to be treated in too timid a fashion. I think the Australian community is mature enough, tolerant enough, reasonable enough if it comes to this, and I hope it doesn't because I hope the Senate passes the legislation, to see the Native Title Act to give certainty where there is now potential chaos, not as a racial issue, because it is not a racial issue. It is a land management, investment, security, welfare of Australia issue.[19]

The effort to portray anyone who disagreed with Howard's Ten Point Plan as 'extreme' provoked a journalist to ask, 'What about the criticisms by the church leaders though, they are hardly radical or extreme?' Howard replied with a further strategy, namely, pointing out the divergences of opinion within churches. As we saw in chapter one, Howard sprang from an exceptionally activist church with a history of political controversy. However, as we also saw, the more important dynamic in his background was his family's resistance to Methodist social activism. Howard knows that church leaders do not always reflect the views of all their congregants. He went into detail:

> [T]he church . . . has, not only many denominations, but many positions within denominations and it has many spokesmen and women and committees. And you can't assume that, for example, [Anglican Primate] Archbishop Carnley speaks for the entire Anglican Church, he speaks essentially for himself and some body of opinion within the Anglican Church. I have heard comments from sections of the Catholic Church, [then Director of Uniya Jesuit social justice centre] Father Brennan does not speak for the National Council for the Collective Catholic Bishops, any more than [then Baptist Union President] Tim Costello speaks for the entire membership of the Baptist Union, or than [NSW Synod Board of Social Responsibility chief executive] Harry Herbert talks for the entire membership of the Uniting Church . . . At the end of the day nobody owns the moral conscience of this nation.

> At the end of the day each of us has got to make our own individual moral judgement . . . I have great respect for the role of the churches in the Australian community . . . But at the end of the day we all make our own moral judgements, they don't have a superior ownership of moral issues.[20]

Foreign Affairs Minister, Liberal Member for Mayo and practising Anglican Alexander Downer was still blunter: 'What do we think if Harry Herbert is on television saying Howard is a shocking person and Downer is a dickhead? We think, "There goes Harry Herbert". "The churches" does not mean Harry Herbert.'[21]

When all else failed, Howard accused churches of abandoning their proper role to become merely 'partisan'. In 2004, Howard delivered another sermon to church leaders. There was no particular controversy to elicit it, but his unsolicited advice was widely interpreted as, in the Adelaide *Advertiser*'s words, a 'pre-emptive strike during an election year in which social issues are expected to dominate'.[22] He told the paper, 'I think that church leaders should speak out on moral issues, but there is a problem with that justification being actively translated into sounding very partisan'. He warned church leaders not to engage in 'political' debate, which often led to their being 'particularly critical of our side of politics'. His worries were altruistic: 'I think . . . the unity of the church . . . stresses and strains when [congregations] hear from their leaders . . . about issues that are bound to divide their congregations'.[23] The complaint is common. For example, Downer added to his criticism of Harry Herbert, the Uniting Church's New South Wales Synod officer responsible for speaking on social justice questions, that he 'is a bourgeois Leftie'. As such, Herbert appeals, in Downer's view, to a constituency more political than theological:

> There are people who are of the centre right in religious groups and there are people who are lefties . . . Day in and day out,

> Harry Herbert comes out and kicks the shit out of the Liberal Party . . . Activist bourgeois Lefties like Harry Herbert because he's part of their sort of paradigm.[24]

Instead of indulging in 'partisan' politics, both Howard and Downer exhorted church leaders to stick to 'spiritual leadership'.[25] Neither said what that was, nor where to find the boundary between spiritual and political. The difficulty was summed up in a letter to the *Advertiser* the next day from Father Peter Gardiner of All Saints Catholic Church, Port Augusta the day after Howard issued his unsolicited advice:

> No, Mr Howard, we will not remain silent . . . When I read something in the Gospels that supports the incarceration of men, women and children in concentration-camp-like conditions, who have committed no crime, nor been charged with any crime, then I will be silent. When I see anything in the Gospels that supports the vilification of a desperate people and the continuance of outrageous lies, in the disgraceful 'children overboard' saga, then I will say nothing. When I see anything in the Gospels that tells me to remain silent about the lies regarding the illusory weapons of mass destruction and the subsequent, and real, massacre of up to 10 000 innocent Iraqi lives, then I will say no more.[26]

Less theologically, *Advertiser* columnist Rex Jory pointed out that clergy, no less than anyone else, enjoy freedom of speech in a democracy, and have particular expertise arising from seeing 'first-hand the anguish and the hardship individuals face in their daily lives . . . Why shouldn't they rail against authorities which do too little to help the victims of social injustice or neglect?'[27]

It is hard to see, in practice, how a church body could possibly live up to Howard's prescription. Perhaps, when he said that church leaders should speak on social issues but without becoming 'political', he meant that churches' policy recommendations are acceptable as long as they do not match any party's actual policy.

Then churches would be always in the position of advocating policies that no one was ever likely to implement, and being prevented from endorsing policies with which they agreed. In fact, if a political party did adopt a church's policy proposals, the church would promptly have to abandon the policy as now 'political'.

Howard's theological tussles did not stop outside the party room door. In 2000, a group of Christian Liberal politicians threatened to cross the floor over the Northern Territory's mandatory sentencing system. Magistrates were obliged to impose tough sentences, including gaol, for sometimes trivial offences, and on young offenders. These laws were more frequently invoked against Indigenous than non-Indigenous offenders, falling especially hard on those from remote communities (partly because of the greater difficulty of getting away with even a minor crime in a small community where everyone knows everyone). Consequently, the system was widely condemned as racist, in effect if not in intent. Many of the petty crimes had all the appearance of desperation in the face of poverty. Sentences which shocked the nation included twenty-eight days for receiving a bottle of spring water valued at one dollar, fourteen days for stealing two cartons of eggs, one year for a homeless person who stole a towel to keep warm at night and one year for stealing cordial and biscuits from a building site. In the face of such damning examples, it took Howard's considerable skill to bring the right's God back under party discipline.

•

The 1996 federal election that swept Howard to power included some remarkable swings in particular seats. The electoral venom in seats where race issues had run hottest suggest the Howard message of fear had penetrated. Pauline Hanson in Oxley and then National Bob Katter in Kennedy rode a racist wave to substantial swings. And Robert Tickner, Keating's Aboriginal and Torres Strait Islander affairs minister, scarred by the Hindmarsh

Island campaign, was tossed from his NSW seat of Hughes with an eleven per cent swing. The new member for Hughes was Danna Vale, subsequently Howard's veterans' affairs minister.

Vale saw her surprise election as a religious vocation. Her evangelical awakening started along with her parliamentary career. Previously, 'I always knew about God, I just didn't bother him very much . . . I didn't go to church, but I sent my kids to Catholic schools'. She added that she had 'woken up one morning with the strong feeling that, if I didn't stand for preselection, I'd one day have to explain to God why not'. Since being elected she claimed, 'I've been on a spiritual journey rather than a political one'. She found parliament a strange and often alienating place: 'You're always on the edge of a plank and someone's wobbling the other end'. As a result she learnt, 'There's only one person in this building I can trust, and that's Jesus Christ'. She was further sustained when a visiting pastor drew her attention to Psalm 91, one particular verse of which became a guiding thread in her parliamentary life: 'For he will command his angels concerning you, to guard you in all your ways. They will lift you up in their hands, so that you will not strike your foot against a stone'.

The voters who tipped Tickner out in her favour may have been surprised by what they got. With Jesus at her side, Vale did not see her mission as sitting quietly while others made the running. Her most prominent public moment came when Independent Member for Calare Peter Andren and Greens Senator Bob Brown introduced private members' Bills to overturn the then Country–Liberal Party Northern Territory government's mandatory sentencing laws.

The widely publicised instances of Aboriginal teenagers receiving jail terms for misdemeanours such as stealing paint from a school storeroom or biscuits from a work site attracted criticisms of 'Dickensian' punishments. Children were mandatorily imprisoned after voluntarily confessing to minor misdemeanours and this raised the fear that the system punished hardest those making an effort to reform. When a young inmate died in his cell just before he was due for release from a mandatory twenty-eight-day sentence, the issue, already under scrutiny from a Senate committee, became a national scandal.

Vale and a group of other Liberal MPs flagged their intention of crossing the floor to support one of the Bills. The other named dissenters were Peter Nugent, Brendan Nelson, Christopher Pyne, Petro Georgio, Bruce Baird and Kerry Bartlett. Like Vale, Baird and Bartlett are both members of the Parliamentary Christian Fellowship (at time of writing, Baird is its president). Pyne and Nelson are often mentioned as examples of the 'Catholicisation of the Liberal Party'.[28] Fellow Catholic Kevin Andrews, who sponsored the private member's Bill to overturn the Northern Territory's euthanasia law, also spoke in the party room in favour of federal intervention.[29] The make-up of the dissenting group suggests at least prima facie support for Hans Mol's observation that race is one area where religiosity and conservatism do not go together.

Although Liberals are officially free to follow their consciences on any issue, unlike their Labor counterparts, who risk automatic explusion if they vote against their party, the group was clearly given to understand that any vote against the government would spell career disaster. Seven dissenters in the House of Representatives could have produced a majority against the government which, Howard told them, would inflict damage beyond the mandatory sentencing issue. Amid the furore, many inside and outside the parliament proposed a conscience vote, allowing both Howard supporters and dissidents to emerge with their honour intact. With the memory of the euthanasia laws debate still fresh, there seemed an attractive symmetry in following that with another intervention in Northern Territory law, again mandated by conscience, to protect the most disadvantaged of juvenile offenders. The 'States' rights' argument that had complicated the euthanasia issue was, if anything, weakened, because between the euthanasia debate and the mandatory sentencing controversy the Northern Territory had held a referendum on Statehood. The 'no' result meant that Territorians had, in effect, voted to keep their parliament under federal authority.

Christian churches were prominent among conscience vote advocates. The National Council of Churches, representing fourteen Christian denominations, denounced the Northern Territory practices as a breach of human rights. The occasion provided a rare opportunity for public discussion about which issues should attract a free vote. Howard set out his position in an interview on ABC TV's *Lateline* program:

> Tony Jones: Now, why have you refused to give your own party members a conscience vote on this?
> John Howard: Because it's not a conscience issue—it's not. I mean, it is not—it is not—the question of whether you have mandatory sentencing is quite different from something like euthanasia or abortion. Those things go to the very essence of somebody's religious or philosophical or moral view, whereas mandatory sentencing, although people feel very strongly about it, is of a completely different category and there won't be a conscience vote. If you have a conscience vote on mandatory sentencing then you might as well have a conscience vote on just about everything . . .
> Tony Jones: Let me ask you this, though: when you heard of the death of that young child in the prison, did it not strike you that this might be a moral issue?
> John Howard: Well, I—Tony, when I heard of the death of that young child I was distressed like any other Australian, but . . . you can't just say, on the basis of that one very sad and tragic incident, that that of itself justifies overturning what is—if you believe in any kind of federation—is traditionally one of the things that states do, and that is manage their criminal laws.[30]

Howard gave the *Canberra Times* a still more circular justification: 'We took the view that you maintain free votes for those things that are indisputably likely to attract them such as the issues like abortion, euthanasia, capital punishment'. That is, leaders don't *give* free votes; issues *attract* them.

Vale proposed a compromise. She would put up her own private member's Bill, which was less sweeping than either the Andren or Brown versions but prohibited mandatory sentencing of juveniles, including seventeen year olds, who were treated as adults under Territory law. At a Coalition party room meeting, all the dissenters were allowed to speak. But, according to one unnamed participant quoted in that week's *Sunday Age*, it was clear from Howard's opening comments how the decision would go:

> In a kind and gentle way he completely gutted these people . . . Everyone knew the Vale Bill was dead but no one said so. The boss made it clear that he disapproved of it and that he would not be intervening. But he gave them their heads, that's the clever part of it. He shut off the oxygen but it was done from a distance. They were writhing and kicking around in a very uncomfortable state, but it was nothing to do with him, his hands were clean—he just happened to have his heel on the hose, that's all. They were not going to cross the floor, nor were they going to be given a conscience vote, nor were they going to be forgiven if they did cross the floor . . . They knew that if they did cross the floor they'd be completely ostracised . . . You know if it's happening, they don't have to tell you.[31]

Brendan Nelson confirmed the pressure:

> No one actually said to me you go and vote with the other side and that's the end of you, or your preselection's in trouble. There was none of that. But anyone who's reasonably intelligent in this game knows that if you do go and vote against the view of the Government, it's not without some

> sort of penalties. Your colleagues would maintain a sense of distrust in relation to you.[32]

There would be no rerun of the 1988 episode discussed in the last chapter, when four Liberals crossed the floor to vote with Hawke Labor in favour of multiculturalism. In government, and at risk of displaying a failure to control the House, the stakes were too high. Even so, Vale felt she could not meekly support the government line:

> I'm a mum. I was a juvenile justice lawyer before I came here. We started a community aid panel as a sentencing option. I do respect States' rights, and I wouldn't have challenged [similar sentencing laws in] Western Australia. But the Northern Territory voted not to become a State. That put me in a direct line of responsibility for young people in the Northern Territory.[33]

As with many in the euthanasia debate, personal experience played a part. Vale revealed that her own son had been in trouble with the police and had been able, with appropriate help, to put the episode behind him. Northern Territory teenagers were being denied comparable chances, she felt.[34] Prevented both from crossing the floor and from proposing her own Bill, Vale considered her options:

> [*Sydney Morning Herald* journalist] Margo Kingston wrote an article about me called 'A Christian Liberal's Lonely Crusade'. I don't usually talk about Christianity, but when she outed me as a Christian, that reminded me to pull out the power of prayer. So when the party decided not to intervene, I went to Plan B: the power of prayer . . . I contacted as many as I could of the churches in my electorate, asking them for prayers for guidance for the prime minister and cabinet. I even asked [Anglican] Archbishop [of Sydney] Harry Goodhew. I also sent letters to the prime minister and

> cabinet, so they'd know they were being prayed for . . . And I sent around copies of Psalm 91. Well, it was [former Northern Territory Chief Minister] Shane Stone who brought in mandatory sentencing, after all—so I put the two crucial verses in bold type, and, where it says, 'You will not strike your foot against a Stone', I spelled Stone with a capital S, just in case some in the party room were a bit slow![35]

In the end, all the dissenters were persuaded to vote with the government. The trade-off was, first, an undertaking from the prime minister to meet Territory Chief Minister Dennis Burke to try and persuade him to soften the laws (though Burke explained that he would be meeting Howard to explain how the laws worked and why they were necessary to Territorians) and, second, that there would be a set-piece debate on the Andren Bill, in which some dissenters would be allowed to air their views. Vale took this opportunity and began her speech, 'I do not think anything has distressed me as much as this particular legislation has'. She announced that she would be voting against the Bill because to do otherwise 'would hurt my government', but wanted to put on the record that 'I abhor these mandatory sentencing laws'. She concluded:

> I want Mr Burke to hang his head in shame, because when we break down fundamental principles of justice—and one of those fundamental principles is that punishment should fit the crime—we are actually reducing the level of justice for each and every one of us; we are all the poorer. My prayer is that we can all work together for these young people because, my goodness, they need it. That is my undertaking to this House, to the people of my electorate and to the young people of the Northern Territory whom I do not know but hope to meet.[36]

Her speech was widely acclaimed as one of the year's more powerful. On her own account, however, she was not prepared:

'When it came to the debate in the House, I couldn't believe how fast it happened. I didn't have a speech ready, so I just said, "Help me, Jesus."' Consequently, she did not want to take personal credit for the speech's substantial public impact: 'I think God put the Spirit on the ears of the hearers'.[37]

Other dissenters were similarly forthright. Nelson argued that mandatory sentencing laws 'violate one of the principles that makes us all Australians'. Pyne listed numerous extreme instances of mandatory sentencing imprisoning people for minor offences (ninety days for stealing ninety cents from a vehicle, fourteen days for stealing a $2.50 cigarette lighter and confessing). He concentrated on the loss of judicial discretion, pointing out that judges and magistrates in the Northern Territory 'are ciphers adopting a law that many of them oppose. They might as well be monkeys making such decisions because they are not being called upon to use their judgment, their experience and their training'. The power to sentence, he pointed out, had been effectively made over to police, since a successful prosecution amounted to an automatic sentence.[38]

So, what did the power of prayer achieve? Howard still refused to intervene; no rebel went so far as to risk their career crossing the floor; Northern Territory Chief Minister Dennis Burke did not, as far as we know, hang his head in shame (still less revise his policy). Nevertheless, the dissident Liberals' speeches kept mandatory sentencing, already high on the nation's agenda, in the spotlight a little longer. The ALP national conference, under pressure from its southern constituencies, compelled its Northern Territory branch to adopt repeal of mandatory sentencing as a policy for the election which, after twenty-three years of Country–Liberal Party rule, they saw no hope of winning anyway. But, against the odds and for a variety of reasons, Clare Martin's Labor Party won. Territorians no longer receive mandatory jail terms for petty offences. On that occasion, the 'power of prayer' proved an effective political strategy at the margins of party procedure, galvanising a block of MPs to the point where, although they did not ultimately break ranks, they used the available opportunities to make statements which exposed the racist effect of the laws and marked race as one issue on which they would not be irrevocably tied to a party line.

•

Probably few politicians drive between Canberra and Sydney; but, during the late 1990s, any who did would have been well advised to stop at the Rimbolin café in Goulburn. Its big neon coffee cup told you it was open. Inside, the talk was as reviving as the dinner. The cook, Catherine, was finishing a Bachelor of Divinity by correspondence. Front of house was composer, conductor and former La Trobe University philosopher Melvyn Cann, who took your order then serenaded you on the violin or dijeridu. He would tell you about the massive reproduction of anthropologist Norman Tindale's map of Aboriginal tribal boundaries which dominated the room. Cann saw learning about and from Indigenous cultures as a first step towards reconciliation.

Together with the steak and kidney pie with pickled walnuts and wine by the glass, you could buy a copy of Cann's book, *Crossing the Floor*. It begins with Cann walking down the main street of Goulburn dressed as a clown named Collywobble. Collywobble reappears throughout the book as a truth-telling court jester, puncturing pretension and interrupting Cann's argument to dispute with the author. When people asked Cann, 'Why are you dressed as a clown?' he replied, 'Why aren't you?' He noted with bemusement that 'Mostly they did not seem to like this answer', and some became aggressive. Walking a rural main street dressed as a clown, experiencing the hostile reactions of passers-by, Cann recalls, 'I had crossed over'—into a world of inverted meanings and upended hierarchies. That is only the first of many 'crossings' the book explores.

Cann recounts how he grew up in Adelaide during what he calls, echoing anthropologist W.E.H. Stanner, the 'Great Australian Silence'. His generation was taught little about Indigenous

Australians, certainly not massacres, dispossession or injustice. Cann takes up historian Henry Reynolds's cry: 'Why weren't we told?' Nevertheless, a couple of experiences were formative: a family visit to the mission at Port Augusta, and getting to know an Aboriginal pupil while at school in Adelaide. Such personal encounters meant he could no longer think of Indigenous people as the abstract, distant and dying 'Them' in his school textbooks. Through such experiences, Cann recalls, 'I had begun to cross the floor'. His floor crossing reached its most intense, emotionally charged moment in Sydney's Redfern Catholic parish. In a ceremony in 1993, Cann was simultaneously received into the Catholic church and given an Aboriginal name and shield by Wirradjuri Elder Uncle Leo Coe and Redfern community leader Mum Shirl.

Cann's book's title is his catchcry for how non-Indigenous Australians should comport themselves. They need to 'cross the floor' to see their country, and their place in it, from an Indigenous point of view. Cann's personal encounters undermined attempts to portray Indigenous people as 'Them', just as Danna Vale, declaring her commitment 'to the young people of the Northern Territory, whom I . . . hope to meet', expressed feelings of connection that led her within a breath of 'crossing the floor'.

Collywobble's creator writes as a committed Christian. His book is dedicated to the members of the Southern Tablelands Fellowship, and has a chapter on Christianity. But just as important to him as his faith in Jesus is his learning from Indigenous religion. The book concludes with an image of Jesus and Mawalan, a mystical Aboriginal figure who reappears throughout the book, sharing a joke. Religion is a crucial theme in Cann's *Crossing the Floor*. He argues that, until Australians recognise the dominant culture's Christian foundations (whether or not we identify as Christians), we cannot properly understand its relationship with other religious worldviews.

•

These days, it is fashionable to contrast 'spiritual' with 'religious'. As a teacher of religious studies, I regularly face classrooms full of people who declare that they are not at all religious, but very spiritual. When pressed, they gloss 'spiritual' as individualised, internal, eclectic, dynamic, anti-institutional and free form. By 'religious', they mean something organised, external, inherited, formulaic, regulated and traditional. Their characterisations reflect what scholars of religion have found people repeating across secular, western societies.[39] My students' tones clearly indicate that to be religious would be a rather disgraceful admission, while to be spiritual is admirable. It is not unusual for prospective students to announce to lecturers that they are enrolling in our courses in order to understand religion 'so that I can show why it is wrong, and persuade people to become spiritual, instead'. The opposition between religious and spiritual comes through in other settings, too. Media representations often indicate approval or disapproval of particular leaders by designating them as spiritual (Gandhi, the Dalai Lama) or religious (Ayotollah Khomeini, Ian Paisley).[40]

Christian fundamentalists tend to share the mistrust of 'religion'. They criticise institutional churches, claiming a return to a pure, pre-institutional 'fundamental' form, with only loose or no links to the denominational structures whence they came. Another significant proportion of people identify themselves as active Christians but do not belong to any church. Rather they belong to various non-denominational parachurch organisations, ranging from political groups such as the Festival of Light and Australian Christian Lobby to networks such as prayer breakfasts for Christian businessmen. I have found this prominently among conservative politicians. Despite the fact that politicians go to church rather more regularly than the Australian average,[41] many who speak about their Christian commitments, including such non-denominational activities as the Parliamentary Christian Fellowship and the Lyons Forum, go suddenly quiet when asked, 'Where do you go to church?'

In Australia's 2001 census, all the mainline Christian denominations shrank; but so did 'no religion', for the first time since it appeared on the form. While some of the difference was made up in immigrant religions (particularly Buddhism and Islam), their increase was not enough to account for the fall in 'no religion'. In Hans Mol's terms, Australia is losing both its religiously committed and its atheists. As in other secular, western countries, a personalised, free-form and eclectic spirituality seems to be replacing commitments for and against religion. My students, who dread to be seen as 'religious' but are proud to be called 'spiritual', point to the wrongs religions have perpetrated: the wars waged, heretics burned, women and minorities oppressed and lands despoiled. We could level the same charges at many other longstanding human institutions, such as political parties, but religion attracts such criticism with unusual force. But religion has positives, as well.

At their best, religious traditions carry the collective memory of generations of committed thinkers, trained and lay, devoting themselves to pressing human problems. The trial and error nature of individual, internalised spirituality has attractions, but it leaves every seeker reinventing their own wheel. Religions tend to have a (more or less) systematised theology, carry institutional weight and have high-status spokespeople to publicise their message. Religions typically address social problems, not just offer self-actualisation. And, for good or ill, religions bind their members into communities. Historically, that has often been their downfall: those outside the community have easily become a dehumanised 'Them'. In modern, plural societies such as Australia, a single religion is unlikely to become a whole community's dividing line. Instead, by bringing together people who might otherwise never associate, religions foster personal connections across the boundaries of race, class and so on, offering one effective bridge across 'Us and Them' divisions.

John Howard and his senior ministers, when they find themselves disputing with church leaders, tell their antagonists to stick to 'spiritual' concerns and not mess with 'politics'. While we seldom find out what they mean by 'spiritual', it seems to mean the opposite of 'political'. When Howard exhorts church leaders to stay on the 'spiritual' side of the floor, he presumably means something along the same lines as my students: sticking to the spiritual means concentrating on the internal, self-focused aspects of religion that might suggest personal behaviours but has minimal involvement with the non-spiritual, political world. In fact, we will see Peter Costello spelling out exactly that view over lunch in chapter nine, urging church welfare agencies to deliver personal transformation, not political opposition.

'We' can all be spiritual. It is an inoffensive category, threatening no one. To be 'religious' is to take on distinctive identifications (Anglican, Pentecostal and so on). In 'Us and Them' politics, 'we' are equal, without problems. If 'we' make demands on government, they reflect genuine needs (for law and order, say, or a strong economy). Only 'they' indulge in special pleading, raising special needs and gaining 'special privileges'. 'They' criticise governments, demand policy changes, speak out, agitate, vote against 'Us'. Well may Howard and his ministers prefer church leaders to sink back into the invisible, spiritual 'Us'.

Faced with meddlesome priests and activist churches, the Howard government responded first and loudest by reproving mainline denominations. Chastisement followed, as we shall see in chapters eight and nine, in the form of financial threats, interspersed with attempts to co-opt churches into the government's own program. Another technique for conservative politicians seeking to tame unruly religion is to encourage a sympathetic alternative. American-style evangelical and Pentecostal churches, aggressively selling both conservative social values and a capitalist-friendly fundamentalism of individual prosperity, proved a safer spiritual home for many of Australia's conservative politicians. Over their third term, Howard and his ministers would become increasingly assertive in courting the votes, and associating themselves with the ethos, of Pentecostal and non-denominational evangelical churches previously dismissed as a parvenu Christian fringe. Howard would open Pentecostal premises at Sydney's Hillsong and Oxford Falls Christian City Church, exchanging compliments with the thousands-strong congregations; Peter Costello would preach Ten Commandments fidelity as the solution to Australia's problems at the inaugural National Day of Thanksgiving and at a Hillsong conference; and, in the 2004 election, other right wing Christians, such as Member for Bass Michael Ferguson, who cut his political teeth campaigning against adoption by gay and lesbian couples and declared 'I love the Lord' in an election night interview, would join Howard's parliamentary ranks. Traditional churches were painted as part of the dangerous 'Them', while a particular, conservative kind of Christianity became increasingly entrenched as a cultural marker of 'Us', even if relatively few of us actually identified with it, or even knew much about it.

Not that encouraging conservative Christianity would prove a total answer. Mol's analysis of traditional Christian denominations also holds true for the newer arrivals. Although ready to go all the way with Howard on many of the sex-and-family topics explored in Part One, and sharing considerable common ground on the economic and welfare issues in Part Three, Australia's Christian right (unlike many of its American models) has shown itself consistently resistant to racism. Though famously conservative on social issues, the Rev. Fred Nile's Christian Democrat party often took a relatively progressive position on land rights issues. A still more pronounced case in point is former Liberal Member for McPherson John Bradford, mainly famous as an ultra-conservative Christian morals campaigner. He resigned from the Liberal Party in 1998, briefly becoming the only Christian Democrat in federal parliament. His cited reasons included a series of disagreements with the government, including over Howard's 'Ten Point Plan' to amend the *Native Title Act 1993*. In the 1998 election, he stood for the Senate, pointedly sharing his ticket with Aboriginal Christian businessman Kerry Blackman. Most strikingly of all, when the Assemblies of God-based Family First burst onto the federal scene for the 2004 election, it was headed by the country's first Indigenous woman party leader, Andrea Mason. Mason brought not only a strong Christian background, but a family tradition of working for improved rights for her people, a point underlined when she was introduced at her campaign launch by veteran Indigenous activist Lowitja O'Donoghue. When the Senate count briefly suggested the Coalition might require Family First support, the Howard government must have started rethinking the hectoring Indigenous policy tone which had gained it votes from One Nation. However, there was one 'Us and Them' binary on which the Coalition might have anticipated at least some conservative Christian support.

Now, we turn to a subterranean assault waged by the right's frightened God against the new 'Them' since 11 September 2001. So deep is the tension between Islam and Christianity, and so tender the wounds, that Howard could not denounce the new 'Them' with quite the same outspokenness he and his backers used to disparage the sacred traditions of colonial Australia's Indigenous 'Them'. Yet, between the lines of conservative political rhetoric about Islam in Australia, we find out much about how religion works, just out of the picture, in the struggle for Australia's soul.

CHAPTER SEVEN

People like that

In late July 2001, Sydney newspapers reported serial gang rapes in the western suburbs, depicting predatory young men with a high-tech game plan, duped young women and terrible ordeals. Piling detail on detail, Sydney's *Daily Telegraph* nevertheless blustered that not enough was being revealed about the crimes: 'politically correct' police, and politicians in thrall to powerful ethnic organisations, were pussy-footing around the fact that the perpetrators were Muslims.[1] Sex, race and crime being the lifeblood of talkback radio, the premier outlet for Howard-licensed 'racial resentment', it was no surprise that Sydney radio 2UE's Alan Jones took up cries of 'out-of-control Lebanese Muslim gangs who hold us and our police service in contempt', attacking 'ordinary Australian girls'.[2] On top of all that, Jones complained that, thanks to rampant police and State government 'political correctness', 'we're not supposed to talk about it'.[3] In fact, police had been issuing statements about serial sexual assault, including the belief that the assaults appeared to have racial overtones, for ten months, with minimal media response.

As the New South Wales Anti-Discrimination Board (ADB) pointed out, 'The attacks became major news' only once 'they were angled as a story about Lebanese, Arabic or Muslim gangs targeting white Australian women'. The ADB also noted another discrepancy: when police first tried to publicise the issue in August 2000, Sydney was in the grip of Olympic euphoria; a year later, when the story finally took off, that euphoria had been replaced by 'a growing moral panic about Arabic or Middle Eastern and Muslim asylum seekers'.[4] The rapes became big news because they could be mixed up in a religious war on a global stage.

This moral panic had not come out of the blue. In 1998, former High Court Judge and Human Rights and Equal Opportunity Commission President Sir Ronald Wilson drew attention to the government's rebranding of desperate asylum seekers as 'illegals', despite their recognition under international law.[5] Subsequent government opinion-shaping added the images of 'queue-jumpers' and 'wealthy, self-serving' associates of 'criminal people smugglers'. The message got through so well that, a month before the gang rapes story hit the headlines, social commentator Hugh Mackay reported that, among his focus group of respondents in the crucial outer-suburban marginal seats, 'Refugees previously referred to as "boat people" are now routinely described as "illegals"' and said to bring 'unacceptable levels of crime and violence'.[6] By the time the year-old gang rape story emerged in August 2001, the carefully nurtured public mood was fertile ground for a seemingly automatic association between 'Muslim', 'Middle-Eastern' and 'criminal'.

At that point Howard was in the fatigue stage of his second term, dented by devastating Coalition losses in the Western Australian and Queensland elections. One factor in the State disasters had been Pauline Hanson's One Nation, which was not delivering preferences to the Coalition parties. One Nation had launched its Queensland campaign with a refugee policy: 'We go out, we meet [the boats], we fill them up with fuel, fill them up with food, give them medical supplies and we say, "Go that way"'.[7] Federally, Howard faced falling polls, a resurgent ALP trading off GST anger and a federal election due by the end of the year. David Marr and Marian Wilkinson describe how, on 8 August 2001, Howard broached using the Navy to implement One Nation's 'push off' border protection policy—an option long championed by his hand-picked department head and ally, Max Moore-Wilton.[8]

The issue promised plenty of traction: just a week later, 345 people arrived on Christmas Island, joined by another 359 the following week. Most were Iraqi and Afghani Muslims. By the end of August, Australia had more than three and a half thousand people in migration detention centres, and more were coming.

On 24 August the diminutive *Palapa* lost its engines, leaving its 438 passengers adrift, without even a radio or positioning equipment, until their dramatic rescue by Norwegian Captain Arne Rinnan of the *Tampa* two days later. Rinnan's increasingly frustrated efforts to land his passengers on Christmas Island, the Australian government's stalling over medical assistance while sending an SAS show of force, the tenuous 'Pacific Solution' and the impact of all that on the 2001 election have been exhaustively told by Marr and Wilkinson. My concern here is the affair's part in the continuing depiction of Muslims as the latest 'Them'.

The Howard government went to extraordinary lengths to prevent the *Tampa* refugees ever setting foot in Australia, or having contact with a civilian doctor, nurse, public servant or journalist (any of whom could have conveyed a request for asylum, ending the charade of keeping the refugees off Australian soil) or lawyer (who might have challenged the government's legal position). Another effect of keeping the refugees in isolation was that, as Marr and Wilkinson noted, the nearest image of them that Australian viewers saw throughout the crisis was a hazy picture of a distant ship, coaxed out of a fully extended long-distance lens. There is nothing like distance for keeping 'Them' scary.

Literature scholar Suvendrini Perera described responses to the *Tampa* asylum seekers, which emphasised common humanity rather than fear, in an article called 'A Line in the Sea'. She recalled that when Arne Rinnan handed his passengers over to the SAS, he exhorted the Australians to take good care of 'my guests'. The people of Christmas Island, prevented from welcoming the *Tampa* passengers, nevertheless prepared bedding, food and accommodation and issued a joint statement by numerous community groups that urged the government to allow the refugees to accept the Islanders' offer of shelter. Gungalidda elder Wadjularbinna issued a media release pointing out that, from an Indigenous point of view, the original European settlers came to Australia as illegal immigrants, arguing that Australia should show the same welcome to those in need which 'the Aboriginal world' had shown them. When the federal government's 'Pacific Solution' finally disgorged the refugees in Nauru, they were met by a traditional welcome dance. Such words and gestures, said Perera:

> . . . signal breaches in the carceral forces separating asylum seekers from the rest of us. They link the inside and the outside . . . our stories and their stories; make simple reciprocal gestures between guest and host, sheltered and homeless, harbour and traveller.

Lest such gestures appear too private, sentimental or eccentric to offer a moral yardstick for a national government, Perera also recalled Canadian Prime Minister Jean Chrétien who, facing questions about the possible terrorist danger from asylum seekers and migrants, declared:

> Let there be no doubt. We will allow no one to force us to sacrifice our values and traditions under the pressure of urgent circumstances. We will continue to welcome people

> from the whole world. We will continue to offer refuge to the persecuted.[9]

Like Chrétien, Howard saw public fear of asylum seekers as a challenge to national identity; but, where Chrétien saw his people's identity threatened by giving way to fear, Howard invoked a mind-spinning paradox to accuse the *Tampa* asylum seekers of illegitimately trying to keep Australians true to our national identity. The refugees were seeking 'to intimidate us with our own decency', he announced as the *Tampa* passengers tried to land in Australia.[10] As with his repudiations of the 'racist' label in the last chapter, Howard reassured us we were fundamentally decent. Sending desperate, sick and hungry people away from our shores in a boat too small to legally carry them and in defiance of international law could not be an indecent thing to do: if it were, decent people like us would not be doing it. Decency seemed to urge the passengers' claim, so not 'they' but 'we' were the real victims, 'held hostage' by our inclination to help people who proved, overwhelmingly, to be genuine refugees from intolerable regimes.

Before Australians had time to reflect too far on these paradoxes, however, all subtleties were burnt away in the blaze of world events. Never mind that many of the *Tampa* refugees were fleeing the very regime that harboured the World Trade Center and Pentagon attackers; the same prime minister who rushed to support the US action in Afghanistan fanned the fear that every refugee was a potential terrorist.[11] The connection was simple: they were all 'people like that'.

•

Probably the clearest instance of attributing negative characteristics to a whole segment of the community was the 'children overboard' affair. The last days of the November 2001 election campaign were dominated by stories about how asylum seekers on yet another creaky, leaky smuggler vessel were said to have thrown their children into the sea in an attempt to blackmail the Australian Navy into taking them to Christmas Island. Though the stories turned out to be groundless, they were unwaveringly recycled by Howard and his then defence minister, Peter Reith. Keeping asylum seekers off Australian shores was, since the *Tampa*, official government policy—with the whole costly machinery of the Navy's Operation Relex to back it up—but the 'children overboard' image allowed Howard to paint the asylum seekers' rebuff as all their own fault. 'I don't want people like that in Australia', an 'angry' Howard told the Melbourne *Herald Sun*, repeating the line in successive interviews.[12] People like what, exactly, was not spelt out. Even accepting the report as true, he could hardly have supposed that every adult on the boat had thrown a child into the water—still less, on every approaching boat—but they had all become 'people like that'.

General allusions to the 'illegal' nature of the asylum seekers' arrival had given way to personal vilification, playing on the most emotional of bonds, that between parents and children. In fact, it was Howard who was throwing children 'overboard'—or, at least, shoving them out to sea. The story seemed tailor-made to build up the picture of asylum seekers as 'Them', a 'sort of people' wholly alien to 'Us', treating even their children in cavalierly self-interested ways 'we' could never comprehend or countenance. It was the latest twist in the line of inference and allusion which linked Muslims, suburban teenage criminals, international terrorists, fundamentalist theocrats and desperate asylum seekers together as 'Them'. Spelling out the connections could only have weakened a set of associations that thrives between the cracks of conversation.

Drawing on detailed polling during the racially charged 1988 US presidential campaign, Princeton political scientist Tali Mendelberg demonstrated in her book, *The Race Card*, that, for white audiences, race remains a powerful political motivator. But, for post-1960s voters imbued with the ideal of racial equality, the most effective racial appeals are the least specific. White audiences who know that racism is wrong need to be able to assure themselves, even as they respond to racially charged triggers, that they are reacting for non-racial reasons. If they cannot assure themselves, the political trigger is much less effective.[13] This pattern is evident in Australian anti-Muslim racism.

Although conservative columnists linked the gang rape story to 'the Muslim community's . . . cultural issues',[14] they did not directly claim, for example, that all Muslim men are rapists. Nor did anyone make the bald assertions that all Muslims are terrorists, queue jumpers, fake refugees or child abusers. Such overt racism would have drawn attention to its own implausibility. Instead, repeated references to 'the sort of people' who would do such things combined into an implicitly racist message that nevertheless contained what Mendelberg identified as an essential element of a successful racial appeal: deniability. So, even as Howard wove together fears about asylum seekers, terrorists in the regimes they were fleeing and unproven allegations of child abuse, he vehemently denied any racial or religious overtone. Refugees would be repelled wherever they were from: 'white or Japanese, or North American or whatever—it is a question of protecting our borders'. He could not be appealing to racism, he reassured voters, in phrases reminiscent of his Native Title soothing discussed in the last chapter. Such charges must be nonsense because, not only was he himself innocent of racism, but so was his audience: 'I don't find any racism in the Australian public'.[15] It was just that the refugees were 'people like that', so absolutely foreign that they might reasonably be denied even a hearing.

As a result of such implicit appeals, from illegals to rapists to terrorists to child abusers, Australian Muslims were repeatedly made to bear collective opprobrium in ways other communities were not. For example, Anne Summers wondered why the perpetrators' ethnicity and religion seemed an essential part of the Sydney gang rape story, whereas the equally attention-grabbing 1986 gang rape and murder of Sydney nurse Anita

Cobby had not resulted in comparable blame sharing among all those who bore the perpetrators' Irish surname, Murphy.[16] Similarly, we might wonder why not all those of Irish Catholic extraction are suspected IRA operatives, and why not all white Australians are taken to be potential child abusers. By contrast, Muslims were portrayed as collectively responsible for other people's perceptions of them, even when the perceptions were groundless or the result of deliberate misrepresentation.

In the week following 11 September 2001, the *Toronto Star* newspaper commented:

> 'Acts of war', 'acts of terror', 'we're at war', 'hunt down and smoke out', 'wanted dead or alive', 'evil-doers', 'mass murderers' and 'barbarians' who 'slit' women's throats. If the war on terrorism was fought with rhetoric, US President George W. Bush may have won it by now.[17]

From the beginning, Bush seemed to be commissioning his troops for a cosmic showdown between the forces of evil and the forces of righteousness. All that paled, though, against his announcement of a 'crusade' on terror and his identification of Iraq as part of an 'axis of evil'. Both were taken as placing his government's actions in the Middle East in a historical continuum with the medieval church's crusades against Islam. For Muslims, the overtones were of unprovoked, ideologically driven Christian brutality. Two days after the 'crusade' remark, Bush's office issued a retraction, saying that all the president had meant was that the response to terrorism would have the characteristics of a 'broad cause'.[18]

Taken at face value, the apology implies staggering verbal ineptitude—what a monumental brick to have dropped in the most diplomatically sensitive environment since the end of the cold war! What extraordinary, gratuitous offence to offer at the very moment you are trying to assemble friends—a slip which could almost seem calculated to produce a coalition of the affronted.

Observers of US political rhetoric might draw a different conclusion. They might, for instance, see Bush mirroring the Christian right strategy identified by Cynthia Burack, which we encountered in chapter four. She pointed out that Christian right leaders regularly 'practise small duplicities—such as apologies—in order to be misunderstood by the major population', while simultaneously 'narrowcasting' to their 'born again' constituencies. That the speakers apologise when addressing a mainstream public does not alter the underlying message.

For those disinclined to see the most powerful man in the world as a hapless blunderer, Bush's crusade 'slip' and belated retraction can be read as just such a double entendre: the evocation of Christian religious warfare might have been, not an unintentional clanger, but a deliberate 'narrowcast' to a Christian fundamentalist audience waiting for just such a clarion call; the retraction, a necessary hosing down without removing the original message.

Following the 'crusade' comment, Bush went to some pains to neutralise the comment, at least as far as his secular and international audiences were concerned. He was shown visiting a mosque, meeting Muslim leaders and repeatedly describing Islam as 'a religion of peace'. The 'c' word dropped from his vocabulary, though he has persisted with religious allusions such as the idea, echoing a famous line of Kennedy's, that 'the liberty we prize is not America's gift to the world, it is God's gift to humanity'. In Bush's hands, though, it comes to sound as if America, the delivery boy, is charged with seeing the gift gets through to its recipients, whether they want it or not.[19] Bush's iconography of an anointed 'Us' facing down a religiously threatening Muslim 'Them' required delicate execution.

Howard's messages about Muslims have been much less ambiguous. In Australia, explicitly religious language cannot be relied upon to carry the automatic positive vibes it does for substantial American audiences. Rather, religious appeals in Australian politics work more along the lines of the 'implicit' racial appeals described by Mendelberg. In our much more secular political environment, overt religiosity is likely to seem suspect in the same way that race does to post-1960s Americans. Not that religious appeals don't work in Australia—they just have to be deniably vague, so their subliminal appeal is not interrupted by rational dissociation.

Having announced no crusade, Howard had less need to visit mosques, or make protestations of admiration for Islam. Instead, his portrayal of Muslims as the new 'Them' picked up the half-spoken list of associations forged during the gang rape and asylum seeker episodes. Muslims remained firmly 'people like that', even when he was expressing sympathy with their plight. The chasm between 'Us' and 'Them' was obvious, for example, in his response to the deliberate burning of a Brisbane mosque shortly after 11 September 2001. Although newspapers reported his comments under the heading 'PM Outraged', his indignation proved conditional: 'If it is an act of vandalism or vilification, I condemn it unreservedly'. He continued, piling on the qualifications:

> Islamic Australians are as entitled as I am to a place in this community. If their loyalty is to Australia as is ours, and their commitment is to this country, we must not allow our natural anger at the extremes of Islam . . . to spill over onto Islamic people generally.[20]

By purporting to know the hearts of one part of the population ('ours') while raising doubt about the loyalty and commitment of another ('theirs'), he drew a sharp division between Australians. And he placed himself firmly on the righteously angry, unquestioningly loyal, non-Islamic side.

Incidents like the mosque torching were the visible crest of a wave of street-level anti-Muslim harassment, with women and children its most frequent targets.[21] Barely a year later, Australia's response to the October 2002 Bali bombing raised the fear that 'acts of vandalism or vilification' against Muslims were no longer the exclusive work of individuals, but had become official policy. ASIO agents conducted highly public raids on the homes of people suspected of having attended past public lectures by Bali-implicated cleric Abu Bakar Bashir. They broke into family homes during the evening or in the early hours of the morning, handcuffed parents in front of their children and confiscated personal belongings. Victims described violent methods that seemed less about catching suspects than about intimidating communities. That the raids took place during Ramadan made the insult seem still more calculated. But the wider public got to see an impressive story of a strong, security-conscious government.

It seemed a heavy-handed form of intelligence gathering—and a singularly ineffective one, as it produced no charges, let alone convictions. As the lawyer for one of the raided families put it, 'If [ASIO] had given our client the courtesy of asking him to provide information, or let them interview him or even come to his house, he would have opened his doors and made them a cup of tea'.[22] In fact, as the Asia Pacific Human Rights Network reported, at least one of those raided had already contacted ASIO and offered to be interviewed. ASIO officers refused his offer, only to come crashing through his front door at dawn two mornings later.[23]

We might expect that violent images of armed men breaking into the homes of sleeping families would evoke fear of government terror tactics. In fact, the depiction of Muslims as the new 'Them' had progressed so far by this time that opinion polling found the government's standing enhanced as strong on national security.[24] Howard declared himself 'one hundred per cent' behind the raids on Indonesian Muslims:

> These raids relate to investigations concerning individuals. People who claim that this is in some way targeting Islamic sections of Australia are just, in my opinion, deliberately

> trying to create a difficulty that does not and ought not exist.[25]

That the raids used unnecessary force and maximum family disruption at the time of greatest potential religious offence to obtain no evidence against people who had, in some cases, already come forward all melted into a perfect example of Mendelberg's 'denial'.

While endorsing actions which reinforced the updated version of 'Us' and 'Them', Howard's spoken responses tended to be brief, ambiguous and elliptical, leaving plenty of room for denials of racism, but also plenty of cracks in which implicitly racist messages could thrive. One issue, though, elicited a long exchange in which the shifting, unpin-downable nature of 'Them' became strikingly apparent. As such, it offers a number of insights into the reasons for Howard's (to some) inexplicable success. Sydney radio talkback host John Laws asked Howard how he felt about NSW Legislative Councillor and maverick Uniting Church minister the Rev. Fred Nile's suggestion that Muslim women should not be allowed to wear full body and head coverings in public because the clothes might conceal weapons. As Laws put it, 'We don't even know if they're women because they're that covered'. Howard gave his customary reassurances of Australian decency, tolerance and commitment to equality: 'We have to respect each other in these things. It's just a question of civilised living. If you've got a religious faith and providing you're not flinging it in somebody else's face, then you should be allowed to practise it'. Nevertheless, Howard also inserted his 'I understand . . .' formula, encountered in previous chapters:

> I don't have a clear response to what Fred has put. I mean I like Fred and I don't always agree with him, but you know Fred speaks for the views of a lot of people . . . No, look, I understand what he's getting at . . .

In the process, the prime minister licensed a sharp contrast between Muslim women and 'the Australian way of life':

> I want everybody in this country to live according to the modalities of Australia . . . People coming to this country, whether they're Islamics [or not] . . . must understand that when they come to Australia they . . . can't cherry pick the Australian way of life. I mean, people have to sort of, they have to take the good with the bad and things they don't like, well they've got to live with them because that's the nature of our society.

Howard's next comments, though, might have opened him to the accusation of doing some cherry picking himself:

> We do respect very strongly equality of men and women. I think that's very, very important. And I think practices of any religion that don't meet that expectation will inevitably draw some disapproval and some criticism.[26]

This was the prime minister whose attitude to the equality of the sexes led him to rejig the political environment to encourage partnered mothers out of the paid workforce, reinstate 'chairman' for convenors of Commonwealth boards and committees[27] and propose an amendment to the *Sex Discrimination Act* to allow the Catholic Education Office to offer men-only teaching scholarships.[28] Given his particular concern about 'practices of any religion' that contravene equality of men and women, we might also wonder about his silence on the ordination of women in the Catholic church and the consecration of female Anglican bishops.

Much of the discussion on Laws's program hinged on how much covering Muslim women are obliged to wear. Laws put it to Howard that 'apparently it's not mandatory in the Qur'an for them to do that'. By most standards of religious freedom, whether a practice is mandatory or not is irrelevant—the point is that people are free to worship in the way they choose. Howard, though, would have been happy to adjudicate, if only he knew a bit more:

> Well, I'm not precisely sure of what the rules of the Muslim religion are on this question . . . I have got to frankly myself have a better understanding of just how fundamental that is . . . Now I can't make at this stage a judgement. I've just had this flung at me. I'm not sufficiently apprised of the tenets of Islam to fully understand that.

Laws reassured with a relevant authority: 'Well I think dear Fred is, in as much as he [has] obviously looked at the Qur'an, and the Qur'an doesn't state that it is necessary to have the full covering'. Not religious freedom, but religious compulsion was the issue. (Imagine if the government decreed that Catholics could take communion, since it is compulsory, while Protestants, for whom communion is less central, could not.)

Still more alarming is the public airing of their naivety about religious orthodoxy. We can imagine the response of Fred Nile, founder of the 'family values' oriented Festival of Light, at a similarly ill-informed argument about his interpretation of Christianity. Suppose that, after reading the New Testament, a member of a non-Christian faith told Nile that there is no Biblical reason why Christians should support 1950s nuclear families over other forms: since Jesus was often at loggerheads with his parents and siblings, while Paul argued that marriage is only a second best to celibacy, the government should ban Christian heterosexual couples from flaunting their family form in public. We cannot imagine Nile accepting such an interpretation; but that is the level of argument Laws and Howard calmly accepted on behalf of Muslim women.

Howard's responses were a masterpiece of double entendre. On one hand, he made noises about tolerance and inclusiveness: we respect religious diversity. Laws and Howard assured listeners that 'most Muslims . . . overwhelmingly' are 'a delight to talk to'. In the same breath they both firmly cast Muslims, and especially Muslim women, as 'Them', whom 'we' assess. When pressed, rather than affirm religious freedom, Howard cast his response in terms of needing a better understanding of Islam. His listeners could infer that, once convinced that the chador was merely 'optional' for Muslim women, he would be happy to ban it—not only for public safety but for their own good:

> Laws: But wouldn't it be better if they were less conspicuous at this time?
> Howard: Well, obviously, consistent with their religious beliefs.[29]

In suggesting that Muslim women would do better to abandon non-compulsory religious traditions, Howard effectively supported repression. The problem, in other words, was Islam, not prejudice.

The tactic of making Islam responsible for other people's perceptions, even when the perceptions are incorrect, was repeated in 2003, when Federal Education Minister Brendan Nelson wrote to his State counterparts asking for extra scrutiny of Islamic schools to allay fears that they were encouraging 'anti-Christian and anti-Western sentiments'. Curiously, Nelson claimed not to be reflecting his own concerns. He was reportedly 'confident' that no such sentiments were being taught, and praised the Islamic schools' charter for promoting peace and mutual respect, making it unclear what the requested scrutiny would achieve. Nelson told State ministers the fears came from 'concerned citizens', and he was worried that their negative perceptions might spread.

Nelson's declaration of personal confidence in Islamic schools was corroborated by the chair of the Australian Council for Islamic Education in Schools, Mahomed Hassan, quoting a letter he had received from Nelson two months earlier, praising the schools' charter. So, the fact that Nelson then aired doubts to

State ministers struck Hassan as 'hypocritical'. Tabling the Nelson letter in the Queensland Parliament, State Education Minister Anna Bligh argued that Nelson's first recourse should have been to allay the fears of the 'concerned citizens' himself. Instead, she argued, 'By issuing a "please explain" to State education ministers on the quality of Islamic schools he has used his position to add weight to these unfounded fears and to pour petrol on the fire of prejudice'.[30] She might have added that putting the onus on Muslim schools to counter allegations he knew to be unfounded, rather than trying to correct the prejudice at its source, furthered the perception of Muslims as 'Them'. Once again Islam, not prejudice, was made to seem the problem.

The schools controversy erupted around the same time as another initiative which laid the government open to charges of implicit racism, the 'fridge magnet' campaign. Like the post-Bali raids, the medium seemed to be the message. In 2003, the federal government posted every household in Australia a booklet and fridge magnet with information about what to do in the event of a terrorist strike, phone numbers to ring to report suspicious behaviour and space to write in items of household information such as the location of the gas meter (the relevance of the latter in avoiding terrorist attack was left to the householder's imagination). As University of NSW political scientist Matt McDonald pointed out in a detailed analysis of the anti-terrorism kit campaign, international relations theory has long noted the way governments 'constantly attempt to create fear of "others" outside the nation as a means of garnering support for specific practices and achieving or maintaining support for the government itself'. Viewed in that light, the kit's purpose seemed to be 'augmenting . . . domestic fear of terrorism'. Its mission was arguably to 'reiterate to Australians the new dangers and insecurities . . .' while indicating 'that the government was "doing the job" of security'.[31]

McDonald saw the kit as part of a government strategy to facilitate the passage of two controversial pieces of legislation then being debated in parliament. The ASIO Legislation Amendment Bill promised ASIO the powers to detain, incommunicado and without legal representation, people—including children as young as fourteen—suspected of being connected with, or having information about, terrorism. The Security Legislation Amendment (Terrorism) Bill included a twenty-five-year or life term for a designated 'terrorist act' and gave the Attorney-General power to proscribe terrorist organisations. Given the controversy surrounding these Bills, and the fact that they seemed to curtail civil liberties in ways unnecessary to the goal of containing terrorism, one could equally see the legislation, and the publicity surrounding it, as further 'fear augmentation'.[32] The bills painted a 'Them' so dangerous (even when they are children) that normal civil liberties should not apply. Coupled with the anti-terrorism kit's invitation to spot suspicious activity and dob in anyone whose behaviour did not 'add up', the new ASIO powers arguably offered not increased security, but a heightened sense of a half-visible menace.

•

Later in 2003, Federal Treasurer Peter Costello told tertiary students about his faith. The venue was the National Student Leadership Forum on Faith and Values, a parliament-sponsored annual conference introduced under the Howard government and modelled on a Washington program of the same name. Delegates get to quiz politicians about their faith, and meet international guests such as Fiji's successful coup leader, subsequently elected president and constitutional reformer, Sitiveni Rabuka. As well as living exemplars, students also study historical leadership models, such as Jesus of Nazareth, missionary Albert Schweitzer and Mother Teresa.[33] The Forum—both in its Australian and US incarnations—is associated with the international prayer breakfast movement, a networking and strategy powerhouse whose religious right associations we explore further in Part Three.

Costello tied his discussion of faith and values to events of the day:

> You would have seen yesterday, the big explosion in Jerusalem, maybe like me you watched the TV and you have seen video of the suicide bomber who did that. He was holding a rifle in one hand and a Koran in the other. He had faith and he had values, you can't deny that. He probably had more faith than all of us put together, but were they the right values?

Adopting the tone of a worldly wise uncle, the treasurer warned his youthful audience that, as students, they might encounter a dangerous philosophy called postmodernism. According to him, it would try to teach them that all values are equally good and you can therefore believe in anything you like. But, he stressed, the example of the suicide bomber proved that not any values would do. Instead, students were better off with 'the ethic and the faith background that we come from', which Costello praised for recognising 'the value of life over death'.[34] He could hardly have been blunter: choose 'our' life-affirming Christianity over 'their' death-dealing Islam.

The explicit casting of Muslims as a religious 'Them' through references to community tragedy, women's dress, the school system and even suicide bombing has to be understood against the background of the concurrent public conversations about religion which were taking place at the time. One conversation, often loud and explicit, was about Islam. It portrayed Muslims as outsiders-within-the-nation, probably teaching their children extreme anti-Western views, and as potential terrorists (especially when wearing distinctive, religiously marked dress). That conversation gained volume from the stereotypes of terrorists and asylum seekers purveyed, and intensified, by public policy moves such as the anti-terrorism kit and the ASIO and security Bills.

Another conversation, then still often muted and carried on, at first, more between the lines than in the headlines, was about

Christianity. It portrayed 'Christian values' as 'tradition' related to nationalism, civic order and public safety. The two conversations came together most obviously in Costello's speech, where the traditions of Jesus of Nazareth, Mother Teresa and Albert Schweitzer became 'our' values and 'faith background', contrasted to the misguided faith of a Qur'an-clutching suicide bomber. Such a blatant comparison between 'our' fine spiritual values and 'their' dangerous religion was exceptionally blunt. But, as we've seen repeatedly, the right's God works most powerfully just off-screen; the fear of 'them' is most effective when 'we' and 'they' are only obliquely marked out, because a more specific definition is able to be contradicted, thus blunting its force. The confluence of the two religious conversations in Australian public life during the Howard government's second and third term created a space in which the pictures of an embattled 'Us' protecting 'our' values and a menacing 'Them', driven by the frightening values of a strange religion, could flourish by remaining half-articulated and, consequently, barely challenged.

Between these two conversations, there was growing talk about 'values'. Everyone seemed worried about who's got them, who needs them and how to impart them; but no one said what they were. All the talk assumed that everyone knows what 'values' are. No one questioned them: apparently, everyone *does* know what everyone else means when they talk about 'values'. Except me. I found myself increasingly confused.

This wasn't happening only in Australia. In the 2004 US Democratic Primaries, people were talking about whether the Democrats would be able to repel the Republicans' attacks about 'values'. Did I get that right: the party that has been embroiled in one scandal or another since even before its election and which was now being denounced by a series of former insiders for lying, cheating and sending young Americans off to die for a cause completely unrelated to the stated goal, is the presumed values winner? While I was musing upon this, along came the Australian values debate.

Howard began it with an apparently off-the-cuff remark about the drift of students from State to non-government schools. The State system, he said, had become 'too politically correct and too values-neutral'. He glossed the remark by explaining that parents were frustrated with a lack of 'traditional values'. A *Sydney Morning Herald* editorial made me feel I was not, after all, quite alone in my confusion: 'these phrases are code—but for what it is hard to say'.[35] The only clue Howard offered, either in the initial interview or in any of the numerous follow-up pieces, was that some schools 'think you offend some people by having nativity plays'. Searching earlier sources, the *Herald*'s Mark Riley found that this was not the first time Christmas traditions had come in for prime ministerial championship. In 2002, Howard had inveighed on Melbourne radio against kindergartens' alleged 'banning' of Santa and department stores' dropping nativity scenes from Christmas displays, which he labelled 'not very impressive' and 'a cave-in to political correctness'. Riley also unearthed a piece of vintage Howard outrage over NSW Premier Bob Carr's 1997 intervention to stop a NSW State school's annual passion play. In fact, the State government had intervened not on religious grounds but because parents had complained that the whipping, spitting and humiliation scenes were too graphic for young children. Riley concluded that the collection of instances—'Easter plays, Christmas nativity scenes and old Saint Nick'—indicated that '"values" has become his shorthand for "religious values"'.[36] In fact, the traditions cited all relate (though tenuously in Santa's case) to a single religious tradition. Riley's *Herald* colleague, Linda Doherty, was more precise, pointing out that to 'Howard, his ministers and talkback radio callers', 'values' referred not to just any religion, but meant Christian values.[37] Similarly, the language of 'banning' evokes religious censorship, raising the theocratic ghosts of 'Them'.

Since his 1995 campaigns against 'political correctness', Howard had given 'censorship' an additional meaning—the 'pall' of elite prohibitions which, he claimed, the 'chattering classes' had draped over the social landscape, and which the silenced 'we' pierced only at our peril. While the kindergarten 'banning' of Santa conjures up images of spiky-haired teachers barricading doors and chimneys against the white-haired old fellow's doddery efforts to reach the innocents within, it is hard to see how it could mean more than the fact that the (unnamed) kindy decided to hold a Santa-less Christmas party. (The childcare centres I've had to do with lately enjoy an annual visit from the Christmas Fairy, a trend I had put down not to ideology but to scarcity of fathers willing to don the furry red suit in midsummer—no one to my knowledge has interpreted Santa's absence as a 'ban'.)

During an interview with Sydney talkback host Alan Jones, Howard did cite one concrete instance: a Queensland Education Department suggestion that schools replace Christmas observance with a celebration focusing on year's end and holidays. This, Howard said, was an 'attempt to sort of bland down any kind of traditional approaches in our country'. That blanding down was a symptom of political correctness, and had fostered the growth of discourtesy, incivility and, he suggested later in the interview, even the kind of street violence that produced that week's other big news story: the fatal kerbside death of cricketer David Hookes.[38]

Far from blanding down, the multicultural classrooms I know have preferred a multiplicity of religious observances, with children introducing one another to their respective traditions. Howard's claim of secularist censorship surely belongs more to the overheated religious atmosphere of North America where, in 2004, courts considered whether the Pledge of Allegiance should be said in schools (with its polarising cold war addition 'under God')[39] and whether the Ten Commandments could be displayed outside court houses (many of them, it turns out in a truly American twist, placed there originally by Cecil B. de Mille to promote his movie of that name).[40] Those are just the most recent in a long string of court battles over the detail of what religious references may be made in US public life (known in legal shorthand as the 'plastic reindeer test'—if a Christmas tableau contains reindeer and other secular decorations along with the nativity scene, it is a cultural rather than religious image and therefore permissible).[41] One possible lesson from the bitter American fights, where successive judgments deal body blows to one side or the other, is that the more rigidly people's deepest commitments are excluded from public life, the more easily people retreat into resentful fundamentalism of the kind that exploded into the Oklahoma bombing.[42] Howard's out of the blue musings about 'politically correct, values-neutral' public schools seemed an attempt to translate that vote-rich feeling of frustrated exclusion, to heat up Australia's traditionally much more laid-back religious climate.

•

Sociologists of religion have long pointed out that as societies become more secular, religion comes to be seen in increasingly instrumental terms. It becomes less a system of beliefs relating to a cosmic order that makes claims upon us than a toolbox of therapeutic and goal-setting techniques that can be adopted selectively to achieve individual ends (the personal fulfilment theology of Norman Vincent Peale's *The Power of Positive Thinking* is a paradigm).[43] Such theories flourished in the 1960s and 70s as mainline denominations' membership rapidly ebbed from their post-war crests and the religious marketplace seemed suddenly flooded with new age and Eastern-inspired movements that offered goal-oriented fulfilment, often with only the most minimal demands on the converts. The growth of prosperity oriented, unblushingly aspirational evangelical and Pentecostal churches in the outer suburbs of large cities was a related development.

A number of strands in the late 1990s suggested a further, more overtly political development in the use of religion as instrumental. People remained willing to appreciate religion as producing desirable outcomes, but they embraced it on others' behalf. '*I* am sufficiently sophisticated not to need religious beliefs to make me moral/obedient/compliant/generous/truthful', their behaviour suggests; but 'religion is a good thing for other people to have'. This type of thinking helps explain the appeal to a highly secular electorate of an apparently sincere—but not too in-your-face—religiously committed prime minister. More, it explains the attraction of social programs which carry a (particular, conservative kind of) religious aura, especially when promoted by increasingly confident evangelical networks.

Howard's 2004 remarks were not the first time the drift from State to private schooling had been linked to a quest for 'values'. The *Sydney Morning Herald* ran a major series of articles in mid-2003 documenting the transfer in federal government funding from State to private schools, which the paper declared to be expanding 'on a runway trajectory'.[44] The *SMH* found parents who professed no religion but hoped schools would instil 'values' they themselves felt incompetent to convey.[45] When Howard's comments reopened the issue in 2004, the paper ran a follow-up article maintaining that parents who denied any religious conviction nevertheless deliberately sent their children to Christian schools in quest of 'a better sense of discipline' and tending to their 'spiritual and social needs'.[46]

Similar thinking is likely among those who, though lacking religious convictions of their own, support the religiously inflected 'family' positions we explored in Part One, and the contracting out of government welfare services to church agencies which we will encounter in chapter nine. On one hand, such people draw a distinction between religion (meaning Christianity) and the allegedly associated values: 'I'm not a believer, but . . .'. On the other hand, they affirm, probably more strenuously than many religious believers, an indissoluble nexus between faith and morality: even if you don't accept the theology yourself, you (or perhaps those more at risk of moral lapse—single mothers, children, the unemployed) stand the best chance of learning the morals, receiving the standards and absorbing the principles from people who do. To the holders of such views a prime minister who not only apparently believes in dogma that they themselves cannot, but also enacts it on the nation's behalf in the form of 'mutual obligation', upholding exclusively heterosexual marriage and so on, is a highly attractive option.

Parents with minimal knowledge of Christian tradition, who choose low-fee Christian schools in a quest for 'values', may not realise that such schools, which have enjoyed substantial growth over the last decade, by and large represent only one, fairly narrow, strand of Christian thought. Facing questions about his government's redistribution of taxpayer funds to non-government schools, Howard told the House of Representatives:

> [U]nder this government about 300 non-government schools which charge on average less than $2000 in fees have been established . . . You are not talking here about King's, Abbotsleigh or Riverview; you are talking here about schools for the battlers who want a bit of choice . . . I have been to many of them and they are on the outskirts of the cities of this country.[47]

Most of the growth has been in small religious schools such as those associated with the non-denominational, Bible-based umbrella group Australian Associations of Christian Schools (AACS) which, by 2003, covered over 75 000 students in 260 schools.[48] Many of the parents the *Sydney Morning Herald* surveyed, who had chosen to send their children out of the State system in quest of 'values', had opted for AACS schools. Students and their families are not required to subscribe to any creed, but all staff, both teaching and non-teaching, must subscribe to the Association's Statement of Affirmation. The Statement positions the Association well towards the conservative end of the Christian spectrum. For example, all staff accept that 'the Scriptures of the Old and New Testaments are God's infallible and inerrant revelation to man' and 'the supreme standard by which all things are to be judged, and an authoritative guide for all life and conduct'.[49]

According to AACS Executive Officer Peter Crimmins, schools differ in how they interpret 'infallible and inerrant', usually taken as meaning that all parts of the Bible are literally true (rather than open to interpretation as metaphor or poetry, say, or the historically and culturally conditioned views of people in a particular time and place). He estimated that 'fewer than twenty per cent' would teach creation science (the fundamentalist belief that the account of God's creation of the world in the Book of Genesis is literally true) as opposed to evolution in the science curriculum, but others would cover creationism as an alternative view or point out that it is a view some Christians hold. AACS staff also affirm that 'Christ is the Head of the Church and will come again to judge the world and complete the salvation of His people and the Kingdom of God'. Such language, with themes of Biblical inerrancy and a strong sense of future fulfilment, hark back to the *Fundamentals* booklet series, published in America and circulated throughout the English-speaking world early last century, from which fundamentalism takes its name.

More than half of AACS schools (152 in 2003 with over 43 000 students) belong to the subgroup Christian Schools Australia (CSA), which has a still more distinctive Statement of Faith. For CSA, the Bible is not merely inspired, inerrant and infallible, but also 'the only absolute guide for all faith and conduct' (not merely 'authoritative', as for AACS). It is also 'indispensable and determinative for our knowledge of God, of ourselves and of the rest of creation'. CSA has a bleak view of religious diversity: 'Salvation from the penalty of sin is found only through the substitutionary, atoning death and resurrection of the Lord Jesus Christ'. It also states that 'All people have sinned, and, if outside of Christ, are in a fallen, sinful, lost condition, helpless to save themselves, under God's condemnation and blind to life's true meaning and purpose'.[50]

Such positions, at the fundamentalist end of Protestant tradition, tend to be associated with political conservatism, particularly on the sexuality, family and national security issues so central to Howard's version of culture wars, and a damning view of non-Christian religions. In other words, on Howard's account, his government selectively transferred public funds to support substantial growth of schools in outer suburban, often marginal electorates whose theological positions are likely to correlate with support for the more repressive elements of Howard's social policy. He must also know that numbers of Australian schools have now replaced evolutionary theories with Biblical 'creationism'—because, again on his own account, he has visited 'many' of them. Given his concerns about religion that threatens the equality of the sexes, we might also wonder how schools that take the Bible to be an infallible, inerrant and absolute standard of knowledge and conduct interpret some of the New Testament's grumpier instructions such as 'wives, submit yourselves to your husbands as to the Lord', or even, 'Let a woman learn in silence and all submissiveness; I do not permit a woman to teach'.[51]

In the 2004 election, the rising Family First Party may have looked a poor bet to support Coalition attacks on Indigenous Australians, but at least some candidates must have seemed attractive allies for the newest 'Us and Them' crusade. For example, Victorian candidate Danny Nalliah, whose nondenominational Catch the Fire Ministries made headlines in 2003 when it was involved in court proceedings for allegedly vilifying Muslims, had also distributed a leaflet inviting churchgoers to 'spot Satan's strongholds' in their local area and 'pull these strongholds down' with prayer. How would the faithful know they'd found a stronghold? Nalliah's leaflet advised them to target 'brothels, gambling places, bottleshops, mosques, temples', as well as 'Freemason/Buddhist/Hindu etc.' and 'witchcraft'.[52]

Howard's vague appeals to bland-sounding 'values' work in the same way as his allusions to his Methodist childhood: they add a quasi-religious weight to his frequent nostalgic invocations of 'the way things used to be', without being religiously specific enough to mark him off from the secular, amorphously spiritual 'Us'. The combination contributes to a politically invaluable persona for a prime minister in a highly secularised electorate, where religion (meaning some vaguely apprehended kind of Christianity) is seen as a good thing for other people to have. It makes particularly effective politics in a climate of increasing fear and suspicion, exacerbated by government demonstrations of toughness, on top of increasingly crime-reliant nightly news. Religious values, even if we don't ourselves share them, promise sincerity, right-mindedness and safety in an uncertain world. How much stronger and more reassuring the promise appears, when the world beyond our vulnerable borders is portrayed as teeming with a religiously fanatical, potentially criminal 'Them'.

Howard's social conservatism was the most visible part of his transformation of Australia's soul. However, before he became famous for his back-to-the-future vision of sex and race relationships, Howard was known as an advocate of economic 'reform'. Seeking the passion behind his transfiguration of Australia, we turn now to investigate his relationship with the right's ultimate 'power greater than ourselves'—the Market.

PART THREE

Market Values

CHAPTER EIGHT

Think tanks

So far, we have explored the ways in which Howard and his government harnessed the themes of 'family values' and 'racial resentment' to entrench their conservative vision of Australia. Both themes provided crucial rallying points for him, often below the radar of much political commentary, to generate support in the thick of culture wars. This ensured Howard's return to the Liberal leadership, his path to the prime ministership and his re-election. Though social conservatism distinguished Howard's prime ministership, his longest established public commitments were economic.

From early in his political career, under Fraser, Howard became increasingly identified with the then emerging *laissez-faire* wing of the party, with smaller government and a deregulated labour market as enduring priorities. Between 1975 and 1983, he served first as minister for business and communications, then minister for special trade negotiations and, from 1977, as treasurer. In these commerce-related portfolios he began the strategy, which we have seen so effective in social policy, of bringing in piecemeal and by stealth reforms which neither the party nor the public was ready to accept up-front. Celebrating Howard's thirty years in parliament, biographer David Barnett pointed out that Treasurer Howard 'argued the case for economic reform to dubious colleagues, including the boss'. Not content with arguing, he also forced the issue:

> He chipped away at the elaborate structure of financial regulations until reform became inevitable, persuading cabinet to agree to the deregulation of the government borrowing rate. He then raced out of the cabinet room to issue a press statement before anyone picked up on the implications.[1]

Once in the prime minister's suite, he could follow through more directly.

Howard's governments have overseen the neo-liberal icons of industrial relations upheaval, ushered in by the waterfront dispute within his first months of power, the push to privatise Telstra and the once-abandoned GST. In other words, he implemented, step by step, the economic agenda that had been foreshadowed during his time as treasurer and elaborated during the Liberals' period in opposition by successive position papers from the neo-liberal think tanks, such as the dry Institute of Public Affairs, and lobby groups like the anti-union H.R. Nicholls Society. Like his social policy, Howard's economic achievements have attracted a sizeable literature, if perhaps not all as poetic or as glowing as David Barnett's hailing of:

> . . . that glorious time when, like a cicada emerging into the light from those years underground, he arrived at the Lodge to fulfil his destiny of changing a stumbling boom-bust economy into one *The Economist* league table shows to be the best run in the world.[2]

Nevertheless, his economic vision and determination is well documented.[3]

One striking aspect of Howard commentary is that his social and economic transformations of Australia have usually been considered independently of one another. Either commentators analyse his race, gender, sexuality and border protection policies, or they discuss his economic, industrial relations and financial reforms. The two halves of the prime ministerial personality—interventionist social policy and deregulationist economics—can often seem so disparate that they are analysed independently, as if they belonged to two different people.[4] When his marriage of these two strands—social conservatism and economic radicalism—is raised, it is usually as an indication of Howard's uniqueness. Admirers and critics alike see the blend as his distinctive contribution to Australian politics. For example, Liberal Party expert Judith Brett has described Howard as 'the most creative political leader Australian Liberals have had since Robert Menzies', because he:

> tirelessly reworked the images, themes and arguments of Liberal party philosophy so as to respond both to the social and economic changes Australia has experienced since Menzies' retirement and to a changed Labor Party.[5]

Brett usefully shows how Howard recast the 'Australian legend', with its themes of mateship, a volunteer ethos and egalitarianism, to his own mix of socially illiberal and economically liberal ideas. Similarly, communications scholars Cathy Greenfield and Peter Williams identify a 'particularly Australian version of a wider neo-liberalism'. The local characteristics are 'a blend of economic fundamentalism, neo-assimilationist social agendas, privatisation of infrastructure and of risk, and nostalgic politics'. They see the mix as so closely associated with 'the leadership role of the Prime Minister' that they refer to it as 'Howardism'.[6]

By contrast, this and the following chapters argue that we cannot understand Howard's economic neo-liberalism in isolation from his social conservatism, and that his genius lies not in inventing the marriage of economic neo-liberalism with a highly regulated social world, but rather in importing the blend from an arena where it was already well developed, namely, the further fringes of the American religious right. Howard's skill was in stripping this fundamentalist melange of its overtly theological trappings—American strategists had already begun a similar toning down, but most Australian audiences required the religion to be even less visible.

To understand this we need to look, first, at the international currents of right wing thought within which Howard merged economic liberalism with social conservatism. Next, we examine the think tanks in Australia, through which such ideas have long been fed to the Australian media, government advisors and, to a lesser extent, academics. One might think that, in such a secular society as Australia, there would be little point in think tanks engaging in religious discussion; but, we shall find, the theological agitprop encountered in chapter five is all in a day's work for some prominent think tanks, and it contributes a significant component of the ideas which sustain government intervention in family life, together with minimal government regulation in economic matters.

One important target for both the economic and theological right is welfare. The next chapter looks at the transfer of government welfare services to church agencies, often against the advice of church agencies themselves. The consequences of this move are much more than economic. The reasons church agencies can deliver welfare more cheaply than government include often paying their employees lower than market wages, along with extremely low rates of unionisation. While these patterns might suit charities devoted to 'picking up the pieces' with the help of volunteers, delivering government welfare services this way raises political questions. Moreover, the deeper church agencies are built into government processes, the less they are able to carry out their historic role as critics of government policy and watchdogs of egalitarian traditions.

Numerous observers have pointed out the obvious contradiction between repressive social conservatism and permissive economic liberalism. Obvious, that is, until we understand the peculiar, quasi-theological philosophy which underlies it. Chapter ten uncovers links between Australia's conservative government and a bizarre, but influential, American theology of Christian supremacy known variously as theonomy, Christian Reconstructionism and Dominionism, though some prefer its old-fashioned name, theocracy. There, we explore the Australian connections with Dominionist thought—connections by no means confined to a lunatic fringe but, on the contrary, extending right into the Howard government.

•

American commentators sometimes oppose strands of recent right wing thought as 'Wall Street' versus 'Main Street'. On Wall Street sit economic libertarians with often progressive social values—in Australian terms, think Paul Keating or John Hewson. Main Street worries about family and social policy—for an Australian counterpart, think of the Lyons Forum agenda discussed in Part One. Their interests do not obviously synchronise—in fact, Main Street conservatives can blame Wall Street economic reforms for much of the pressure on families. Just ask Ronald Reagan, who defeated Jimmy Carter on a wave of small-town Christian conservatism, then almost immediately alienated those supporters by ruling for the big city's big end.

In the USA, after Reagan, Main Street and Wall Street made common cause, substantially through the efforts of an increasingly politically influential Christian right. Think tanks such as the Heritage Foundation and political organisations like the Christian Coalition and National Prayer Breakfast movement provided crucial policy goals, strategy and people power. Their campaign was helped by televangelists such as former presidential hopeful, TV's *700 Club* host and Christian Coalition founder Pat Robertson, and Focus on the Family President James Dobson, whose radio programs had an estimated audience of over five million in the mid-1990s. Together, the various strands of the religious right provided a philosophical framework which reconciled the apparently contradictory goals of getting government regulation out of the economy and, simultaneously, into the home.

The Howard government, over successive terms, imported policies normally associated with the American Christian right. Tightened censorship, opposition to gay and lesbian marriage and parenting, reopening the debate on abortion and capital punishment, overturning euthanasia law, a preference for faith-based over government welfare and schools, intolerance of Muslims, suspicion of outsiders, hostility to 'activist' judges and a claim to exclusive, inside knowledge of 'values' are all hallmarks of these right wing movements associated with such figures as Robertson, Dobson, Christian Coalition founding executive Ralph Reed and Moral Majority founder Jerry Falwell. But Australia has pronounced differences from the American political culture that gives those opinion-shapers so much oxygen. Indeed, in 1979, a deciding factor in the Reagan campaign's trouncing of Jimmy Carter was that some forty per cent of Americans described themselves as 'born again' Christians. (That one of those forty per cent was Carter himself could not make up for the fact that Reagan, at most a nominal churchgoer, excelled at talking the evangelical talk.)[7] Lacking the large conservative Christian voter base that sustains such organisations in America, Australia is no easy haven for religious right ideas; yet, the current combination of social conservatism and free market economics looks remarkably like the American phenomenon, imported by a range of business, political and religious leaders.

Howard's 'white picket fence' nostalgia, often communicated through symbols and suggestions rather than explicit statements, has proved a vote winner. That alone should warn us not to attribute it just to his own suburban socialisation or native political genius. This is but one illustration of why Australian politics cannot be understood as an isolated political culture, because American neo-conservatism also arrived across the Tasman.

In New Zealand, where the Mixed Member Proportional (MMP) electoral system rewards small, special interest parties, the 'family values' flag has been waved since the 2002 election by United Future New Zealand, a hybrid party formed out of the rump of the Future Party, which was avowedly Christian, and the centrist United Party. Through an appeal to 'common sense', their socially conservative and ambiguously Christian offspring won an unexpected eight seats in the 120-seat parliament, providing Helen Clark's minority Labour government with a confidence-and-supply partner. United Future's leader, Peter Dunne, is unique in the NZ Parliament, having served in both Labour and National governments but, until the last election, had no known association with religious politics. His deputy leader, Anthony Walton, is the senior pastor of The Rock, a fundamentalist megachurch on Wellington's outskirts, and he does not sit in parliament. Dunne's parliamentary number two is Gordon Copeland, a layman who was raised Pentecostal but converted to Catholicism in adulthood.

After the election the New Zealand press revealed, as if out of the blue, that several other United Future MPs had conservative religious affiliations, and were on the record defending such policy departures as publicly identifying HIV carriers and offering a $100 reward to marrying couples (so as to encourage the institution of marriage). In office, United Future retreated from such electorally untenable positions, yet expresses its policy in terms reminiscent of the American religious right. For example, a condition of the confidence-and-supply agreement with Labour was an office, modelled on the one in Ronald Reagan's administration, to vet all legislation in the light of its impact on 'the family' (a move whose conservative impulses the Labour government tried to partially subvert, by insisting on the plural, 'Commission for Families').[8] United Future also vehemently opposed Labour's plan for same-sex civil unions. The parallels with Australia's Family First Party are glaring—not only in policy specifics, but in campaigning technique, such as playing down religious connections in favour of neutral-sounding terms like 'family', 'commonsense' and 'mainstream'. But Family First's 2004 eruption onto the federal stage was arguably only possible because so many of the same techniques had already been well road-tested, and the electorate well primed to respond, over eight years of Howard government.

If Howard's social conservatism is said to be the result of his personal background, it strains credibility to argue that these conservative 'family values' oriented political movements all arise, and succeed, because of their respective leaders' coinciding personal histories and character idiosyncrasies. George W. Bush exemplifies American right wing religiosity. His combination of stringent welfare cuts with back-to-the-family nostalgia picks up, and intensifies, the agenda laid down by Ronald Reagan.[9] We best understand neo-conservative success in the USA and beyond by observing the steady growth of right wing activism since the 1964 defeat of then seemingly extreme Republican presidential candidate Barry Goldwater. Indeed, William A. Rusher, a founder of both the conservative *National Review* and the Draft Goldwater Committee, has argued that 'the most important event of 1964 . . . was not Johnson's landslide . . . [but] the fact that the Goldwater campaign introduced the conservatives of America to one another'.[10]

•

Part of the growth of right wing activism was the flowering of think tanks—privately-funded policy institutes whose staff typically work at the intersection of economic and social research, lobbying and public relations—that pushed a right wing economic agenda. Until then, the unfashionable free market position had been promoted by the likes of the Mont Pelerin Society, which was founded in 1947. By the 1990s, one international directory listed about 700 independent 'policy institutes',[11] predominantly supported by business and promoting business friendly policies. Alongside the free market expansion went a quieter movement of religiously oriented think tank activity, often sponsored by wealthy 'born again' business donors. Just as the economic agenda of organisations such as the Mont Pelerin Society and its offshoots were becoming increasingly assertive from the 1970s and increasingly influential among parties of the right, so the conservative social agenda was pushed by their religious counterparts. These aimed to challenge a perceived leftism among the so-called 'mainline' churches (such as the Methodist church) and associated organisations, such as the World Council of Churches. Christian right objections are often expressed as opposition to the moral decadence and 'relativism' which they saw as entering the churches with the 1960s generation—through America's 'summer of love' and, in Australia, Whitlam and the 'chardonnay socialists'.

In the early 1970s, right wing activist Paul Weyrich, frustrated with a Nixon administration he saw as too liberal, sensed that some conservative members of Congress shared his views but lacked the resources to mount a strong case. His response, backed by a wealthy Colorado brewer, was to found what became the Heritage Foundation in 1973. By 2003, it commanded an annual budget of over US$25 million.[12] The Foundation aimed to provide 'intellectual back-up' for conservative positions on a range of issues, including vigorous critique of welfare, wage and price controls and *rapprochement* with Eastern Europe. Its staff peppered congressional offices with conservative position papers, while Weyrich went on to found a series of political action committees, beginning with opposition to an Inland Revenue Service plan to end tax exemptions for Christian schools that practised racial segregation.[13]

A still more explicitly religious example is the Institute on Religion and Democracy (IRD) that was founded in the USA in 1981. Its roots in earlier right wing reform movements within the United Methodist Church go back to 1966.[14] It opposes what it sees as the mainline churches' promotion of 'a secular agenda of the Left instead of the timeless message of Jesus Christ'.[15] In place of the 'impossible compromise between Christianity and Marxism' (citing Pope John Paul II), the IRD promotes anti-communism and free market economics.[16] Its early projects targeted the World Council of Churches, claiming development aid money was supporting terrorists.[17] Today, it has specialist committees devoted to the reform of the perceived leftist bias of three mainline American denominations—the United Methodist, Presbyterian and Episcopal churches[18]—whose threats include 'public policy advocacy that may reflect leftist positions', 'unrelenting pro-homosexual advocacy and undermining of the family by church leaders' and 'church officials who embrace a radical feminist theology'.[19] The IRD has also campaigned against the Kyoto accords and government welfare, and for the 2003 invasion of Iraq.

The IRD concentrates on practical politics at the church level. For example, it promotes candidates for church councils and synods, so they can then campaign for conservative causes within their denominations. It also maintains a permanent stream of media releases and public comment. Its United Methodist Action subdivision says it:

> goes to church agency meetings, studies church publications, and interviews church officials . . . [and] publishes its findings in news publications as well as in its own UM Action Briefing. The Briefing . . . provides . . . specific action items individuals may take to affect positive change and reform.[20]

Not surprisingly, the rest of the United Methodist church is inclined to interpret these actions and press releases as intended to foster ideological division.[21]

The Acton Institute is another religious and political lobby group founded in 1990. Although it espouses conservative views of marriage and family, its main concerns are economic and environmental. For example, it publishes the journal *Markets and Morality*, which promotes theological justifications of neo-liberal economics and runs a program called Environmental Stewardship to promote the view that 'sound ecological stewardship' requires 'a vigorous commitment to property rights'.[22] In other words the free market is, once again, the answer—and government should just let rich people and corporations sort these things out for themselves.

To reconcile social conservatism (authoritarian government) with economic liberalism (limited government), the various organisations share a vision of government supporting corporations and Christian social services (such as schools and welfare), and enforcing a narrow version of families against social and cultural diversity. Indeed, Howard has argued that economic restructuring is so unsettling that traditional families are a necessary defence. (This philosophy reveals itself in detail in chapter ten.)

The organisations just described are but the tip of 'Wall Street-meets-Main Street'. Add in the culture wars focused Traditional Values Coalition, Eagle Forum and Concerned Women For America, the more economically oriented American Enterprise Institute and their numerous offshoots, front organisations and related movements, and the combined pressure on government and public opinion is substantial. But generating ideas and lobbying alone is not enough. Even the best policies need organisation and a public groundswell. Controversies, such as the 1924 Scopes trial over the public school teaching of evolution and later campaigns against sex education, had left the religious right with an image of ignorant, unsophisticated and marginalised political nobodies. Part of the task of getting ideas into law was building a movement confident enough to defend them, ready to vote on them, powerful enough to be taken seriously and prepared to hold legislators to their promises.

To sum up the modern US religious right in a single person: Pat Robertson. Not that everyone associated with the movement identifies with him; on the contrary, his Pentecostal tongue speaking and faith healing made him long an object of suspicion to many other central figures, such as Moral Majority founder Jerry Falwell. But Robertson has traversed in person many of the defining shifts in the movement. Like many others, he supported Jimmy Carter's presidential campaign not so much on political grounds as because of the desirability of a born-again president.

When Carter turned out to be, after all, a Democrat—and a moderate one at that, refusing to consign either homosexuals or abortionists to damnation—Robertson, like many on the religious right, felt betrayed. By the late 1970s, he was urging conservative Christians to ditch politics: 'There's a better way, fasting and praying'.[23] Reagan's 1980 candidature brought new hope for fundamentalist politics, though, and a strategic rethink. Reagan was the featured guest at the National Affairs Briefing, a meeting of evangelical conservatives. Warming up the crowd before the star's appearance, Robertson announced that God was telling Christians:

> Be fruitful and multiply. Take dominion. Subdue the land in [God's] name. We are to fight a war. Our weapon is faith. We are salt and we are light. We can move the hand of God in a mighty crusade of holiness.[24]

One evangelical observer expostulated, 'We've got a bunch of TV preachers who want to establish a theocracy in America, and each one of them wants to be Theo'.[25]

When Reagan, too, proved a disappointment, Robertson resorted to a still more direct form of politics: in 1988, he announced his candidature for president. Despite shocking his opponents with early success in the pre-primary Iowa 'straw poll' and a series of first or second placings in the early primaries, Super Tuesday was the end of his road. George Bush Sr became the determinedly non-fundamentalist Republican candidate.

At the US Republican Party's 1992 Houston Convention, with Clinton in the White House and fundamentalist nerve failing, conservative columnist Pat Buchanan declared, 'There is a religious war going on in this country. It is a cultural war as critical to the kind of nation we shall be as the Cold War itself. This war is for the soul of America'.[26] Conservative evangelical radio star and Focus on the Family founder James Dobson is famous for a similar expression, comparing the culture wars to the other great touchstone of American political history:

> Nothing short of a great Civil War of Values rages today throughout North America. Two sides with vastly differing and incompatible worldviews are locked in a bitter conflict that permeates every level of society . . . The struggle now is for the hearts and minds of the people. It is a war over ideas. And someday soon, I believe, a winner will emerge and the loser will fade from memory. For now, the outcome is much in doubt.[27]

Such statements sounded, to outsiders, like post-1988 cries of despair.

'Columnists were writing the epitaph of the Religious Right', Robertson acolyte Guy Rodgers recalled; but to insiders the movement had merely transformed again. While commentators concentrated on the White House and Congress, Robertson packed up the wreck of his presidential bid, hired seasoned right wing student activist Ralph Reed and founded the Christian Coalition. The new organisation concentrated on spreading through local and community organisations, targeting school boards, city councils and local issues. The Christian Coalition, Rodgers explained:

> had a training manual for organizing the grassroots. They had a strategy. They had a plan . . . I think, as much as anything else, that what sets us apart as an organization is

> that the people who were at the top of it, from Ralph to me and my staff, were all political people.[28]

While think tanks such as the Heritage Foundation and American Enterprise Institute shaped policy goals, the Christian Coalition brought campaign experience. Voter registration materials were handed out in churches, to be returned via the collection plate. Volunteers learnt to avoid speaking 'Christianese', which would alienate those not attuned to it; to book meeting rooms to fit half the expected crowd, so the resulting 'standing room only' would portray a popular groundswell; to write name tags in block letters so speakers could address people in the front few rows by their first names.[29]

At last, the strategies were in place to fulfil a plan first mooted in the early 1980s. Back then, Tim LaHaye, a prominent American fundamentalist and most recently famous as co-author of the monumentally successful *Left Behind* series of apocalyptic bestsellers, proposed on Pat Robertson's *700 Club* television show that:

> There are 110 000 Bible believing churches but there are only 97 000 major elective offices in America. If we launch one candidate per church, we can take over every elective office in this country within ten years.[30]

Heritage Foundation founder Paul Weyrich summed up the goal: 'If you want to have an influence on politics . . . elect people at the local level. Grow the movement from the bottom up. Don't worry about the presidency; the presidency will take care of itself in due course. And train people.' Interviewed during Clinton's presidency, Weyrich discerned a national political climate ready to respond to a conservative president when one should arise:

> We have lots of friends now on city councils and country boards and school boards and in state legislatures—something we never had before. This is why we can seriously talk now

> about fundamental changes in Washington, because you've got governors and legislators and mayors who are speaking up . . . Heck, when Reagan was president and wanted to do some of the very things we're talking about now, he didn't have a mayor in the country outside of some small town in the middle of Tennessee who was willing to speak out in his behalf. Now you have big-city mayors who are willing to say, 'Yes, we will handle this if you give us the flexibility', and governors, including some Democrats, who will say, 'Yes, reform welfare this way and we'll handle it for you and do it more cheaply' . . . In the eighties, the whole infrastructure was in the hands of the status quo and they screamed bloody murder when Reagan tried to change anything.[31]

The religious right's reported death turned out to have been merely its shift of operations to more productive ground, out of the media spotlight and into church and parachurch networks. Christian Coalition executive Ralph Reed summed up his organisation's technique: 'I do guerrilla warfare. I paint my face and travel at night. You don't know it's over until you're in a body bag. You don't know till election night'.[32] A deliberate strategy was turning Main Street and Wall Street from enemies to friends. Pushed by Reed, the Christian Coalition identified tax reform as the alliance-building issue. He recalled:

> We decided our top legislative priority for the 103rd Congress would be a tax cut for middle-class families with children. We held a news conference and announced that; then we began to meet with members of Congress and lobby them. [Economic conservatives] supported a tax cut because they were against big government and for lower taxes. We supported it because we were pro-family . . . When it came time for a vote, we ginned up our phone banks, we got it on Christian radio and television, and they got more votes for a Republican budget than they had gotten in ten years—because there was family tax-relief in it.[33]

He ranked the decision one of 'the critical turning points for our movement', and the movement as crucial to the decisive Republican 1994 victories which delivered significant majorities in the House of Representatives and numerous state legislatures, as well as eleven new governors. This produced a fundamental shift in the American political climate, summed up in then House Leader Newt Gingrich's conservative 'Contract with America'.

•

We can trace comparable developments in Australia. Founded in 1943 by Charles Kemp (father of the Howard governments' David and Rod), the Institute of Public Affairs calls itself 'Australia's oldest and largest private-sector "think-tank"'. An IPA form letter, dated soon after John Howard's election as prime minister, stated:

> Although measuring success is difficult in our business, IPA's influence is clearly significant. Our views appear frequently in the media. We are regularly asked to write for newspapers and other publications, to comment on radio and television, to give public talks (with over 100 delivered in 1995), and to make submissions to public inquiries. Our masthead magazine, *IPA Review*, has one of the largest per capita circulations (7800) of think tank journals around the world. Our publications are distributed to Federal and State politicians, to many educators and libraries, and to 4500 subscribers.[34]

Long associated with the 'dry' end of the Liberal Party, IPA's primary concerns have always been economic. From the mid-1980s, however, it began pushing 'family' issues as well, with regular opinion columns in Rupert Murdoch's *Australian* that argued for more durable marriage and more difficult divorce, for example. It also enthusiastically joined the anti-sacred site clamour, publishing a number of Ron Brunton's attacks on the validity and authenticity of Jawoyn (Coronation Hill) and Ngarrindjeri (Hindmarsh Island) traditions.[35]

An even stronger line on social issues emerged from the Centre for Independent Studies (CIS).[36] The CIS was formed in 1976 in the garage of high school maths teacher Greg Lindsay, still its director. Its rags-to-riches origin myth tells of its founding conference, reported in Paddy McGuinness's appreciative newspaper column headlined 'Where Friedman is a Pinko'. That led to a wave of supporters, notably Western Mining Corporation's CEO Hugh Morgan in 1980.[37] His largesse rescued Lindsay from among the 'lawnmowers and the odd spider', just in time for Lindsay to help with what became the first of Morgan's many standoffs with churches over land rights (discussed in chapters five and six). Morgan not only gave generous financial support, but served as chairman of the Centre's Board of Trustees through the mid-1980s.

Morgan's new protégé launched what is now a more than twenty-year campaign against perceived church leftism. In 1983, for example, CIS published conservative economist Geoffrey Brennan's anti-welfare *The Christian and the State*.[38] The following year, it issued a collection of essays, edited by Brennan, called *Chaining Australia: Church Bureaucracies and Political Economy*. The title was a pun on a combined churches' social justice statement, *Changing Australia*.[39] In 1999, the Centre formalised its growing list of church-related publications into a program called 'Religion and the Free Society'.

Diagnosing a church consensus 'dominated by state-welfarist and interventionist' economics, the program aimed to re-educate 'clergy, theologians and lay church workers' because, 'if one can shape the thinking of leaders and intellectuals, then one is more than half-way towards changing the ideas of their communities and institutions'.[40] Its desired outcome was, 'at a minimum', to foster 'religious thinking . . . that rejects welfarist/interventionist models'.[41] The program also sponsors seminars for church and business leaders and an annual 'Acton Lecture on Religion and

Freedom', where speakers link conservative theology with free market economics. Past Acton Lecturers have included conservative Catholic Archbishop (subsequently Cardinal) George Pell, evangelical Anglican Bishop Robert Forsyth and George Weigel, a US-based papal biographer, conservative Catholic theologian and co-founder of the controversial National Endowment for Democracy (which distributes US taxpayers' funds to political parties around the world friendly to US military and corporate interests).

By mid-2004, the CIS catalogue listed sixteen religion-related titles, offering theological justifications for opposing environmentalism and anti-discrimination legislation and promoting capitalism and small government.[42] These tie in with its anti-welfare 'Social Foundations' and 'Taking Children Seriously' programs, with titles such as *Divorce Law and the Future of Marriage* and the pro-income splitting *The Taxation of Shared Family Incomes*. Poverty, the publications argue, comes from failures of individual responsibility, while children's rights movements are part of the 'ideological attack' which has 'undermined the family in the west'.[43]

CIS is Australia's most prolific think tank source of conservative 'family values', loosely tied to Christian theology. However, other right wing think tanks have also turned from solely economic to social issues. Another to span the economic and social right through the 1990s was the Tasman Institute. Founded in 1990, Tasman was a copious generator of position papers and policy goals, though later more active through its economic consultancy arm, Tasman Asia Pacific.

Western Mining Corporation was again well represented on Tasman's Advisory Council with its chairman, Sir Arvi Parbo, and CEO Hugh Morgan, along with WMC board member Dame Leonie Kramer.[44] One-third of the twenty-one corporate members listed in Tasman's 1995 Annual Review were from energy-related industries (BHP, CRA, Esso, MIM, Shell Australia, WC, Woodside Petroleum), along with organisations such as the Electricity

Corporation of NZ and the National Association of Forest Industries. Under its 'flagship' project, called 'Markets and Environment', the Institute described itself as particularly concerned with issues 'which have important implications for investment in Australia's resource based industries'.[45] Its corporate sponsors were apparently happy for it to interpret that brief broadly to include, for example, yet more of anthropologist Ron Brunton's attacks on the Hindmarsh Island claims[46] discussed in chapter five, even though any mining potential on the island remains its best kept secret of all. Rather than minerals, Hindmarsh Island's relevance seemed to be its carefully nurtured iconic status as the test case of 'fabricated' Indigenous tradition.

Tasman also made academics a target, declaring that:

> Universities, particularly in the humanities and social sciences, have increasingly not pursued fearless enquiry, have not upheld the scholarly duty to truth and the pedagogical duty of cultural transmission, to the degree they should. Moral grandstanding has too often supplanted the more humble scholarly and pedagogical duties.[47]

Indeed, Hugh Morgan and his WMC offsider Ray Evans (described by Robert Manne as the Australian right's '*eminence noir*') ranged well beyond immediate mining concerns, founding or supporting organisations that opposed Indigenous self-determination,[48] campaigning for conservative values in education[49] and promoting right wing social and economic agendas in Christian terms,[50] among other things. Morgan and Evans were also active supporters of the H.R. Nicholls Society, which campaigns for deregulated industrial relations, and the constitutionally focused Samuel Griffith Society that opposes so-called 'judicial activism' among members of the High Court.

In 1994, Evans (like Howard, an Anglican convert from childhood Methodism) supported a new inter-denominational group formed in Melbourne by three disgruntled Uniting Church ministers—Reverend Dr Max Champion, Reverend Dr John Williams and Reverend Ross Carter. The Galatians Group took their name from the text:

> In Christ, there is neither Jew nor Greek, slave nor free, male nor female, for you are all one in Christ Jesus.[51]

The verse has often been a slogan for the Christian left with, for example, 'neither male nor female' providing justification for moves to ordain women to the priesthood. The Galatians Group took Paul's emphasis on unity to mean sameness, and so devoted itself to opposing the Uniting Church's commitments to multiculturalism, widely accessible welfare and a bilateral 'covenant' with its Indigenous body, the Uniting Aboriginal and Islander Christian Congress. In effect, the Galatians Group launched a theological version of what would become the Howard conservatives' 'no special privileges' view of equality: we are all equal, so it is wrong to pick anyone out for help. In other words, the government should support only the mystical 'Us'—hardworking, white, Protestant families and those prepared to act like Us.

Like those more famous Morgan/Evans offspring, the Galatians Group held annual conferences with invited speakers (many of whose connections to either the Uniting or any other church were obscure) and then published the proceedings. The national conferences aimed to undo what the group saw as the church's 'straitjacket fitted by the judges of current fashions in political correctness'.[52] That translated to opposition to the Uniting Church's 'covenanting' process aimed at achieving reconciliation with Indigenous peoples, disapproval of multiculturalism, a commitment to free market principles and suspicion of government welfare.[53]

The Galatians Group was active from 1994 until 1999, then went quiet. Its founders, though, did not. For example, in 2004, Champion took over the chair of Reforming Alliance, an American-style vanguard movement within the Uniting Church.

Rather than lobbying from without (in the manner of the Galatians Group), Reforming Alliance and its evangelical counterpart, Evangelical Members of the Uniting Church (EMU), aim to change from within, by electing conservative Synod and Presbytery representatives and circulating position papers aimed at changing opinion in the pews.

The theological right has also found audiences beyond the churches. The economic libertarian Society of Modest Members is a pressure group of federal dry MPs formed in 1981 by a group of Coalition MPs 'suffering under the yoke of the Fraser socialist government'.[54] Though not a religious organisation, it has included both Champion and CIS Religion and the Free Society founding director Sam Gregg in its speakers' program. Gregg encouraged the Modest Members to see neo-liberal economics as a response to the Christian doctrine of sin,[55] a view that was apparently congenial to the group's objective of promoting 'the competitive market as the best means of providing for human well being' and its commitment to 'personal advancement through initiative and hard work in a society that provides opportunities, as opposed to one with an anti-success culture and a focus on redistribution'.[56]

IPA, CIS, Tasman, the Galatians Group and Morgan and Evans have attacked the churches on economic and welfare issues. However, as the American Christian Coalition discovered in the early 1990s, an economic right agenda is hard to sell in the pews. On the face of it, regressive taxation, reduced welfare and cut-throat competition contradict Christian compassion, altruism and advocacy for the downtrodden. 'Sell all you have and give the money to the poor', Jesus instructed a rich man inquiring after salvation. Many Christians were dismayed to find Jesus co-opted in support of lower taxes for the rich and harsher demands on the poor. It is not immediately apparent why Christian activists would support such campaigns. For the Christian Coalition, a conservative 'family' agenda proved a crucial component of its economic activism, but not necessarily because of any obvious connection between social conservatism and economic liberalism. Rather, the former provided a more readily graspable *raison d'être* for right wing Christian political activism. The economic agenda was then able to follow, less startlingly, in its wake.[57]

Like its US prototype, Australia's think tank movement has spawned a plethora of small, single-issue lobby groups where a loud social conservative message carries neoliberal economic riders. One example is the National Fathering Forum, founded in February 2003 and generating a series of follow-up events, including a National Strategic Conference on Fathering. The Forum was the offspring of evangelist couple Warwick and Alison Marsh of Australian Heart Ministries. Events under its umbrella typically open with the Lord's Prayer ('Our Father . . .'). The initial February 2003 meeting brought together thirty-five delegates, described in the Forum's report as including 'a wide range of Men's Groups, Family Law Reform Groups, Education and Training Institutions, Academics, Social Researchers and Psychologists, Drug Rehabilitation Organisations, Prison Charities, Social Reform Networks, Church Groups, Journalists and Media, Family Focused Charitable Organisations and Fatherhood Institutions'. The group produced a 'Twelve Point Plan' to 'turn the tide of fatherlessness'. Launched by Mark Latham, the plan addressed such concerns as the disproportionate incidence of male suicide, imprisonment, substance abuse and gambling and the need for role models. Among all that, it carried messages with significant economic and industrial relations ramifications.

For example, it related male unemployment to the claim that 'Gender, race, disability, cultural and ethnic identity are no longer the opportunity barriers they once were', but that 'proactive policies' to address them had 'inadvertently' created 'a new disadvantaged group', men. Given that a man's average weekly earnings the previous year were more than one-and-a-half times a woman's, with the gap widening thereafter, and that men continue to hold the overwhelming majority of senior political and corporate positions where decisions shape others' destinies, the argument requires a curious view of disadvantage. To rectify the new cultural and political exclusion of men, the Forum (guided by speeches from the male Minister for Family and Community Services, Larry Anthony, his male parliamentary secretary, Ross Cameron, various male community leaders and a number of politicians from the major parties, both of which have been led by men through their entire histories) recommended that 'it is now time to reassess the relevance of outdated affirmative action policies and consider a return to merit based selection where only the best person for the job is offered employment'.

The call is somewhat misleading given that Australia's affirmative action program has never included employment quotas for target groups and was aimed at selection on merit, being specifically designed to ensure that 'only the best person for the job is offered employment' (even if they happen to be female, from an ethnic minority, homosexual or to have a disability). In other words, the call seemed to have more to do with purveying an ideologically driven picture of Australian social, economic and cultural realities than with changing actual injustices. In fact, the call could be read as an exhortation in the name of love and compassion to unpick what remained of government assistance for those historically excluded from the market, leaving the strong to slug it out between them.

Though Howard himself did not join the 'Jesus loves the market' chorus, he proved highly adroit at alluding to its themes while letting fall just enough religiously inflected allusions to align himself with its proponents. And, as we shall see in chapter ten, there is a good reason for doing so. The strange permutation of Christian theology by which 'blessed are the poor' comes to mean 'blessed are the rich' gives philosophical justification for the otherwise awkward blend of economic liberalism (government out!) and social conservatism (do what the government says!). Moreover, a school of thought that favours redistributing resources from the poor to the rich while reducing individual freedoms requires some legitimising framework if it is not to look like cynical opportunism. Vaguely religious allusions, painting the approach as guided by (Christian) 'values', help provide one.

Once the Liberals got rid of John Hewson (and Alexander Downer got rid of himself), they had a leader embodying both Wall Street and Main Street conservatisms. What to call the Australian street joining those foreign thoroughfares? In the back-ways of Earlwood, we find an appropriate image. A few blocks south of Howard's boyhood home and church, Manildra Street runs between busy Homer Street and Wolli Avenue. Perhaps the Howard boys ran along it to reach the grass and swings at the S.J. Harrison Reserve. Its quiet, unpretentious brick fronts and neat fences could have been the props for his *Future Directions* manifesto's cover. But Manildra has a more recent Howard connection. It is the name of the ethanol company run by Howard's friend, and generous Liberal Party donor, Dick Honan. The company became a household name through Howard's alleged misleading of parliament over whether the two had met, in the process of working out an altered excise regime that substantially benefited Honan's local product over imported ethanol. The affair came to stand for the politics of privilege, benefiting the big friend over small competitors. I hope Manildra Street residents will not take it amiss, then, if I borrow their address as a metaphor for Australia's own blend of Wall Street big-business-friendly economics and Main Street suburban family values conservatism.

Howard's distinctively Australian Manildra Street blend drew on many of the same religious source materials as inform America's Main Street, but used them in a different way. In America, the Christian Coalition worked hard to associate tax cuts and small government with conservative 'family' ideology so as to garner support for otherwise unsettling economic reforms. In Australia, the need to sell economic reform in religious terms is not nearly as pressing as it is in the United States' much more religiously charged electoral climate. However, in Australia no less than in the US, the unsettling effects of economic reform still needed to be softened, and the program made alluring to a nervous electorate. The loss of permanent jobs, reduced government services and greater insecurity which come with the neo-liberal economic agenda leave people feeling the need for some kind of social safety net. The kind of politics which privileges big friends and rewards the wealthy needs a moral justification if it is to look like anything more than rampant opportunism.

Howard's suburban Methodist myth making endowed both the economic and social dimensions of his Manildra Street political persona with the force of conviction politics. It reassured that his political commitments, economic as well as social, sprang from personal faith rather than political expediency or business pressure. Meanwhile, the Centre for Independent Studies, the Tasman Institute, the Institute of Public Affairs and the Galatians Group poured out socially conservative pamphlets, books, sermons, opinion columns and letters to the editor which provided a reassuring vision of a deregulated society as filled not with scary, rapacious corporations, but with family oriented, self-reliant, culturally homogeneous individuals. While their social policy projects promoted a recognisably religious right family agenda, the think tanks also addressed what is arguably their number one theological goal, making the religious case for capitalism against what they see as mainline churches' leftist preoccupations.

•

Whether we trace Howard's Manildra Street blend of social conservatism and economic radicalism to his youthful Methodism (as the commentators discussed in chapter one suggest), or whether we see it as the product of his mature political genius (as argued, for example, by Greenfield and Williams), one consequence is that it comes to be seen as the result of personal idiosyncrasy. Any perceived meanness or Machiavellianism belongs to one leader. The corollary is, of course, that Howard's departure sees it finish.

No doubt Howard's social conservatism is a part of his personality, not just his politics. It resonates with his *Saturday Evening Post*-reading family background as well as his later life. His economic radicalism is less obviously related to his biography—one has only to recall small business owners' irritation at the GST and extended shopping hours to realise that he cannot be said to have directly translated his family's experience into his economic vision for Australia. Rather, as David Barnett's biography makes clear, his economic thought developed over the course of his political career, the hard neo-conservative stance of his prime ministership being the end product of a long transition.

The point I make in this chapter, though, is that his particular Manildra Street blend of the two stances, social conservatism and economic liberalism, put him in sync with the major currents swirling through international right wing thought: pouring out of the think tanks, being recycled through the New Right columnists and taken up by talkback demagogues, seeping through grassroots congregations and penetrating parliaments, electorate by electorate. It may well be that, without those international currents, Howard would hold a similar personal collection of views. But, without the Mont Pelerin economic liberals, the measurable successes of the US Christian Coalition (not least in electing a president with whom Howard could so comfortably go all the way) and, at home, the IPA and CIS family-and-market activists and even the quiet agitation of the Galatians Group, National Fathering Forum and related groups, Howard would have looked less like an international leader riding the crest of a wave and more like an aging eccentric whom the world was sweeping past. As he famously observed, the times did, indeed, suit him.

Using the US right's favourite medium of talkback radio, particularly with Liberal insider Alan Jones, Howard spoke the recognisably American language of 'political correctness', 'racial resentment', 'traditional family'. He postured tough on drugs and terrorism, flirted with capital punishment and brought the previously near-invisible issue of gay marriage to front page wedge status. He delivered tax cuts to the rich and encouraged segregated Christian schools, attacked the public broadcaster and espoused a proud arts philistinism, while speaking knowingly of 'values'. He clothed an assumed patriarchy in talk of family 'choice' (to have the mother at home) and 'male role models' (except at home), while taking away choice for gay and lesbian couples wanting to adopt children or have them by IVF. Headline by headline, he remoulded Australia in the American right's image. The shift in conservative politics is bigger than him, and bigger than Australia. His stunning 2004 election clean sweep of both Houses did not so much entrench his personal dominance as confirm his position's congruence with the bigger cultural shifts that he rode to power in the first place. It is hard to imagine any Liberal leader in the near future moving out of Manildra Street.

On the social front, Costello is regarded as less conservative than Howard. This impression gains from his republicanism and his readiness to apologise to Indigenous Australians.[58] However, there is surprisingly little public record of his stances on such matters as legal equality for gay and lesbian couples, publicly funded abortion or the desirability of a full-time stay-at-home parent. For example, in March 2001 ABC Radio National's *Background Briefing* endeavoured to go behind 'the smirk on the hard face of economic rationalism'. It sought the treasurer's views on Aboriginal reconciliation, immigration and football. On 'family' issues, however, they recorded only the ambiguous statement: 'We just ought to get the governments out as far as possible, out of family lives, you ought to let the non-government institutions of society, like the family and the school and the community and the church take a lot of the slack'.[59] The program discussed his founding involvement in the economic libertarian

H.R. Nicholls Society, but not in the socially conservative Lyons Forum, well documented at the time by journalists such as the *Age*'s Nikki Savva (subsequently his media officer).

In 2004, Costello finally began to fill out the picture. A series of appearances at religious events gave some hints about where a Costello government's social priorities might lie. That May, he appeared at the inaugural National Day of Thanksgiving celebration, modelled on the American Thanksgiving, which reminds Americans of their nation's Christian origins. The Australian Thanksgiving is sponsored by a lengthy roll-call of nondenominational and para-church evangelical and Pentecostal organisations, though not one mainline denomination. Costello identified a series of social problems, such as marriage breakdown, drug abuse and 'moral decay', which he saw summed up in violent rap lyrics. His preferred solution was a return to the Ten Commandments. His appearance was controversial because one of the event's sponsoring organisations, a parachurch body called Catch the Fire Ministries (whose pastor Danny Nalliah would stand later that year as a Family First candidate), was then involved in court proceedings in Victoria, answering allegations that it had religiously vilified Muslims. The law is not the way to deal with religious vilification, Costello told his audience, adding, somewhat paradoxically, that the answer to Christian-Muslim differences is a return to 'Judaeo-Christian values'.[60]

He repeated the Ten Commandments prescription just over a month later before a 21 000-strong audience at the opening night of a conference organised by Sydney's Hillsong church. Anticipating scepticism from the next morning's 'editorial writers', he urged people not to pay too much attention to what the papers might say, since 'Christ has changed more lives than editorial writers'.[61] His Hillsong appearance was also controversial. Hillsong, whose Senior Pastor Brian Houston is the author of a Biblically based get-rich-quick program entitled *You Need More Money*, is a prominent base for 'prosperity gospel' theology in which wealth is interpreted as a sign of God's favour, its absence as the opposite. Hillsong's teachings, spread through CD and tape sales estimated at two million a year, reach far beyond Sydney and even Australia.[62] The church's 15 000-strong weekly congregation is said to be Australia's largest. It is also the spiritual home of the revived Lyons Forum's convenor, Alan Cadman, whom we met in chapter two and encounter again in the next chapter supporting an Australian version of US-style 'faith-based' welfare programs, and of 2004 parliamentary rookie Louise Markus, who previously worked in Hillsong's own version of faith-based social services.

There is little to suggest that Costello stands anywhere other than squarely in the stream of socially conservative right wing Christian thought. In the light of the international currents swirling through the right, that is just as well for his career prospects. The federal Liberals' turn-of-the-millennium ideological homogeneity is no mere consequence of local pushes but, rather, reflects wider currents of the economic and religious right internationally.

Back in 1986, political scientist Dennis Altman predicted:

> I suspect there are people on the New Right who are very aware of the electoral appeal of bashing feminism, gays, humanism and small 'l' liberals; read the columns that appear in the *Weekend Australian* carefully and you see the groundwork for this sort of campaign.[63]

Altman implied cynical populism rather than ideological commitment. But the appeal to 'family values' conservatism is more than that—it is an essential contributor to the plausibility of New Right thought. And, like its American counterpart, it requires a political strategy to turn all the position papers into vote-winning positions.

In April 2004, the *Sydney Morning Herald* reported 'the movement of God into the NSW Young Liberals'. The archconservative Catholic Opus Dei movement, based at University of New South Wales residential quarters Warrane College, is associated with the dramatic growth of the Randwick–Coogee Young Liberals, with nearly a quarter of the branch's eighty-eight enrolled members giving the college as their home address. Moderate Liberals described the move as a 'takeover by the religious right of the Liberal Party'. The new members had a champion in NSW Legislative Councillor David Clarke, famous as the country's first self-professed Opus Dei-linked parliamentarian.[64] Federally, observers noted 'hothousing' of young Christian right wingers by conservative NSW MPs, including Tony Abbott, Bronwyn Bishop and Ross Cameron. The new recruits gained experience on the members' staffs, ready to push conservative stances on issues such as abortion, stem cell research, homosexuality and the age of consent.[65]

The same *Sydney Morning Herald* article reported the Greenway branch of the Liberal Party had preselected Louise Markus, a lay worker at the highly evangelical—and entrepreneurial—Hillsong church at whose conference Costello spoke in July 2004. Though Markus was, of course, preselected by the Liberal Party, not the church, the *Sydney Morning Herald* reported that the Liberals' State director, Scott Morrison, 'himself a man of "strong religious views"' and fellow Hillsong member, responded to questions about her preselection by 'launch[ing] into a pitch for the type of "faith-based programs" that Hillsong had established to address social problems'.[66] In the eyes of his election-galvanised party, intimations of church–state blurring posed no problem.

Although Hillsong only attracted national attention once it had the double blessing of the federal treasurer and its own Liberal candidate, its Liberal friendships go back some time. In the week after the 2002 Bali bombing, Howard took time out from his hectic round of commemorations, condolences and security briefings to open the church's $25 million complex. Houston welcomed him to the stage: 'I know our PM is amongst friends tonight'. Howard seemed to know it, too, as he marvelled, 'You started with 45, I'm told. Forty-five! I don't believe it. I cannot believe that there were only ever 45 in this congregation. You've gone from 45 at your first service in 1983 to a congregation of over 14 000! I've got to tell you that I don't think there's any side of Australian politics that could do a branch stack as good as that.'[67]

Hillsong is a congregation of the Assemblies of God, the denomination from whose ranks sprang all the leading figures and almost all the candidates for the Family First Party, though the party consistently disclaimed an Assemblies of God identity. The Assemblies of God was formed in Australia in 1937, and is part of the family of churches called Pentecostal. The name commemorates the Day of Pentecost, described in chapter two of the New Testament book of Acts, and historically celebrated in Christian churches on the Sunday closest to forty days after Easter. On the original Pentecost, Jesus' disciples, left at something of a loose end after his resurrection and ascension, experienced an ecstatic transformation in which they heard a sound 'like a mighty rushing wind', saw 'tongues of fire, distributed and resting on each one of them', and felt what they interpreted as an outpouring of the Holy Spirit. This gave them a mysterious ability to speak in other languages, so that people from all over the Roman Empire were able to hear the Gospel preached in their own languages. At the end of the nineteenth century and beginning of the twentieth, some Christians in America and Britain began to have similar experiences, though, unlike the disciples in Acts, their ecstatic speech came out in languages no one could understand unless the hearer, too, was divinely inspired. They understood their experiences as 'baptism by the Holy Spirit', and regarded it as a crucial, subsequent stage of salvation, which followed on from the 'water baptism' most Christians undergo as babies. The noise, intensity and emotional flavour of their worship, together with the fact that it arose most of all among the poor and involved what one Los Angeles newspaper called a 'hideous mingling of the races', meant that the early Pentecostals were ridiculed and marginalised by traditional churches. The idea that believers required a 'second stage' Spirit baptism to complete their salvation was also doctrinally controversial, implying two classes of believers—those who had received the Spirit and those who had not.

Early in the twentieth century, finding themselves marginalised from existing churches, a number of Pentecostal groups formed their own denominations, including, in 1914, the Assemblies of God. From gatherings of the poor and outcast, Pentecostalists worked hard for social acceptance and public influence. Today, a number of such churches have business schools attached to them, and many are associated with networks for Christian businessmen (it does seem to be usually men). The path towards respectability has included for many churches an unabashed enthusiasm for wealth and visible success. Hillsong Pastor Brian Houston promoted his book *You Need More Money* by advising Christians to get over being uncomfortable talking about money: 'If you can change your thinking and develop a healthy attitude to money, I believe you will walk in the prosperity and blessing of God and never have a problem with money again'. To help, the book promised 'to tell you why you need more money and secondly *how* you can get more money'.[68] Houston was elected National President of the Assemblies of God in 1997. In 2000, substantially under his guidance, the Assemblies of God joined a larger Pentecostal federation, the Australian Christian Churches, together with Apostolic churches (a group of denominations that grew out of the 1904–5 Welsh Revival), smaller Pentecostal denominations and independent congregations, covering an estimated 170 000 churchgoers.

Divine inspiration delivered through tongue-speaking gives Pentecostalists a prophetic direct line. Some branches, such as the various Apostolic churches, even call their mode of governance 'theocratic', meaning that in theory no detail of church organisation, however minute, is decided without verbal guidance from God. That, plus the desire for influence in high places so as to bring God's will into national life, can lay some Pentecostals open to allegations of entertaining more far-reaching theocratic aspirations. In fact, some members of Pentecostal churches are extremely uncomfortable with the new mood of overt political activism. Equally, direct-line-from-God political activism can be found at the conservative ends of the traditional denominations.

In the next two chapters, we look at the features of Howard's agenda most shaped by these external forces, and we glimpse what an Australia rebuilt on Manildra Street lines might look like. We have only begun to hear from the God of the radical right.

CHAPTER NINE

Church, state and charity

Facing the electorate in 1996, Howard assured us that the goods and services tax (GST) was not an issue: 'There will never be a GST. Never ever. It is dead in the water'.[1] When John Hewson, Liberal opposition leader in the early 1990s, received his GST *coup-de-grace*, the *Financial Review* mused on the irony that the churches had been instrumental in his despatch, yet they and the Coalition seemed to 'share a constituency'.[2] Hewson's fate, therefore, must have stung. In 1993, he faced the election every commentator said he should have had on a plate. The populist Hawke was supplanted by the more aloof Keating, still scarred by his long stint as treasurer, as a reform-weary electorate reeled from what Keating regrettably called 'the recession we had to have'.[3] A decade on, the shorthand nickname for the 1993 election is still 'unlosable', always in ironic inverted commas because, of course, the Coalition lost.

Hewson, a former economics professor, had waged an economic purist's campaign, effectively outsourcing party policy to the accounting firm Access Economics.[4] It wasn't the message to offer an electorate who saw fast and furious economic reform as one of the main reasons to hate the incumbents, and it particularly annoyed the welfare lobby, who saw increased poverty throughout the package, above all as a consequence of its centrepiece, a GST. As big providers of welfare and also with a long tradition of campaigning against causes of poverty, the Christian churches were particularly stringent critics. Catholic, Uniting and Anglican churches, on their own and in collaboration with other denominations, produced a barrage of commentary arguing that the proposed GST would benefit the well off with cheaper luxury goods while making basics, such as food, more expensive. In October 1992, Geoff Kitney wrote in the *Australian Financial Review* that the churches' criticism of Hewson's *Fightback!* manifesto was 'potentially very damaging for the Coalition' in a controversy which, he said, had seen 'the Catholic Church becoming more deeply embroiled in the national political debate than at any time since the bitter State aid debates'.[5]

Probably even more damaging to the Liberals than the churches' statements was Prime Minister Paul Keating's skill in taking up church objections and turning Coalition rejoinders back on their source. So, when opposition front bencher Fred Chaney accused church critics of Coalition policy of being 'conditioned by a left view rather than a Christian view',[6] Keating promptly branded the Coalition 'anti-church' with such success that Liberal and National backbenchers warned their party rooms that the 'leftist' tag risked offending many churchgoing voters.[7] In a similar vein, when then Liberal Senator Richard Alston attacked the Australian Catholic Social Welfare Commission's statement 'Taxation on Food' as 'mealy-mouthed' and a 'second rate polemic parading as moral argument', Keating savaged Alston's 'arrogant and nasty' response.[8]

When Howard resurrected the GST for the 1998 election, he knew he was going to have to face down the same kind of church comment that proved so damaging to Hewson. He needed a way to neutralise their criticism. In fact, the GST was just the most visible part of an economic restructure that overturned many longstanding assumptions about welfare, inequality and the relationship between churches and government. And, as we've seen throughout this study, Howard's right relied on being able to mobilise half-submerged religious sentiments without being specific enough to either arouse secular anxieties or provoke a theological rebuttal.

Howard's appropriation of history poses the question: Does religion incline people to left or right? As we saw in chapter six, the *Financial Review*'s view that churches and the Coalition 'share a constituency' is only partly true—at least in the Howard era, when the Coalition moved further from churchgoers' unusual levels of racial openness. But it is true that, overall, churchgoing aligns with greater conservatism, particularly in relation to issues such as patriotism, law and order and defence, as sociologist Hans Mol found. Numerous other Australian studies have revealed similar patterns: more regular churchgoing increases conservatism and less regular attendance weakens it.[9] Although Catholics have a much-cited historic tendency to vote Labor, even they increase their support for the Coalition parties as they increase regular church attendance (as opposed to being merely cultural adherents). However, race is not the only exception to that general pattern. Political scientist Rodney Smith noted, for example, that: 'Religiously affiliated Australians view the unemployed more favourably than secularists, while church attendance and placing a high importance on religion both seem to reduce anti-welfare sentiments'. Smith's account repeats the pattern we saw in relation to race, in that it is the practice of actually going to church that protects against intolerance. Holding spiritual beliefs, alone, produces, if anything, the opposite effect: 'beliefs in God and heaven', as distinct from religious attendance, 'seem to be associated with increased anti-welfare feelings'.[10] As with race, welfare holds out tantalising buttons for gentle, surreptitious pressing by a political party willing to appeal to the more intolerant potential of the 'spiritual but not religious' mass of the population.

Howard-style welfare reform conjured its own 'Them': welfare recipients—indolent, undisciplined and ready to shuffle their problems on to the state—who bludged off the decent, hard-working, thrifty and family oriented 'Us'. Such pictures evoke the grim theological traditions of human beings as sinful, selfish and lazy, in need of constant pestering to do our duty. The welfare buttons created for the occasion were 'self-reliance' and 'mutual obligation'—the idea that support in hard times is not a right the state owes to citizens but a privilege in return for which beneficiaries must 'put something back'. Such terms push well out of view any idea that unemployment is produced by the economy, let alone ever deliberately used as an instrument of economic policy.

As we saw in relation to the vilification of Muslims in chapter seven, indirect, implicit political messages of intolerance work best when the unworthy message is not named for what it is—bringing it out in the open risks showing people what they've been conned by, and having it refuted. Church criticism of the Howard welfare shake-up, with the churches' explicit invocation of a God biased towards the poor, threatened to make the 'personal responsibility' dog whistle loud and undeniable while countering it with a more inclusive, loving vision of people's responsibility to one another. It ultimately threatened to send Howard the same way as Hewson. The trick was to silence, or at least circumvent, the churches' actual messages about unemployment and welfare—which tended to emphasise such awkward values as love, compassion and a bias towards those in most need.

Howard's right was locked in a strange ambivalence about churches. They did not like churches to criticise them, so that the government regularly denounced ecclesiastical 'meddling' on everything from Native Title to war to tax reform. On the other hand, judging by Howard and his ministers' pronouncements, they liked churches to deliver cheap welfare, pick up the pieces in the wake of shrinking government assistance, and provide a vocabulary to fill out such shadowy concepts as 'personal responsibility' and 'mutual obligation'. Moreover, Howard and his team readily blurred the lines between church and government. This chapter shows how the churches were at least partly silenced, while the government played religious cards just out of the frame.

•

One of the longest-standing strands of the churches' public activity in Australia is social welfare. For almost as long, Australian churches and politicians have debated who should be responsible. Early in the nineteenth century, the general assumption was that welfare activities belong in the realm of 'charity' or 'philanthropy', dictated by individuals' generosity rather than being part of the government's duty to its citizens. In any case, state aid to religion and the churches' disciplinary function in the convict colonies meant that boundaries between church and state scarcely existed. Stronger church organisations and increasing financial resources through the nineteenth century meant greater independence and an end to state aid. They also led churches to more hands-on involvement in the lives of the poor. For example, churches extended their welfare activities in response to the 1890s depression.

The increasing first-hand observation of working-class conditions led churches to revise many of their assumptions. The depression gave them a sharper view of the relationship between labour and capital, which led to stringent criticism of inequality.[11] Consequently, some clergy began to rethink the basis of charitable welfare provision, coming to the conclusion, to quote one historian, that, in place of private philanthropy or church charity, it was for 'the State itself . . . to direct and finance welfare work' but 'acting within guidelines drawn by the churches'.[12] With that came a renewed interest in the ideas of Christian socialism, which had flourished in England in the mid-nineteenth century, and even older traditions. For example, Methodists stuck to the stance of their eighteenth-century founder, John Wesley. Despite his own phenomenal philanthropy, Wesley severely criticised the idea that individual acts of largesse would, alone, rectify injustices inherent in society's organisation. He was, consequently, an early advocate of government responsibility to address the structural causes of unemployment and working-class poverty.[13]

As the churches saw it, governments have several advantages in undertaking the task of welfare, including universal reach and the ability to raise funds equitably and consistently through the tax system, rather than relying on the variable surplus which individuals or businesses might choose to donate in a good year but hang on to in a lean year. There is also an issue of perception: government is responsible equally for the well-being of all citizens, so it is less likely to be open to suspicions of favouring some (perhaps, co-religionists) at others' expense, or enforcing arbitrary divisions between 'deserving' and 'undeserving' poor. At a more philosophical level, church advocates of government welfare over private charity argued that caring for the least well off is a universal obligation, not an option, and so should not be left at the mercy of philanthropic whim.

Although government responded with the mechanisms of the welfare state, expanding government welfare activity has never, in practice, absorbed all of those whose needs are not adequately taken care of by the market or the family. Non-government organisations have remained important for those who fall through the gaps. Varying philosophical commitment to greater or lesser state involvement has altered the balance from time to time. The Howard government has consistently moved social welfare services out of the public sector and into a 'social coalition' of community organisations, supported by a mixture of government and philanthropic funding.[14]

In particular, Howard has promoted two safety nets to protect people from the effects of shrinking government. One is 'the family'. In a 1995 speech to the Australian Council of Social Services, Howard declared 'a stable, functioning family' to be 'the best welfare support system yet devised'. The half-spoken theology of marriage as a remedy for sin and 'the family' as the moral stop-gap for fallen humanity (as discussed in chapter four) has concrete economic outcomes. It provides a moral justification for moving a substantial part of the welfare responsibility off the tax system and on to individuals. Raising the bars for student allowances and refashioning the rules for youth unemployment benefits reinforced the idea that, while depending on the government is morally corroding, dependency on your own parents is not (no matter how much they struggle). In 1997, Howard protégé Tony Abbott, the self-confessed unwed father whose concerns about 'teenage promiscuity' have resurfaced throughout his political career, moved to amend the *Sex Discrimination Act* to allow discrimination between married and de facto couples under the age of twenty-five for the purpose of student allowances, so only the married would get the higher 'independent' allowance. De facto couples would, in effect, be substantially more dependent on their own parents. He feared that to do otherwise offered students 'an incentive to shack up' sooner 'than it might be good for them'. Why it should be good for twenty-four year olds to marry but not to live together he did not make clear. The consequent strains on the many adult de facto couples paled beside the perceived moral danger to a few.[15]

If families can't fill the gap, the second fallback is churches and non-government charities. Again, although we heard a lot about 'spiritual values', the bottom line was dollars and cents. The Howard government encouraged church and charity organisations to bid for government money to provide services which otherwise would be provided by government agencies. The tendering system has always been controversial. The principle of trying to compete on price has sometimes caused the tendering agencies to worry whether the quality of services risks being compromised. Another concern is that the conditions of contracts entrap such agencies increasingly in the government's systems, weakening their ability to offer independent critique and advice about the services concerned. To learn from the US experience, faith-based contracts can reward government-friendly churches.

One significant move towards outsourcing welfare was replacing the government's Commonwealth Employment Service with the private Job Network. In late 1999, Employment Services Minister Tony Abbott announced the results of the second round of tenders for job placement services: $700 million worth of contracts had been won by church employment services, out of a total of three billion dollars awarded.[16] In 2004, Howard announced another major outsourcing move: the Stronger Families initiative would give $365 million over four years to church charities to 'support early intervention to help children and families where there is a strong likelihood that these children would not otherwise grow up in a stable and supportive environment'. At the heart of these, and similar, initiatives lies a strong belief that welfare is best delivered by someone other than the government. But not just anyone: Christian agencies, the Howard government argues, have a competitive advantage. Howard told an audience at Sydney's Wesley Mission of his 'very strong belief', often repeated, that:

> The organisations that are best able to deliver these services are in fact organisations like Wesley Mission: they know the problem, they've had coalface experience, they know even better than the sternest bureaucrat in the Department of Finance and Administration how hard it is to raise money and therefore how prudent you have to be in the spending of your donors' dollars.

The church charities' strength went beyond their practical experience. Howard concluded:

> I've long admired the work of Wesley Mission, as I do the work of great organisations [such] as the Society of St Vincent de Paul and Anglicare, and the Salvation Army, and the

> Smith Family . . . and I therefore believe very strongly, that the best way that we can help those underprivileged and marginalised people as a Government is to help those great organisations that fuse practical experience with a sense of mission, a sense of commitment born in the main, but not exclusively of course, by the great Judaeo-Christian ethics that instruct and continue to influence our community.[17]

Tony Abbott had developed the same line in defending the church agencies' share of the Job Network:

> The fact is, these agencies do an extremely good job and why shouldn't people who work for organisations like the Salvation Army and Mission Australia be expected to uphold that ethos of love and compassion and the brotherhood of man, which helps to give them their very unique and special and magnificent identity.[18]

Alan Cadman, Liberal Member for Mitchell and Hillsong regular, agreed. Christian agencies shone in the tendering process, he said, because they were the ones 'prepared to go the extra miles and spend the extra time'[19] to see results. Peter Costello told an Anglicare lunch that the welfare state could never supplant charities because such agencies 'bring an extra dimension to their work to the extent they are staffed by people of strong religious or moral conviction' and, consequently, their work 'enriches the giver as well as the receiver'. He explained:

> In a complex web of relationships between givers, service providers and those in need, all are drawn together and benefit in different ways . . . They have stepped outside their roles as taxpayers and income beneficiaries. They are not relating now through the tax file number and the bank account. They are relating as people.[20]

For Costello, it was government's job to help the process along. He acknowledged one problem charities faced was that 'a lot of people will think to themselves, that since they are already paying tax they are contributing enough to the needy'. To overcome it, he advocated 'limited government' which, he said, 'allows the non-government associations to develop and prosper and deepen the social relationships in a community'. Cutting government services, on that view, was not placing a burden on the poor, but making space for charity.

While charity benefits everyone, welfare, according to the Howard government, holds definite moral dangers. Abbott argued that universal welfare, for example for those unable to find work, could undermine people's work ethic, eroding 'those sturdy values of responsibility, self-reliance and neighbourliness'. As a result, 'for many people, working has become more trouble than it's worth'.[21] So how did charity, as opposed to government welfare, avoid those degrading effects? According to Abbott, when he was employment services minister, tackling poverty meant tackling unemployment; and that meant understanding that the problem was not 'lack of training' or 'lack of jobs', but people's disinclination to work. They resisted 'for all sorts of reasons', he said, but the bottom line was that they gave up too easily: overall, their own moral failings stood between them and lifelong earning.[22] And who better to have charge of those morally at risk than churches? Costello further explained, 'People of religious and moral conviction' who staff church charities are 'willing to share their values in support of treating underlying causes of poverty'.[23]

As we found in the 'values in schools' debate in chapter seven, the Howard government relies on the view of a substantial number of voters that, even though 'We' may not need religion to get through life, those (children, single mothers, the unemployed) at greater risk of moral lapse than 'Us' are best passed into the hands of people who do have sincere religious convictions, as they will be able to convey a moral message with a force which the rest of us might lack. Costello gave examples. Framed by the panoramic harbour views at Sydney's WatersEdge restaurant, he urged church charities to press home a message of 'changed lives' which can address 'the causes of poverty' rather than merely buffering people against its effects:

> Income support provides insulation against poverty but it does not treat the cause of poverty . . . A homeless man who is drug or alcohol dependent will probably be entitled to income support . . . [which] should be enough to provide food and shelter. But it doesn't in his case because the money he receives is always spent on the wrong thing. And it always will be until you treat the cause of the poverty which is alcohol and drug dependence.

A second example he cited concerned 'a family on average wages' which breaks up, leaving the same wage now having to support two households. 'Things would be a whole lot better if we could treat the cause of the problem which in this case is the marriage breakdown.' He concluded:

> To the extent that the people involved in helping others can help those others to deal with these problems they will make a very big difference. If the churches can point to lives that have been changed it will make a big difference; more than anything else it would demonstrate that faith is not a lost cause. The public would take a whole lot of notice.[24]

Costello's point at the Anglicare lunch was not just to assure his church charity worker audience that their work was appreciated. He brought chastisements, as well as congratulations. He was worried that the public was losing faith in churches and their agencies, and he dispensed advice about how to regain that trust, so 'hard won but easily lost'. The problem, as Costello saw it, was church leaders talking out of turn about 'what they perceive to be moral issues'. This, he thought, had been particularly rife in recent debates:

> The church leaders had a lot to say about Australia's involvement in Iraq. When the Government was reforming the tax system I was amazed how many church leaders were, in fact, tax experts who had sized up the moral dimensions of a value added tax.[25]

To rub salt into the wound, according to Costello, churches were mouthing off about matters beyond their ken at the very same time as overlooking 'people who really had engaged in moral failure' within their own ranks, an allusion to the clergy sexual abuse scandals then engulfing Anglican and Catholic churches, in particular. On the way to his Anglicare engagement, Costello spoke to Sydney Radio 2BL, foreshadowing his speech:

> If you think of the trouble that the Anglican church has had with the sex abuse issue in Queensland . . . it strikes me, that there is a bit of a crisis of confidence in the voluntary and charity agencies, and what I want to do is address those issues today and try and give some reasons why we need these agencies and . . . what they can do for the public to rediscover trust and faith in the agencies.[26]

Costello's mention of 'the trouble that the Anglican church has had with the sex abuse issue in Queensland' might have been more accurately phrased 'the trouble that the Howard-appointed Governor-General has brought upon the Anglican church in Queensland'; so it was probably prudent that he did not elaborate once he got to his Anglican audience. Instead, he drove home four simple messages. First, he, like Howard, was sure that in the good old days churches used to keep out of public debate. Their intervention on political issues (such as the Iraq War and the GST) are only recent departures, he claimed.

Second, when they do join in public debate, the matters they raise are only 'what they perceive' to be moral issues. Who among us, Costello seemed to imply, can claim to know whether, say, complicity in taking thousands of lives on spurious grounds (as in the Iraq War), or introducing a tax regime which arguably benefits the most well off at the expense of the aged, infirm and unemployed (as many analysts claimed of the GST), is 'really' immoral? This, remember, was the man we heard in chapter seven warning impressionable students at the National Student Leadership Forum on Faith and Values against postmodernism, which teaches (according to Costello) that morals are merely a matter of opinion. When it came to the GST and Iraq cases, though, he seemed to be saying exactly that, so church leaders who claimed that such issues involve moral absolutes were merely peddling their own 'perceptions'.

Third, in any case, no one need take church criticism on those issues too seriously because clergy have not dealt with the moral logs in their own eyes. And, fourth, unlike the Howard sermons to churches discussed in chapter six, Costello did tell his audience of church workers what their job was: changing lives from within, leaving externalities to others. The alcoholic, drug-addicted street person and the couple at risk of marriage breakdown needed what only churches could give. No evangelical pulpit thumper could have put it more clearly: churches' business is personal rather than social transformation. Not that he feared churches' social criticism might damage the Coalition—on the contrary, his concern was all for the churches. He was worried that they were losing credibility with the public, and so he had taken time out of his busy treasury schedule to advise them on how to 'keep the public trust' and persuade the public that 'faith is not a lost cause'.

Those messages were repeated two months later, when it was Foreign Minister and Member for Mayo Alexander Downer's turn to damn church comments on politics.[27] Delivering the annual lecture that commemorates long-serving South Australian Premier Thomas Playford Jnr (premier from November 1938 to March 1965), Downer applauded the 'central role' of 'the Christian churches [and] . . . other great religions, such as Judaism, Islam, Hinduism and Buddhism' in 'providing a moral compass to an increasing[ly] materialistic world', before lamenting the 'partisan politicking' which, he felt, had seduced church leaders in recent years. He argued that people were losing 'much-needed spiritual sustenance' as their religious leaders succumbed to the temptation to 'be amateur commentators on all manner of secular issues on which they inevitably lack expertise'. He went further, accusing clergy of 'hogging the limelight' (presumably from its rightful occupants on Capital Hill) and taking on 'complex political issues' in quest of 'cheap headlines'—travesties which, he declared, 'would have been inconceivable in the Playford era'.

His blast did not seem to work: three months later, he was telling the National Press Club that 'the usual suspects in the clerical elite' remained 'unstoppable and invincibly ignorant', giving way to 'weird kinds of self-disgust' (as though to criticise one's government is to hate oneself). He went on: 'Who can explain this moral equivalent of the cultural cringe, except perhaps as an aberration of the elites in the dwindling days of their influence? I am inclined to regard it as a reflex action and to think that they simply can't help themselves'.[28] One of the 'usual suspects' was an unnamed archbishop who had accused the Howard government of 'destroying our international reputation, brutalising the Australian people's attitudes and making us a less compassionate people'. When I dug up Downer's mystery source, it turned out to be Anglican Archbishop of Adelaide Ian George, quoted in a 1998 article headed 'Howard, Beazley lashed over race' with the strap, 'Church and political leaders have condemned the two major political parties for silencing the critics of their tough stand on asylum seekers'.[29] It took some rhetorical skill, therefore, for Downer to portray that one as 'partisan politicking'!

Another 'usual suspect' was Anglican Archbishop Peter Carnley who, Downer said, had 'announced to his Synod, on the slenderest evidence, that "Australia's policy on asylum seekers had affected its reputation around the world"'. You'd think Downer would have been pleased: the Howard government regularly justified its asylum seeker policy as sending a message to the rest of the world. Perhaps Downer was really more stung by another issue Carnley raised in the same speech: changes to the charity laws to strip tax deductibility from those who criticised government policy. That, Carnley reproved, was 'the kind of thing that one might expect from a quasi-totalitarian regime, hell-bent on controlling information and stifling public criticism'.[30]

Then, in February 2004, came Howard's own 'keep out of politics' speech. Churches, he said, were often 'particularly critical of our side of politics'. Like Costello, it wasn't that he feared any punches they might land; his motivation was altruistic. He was concerned that church leaders risked 'dividing their congregations', and so he had called a special press conference to alert them to the danger. There was, he said, a great 'spiritual hunger' in the Australian community, which church leaders could fill, but only if they stopped interfering in what doesn't concern them—namely, politics.[31]

All the speeches were readily picked up by conservative commentators.[32] Repeated church criticism of Coalition positions prompted a determined effort by the Howard government to show that churches are Johnny-come-lately interlopers in the political arena, that they do not know what they are talking about and that they should probably not be talking about it anyway.

In fact, as we saw in chapter one, church commentary on social issues is nothing new. Indeed, the 1950s Methodist church activism of Alan Walker and his colleagues was no more an aberration from an apolitical rule than contemporary clerical outbursts. On the contrary, almost from the first arrival of Christian churches in Australia, clergy have been enthusiastic participants in public debate, often as irritants to the establishment. For example, in the nineteenth century, church leaders campaigned against transportation and for equal wages for Chinese labourers, universal franchise and republicanism. And when they did, they encountered similar charges to those levelled by the Howard government.

At first, with church structures still embryonic or non-existent, such interventions tended to be by individuals. Activist clergy churned out books, pamphlets, journalism, letters to the authorities and presentations to government committees, attempting to change public policy and setting out their theological reasons. Australia's first Roman Catholic vicar-general, Reverend Dr William Ullathorne, fought transportation through his pamphlets 'The Catholic Mission in Australia'[33] and 'The Horrors of Transportation',[34] earning an invitation to give evidence to the House of Commons Select Committee on Transportation, chaired by Sir William Molesworth.[35]

The anti-transportation campaign was one sliver of common ground joining Ullathorne and the vehemently anti-Catholic Sydney Presbyterian Reverend Dr John Dunmore Lang, who published similarly and also gave evidence to the Molesworth Committee.[36] Lang was then just beginning his political transition from Tory bourgeois moralist to the radical republican who eventually took his seat in the New South Wales Legislative Council on a platform of no transportation, no gerrymander and greatly extended franchise.[37] The constant in his turbulent public career was the confetti of representations, letters, petitions, newspaper articles, books and pamphlets with which he showered the public and government officials in Australia and the United Kingdom.

These regularly invoked his authority as 'senior minister of Scots Church'[38] and spelt out how he understood the relationship between his roles as political activist and minister of religion. Then, as now, critics admonished that 'a professed minister of religion' should not 'meddle' with politics but 'mind your own proper business and leave these things to other people'.[39] Lang retorted that politics was as much his business as anybody's. For example, he claimed republicanism, underpinned by political equality, universal suffrage and popular election, as the only Biblically endorsed system of government.[40] When detractors labelled his ideas '*Chartism, Communism* and *Socialism*', he retorted that in that case those 'isms' must, like his own 'objectionable principles', have originated in 'that *Word of God which endureth for ever*'.[41]

Race also brought church people into conflict with the government. Henry Reynolds has drawn attention to the role of Australian and English evangelicals, the 'Exeter Hall' reformers, in nineteenth-century campaigns for Indigenous peoples. Lang's campaign to liberalise the rules on Chinese immigration brought five hundred Chinese mourners to the head of his funeral procession.[42] Congregationalist Reverend Dr James Jefferis argued in the 1870s for equal wages for Chinese and Australian workers. They all regularly drew the same charges that the Howard government would so regularly recycle, more than a century later. Churches were accused of dangerous innovation by taking to political comment, told not to meddle in matters too complex for their understanding, accused of political grandstanding and warned against abandoning their 'real' responsibilities—whatever those may be.

At times, politicians feared that church criticism was not going to stop at commentary from the sidelines. In 1877, newspapers alleged a Wesleyan Methodist attempt to take over the South Australian Legislative Council. Even then, the 'partisanship' charge had a tired ring. The *Methodist Journal* dusted off the standard rebuttal, from the 1820 Liverpool Minutes, read annually to Wesleyan ministers: 'we as a body do not exist for the purpose of party'.[43]

Industrial relations was another arena in which church spokespeople were regularly accused of 'partisanship' and of abandoning their 'proper' business. In the aftermath of the 1890 Maritime Strike, Roman Catholic Cardinal Moran's qualified pro-unionism, Anglican Bishop Barry's moderate socialism and the full-blown Christian socialism of Congregationalist Reverend Dr Thomas Roseby and Anglo-Catholic Reverend H.L. Jackson alike drew the charge of misplaced allegiance, together with admonitions that social questions do not belong in the pulpit.[44]

Historian Richard Ely described the active interventions of clergy in the debates prior to Federation, both locally and on the national stage. They addressed not only the predictable topics of religious freedom and the status of clergy in the new commonwealth, but also the nature of social justice and the desirability of Federation itself. As Bathurst was preparing to host the 1896 People's Convention, for example, its churches observed a 'Federation Sunday'. Sermons with titles like 'The Federal Lord' interpreted the fellowship of colonies in terms of Christian love and unity.[45] Church services focusing on social issues—and promoting a particular angle—remained common after Federation. For example, A.E. Talbot, Dean of Sydney's St Andrew's Anglican Cathedral from 1912 to 1937, made the cathedral the venue for an annual Eight Hour Day Service.[46]

Church criticism of government policy under Howard, then, merely continued a venerable tradition. Industrial relations proved an election campaign flashpoint between the Coalition and the churches, with all the hallmarks of a *Fightback!* rerun. On 21 February 1996, in the final weeks of the campaign that saw Howard ushered into office, one hundred members of religious organisations signed an open letter endorsing the then Labor government's approach over the opposition's. Keating joined in, invoking the pope in his party's support. Opposition leader John Howard retorted by quoting a papal encyclical, *Centessimus Annus*, defending voluntary unionism. In the same breath, Howard added:

> I don't want His Holiness involved in the election campaign . . . I don't think Catholics or non-Catholics in the Australian community want His Holiness involved . . . I'll be very happy to argue the Christian credentials of anything I put forward in this election campaign.[47]

I always thought it a pity no one took him up on the offer, since a robust theological debate over, say, welfare cuts, education spending and attacks on Indigenous rights might have livened up his famously highlight-free 'small target' campaign. Theological pressure on the Coalition kept up nonetheless.

In April 1998, when the Howard government supported the proposed Multilateral Agreement on Investment, which would have overridden national governments' environmental, labour and human rights protections in the name of international competition, the New South Wales Synod's Board for Social Responsibility of the Uniting Church in Australia called the agreement 'from a Christian point of view . . . idolatrous'.[48] The following year, the National Council of Churches said that Industrial Relations Minister Peter Reith's employment proposals fell 'far short of what is required', citing sources ranging from the Australian Catholic Bishops' Conference and Orthodox bishops to Salvation Army founder William Booth.[49] Welfare was another hot spot with, for example, two Uniting Church bodies, UnitingCare Australia and National Social Responsibility and Justice, calling aspects of mutual obligation 'unacceptable' and 'inappropriate'. A proposal to subject people with disabilities to the job seekers' activity test (which checks job seekers' genuineness in looking for work) the Uniting Church bodies found 'morally repugnant'.[50]

Downer's wistful comment that church criticism of government activity would have been 'inconceivable in the Playford era' flies in the face of history. Australian clergy have regarded an active, even controversial, role in public debate to be part of their core responsibility for almost as long as there have been clergy in Australia. What had changed was not that churches had begun lobbying, but that government had grown hypersensitive to criticism. Those who, before the 1996 election, bemoaned the 'pall of political correctness' which, they claimed, stifled freedom of speech in Australia, spent the next eight years radically limiting what can be said and by whom.

But there were still greater ironies in the Howard government's sermons to church leaders. At the same time as the government was telling churches to keep out of public debate, various political supporters were mobilising conservative, American-style evangelical and Pentecostal churches to promote right wing policies and politicians. The new mood saw increasingly assertive 'born again' political activists who favoured individual enterprise and reduced government support for a whole range of sinners. In addition, Howard and his government were going to extraordinary lengths to blur the lines between church and state, building church agencies into its own structures. The welfare system was its front line.

•

One consequence of tendering out government services to church agencies was tethering those agencies to non-welfare aspects of government policy. A prime example of the ironies inherent in being willing to build church agencies into a wider policy agenda, while at the same time exhorting them to keep out of politics, was the Job Network. It outsourced the work previously done by the Commonwealth Employment Service (CES) of matching unemployed people with available jobs.

Churches gained their foothold in the Job Network via the tendering system. One of the grounds for awarding tenders was price.[51] One likely reason for the tenders by church agencies being so successful is that, as not-for-profit organisations, they could provide cheaper services than private enterprise. Another way of putting then employment services minister Tony Abbott's declaration that the religious tenderers succeeded because of their 'ethos of love and compassion' is that their 'ethos' enables them to perform sacrificially what others do in terms set by the market. Churches and charities, offering much-needed services on tight and unpredictable budgets, have historically relied heavily on the labour of volunteers, while paid workers have often been employed at lower rates than they could command in comparable secular employment. A sense of vocation is, in some ways, the unofficial trade-off for reduced pay and conditions. Consequently, in many areas, 'volunteerism and amateurism are two hallmarks of church life'.[52] Both the tendering advantage and the industrial pitfalls show clearly in the following example.

In 1999, when the Job Network was still new, Tim Costello published his *Tips From A Travelling Soul-Searcher*, which describes one highly successful tenderer called WorkVentures. Costello reported that WorkVentures 'created a lot of employment for disadvantaged people, achieving a multi-million-dollar turn-over'.[53] Costello attributed WorkVentures' success to its integration with its staff's private lives. One called her work 'a career without a salary'. The founder dreamt of the project evolving into a 'living-working village', where 'work is so meaningful and integrated with life that the distinction between the two disappears'.[54] Costello cited a study of WorkVentures by Melbourne theologian Gordon Preece who, in Costello's words, saw 'the WorkVentures success as due in large part to its workers' approach'. This included being 'willing to blur the lines between paid and unpaid work'.[55] The government's view was that such willingness made for better service. The barely spoken implication was high staff input—in Alan Cadman's encomium, being willing to 'go the extra miles and spend the extra time'.

The issue in tendering was not quality alone, however, but a relationship between quality and cost. One way to get high quality for a low cost is to make some of that staff input unpaid. In the Jobs Network tendering system, WorkVentures and similar organisations were pitted against commercial job placement services, which are required to operate at a profit and whose employees do not have the luxury of pursuing 'a career without a salary'. Translating 'extra miles' out of Cadman's New Testament phraseology,[56] it is hard to see what it means other than that the successful religious agencies were the ones whose employees did more work than they were paid for.

Within a couple of years, Howard's treasurer was able to count the benefits. Launching the 2002 Salvation Army Red Shield Appeal, Peter Costello frankly admitted:

> [W]e have learned in Government . . . that services can be delivered through the voluntary association much more effectively because of the quality of character of the people that staff the institution. And I was watching some of these pie graphs up here, as Treasurers are wont to do, during our breakfast, and the overheads and the administration are so much lower in the delivery of services. If I could get some of those efficiencies in the delivery of my services I would be very happy. I watched even some of the bankers on my table here enviously looking at the low overheads.[57]

One reason they could not 'get those efficiencies' is that neither bankers nor government can tap (directly) the Salvation Army's culture of sacrifice. Coming from a treasurer, 'quality of character' is a touchingly euphemistic way of expressing the fact that, for example, the Salvation Army's US Commissioner, 'head of a national enterprise with a [US]$2.1 billion budget', has an annual salary of 'about [US]$13 000 a year'. An article comparing the Salvation Army to the Red Cross points out that the latter's US CEO, heading a similarly sized operation with comparable programs, draws US$450 000. From the commissioner down, Salvation Army officers are encouraged to see their income as a 'living allowance' rather than a salary, and to forgo personal possessions so that 'When officers are transferred, they simply take down a few personal pictures, gather up their clothes and walk out the door. Everything else, right down to the sheets and silverware, belongs to the Army'.[58]

It is difficult to imagine a Liberal government—or, for that matter, a bank—endorsing so communistic a mode of life for the employees delivering its services; but the privatisation-loving treasurer had no problem accepting at second-hand the efficiencies such collectivism produces. Moreover, we might wonder why a government so wedded to leaving things up to the market is ready, in the case of welfare, to abandon the all-powerful market in favour of a sector that directly undercuts it.

One result of government reducing its welfare commitments is that more and more of the welfare burden is shifted to churches and charities, supported by cut-price government input. As the ABC's Sally Loane put it to the treasurer, church agencies are important 'because they do fill in a lot of the gaps that Government used to do'. The alternative was that 'the Government is going to be more in demand, more tax, more money'. Costello replied, 'Absolutely'. He added that Americans 'are very good in relation to their philanthropic and charitable institutions', which he accounted for by 'the fact that they have more limited government', meaning that 'the private citizen feels that they have a bigger obligation to step in'.[59]

There are other consequences to the 'voluntary' view of welfare. One is that more workers are likely to find themselves expected to provide cheap services for minimal return—not by choice, but because of a fundamental change in the way welfare is delivered. In that case, welfare workers would surely experience substantial personal and family pressures—or find other careers.

One traditional bastion against such pressures has been trade unions. Church agencies' mix of volunteer workers and paid workers organised around a volunteer ethos means that church employees are among the least unionised in the Australian workforce. One effect of the church–state blurring brought on by the Commonwealth Employment Service's replacement by the Job Network has been to reduce substantially the rate of unionisation among job placement workers. Anecdotal reports suggest that up to eighty per cent of CES employees were union members, making the CES the Community and Public Sector Union's 'flagship portfolio'.[60] By contrast, in church-based agencies unionisation is estimated at a fraction of that rate.[61] If that effect did not stand out in public commentary, it did to the initiators of the change. Speaking on ABC TV, Tony Abbott boasted that one of the Jobs Network's achievements was eroding 'the . . . union-dominated, bureaucratic monolith of the CES'.[62] Religious agencies were used by government in a political agenda beyond the immediate question of delivering job placement services.

Another consequence of churches receiving government funds was that they then found it harder to criticise government policy.[63] Indeed, refraining from criticism was increasingly one of the terms of a contract under Howard's governments.[64] According to Melbourne City Mission Chief Executive Ray Cleary, that restraint:

> eats at the very heart of the mission and the value base of church-based agencies, which are there to demonstrate God's preferential or special interest for the marginalised and those at risk.[65]

Even without explicit 'no-criticism' clauses, there is always the fear of losing future contracts. Either way, church agencies, being increasingly built into the same set of mechanisms as the government departments they previously challenged, may find it harder to distinguish government's goals from their own.

In 2003, the Howard government introduced a Charities Bill to tidy up the definition of what counted as a charity for the purposes of tax exemption.[66] The Bill's effect was to rule in as charities any non-profit organisation for the public benefit, except for those with a 'disqualifying purpose'. Three activities could rule out a non-profit organisation if they were more than 'ancillary or incidental to the other purposes of the entity concerned'. The fatal three were 'advocating a political party or cause', 'supporting a candidate for political office' and 'attempting to change the law or government policy'. Although the Bill was eventually withdrawn, its threat remained. Moreover, the Board of Taxation stated that 'if the Tax Office receives information [about a charity] which . . . confirms the advocacy role as dominant, it is likely the [charitable] status will be revoked'.[67]

The Green Party worried that, even though 'the advancement of the natural environment' was specifically mentioned as a possible public benefit, the nature of environmental advocacy would make environment groups particularly vulnerable. Planting trees, weeding a nature reserve or bottle-feeding marsupial orphans would presumably be acceptable, but campaigning for a carbon tax or greener building codes could demolish an organisation's tax deductibility and GST exemptions. Indeed, the Greens' online comment on the Bill succinctly noted, in relation to the prohibition on 'advocating a political party or cause': 'It is hard to think of a cause which isn't political!' while 'attempting to change the law or government policy', according to the Greens, 'speaks for itself'. The Greens also pointed out that charities would be unfairly singled out, since businesses 'can tax-deduct all their costs for advocating, promoting, advertising and lobbying for their own interests'.[68]

The National Council of Churches in Australia (NCCA), covering fifteen churches including the Catholic and major Protestant and Orthodox denominations, made a submission to the Board of Taxation on behalf of its aid arm, Christian World Service. It argued that its work with partner councils of churches overseas did not permit a neat distinction between charity and advocacy. The submission paraphrased the famous saying of Brazilian Catholic Bishop Helder Camara, 'When I feed the poor, people call me a saint; when I ask why the poor have no food, they call me a communist'. The NCCA's version was, 'The Bill appears to state that helping the poor is considered praiseworthy but advocacy regarding why the poor are poor could well constitute a disqualifying purpose!'. The NCCA saw advocacy not only as a necessary aspect of its work to alleviate poverty, but also as a matter of public accountability to its donors: 'The sector owes it to the community to share with it the learnings and insights gained from its work'. Disqualification for 'attempting to change the law or government policy' the NCCA found 'very strange and indefensible'. It maintained that:

> the law or a government policy should reflect evolving human considerations, and, hence, should not be inflexible. It should be beyond dispute that a law or policy needs to be changed if experience or new learnings indicate that that law or policy . . . did not serve the community.

Given charities' public obligation to share their coal-face knowledge, it argued that:

> The charity sector . . . be considered the Government's 'eyes and ears' . . . uniquely placed to observe and provide feedback on the effects of its laws and policies, to reflect on and critique government policy, and if appropriate . . . advocate for a change.

The NCCA shared the Greens' concern that the definition of 'political cause' is so broad that almost anything could fall foul of it. The Council gave examples of its activities which had produced tangible public benefit but which might, in future, breach the Bill's restrictions. The Campaign to End Child Prostitution in Asian Tourism resulted from a partnership between the NCCA and churches in the Asian region 'who were appalled by the brazenness and extent of child prostitution in their midst'. It produced the 1994 Act empowering Australian courts to try Australians for sex crimes committed overseas. The government may have been less impressed by another of NCCA's self-proclaimed successes: its efforts 'to raise awareness, and, as appropriate, critique government policy in relation to refugee and asylum seeker issues'. Although it could not claim major policy changes on that front, the NCCA maintained that, 'Moved by humanitarian and moral grounds, community and government attention has been drawn to the plight of children in detention, acceptance of minimum standards in detention centres, inappropriate management of detention centres, the Pacific Solution, etc'. It added, dryly:

> While the government may not have been eager to receive the critique, the changes have been advocated to enhance the community benefit. The broader point is that such advocacy is carried out in the interests of a humane Australia. This is acceptable in a democratic society.

The NCCA also worried about another disqualifying clause, namely, that charities would be ruled out if they undertook 'unlawful activities'. The NCCA argued that civil disobedience might well be a legitimate undertaking for charities in 'an enlightened society',[69] a worry also shared by the Australian Council of Social Services.

The fears of non-government organisations (NGOs) were not allayed by the fact that, at the same time as the Charities Bill was being debated, the Liberal Party-aligned think tank, the Institute of Public Affairs (discussed in the previous chapter), received a $50 000 contract to investigate the relationship between government and NGOs. Its research concentrated on 'the right of government and the taxpayer to know enough about an NGO to make an informed judgement about granting access and resources'.[70] The Greens commented, 'Given the IPA's track record, this begins to look like a concerted attack on community groups and public debate'.[71] In other words, the fact that the government had skirted the usual sources of background information and research, and gone instead to an organisation with a long history of ideological campaigning on topics such as the environment, overseas aid and Indigenous issues (as discussed in chapter eight) in ways that have generally helped conservative governments against more progressive groups, gave the move a look of paying to get the advice you want.

Given the IPA itself is an NGO that exists to lobby, regularly attempting to change the law and government policy, its position was equivocal. It opted for a strong market model, arguing that what was really needed was enough disclosure to donors about what their money was being used for to enable them to decide, if they wished, to give it elsewhere. 'Disclosure to donors, not limits to non-partisan advocacy, is the answer to the scrutiny required for the public support of charity work.' Significantly, in the light of the issues canvassed in the last chapter, the IPA did not argue for disclosing donors' identity to the public (a move that would have bothered business-funded private think tanks much more than charities). It listed 'adoption of lobbying as a dominant activity', 'involvement in the political process' and 'undertaking violent protest and illegal activity' as factors that had had 'a deleterious impact on the [charity] sector'. The IPA felt that 'Giving aid to the poor, planting trees, and writing letters to foreign governments on behalf of political prisoners' were all 'unambiguous' instances of charity; but that a more sinister element had entered much ostensibly charitable work:

> The charity no longer gives direct aid to the poor, it wants to use the tax system to achieve equality. Does lobbying to create more generous unemployment benefits or a more progressive tax system constitute charity for the poor, or is it the pursuit of an egalitarian ideology? Is lobbying to tax hydrocarbons a public benefit or the pursuit of an environmental ideology based on assumptions of resource depletion? Is lobbying for an International Criminal Court the pursuit of human rights, or the pursuit of an anti nation–state ideology?

Like Downer, Costello and Howard in their strictures on churches' political activism, the IPA invoked a good ol' days image of when charities stuck to dispensing soup to the deserving poor, leaving the policy prescriptions to government and (as the Greens argued) business. It lamented:

> The methods, as well as the scope of charities have changed, and in doing so, so has the purpose of charity. Lobbying means activity to change policies in favour of the view of charities, which are almost invariably that more public resources should

> be devoted to their favourite cause. Charity work is no longer unambiguously good, or for the public benefit. It may be altruistic, but increasingly it is imbedded in a political framework that seeks to use public power for system change.[72]

The trouble is that, no less than Howard and his ministers' wistful invocation of the days when churches minded their own spiritual business, the IPA's soup kitchen nostalgia harks back to a fiction. From the great eighteenth- and nineteenth-century evangelical campaigns against the slave trade and for woman suffrage, universal education, temperance and poor law reform, church and charity activity has had a distinctly political edge, with changes in law and policy as prominent purposes.

•

The proposed Act would have been administered by the Australian Taxation Office, so its championship fell to Peter Costello. Costello had previously drawn headlines with speeches advocating a renewed voluntary sector, arguing that civil society risks serious erosion unless government is 'alert to deal with any threats . . . to the voluntary sector', that where government 'can support the voluntary sector, without smothering it, it should do so', and that government's overriding principle in dealing with voluntary organisations should be 'first, do no harm'.[73] Yet the Charities Bill, by telling churches and charities what were and were not legitimate uses of their donors' money and, especially, by threatening to limit many charities' financial viability if they criticised the government, suggested a political correctness with far more concrete silencing consequences than the kind Howard had been wont to complain about when in opposition.

Costello's media release announcing the draft contained one curious qualification, which gives an insight into Coalition-style political correctness. Charities had to fulfil a 'public benefit', and that could include closed and contemplative religious orders, provided they undertake regular 'prayerful intervention' at the request of the public. In other words, the public benefit doesn't have to be visible or tangible (like dispensing soup). Contemplative orders, presumably, are the kind of model religious people who stick to the spiritual. But what, I found myself wondering, if a closed order began to pray (at public request) for a change in government policy? What if they interceded for refugees, or asked God to move politicians' hearts against legal abortion? Charities were free to lobby God, the Bill implied, but not the government. They could appeal to Jesus, but not voters. You'd have to think that the 'spiritual matters' which Howard and his ministers wanted churches to confine themselves to didn't rate very high on the government's potency scale. The Howard government's use of religion was highly selective. Somehow, political prayer didn't seem as divisive as political advocacy. The power of prayer, locked in a cloister, was safely contained. 'Spiritual' turned out to be anything that doesn't obviously stand in the government's way. No wonder they wanted churches to confine themselves to it.

As Howard and Costello's enthusiastic welcomes at Hillsong imply, not all church people are suspicious of the Liberals' economic agenda. And the more sympathetic seem to find the government's 'churches out of politics' advice even harder to follow than the critical traditional denominations do. Indeed, in 2004 the Assemblies of God was associated with the federal launch of a new political party. As well as gaining a Senate seat, Family First exerted considerable influence even before the election, its leaders meeting Howard personally to extract the family values promises that would ensure its preferences in most states flowed to Liberal candidates. (There were two exceptions—Warren Entsch, who had publicly supported gay marriage, and Ingrid Tall, who had never done so but identifies as lesbian.)

The 2004 election revealed conservative Christian political enthusiasm even beyond the new party. That is evident not so much in the election of born-again candidates (previous parliaments have seen plenty of those), as in their exceptional assertiveness about faith-based politics, and the prominence of religion in their campaigns. Even Howard, who described himself to ABC-TV religious affairs show *Compass* as only an occasional churchgoer, seemed to be repackaging himself for a conservative Christian market. His appearances at various aspirational, 'prosperity Gospel' conservative churches earlier in his third term were reinforced during and immediately after the 2004 campaign.

When Howard launched Western Australian Liberal Don Randall's campaign for Canning at the Perth Christian Life Centre, Randall welcomed the prime minister by saying that the country needed a Christian leader, and that Latham, as 'an atheist or agnostic or whatever he calls himself these days', would feel less welcome in that environment. Howard responded by apparently hosing down Randall's enthusiasm: 'Although I come from a Christian tradition myself, I respect fully the secular nature of our society'. But this reply fits the pattern of muted retractions, examined in chapter seven, in both Howard's and Bush's technique for sounding moderate to the general public while sending a more extreme message to a narrow target group. In Howard and Randall's Canning double act, their coding addressed religious conservatives (Randall) while at the same time reassuring the secular (Howard). The conservative Bible-belt target audience could go on believing Randall's view, rationalising the prime minister's distancing gesture as a necessary compromise for the sake of the 'politically correct', secular 'elite'.

Even more striking was Howard's first public appearance after the election was won. Although he had been up into the small hours on election night, ABC News reported on the Sunday morning that 'Prime Minister John Howard has begun his fourth term in office with a quiet day . . . Mr Howard turned out early for church at Lavender Bay in Sydney this morning, saying he would be spending the rest of the day relaxing'. Newspapers went into more detail, with photos of a navy-suited Howard emerging, alone, through the gothic arch and down the front path of the church where his daughter's father-in-law had preached on the theme of national leadership. We would be hard pressed to find a better icon of the shift the 2004 election had brought in Australian political culture. No Janette in the photo and, despite the family connection to that particular church, no Melanie or her husband. Howard, whose religion had previously sounded more nominal and family-oriented than fervent and personal, was rebranding himself: on day one of his fourth term, Australia suddenly gained a faith-based prime ministership.

Examining John Howard and Australia's soul, we have come up repeatedly against the questions, 'What are spiritual matters?', and 'Are they different from political ones?', and 'How can you tell?' When the coded language of 'family', 'community', 'spiritual values' and 'ethos of love and compassion' seems to translate into reduced services, reduced pay and the stealth aspect of the Howard government's ongoing war on trade unions, it's hard to tell what the words really mean. In the next chapter, we delve into the spiritual underpinnings of Howard's vision for Australia.

CHAPTER TEN

God under Howard

God must find the weeks when parliament sits a challenge. Each sitting day starts by inviting God into the chambers:

> Almighty God, we humbly beseech Thee at this time to vouchsafe Thy special blessing upon this Parliament, and that Thou wouldst be pleased to direct and prosper all our consultations to the advancement of Thy glory, and to the true welfare of the people of Australia.[1]

God under Howard was sometimes humbly besought to prosper, and sometimes confidently implicated in moves to prevent the dying from dying, deny gay couples equal rights with their straight neighbours, reinforce racial resentment and keep Muslim refugees at sea, lower Australia's abortion rate and taxes, impart 'values' and a sense of obligation to children and the unemployed and undermine trade unions. Meanwhile, Howard adroitly sidelined the 'power of prayer' in attempts to repeal the Northern Territory's mandatory sentencing laws and keep young Indigenous Territorians out of jail. Increasingly, God was called upon to direct and prosper the resurrection of the political hard right.

Providence was in demand internationally, too. We encountered in chapter eight the think tank and lobby group activity that issued the kinds of policies examined in the other chapters. That activity is upheld by an elaborate, and liberally financed, structure of prayer, policy and networking. Though that American God looks, at first glance, unfamiliar in Australia, it rules a seldom-noticed layer of right wing religious activism that is well established and rapidly expanding here. This religious right, adept at evangelising capitalism and marketing faith, connects Australian parliamentary conservatives with their colleagues around the world and provides the philosophical justification needed for the Howard Liberals' apparently contradictory 'Manildra Street' blend of economic radicalism and social conservatism.

•

While the Christian Coalition was training activists and mobilising the American grassroots, it benefited from long-established, backroom patterns of association between a particular, conservative brand of Christianity and political power. This tendency's most visible manifestation is the Washington National Prayer Breakfast. Prayer Breakfasts began in Seattle in 1935, when evangelist Abraham Vereide was worried that socialists were poised to take over local government. Vereide dreamed of bringing religion to the powerful, turning from Christianity's historic mission to reach the down and out to minister instead to what he called the 'up and out'.

In 1942, he and his breakfast arrived in Washington. The first group began among House of Representatives members, followed by groups in the Senate and various federal agencies.[2] With the blessing of Eisenhower, and every president since, Congressional Prayer Breakfasts became annual from 1953. The movement rapidly expanded. Today, some 3500 to 4000 people gather each February—by invitation and payment of $US425 a head—to pray with the president.

The annual power breakfasts, supported throughout the year by small, intimate prayer cells of business and political leaders, were aimed at building an 'invisible organisation' of Christian leaders all over the country. To resource the groups and sponsor the breakfasts, Vereide founded an organisation known simply as 'the Fellowship' or 'the Family'. When Vereide died in 1969 his then understudy, Doug Coe, took over the leadership. Coe remains at the helm in 2004, and the organisation employs Coe's two sons,[3] one of whom, David, is regarded as Doug's 'presumptive heir to the leadership'.[4]

Vereide's aim was to 'win the nation for Christ, one city at a time'.[5] After the nation, the world. Now Prayer Breakfasts illuminate the public life of countries as far afield as Canada, New Zealand, Nigeria, Zambia, Taiwan and South Korea. Religious affairs journalist Jeffrey Sharlet observed in *Harper's*:

> Steadfastly ecumenical, too bland most years to merit much press, the breakfast is regarded by the Family as merely a tool in a larger purpose: to recruit the powerful attendees into smaller, more frequent prayer meetings, where they can 'meet Jesus man to man'.[6]

Not that the recruits necessarily realise this. The *Los Angeles Times* noted that the invitation to the National Prayer Breakfast in Washington in 2002 was inscribed from 'members of the Congress of the United States of America', and presidential seals adorned 'nearly everything at the event, from the podium, to the registration desk, to the official program'. Consequently, 'It's not surprising that many think it's an official government event', with guests assuring the reporter, 'It's the government leaders who invited everyone. It's owned by Congress'. The event's official host, according to the *LA Times*, was 'an informal . . . committee, made up of members of the House and Senate who meet once a week in small prayer groups', who also took responsibility for the event's program. Coe explicitly denied Family involvement.

The *LA Times* found a different story, though, in the Family's archived private papers and tax records where it claimed, for example, to have spent $US742 604 on the 2000 National Prayer Breakfast. Overall, the *LA Times* estimated the organisation's annual budget at around US$10 million, mostly disbursed on 'salaries, the National Prayer Breakfast, travel for Coe, members of Congress and others, upkeep of Cedars [the Family's Virginia home base] and a roster of Christian groups worldwide'.[7]

According to Jeffrey Sharlet, who spent some weeks at Ivanwald, the Family's training house in Arlington, Virginia, uncovering the Family's structure is 'sort of like peeling an onion'. Close to the inner circle are 'Friends of the Family', further in are 'Members of the Family', and Sharlet found even 'further levels'. The group's documents talk about a 'core', and provide for 'different levels of information, depending on how close you are to the core'. Many of the organisation's activities draw in people who do not realise what they might sniff beneath the outer layers:

> Certainly going to the National Prayer Breakfast doesn't mean anything. And at the same time you could be going to prayer groups once a week with congressmen and it's still a pretty benign thing. It is nothing more than this group of guys not talking about politics but about religion and what they can learn from Scriptures, and that's kind of admirable [to be doing that]. That's most people's level of involvement.[8]

That many participants are unaware of the rest of the onion is no problem:

> That's how they do it, to keep an access to power. They [would] much rather have a powerful person [peripherally] involved than having down-the-line true believers. And that's what makes them more sophisticated than the Christian Coalition . . . you have to sign on with the [Christian Coalition] program 100 percent. [In] this group, it's OK if you

believe something different, because we have access to you now.[9]

The Family uses its access for what George Bush Sr called, at the 1990 Prayer Breakfast, Doug Coe's 'quiet diplomacy, I wouldn't say secret diplomacy'. A strong Family tradition is denial of its own existence, a strategy belied by, among other things, its extensive archives, stored at the Billy Graham Centre at Wheaton College, Illinois. Coe justified the secrecy policy by Jesus' injunction to do good in secret.[10] But the Family's 'quiet diplomacy' produces more than bagels and prayer with the president.

In 1955, the Family's diplomatic goal was a 'worldwide spiritual offensive' against the Soviet Union. A first step was financing the propaganda film *Militant Liberty* for the Defense Department to use to bolster anti-communist opinion abroad.[11] Over the years, the Family has facilitated behind-the-scenes meetings of world leaders to resolve diplomatic impasses. For example, the group claims credit for the deadlock-breaking meetings between the presidents of Congo and Rwanda, and between those of Somalia and Kenya, in each case opening the possibility of peace negotiations between the warring countries.[12] The meetings on the Cedars' salmon-toned lounges did more than pave the way for peace.

In June 2003, Kenya held its own National Prayer Breakfast, with the announcement that it would become an annual event. The Nairobi breakfasters heard religious leaders and politicians give thanks for the country's new government, peaceful transition and stability. The Nigerian President Yakubu Gowan, who had hosted his own country's first National Prayer Breakfast the preceding year, proposed that similar prayer sessions could help other African countries solve their problems: 'God raises the nation that seeks his face'.[13] Some took the hint: Zambia had its first National Prayer Breakfast in May 2004, with the distinctively American slogan, 'A Time for Prayer . . . One Nation

Under God'. The event was 'approved' by the president and organised by Church of God Bishop John Mambo. The Church of God's news service noted that the bishop had refused a government budget for the event, preferring to rely 'on donations from Christian well-wishers'.[14]

Jeffrey Sharlet lists some others embraced by the Family's quiet 'faith-based diplomacy':

> During the 1960s the Family forged relationships between the U.S. government and some of the most anti-Communist (and dictatorial) elements within Africa's postcolonial leadership. The Brazilian dictator General Costa e Silva, with Family support, was overseeing regular fellowship groups for Latin American leaders, while, in Indonesia, General Suharto (whose tally of several hundred thousand 'Communists' killed marks him as one of the century's most murderous dictators) was presiding over a group of fifty Indonesian legislators. During the Reagan Administration the Family helped build friendships between the U.S. government and men such as Salvadoran general Carlos Eugenios Vides Casanova, convicted by a Florida jury of the torture of thousands, and Honduran general Gustavo Alvarez Martinez, himself an evangelical minister, who was linked to both the CIA and death squads before his own demise.[15]

The Family describes itself as an 'invisible' organisation, its members encouraged not to talk about it or their involvement. It retains Vereide's vision of reaching the powerful and, declaring God's covenant with the Jews broken, identifies its converts as the new 'chosen people'.

Being chosen has ramifications many political leaders might covet. Sharlet quotes leader-in-waiting David Coe explaining to a group of Family trainees the significance of the Biblical figure of King David: 'Here's this guy who slept with another man's wife—Bathsheba, right?—and then basically murders her husband. And this guy is one of our heroes . . . God *likes* this guy!'[16]

Actually, in the Biblical account, God does not like David unconditionally: David is forced to admit after the Bathsheba episode, 'I have sinned against the Lord', and is told by the prophet Nathan that because he has repented, 'The Lord will forgive you; you will not die. But because you have shown such contempt for the Lord in doing this, your child will die'.[17] The story is usually taken to show that those in power have both temptation and means for great sin, and so need repentance and forgiveness at least as much as the rest of us. But Coe had a unique slant. Because David had been 'chosen', Coe explained to Sharlet and his fellow residents, his crimes were secondary to his mission. Coe elaborated by turning to one of the residents: 'Beau, let's say I hear you raped three little girls. And now here you are at Ivanwald. What would I think of you, Beau?' According to Sharlet, when Beau responded 'Probably that I'm pretty bad?' Coe reassured him:

> No, Beau. I wouldn't. Because I'm not here to judge you. That's not my job . . . We elect our leaders. Jesus elects his . . . If you're a person known to be around Jesus, you can go and do anything. And that's who you guys are. When you leave here, you're not only going to know the value of Jesus, you're going to know the people who rule the world.[18]

People who know the people who rule the world join 'core groups' or 'cells', defined in Family documents as 'a publicly invisible but privately identifiable group of companions', modelled on communist, mafia and Marine Corps cells. 'Hitler, Lenin and many others understood the power of a small core of people', Sharlet quotes from Family documents. Compared to other church–business networks, Sharlet concluded, the Family:

> is a lot more militaristic . . . We would be told time and time again, 'Christ's kingdom is not a democracy'. That is their model for leadership. They would often say, 'Everything you

> need to know about government is right there in the cross—it's vertical, not horizontal.'[19]

The Family's leaders, according to Sharlet, 'consider democracy a manifestation of ungodly pride' because the people, rather than God, are in charge.[20]

The Family's political ideology shares much with the movement known as 'Dominionism', associated with, for example, the televangelical empire of one-time US presidential aspirant and Christian Coalition President Pat Robertson. Dominionism argues that the way to national salvation is for 'chosen' Christians to occupy all public offices. As Robertson put it, 'God's plan is for his people . . . to take dominion . . . to reign and rule . . . We are not going to stand for those coercive utopians in the Supreme Court and in Washington ruling over us any more'.[21] The most extreme end of the Dominionist spectrum is a movement known as 'Christian Reconstructionism', based on the writings of Rousas J. Rushdoony and Gary North.

Their rationale is simple: God's law is higher than mere human law, so human law should emulate God's. God's law is revealed in the Bible, so the Bible is the charter for modern lawmakers. Not all of the Bible, though—compassion, forgiveness and equality are downplayed in favour of the more authoritarian passages. Far from freeing his followers from the detail of Moses' law, the Reconstructionists' Jesus came 'not to change the law, but to fulfil it'.[22]

Consequently, the Reconstructionist program involves legislating every detail of what its proponents consider to be Biblical law, including capital punishment, possibly by stoning, for a long list of crimes, including adultery, homosexuality, effeminacy, blasphemy, abortion and being an incorrigibly rebellious child. While acknowledging that full implementation will come only gradually, the transition starts now. A crucial step for Dominionists, including Reconstructionists, is restraining the power of the courts, both through legislative assaults on 'judicial activism' and by stacking the judiciary with sympathetic judges. The outcome would be what Robertson began proposing on air from the mid-1980s: Congress could tell the Supreme Court, 'There are whole classes of cases you can't hear, and no one can do anything about it!' Consequently, Congress would no longer be restrained by the traditional 'checks and balances' of America's three-armed system of government.[23]

That is the potential effect of the *Constitution Restoration Act*, drafted by Herb Titus, a Robertson affiliate and regular guest on Robertson's TV show, *700 Club*. Introduced into both houses of Congress on 11 February 2004, the proposed Act removes from Supreme Court review:

> Any matter to the extent that relief is sought against an element of Federal, State or local government, or against an officer of Federal, State or local government (whether or not acting in official personal capacity), by reason of that element's or officer's acknowledgement of God as the sovereign source of law, liberty or government.[24]

In simple terms, an official who makes a ruling on religious grounds (because God is the source of law) could not be challenged.

Though considered from the outset unlikely to pass, the Act has considerable symbolic significance, presented by many conservatives during 2004 as 'the most important item on the conservative agenda . . . significantly more important than who wins the White House this November'.[25] One commentator, comparing the Act with the Bush administration's draft constitution for Iraq, observed, 'If the Act passes, Iraqis would have stronger protection from religious extremism than Americans'.[26]

Dominionism combines the more extreme aspirations of Main Street and Wall Street. As its most strident end, Reconstructionism invokes Mosaic law, not merely to control but, ultimately, to eliminate violators of conservative values. At the same time, its limitation of the state's functions to those described as existing under Moses means that social welfare, state-funded health and education and, indeed, any government activity beyond the maintenance of law and order and defence, would be illegitimate.[27] (Strict Reconstructionists even oppose prisons, since there were none in Moses' day; instead, petty wrongdoers are to be reformed by being sold into slavery for a specified period, while more severe criminals are executed.)[28]

Although the movement occupies one end of the theological fringe, it has considerable mainstream influence. Billy Graham's biographer and respected scholar of the US religious right, William Martin, observes:

> Because [Reconstructionism] is so genuinely radical, most leaders of the Religious Right are careful to distance themselves from it. At the same time, it clearly holds some appeal for many of them. One undoubtedly spoke for others when he confessed, 'Though we hide their books under the bed, we read them just the same'.[29]

While self-identified Reconstructionists remain relatively few, many more mainstream evangelical leaders also endorse Reconstructionist books, invite the authors on to their TV shows and accept some aspects of the position. As one put it:

> A lot of us are coming to realize that the Bible is God's standard of morality . . . in all points of history . . . and for all societies, Christian and non-Christian alike . . . it so happens that Rushdoony, Bahnsen, and North [self-described Reconstructionist authors] understood that sooner . . . There are a lot of us floating around in Christian leadership who don't go all the way with the theonomy thing, but who want to rebuild America based on the Bible.[30]

It has attracted a substantial literature, both for and against.[31] The attractions of Reconstructionism are those of fundamentalism, extended into the political arena, providing apparently straightforward, secure answers in an uncertain world. It justifies its authoritarianism in the face of liberal demands for tolerance and pluralism (or 'moral relativism', as the Christian right often calls it).

The Christian right is training leaders. Pat Robertson's private college is significantly named Regent University—regents being those who rule in place of the monarch, awaiting his return. A small, new university especially for home-schooled teenagers, Patrick Henry College, aims to produce young men and women 'who will lead our nation and shape our culture with timeless biblical values'. College President Michael Farris reports that 'the most common thing I hear is parents telling me that they want their kids to be on the Supreme Court'. They have good reasons for optimism: when still only four years old and with a student body of just 240, the college boasted seven of the White House's 2004 crop of 100 interns. As well, students have been placed in the office of Bush's chief political advisor Karl Rove, with the Bush–Cheney re-election campaign and even with the Coalition Provisional Authority in Baghdad.[32]

Members of the Bush administration associated with Dominionism include former Attorney General John Ashcroft and, Reconstructionists believe, Bush, who pledged on 14 September 2001 to 'rid the world of evil'.[33] Bush does meet—and apparently follows advice from—self-described theocrats, such as a May 2004 Apostolic delegation opposing US support for Israeli withdrawal from Gaza on the grounds that, until Israel is a single nation with a rebuilt temple, Jesus cannot return.[34] Another with Reconstructionist resonances is Supreme Court Justice Antonin Scalia. He set out his views of the divine basis of the American state in a 2002 article, 'God's Justice and Ours', in the conservative Christian magazine *First Things*. He discerned a Western consensus, going back to St Paul, that government is God's authorised 'minister'. As such, government has both the power and the right to deliver divine judgement, including 'the sword' or death penalty. He contended that the ancient consensus has suffered a modern 'upset'—democracy. The death penalty's legitimacy only came into question, he argues, with democracy's 'tendency . . . to obscure the divine authority behind government'.

Scalia also has an unusual view of the American Constitution. He advocated reading it as 'not living but dead—or, as I prefer to put it, enduring', which means taking the framers' intentions as its definitive interpretation. Since the death penalty was not only regarded by the framers as legitimate but, in their day, applied to a much wider range of offences than now (Scalia gave the example of horse theft), it may, one day, be restored to commonplace.[35]

More generally, Reconstructionism offers a philosophical framework within which even non-Reconstructionists can find a justification for the Wall Street–Main Street blend—the combination of economic liberalism and social conservatism that I have called, in its Australian manifestation, Manildra Street. The problem for a Main Street–Wall Street junction has always been the role of the state. Both sides agree that the state's job is to promote human flourishing; they disagree about how.

Wall Street purists think it is best achieved by government providing minimal services (such as defence and law and order) to allow private enterprise to blossom, but keeping out of economic regulation and allowing maximum individual and business autonomy. Though their view involves a drastically limited state, they nevertheless maintain that human flourishing is the goal, and the state best furthers it by keeping out of the way.

Main Street purists think the state has a bigger role, since the human tendency to sin means that, left to ourselves, we are unlikely to find the path to happiness. Consequently, on Main Street the state has responsibilities both in regulating the world in which economic transactions take place, and also in regulating individual behaviour—for example, enforcing the model of domestic life Main Street residents regard as most conducive to human well-being and scapegoating many otherwise inoffensive alternatives.

Reconstructionists take a bold, new look at the question and conclude that both are wrong: the state has nothing to do with human well-being. That is up to God. If God favours you, you will be rich. If you are not rich, it means God has not favoured you, no doubt for a good reason. It is not up to the state to make you well off, comfortable or financially secure. The state's job is to ensure that those who do not choose a godly life are at least compelled to observe its externalities, making society completely unthreatening for those who do. The 'chosen' get to live entirely unfettered by government, whose role is limited to restraining sinners.

A key element of Reconstructionism is belief in Jesus' literal second coming. Human government is a mere stop-gap until then; and the signs, especially in the Middle East, are promising.[36] Even to those who don't share the apocalyptic expectations which underpin Reconstructionism proper, its breakthrough is to absolve the state of responsibility for human well-being—in any form. It does so not by saying that human well-being doesn't matter, but that it is all taken care of elsewhere.

•

Few Australian religious right figures publicly describe themselves as Reconstructionists. But Reconstructionist and Dominionist ideas find their way into speeches and endorsements from those who would not necessarily consider themselves part of the movement. For example, Reconstructionist themes blend into Galatians Group reports. Galatians co-founder and former Western Mining executive Ray Evans offered the group's 1998 conference a paper called 'Gnosticism and the High Court of Australia'.[37] Gnosticism is the ancient belief, heretical to Christians, that nature is evil, the world to be shunned, and believers distinguished by their divine spark of secret knowledge ('gnosis'). Evans drew a circuitous argument, based in a curious history of Christian doctrine, to suggest that Australian politics and law had stumbled into doctrinal error. Labor Prime Minister Bob Hawke's 1991 decision to stop mining at Coronation Hill on the grounds that it would desecrate sites sacred to the Jawoyn Dreaming figure Bula was, according to Evans, one indication of Gnostic heresy triumphant over Christian orthodoxy. The High Court's Mabo judgment was similarly illegitimate because it enshrined in law a 'Gnostic' rejection of Christian doctrinal supremacy.

I first came across a version of the essay in *Quadrant*, and was baffled. Was the Australian right's *eminence noir* really thinking that denouncing the High Court for heresy would bring activist judges under control? It was only after reading the Galatians Group presentation that I recognised echoes of Reconstructionist political theology. Adapting a line from an anecdote about Disraeli, Evans invited his Galatians Group audience to 'fix our cold gaze on the High Court' and remind the judges that their jobs depended on the dominance of Christian orthodoxy over rival belief systems: '"Pray, Your Honours, remember this—no Christianity; no Western civilization; no rule of law; no democracy; no High Court."'[38] In other words, without Christianity as its underlying presupposition, Western civilisation and all it contains, including the High Court, crumbles. High Court judges therefore have a responsibility to maintain the true faith and shun heresy.

Evans's thought intersects with other parts of the Reconstructionist program, such as abolishing minimum wages and labour regulation and abolishing or drastically reducing government welfare by replacing it with 'private and local charity', with 'family as the primary answer to the problems of misfortune, tragedy or indigence'. These are, of course, flagship agenda items in the economic forums with which Evans is most usually associated, and he has enunciated them at many an H.R. Nicholls and Mont Pelerin meeting. Christian audiences, however, hear a specifically theological version[39]—and it is the theology of Reconstructionism and its relations, such as the Family's view of the divine right of the 'chosen', within which the apparently contradictory Wall Street and Main Street agendas become coherent.

Given the influence which Evans, Morgan and their various think tank and lobby group offspring have enjoyed in the Manildra Street transformation of the Australian right, we should not be surprised to hear Reconstructionist-like themes emerging in Howard's political argot. But there are also other Reconstructionist influences in Canberra.

•

Since 1968, Australia's parliament has been home to the determinedly bipartisan and apolitical Parliamentary Christian Fellowship, formed by Labor's Gill Duthie and the Liberals' Merv Lee. It meets on Wednesday mornings during sitting weeks for breakfast and a speaker. Any given event can draw an unpredictable proportion of its total membership, estimated at around sixty in recent years. It also hosts an annual church service for the opening of parliament. Duthie's memoirs recount:

> The Government officially recognised the fellowship as an integral part of the Parliament and took over the cost of printing our orders of service and invitation cards. The President of the Senate and the Speaker gave it their full blessing.[40]

And so it continued for nearly two decades, startling nobody.

In 1986, that year's Parliamentary Christian Fellowship president, Liberal Member for Berowra Harry Edwards, announced a new, more evangelical dimension. Affixed to the opening of parliament service, there would henceforth be a National Prayer Breakfast designed, in Edwards's words, 'to reach out to the "unchurched" among Senators and Members and in all walks of life and from all parts of the country', to 'encourage Australians to recognise their privileges and responsibilities before God'.[41] The Family's US National Prayer Breakfast template had arrived in Australia.

In fact, 'Breakfast' scarcely does justice to a program beginning with evening events and concluding with lunch the following day. For example, on the first Sunday in November 2003, five hundred or so gathered in the Parliament House Great Hall for an inter-denominational evening worship service. They were back at 7.15 a.m. the next day to hear the Governor-General, Major General Michael Jeffery, talk about his faith over breakfast. With that came Bible readings from Prime Minister John Howard (Psalm 67, a harvest thanksgiving), Opposition Leader Simon Crean (Romans 12:9–21, exhorting believers to work hard, love one another and share with the needy) and Vanuatuan Prime Minister Edward Natapei (Matthew 6:19–27, part of the Sermon on the Mount warning, among other things, against storing up possessions or letting money become a god). Interspersed were prayers by Liberal Member for Menzies Kevin Andrews, Air Marshall Angus Houston and Sydney university student Kate Barnett.

A choice of seminar groups followed. The list of instructors suggests breakfasters would have heard a consistent theological message. A session on 'Leadership' was given by Jock Cameron, whom the program did not identify any further but who is a central figure in Prayer Breakfast networks internationally, and whom we meet in more detail shortly. On 'Nation Building', participants could hear Speaker of the Papua New Guinea Parliament Bernard Narokobi, together with former theocratic coup leader and president, described modestly in the program as Sitiveni Rabuka of Fiji. 'Faith in Media' was led by Mark Scott, identified in the program as *Sydney Morning Herald* editor-in-chief. 'Business' was given by someone identified only as Andrew Tyndale.

Tyndale, it turns out, is director and partner of Babcock & Brown international investment bank, with responsibility for corporate finance, focusing on acquisitions, leverage investments and public company takeovers. He is also a colleague of Mark Scott's—not at Fairfax, but as a lecturer at PathFinders evening business course. There, they and fifteen other lecturers associated with Oxford Falls Christian City Church bring students a 'Biblical framework for success, prosperity and business management'. Founder and Senior Minister, Pastor Phil Pringle, introduces PathFinders: 'God's will is that we are successful and prosperous in whatever we do'. He advises prospective students that 'There are fundamental Biblical principles that will determine the success or otherwise of any business venture'. For $450, the course offers modules on Marketing, Accounting and Finance, and Business Management, all designed to provide 'an overview of the key business and management principles with a Christian Context'.

Christian City Church began as twelve people in the Dee Why surf club on Sydney's northern beaches in 1980, but is now the founding member of an international denomination with over thirty churches, preaching a 'prosperity gospel' of worldly success. Lyons Forum strategist and Hillsong congregant Alan Cadman visits occasionally, and regularly invites Pringle to Canberra.[42] Prime Minister Howard officially opened the Oxford Falls premises in 1999.

'Prosperity gospel' theology is the idea that wealth and worldly success are signs of God's favour. Mainstream churches regard it with suspicion, for the obvious reasons: if God wills us to be prosperous, Jesus failed spectacularly—a homeless itinerant, dependent on charity. Moreover, the ethos of prosperity promoted by Pringle and his chain ('We want to have success, really nice lives', he told a *Bulletin* journalist in 2000)[43] seems to directly contradict such instructions of Jesus as 'sell all your belongings and give the money to the poor',[44] warnings that 'it is much harder for a rich person to enter the Kingdom of God than for a camel to go through the eye of a needle'[45] and advice to his followers to renounce acquisitiveness, emulating instead the unburdened existence of birds and wildflowers.[46] Yet Christianity is now by far the most numerically successful world religion, with Pentecostal churches in Africa, Asia and Latin America its biggest growth story. Though such churches' political effects are by no means uniform (for example, evangelical and Pentecostal votes helped secure Brazil's socialist presidency in 2002), Christianity's sheer weight of numbers is due, in no small part, to the potent combination of aggressive sales techniques where business and church go hand in hand. Only a small number of national governments, including Israel, have adopted policies to regulate Christian proselytising.

'Prosperity gospel' theology also sits comfortably with Reconstructionist themes, for example in its conviction that those who succeed are favoured by God and those who don't, aren't. Perhaps because financial success and power tend to go together, it is also often associated with the idea that Christians should try to infiltrate influential institutions. For example, after Pastor of Orange Baptist Church Reverend Robert Griffith met Fairfax editor-in-chief Mark Scott, he enthused that he had found 'yet another of God's secret agents . . . trying to bring the light and life of Jesus into one of the most hostile parts of our society [the media]' as part of the process in which God 'infiltrates every industry, every organisation, every government, every business and every neighbourhood'.[47]

Prayer Breakfasting in the seat of power can have profound effects. Here is what happened to Robert Griffith when he attended the 2001 Prayer Breakfast representing the National Board of Christian Parent-Controlled Schools. While participating in worship in the Great Hall, led by then Liberal MP for Parramatta Ross Cameron ('more like a Pastor than a Politician', according to Griffith), he became overwhelmed by the sense that:

> This was God's agenda—that this was His plan—to bring more and more of His people into the Parliament so that one day, this would be a normal and common event—worship in the Great Hall—rather than just a special occasion . . . I realised on that Sunday night, standing in [the] seat of

> power in this land, that God's agenda is far greater than I ever dreamed. He is calling His people into leadership positions right across our nation . . . He is raising up men and women into leadership in Government . . . As I looked around that magnificent building that night, I sensed the Lord saying very clearly, 'This is my house and I will be worshipped here too, every day—do you believe me?' . . . God wants to saturate and permeate every human institution we can.[48]

During the Breakfast's two days Griffith was repeatedly asked, by different people, to consider entering federal politics—'I began to think someone had stuck a sign on my back without me knowing it!' He felt personally addressed by a song, 'Whom Shall I Send?', about God's call to special kinds of service. In the 2004 election, Robert Griffith stood as the National Party candidate for Calare.[49] He did not lose his sense of divine calling, despite his opponent's massive fifty per cent margin. His tactics during the campaign included 'a combined churches prayer meeting every Sunday from 5 pm in the Blue Room (rear of the Baptist Church, Sale St, Orange)', and, on election eve, 'a combined churches worship from 7.30 pm. Everyone welcome as we lift our hearts and prayers to heaven in anticipation of God's mighty miracle the following day'. On election day itself, supporters were exhorted (via an email instructing, 'please keep this news to yourself') to join: 'continuous prayer all day. Bring your own lunch. Half a day in prayer and half on the voting booth. The battle is being fought in the media, through the letterboxes. But it will be won in prayer . . . Just praise God and pray for more miracles.'[50]

Numerous Christians on both sides of politics, including a number of clergy, have entered parliament with the intention of doing God's will. However, Griffith's inspiration went further than enacting Christian social principles in a pluralistic environment. His Prayer Breakfast revelation was shaped by an experience at the ecumenical service a fortnight earlier to commemorate the victims of the 11 September terror attacks. What others might have interpreted as good manners on the part of a multi-faith congregation and natural emotion in the face of tragedy, Griffith interpreted as an intimation of mass conversions:

> As I was waiting for the service to begin I read these words from Joshua 5:13–6:2: '. . . Then the Lord said to Joshua, "See, I have delivered Jericho into your hands, along with its king and its fighting men."' . . . I expected a 'politically correct' and user-friendly service so as not to offend many people who were of different faiths. Not so. The service was unapologetically Christian from beginning to end . . . Islamic Leaders, Mormons, Buddhists, Atheists and Christians all stood together and prayed the Lord's Prayer. People from every tribe and nation . . . People from every Political and religious faction imaginable stood together and prayed for Christ's kingdom to come and God's will to be done here in this nation and around the world as it is in heaven! . . . I looked in front of me and saw this Islamic leader weeping like a baby—under what I am convinced was the anointing of the Holy Spirit . . . Then this rare gathering of humanity stood and sang the Battle Hymn of the Republic. *Glory, Glory, Hallelujah, Our God is Marching On!* . . . It is a miracle and we are only just beginning to see what God is capable of.

What with that and the Prayer Breakfast, Griffith concluded, God 'challenged me to believe in a BIG God . . . a God who could restore righteousness and holiness and truth to the leadership of this entire nation'.[51]

•

Over the years, the Canberra Breakfast has attracted satellite events. In 2003, it was preceded by the Australian Christian Lobby's national conference, addressed by Howard lieutenant Tony Abbott. After that came the National Assembly of Christian Leaders (NACL) at Old Parliament House, where speakers included then Australian Broadcasting Authority chair Professor David Flint and Superintendent of Sydney's Wesley Mission, now Christian Democrat NSW Legislative Councillor, Reverend Dr Gordon Moyes. Those whose Sunday was not already fully committed could also squeeze in the NACL's National Strategy Summit.[52]

For many of the national Christian leaders, the Assembly and Summit would have provided the opportunity to catch up with old friends. Some, for example, would have recently met in Parliament House, at the National Prayer Council, voting unanimously in favour of a National Day of Thanksgiving to be held the next Pentecost weekend, 29 May 2004. Governor General Michael Jeffery made the official announcement, stating that the Pentecost Thanksgiving would become an annual event. He read out letters of endorsement from Prime Minister John Howard, and from Western Australian Indigenous elder Reverend Cedric Jacobs who, according to news reports, wanted the day to 'encourage the Indigenous people to rise up and thank their fellow Australians for coming to Australia'.[53] Like the Prayer Breakfast, the National Prayer Council was the focus for a cluster of activities, including a lunch for 300 people, hosted by Christian Democrat politician Gordon Moyes, with Sydney's ultra-conservative Anglican Archbishop Peter Jensen as the speaker.[54]

Prayer Breakfast events also continue through the year, and all over the place. For example, there are Australian practitioners of international Prayer Breakfast diplomacy. In 2000, Liberal Member for Cook Bruce Baird visited South Korea 'at the invitation of the Korean Ambassador and . . . sponsored by parliamentarians in Seoul' to 'coincide with . . . their annual prayer breakfast, which is sponsored by the Korean Parliament'. That trip also marked 'the first gathering of the World Parliamentary Christian Association', sponsored by South Korean President Kim Dae-Jung. Baird reported that the World Association has a Korean head, but Baird was one of five invited to be co-convenors, along with representatives from 'the United States, Canada and other South-East Asian Countries'.[55]

At an afternoon tea following the 2003 Canberra Breakfast, Australia's Governor-General, Major General Michael Jeffery, hailed 'the good work being done in the Asia Pacific—under the aegis of the Breakfast', which he traced back to 'the 1970s', well before the Australian Breakfast's 1986 launch. Back then, he recalled:

> An Australian delegation flying the Prayer Breakfast flag jumped on a small plane and visited a number of newly formed Pacific nations in order to meet with, and pray for, leaders of the region.

Presumably, at that time, the flag was of the American National Prayer Breakfast, since Australia's still lay in the future. Jeffery reported, 'These sorts of trips have taken place regularly since that time'. One, in March 2003, led by Bruce Baird and Liberal Member for Deakin Phillip Barresi, visited Indonesia 'in order to forge friendships with members of that country's parliament'. Dropping in on the world's most populous Muslim nation, they discussed 'a common belief in the value of faith' in an effort to 'improve understanding between our countries and address mutual misconceptions'. Two months later, the Governor-General added, breakfast diplomacy once more took off around the Pacific:

> The latest—led by Major General Rabuka and the Honourable Bernard Narokobi in May—covered six nations and involved meetings with Prime Ministers, Governors-General and other heads of government. The mission had two straightforward messages for regional leaders. The first was that God had a love and a concern for them, their nation and their people. The second message was that they were not alone in meeting the demands of leadership, and that they had friends close to home, in the region, that they could call on in time of need.[56]

Labor Member for Franklin Harry Quick described prayer breakfasts as 'a bit of a globetrotting circuit', beginning with Washington in February and ending with Canberra in October. Quick, who became president of the bipartisan Parliamentary Christian Fellowship in 1999, found the 1996 Washington breakfast 'bigger than Ben Hur . . . a Who's Who of American society', and refused subsequent invitations because he felt put off by the 'Bible-waving crowd'. Other breakfast-to-breakfast diplomats have included Queensland Liberal Member for Moncrieff Steve Ciobo and former Liberal Member for Parramatta Ross Cameron, often the source of other MPs' invitations for the trips. Funds have often come from Sydney millionaire construction magnate David Bussau, through his evangelism and development charity Maranatha Trust.[57] ('Maranatha' is the English rendering of an Aramaic expression meaning 'Come, Lord', used by the early Church praying for Jesus' imminent return and by modern Pentecostals looking forward to a literal second coming.)[58] In another Prayer Breakfast link, Bussau's Maranatha-supported evangelism and development charity Opportunity International made Australian Prayer Breakfast founder Harry Edwards its inaugural chair on his retirement from parliament. Ross Cameron's brother and former staffer, Jock, is also a serial breakfaster, for example, accompanying Christian Democrat Leader and then NSW Legislative Councillor Fred Nile to South Korea's 2001 National Prayer Breakfast, which also marked the founding of the Korea–Australia Christian Parliamentary Association, and the World Christian Parliamentary Association Dinner, where Jock gave an address.[59]

•

Australian members and senators wanting a more personal take on faith than they get at the Parliamentary Christian Fellowship attend an informal, low-profile group. They meet late on sitting Monday nights for prayer, Bible study and discussion. From 1996 until 2004, the venue was the office of its founder, Member for Parramatta Ross Cameron.[60] Participants differed as to how public the group's existence was meant to be. Some would discuss it only off the record. According to one member who was prepared to discuss the group, some are inclined to be 'very secretive and Masonic' about it. Labor regular, and Member for Griffith, Kevin Rudd described the group as 'people who are reasonably comfortable talking about issues of personal faith. The main aim is mutual support', he said.[61]

The Monday night group attracts varying numbers from a pool of between twenty-five and thirty, almost all from the Coalition side. Rudd described himself as 'probably the only Leftie there'. In the group's meetings, issues of personal faith and practice take over from politics. Nevertheless, Rudd agreed that the Monday night group's existence has a discernible effect on the parliament's processes:

> One of my Labor Party colleagues said to me, 'Kevin, never pray with the bastards, because if you do it makes it harder to hate 'em. And half of the business of this place is hating them, because we want their jobs.' And in part, the observation is right, because if you get to know these guys, they're just like me, flawed human beings. And while you will not resile from fundamental policy differences, because you know them and realise that they are, within their own paradigm, struggling in terms of their perception of truth and their perception of political praxis—albeit often restricted to questions of private morality—then you have some respect for them, as opposed to people who are not restrained by anything. So . . . you tend to have a greater respect for them. And does that have a political consequence? You're more likely to listen with some respect [when a group member is speaking from the opposite side of parliament].[62]

Not only do group members see themselves as more likely to listen to each other, but some even treat one another differently in the political rough and tumble. According to regular attender and Liberal Member for Hughes Danna Vale, mutual prayer cannot help but change the way political antagonists relate: 'Of course it does, that's human'.[63] Another rare Labor Monday-nighter, Harry Quick, recalled:

> There was an opportunity . . . where, rather than call the media out and do a television interview and heap it on Tony Abbott, I worked with him because of our Monday night thing, to try and get the result for my constituents, rather than point score. But a lot of my colleagues would say you're mad, because you've lost the opportunity to get your name in the paper or on TV . . . It worries the whips![64]

Participants speak of the Monday night group as a home-grown initiative, the personal offspring of the Cameron brothers. In fact, it stands in a longer tradition of informal prayer groups distinct from the Parliamentary Christian Fellowship—for example, a similar group was hosted, until his 1993 defeat, by Liberal Member for Macquarie Alasdair Webster (who, after losing his seat, resigned from the Liberal Party to join Fred Nile's Christian Democrats).[65] It also has international counterparts, usually associated with National Prayer Breakfasts, and often ultimately linked to the Family. For example, in addition to Congress, Family-linked groups meet in the Pentagon and various federal agencies, and in national parliaments around the world.[66] The groups have a number of features in common. All emphasise personal sharing and discourage explicitly political discussion, and all proceedings are strictly off the record. 'Servant leadership' is a common theme. Many of the groups seem to stress commitment to the group rather than membership of a local church, so that these Christian elite networks can become the members' main form of religious practice.

•

Since February 1997, a group of members and senators from all parties have hosted an annual gathering of students in Parliament House to explore leadership. At the 2003 event, as we saw in chapter seven, federal Treasurer Peter Costello warned impressionable students against the dangers of postmodern relativism and seemed to compare the Qur'an unfavourably with Christian values. As outlined in the letter of invitation to 1998 participants, sent out with the signature of Liberal Member for Bradfield and Parliamentary Secretary to the Minister for Defence Brendan Nelson, the National Student Leadership Forum on Faith and Values:

> Is not so much a 'how to' seminar about the technical aspects of leadership. Rather, it is an interactive forum to consider the spiritual values and faith perspectives which underpin effective leadership.[67]

Its content and format mirror a Washington program of the same name.

Washington's National Student Leadership Forum on Faith and Values, just like the US National Prayer Breakfast, presents publicly as an initiative of the Members of Congress while being discreetly sponsored and organised by the Family.[68] Like the Washington model, Australia's version seeks leadership values in 'the lives and ideas of leaders such as Jesus of Nazareth and MK Gandhi among others'.[69] Other 'servant leaders' whose ideas have been studied at past forums include German missionary Albert Schweitzer and Mother Teresa of Calcutta, along with the contrasting leadership styles of Adolf Hitler and Mao Zedong. (The latter two, in particular, Sharlet reports as being also frequently invoked by the Family as examples of leaders who, like Jesus, bind their followers in a 'covenant'.)

Australia's Forums are hosted by a cross-party group of members and senators, with a heavy weighting towards the House of Representatives and the Coalition parties.[70] Practical organisation has so far come largely out of the office of Ross Cameron, with much of the less public work done by his brother,

Jock.[71] In 2000, Ross Cameron described his brother as 'a full-time lay worker' spending two or three days out of every sitting week attached to the Member for Parramatta's office. When I asked whom Jock worked for, Ross replied, 'Well, effectively for me'. Jock seemed to have some of the status of a parliamentary staffer. For example, Jock's name, along with his brother's, was listed in the Parliament House internal phone directory. Other efforts to define Jock's role tend to be even vaguer, such as 'Just an average guy, doing the work of the Lord, supporting people in leadership throughout the Pacific area'.[72] The 1998 Forum, where he spoke on 'the Leadership Strategy of Jesus', introduced him as follows:

> Jock has a background in corporate marketing but a number of years ago decided to leave a promising career to devote his time to developing Australia's young people. His position has variously been described as a catalyst, consultant and motivator.

Trying to get behind the generalities, I asked Jock how he answered the 'what do you do?' question when, for example, meeting people at parties. He replied that he says 'different things to different people', depending on circumstances. Asked how his work is funded, he explained that he is supported by donations from business people.[73] As well as organising the National Student Leadership Forum, his responsibilities include the National Prayer Breakfast.[74]

According to Ross Cameron, the Leadership Forum's purpose is two-fold. On one hand, it facilitates an exchange of views between politicians and potential leaders. On the other hand, it plays an evangelising role within the parliament providing, like the Prayer Breakfast, a chance to reach the 'unchurched' in the chambers:

> It's as much a way of engaging the politicians as the students. It gives us a context to go and say, 'we're talking about faith

> and values, we're using the life of Jesus of Nazareth as a paradigm of leadership'. So, for example, Mark Latham comes. He's an atheist, but he's happy to see Jesus as a paradigm of leadership.[75]

Sure enough, several Latham profiles have referred to his 'fascination' with the historical figure of Jesus, whom he sees as a 'great leader' and an 'incredibly charismatic and inspiring person'.[76]

At times, the Cameron brothers' associations have proved controversial. Out of their efforts to develop 'a network of Christian MPs in Australia, Fiji, the USA and around the Pacific',[77] they became friends with Fiji's then prime minister, Sitiveni Rabuka. He was a key-note speaker at the 1998 Forum, prompting questions in the House as to how appropriate a coup leader was as a leadership role model for Australian students.[78] As prime minister, Rabuka pushed for compulsory Sabbath observance and interpreted his coups as God's will.[79] Jock Cameron, to whom Rabuka has been 'a good friend for many years', responded to criticism of the invitation by saying that Rabuka's 'public image might be one thing, but when you get to know the person, when you get to see what's underneath, you find something totally different'.[80] Rabuka's assessment of his own political impact is shared by others interested in international Christian politicians' networks. For example, in a follow-up interview to his *Harper's* report on the Family, Jeffrey Sharlet recalled during his time at Ivanwald being 'shown a video about the island of Fiji and their leader . . . Well, this is how they [the Family] work, small country by small country. Fiji is now a theocracy. And they take credit for that'.[81]

Ross Cameron, whose 2004 confession of adultery rubbed some of the gloss from his earlier high profile encouraging Aussie men to commit to their women and couples to resist 'no-fault' divorce (see chapter four), embodies the Manildra Street blend of social conservatism and economic radicalism. His economic views are summed up in a theology of wealth, emphasising unrestrained competition and a minimal state:

> People are entitled to the fruits of their labour, so we need minimal taxation . . . Every impost on capital reduces the opportunities of those with the least, so we need to remove restraints on capital . . . At the deep inner core of the left is the belief that profit is morally wrong. But the two most offensive parables [for the left] are the talents [Matthew 25:14–30] and the labourers in the vineyard [Matthew 20:2–16] . . . I was giving a talk to secondary students a while ago, and one of them asked a question to the effect, 'Isn't it immoral that Company X posted Y billion dollars profit this year?' They were saying, 'Shouldn't there be a limit on profits?' That's the kind of thinking that Christ was challenging.

As to his general philosophical orientation:

> I'm on the right wing of the Liberal Party on most issues. My political view is about development of the human person. The heart of Christ was freedom—and freedom comes through having the confidence, skills and optimism to take control of your own life. The state is too often a short-circuiting mechanism in the development of the human person against the circumstances of the market . . . I want the least possible reliance of citizens on the state. I'm against the welfare state on humanitarian and religious grounds. The early church had welfare, but it was also tough—Paul said, 'Whoever does not work, does not eat' [2 Thessalonians 3:10].[82] I'd pretty much repudiate the concept of social justice, it does more harm than good . . . I visited an Aboriginal community five hundred kilometres west of Alice Springs—the dependency I saw there was produced by the strategy of social justice. I'd almost call it evil.[83]

Such views gel well with Costello's, expounded to the inaugural National Day of Thanksgiving, that, as a country founded on

Christian traditions, Australia needs less government intervention and a return to the Ten Commandments.

•

When Australia considered a new constitutional preamble, Howard began it: 'With hope in God'. You might well ask: Which God? God used to oppose greed, from the Hebrew prophets' blasting of those who 'sell into slavery honest men who cannot pay their debts, poor men who cannot repay even the price of a pair of sandals' and who 'trample down the weak and helpless, and push the poor out of the way',[84] to Jesus's warnings that one 'cannot serve both God and money'[85] and his throwing the money-changers from the temple.[86] But the growth of capitalism during recent times has made greed good, with its own God to bless it.

In 1944, economic historian Karl Polanyi wrote what he fondly imagined was a requiem for free market economics, laid to rest by the welfare state. Polanyi said that the competitive market system had 'a claim to universality unparalleled since the age when Christianity started on its career'.[87] In this system, 'The middle class fulfilled their function by developing an all but sacramental belief in the universal beneficence of profits'.[88] That meant that 'Economic liberalism . . . evolved into a veritable faith in man's secular salvation through a self-regulating market', while 'the liberal creed assumed its evangelical fervour only in response to the needs of a fully-deployed market economy'.[89] Interested mainly in economic history rather than religion, Polanyi stopped short of saying that the competitive market system *is* a religion.

Half a century later, Polanyi's circumspection sounded almost coy. By March 1999, American theologian Harvey Cox wrote in the *Atlantic Monthly* that 'Current thinking assigns to The Market a wisdom that in the past only the gods have known. It knows our deepest secrets and darkest desires'. It also controls our actions and demands unquestioning obedience, even when its prescriptions don't seem to be working—all 'Market' failures prove is that we don't believe hard enough. It only takes a few financial scandals, Cox noted, to show up the truth of St Paul's instruction that 'true faith is the evidence of things unseen'.[90]

The nineteenth-century philosopher of religion Ludwig Feuerbach argued that God is a projection: really a human creation. We unconsciously imagine God into a real thing of which human beings then become the objects. Marx borrowed and intensified Feuerbach's projection theory, calling religion the 'reversed world-consciousness' of a 'reversed world', in which we constantly mistake the real for the ideal, and vice versa. To him, religion was:

> the general theory of that world, its encyclopaedic compendium, its logic in a popular form, its spiritualistic *point d'honneur*, its enthusiasm, its moral sanction, its solemn completion, its universal ground for consolation and justification.[91]

Nowadays, those descriptions sound more in accord with The Market. Although it is a human creation, it acts on us daily—rising or falling, plunging or recovering. It has emotions—jittery, nervous, capricious, buoyant or confident. It requires sacrifices and promises rewards but, demanding propitiation, is nevertheless beyond complete human control or prediction. This jealous God demands single-minded loyalty and resents rival deities.

This God also demands a restructuring of the rhythms of social and family life. As just one example, industry groups such as the Business Council of Australia and the Confederation of Australian Industry have long lobbied for the abolition of weekends and holidays.[92] As Howard put it, launching his party's industrial relations policy back in 1992:

> If someone makes a capital investment in this country, they ought to be able to run that capital investment 24 hours a day, seven days a week, 365 days a year, without penalty.[93]

At the output end, this shift to a perpetual working week is signalled in the loss of penalty rates for working (what used to be) after-hours and weekends, while from the consumers' end extended shopping hours mean there is never a break from the duty to keep retail spending up. The removal of scheduled rest days which interfere with the ceaseless cycle of production and consumption is paralleled by the commercialisation of old, mainly religious, festivals, and the creation of new, marketing-based celebrations such as Father's Day. In place of love, this God makes competition the fundamental value. For The Market becomes the measure of everything. This new *laissez-faire* God has remarkable convergences with the Reconstructionist theocrat God that grants total freedom to believers and reserves its wrath for nonconformists.

Let's consider an early Howard example, his government's review of the *Affirmative Action (Equal Opportunity for Women) Act 1986*. The Act was assessed, not for its effectiveness in redressing inequality, but as part of a larger process of reviewing Australian legislation which might have an impact on business's 'competitiveness'. Submissions were invited to address an 'Issues Paper' in which greater equality did not feature as a desirable goal, having been overtaken by competition.[94] It either ignored any criterion by which legislation could be judged other than its effect on competitiveness, or assumed that both aims are served by the same legislation, without conflict. Competition in The Market had become just what Marx found in the religion of his own day: 'moral sanction . . . solemn completion, universal ground for consolation and justification'.

In 2003, when Labor breakfaster Harry Quick declared 'Bible-waving' fatigue and turned down his invitation to the South Korean National Prayer Breakfast, Ross Cameron found a last-minute replacement: Steven Ciobo, the Liberal Member for the Gold Coast seat of Moncreiff, previously held by the invincibly moderate Kathy Sullivan (who in chapter two denounced the Lyons Forum's attempts to co-opt the bipartisan Parliamentary

Christian Fellowship in its campaign against John Hewson). New MPs typically use their first speech to set out their foundational commitments. The more religious sometimes thank God for their election (or, as they usually put it, the 'opportunity to serve'). Ciobo outlined his belief in a higher power—'The foundation of my canvas and the pillar of my purpose is . . . a belief in the supremacy of the market'—and like many a new MP, he thanked his friends, his parents and his wife. He then attributed their mutual bonds to the faith holding them all together:

> The strength all of you have provided me I know flows from your belief in the philosophy of the Liberal Party, the belief in the sovereignty of the individual and their empowerment over the collective, in the responsibility every one of us has in a civil society, in the promotion of the family as the bedrock of any sustainable society and in the limited role for the state in wealth redistribution and market intervention.[95]

Ciobo's creed invokes The Market God, with the Liberal Party its community of faith. But the Market God cannot rule alone. It has proved too dynamic and unsettling. It sabotages family and community life and tears away safety nets. It has had to make Olympian room for another deity, one who brings 'Us' a renewed sense of the security the Market God took away. The repressive God of racism, authoritarian 'family values' and exclusion tries to make 'Us' feel secure by turning our anxieties upon 'Them', corralling Australian tolerance and generosity behind an unbreachable white picket fence. Main Street's God turns us in on ourselves, distracting us from the hard face on Wall Street. At their Manildra Street junction, the two join forces.

Like many in the Prayer Breakfast movement, Howard did not describe himself as a regular churchgoer, though he joined his wife Janette in identifing with Sydney's famously conservative Anglican diocese. (He refused and she did not reply to interview requests for this book.) Howard certainly never called himself a

Christian Reconstructionist—or, indeed, publicly expressed either interest in or knowledge of any particular school of theology. On the contrary, his few public comments about his religious practice suggest that the religion of his childhood has left a fairly amorphous and malleable residue. 'When I go, it tends to be to an Anglican church', he told ABC TV's *Compass* program in 1998, 'but it matters not to me. I would just as easily go to another Christian church, right across the religious spectrum . . . certainly within what I would call the Protestant-Catholic-Anglican traditions it wouldn't make any difference'.[96] But look at the themes he espoused—curbing 'judicial activism' and working to limit the reach of the courts,[97] trouncing 'political correctness', restoring (Christian) 'values', supporting segregated Christian schools aligned with Christianity's most conservative end, stomping on Indigenous religion, painting Muslims as a threat, joining invasions of Afghanistan and Iraq, enforcing a patriarchal, heterosexual family model, re-opening the debate on capital punishment (because 'people close to me' favour it) and, behind it all, a calm 'we know best' paternalistic authoritarianism. He appointed as Govenor-General first (controversially) an archbishop and then (almost unnoticed) a champion of the Prayer Breakfast 'quiet diplomacy' associated with a secretive, theocratic movement that sees democracy as 'a manifestation of ungodly pride'. Howard opened the 'prosperity gospel' Hillsong and Oxford Falls megachurches, the latter the Prayer Breakfast's supplier of Christian experts on leadership and financial success. His policies are the beneficiary of alleged fundamentalist Christian branch stacking and the purging of 'wets'. His achievements are much closer to the aspirations of fundamentalist theocrats than they are to the politically progressive Methodism of his childhood.

•

The last time I saw a stoning was in *Monty Python's Life of Brian*. The blasphemer, played by John Young, taunts his executioners by repeating his offence, louder and louder. When a stone-wielding

John Cleese reproves, 'You're only making it worse for yourself', the man retorts, 'Making it worse? How could it be worse!' and shouts the louder: 'Jehovah! Jehovah!'

The extremes of Christian Reconstructionism, in whose fantasies people would again be stoned for blasphemy, are a long way from Australian political realities. But the faith in which 'blessed are the poor' means 'blessed are the rich', and God's will means repressive social policy, maximum freedom for money and minimum freedom for people, is well and truly here. In God's name, old-fashioned religion has become a cloak for new-fashioned repression and inequality. Under Howard, the Manildra Street Gods have brought their church into the corridors of power.

To say these things is heresy. To denounce The Market God is today's blasphemy. To criticise bad religion brings down the wrath of those who, at other times, are the first to accuse their opponents of being 'values neutral', wishy-washy relativists. Blasphemers are not yet stoned; unlike the sinner in *Life of Brian*, things for us can still get a lot worse. But the worldwide 'Civil War of Values' announced by Focus on the Family's James Dobson in 1990 is being fought out in Australia.

Just as in the USA, it is often a guerrilla war. Its vanguard, like the Christian Coalition's Ralph Reed, metaphorically paint their faces and travel at night, hiding behind bland-sounding choruses and leadership slogans. Noticing and naming the guerrilla forces in Australia's 'Civil War of Values' is a first step to a response. Those who cherish Australia's democratic, egalitarian soul had better repeat heresies: loudly. Jehovah! Jehovah! Jehovah!

EPILOGUE

Reclaiming Australia's soul

Catching the Australian people in the theological act is not always easy, but theology went public at the 1998 Constitutional Convention. God was on the agenda, and the debate tells us a lot about God's public place in modern Australia. At the Convention, two theologies vied for constitutional recognition—one emphasising openness, welcome and generosity; the other, a nervous nation's authoritarian bulwark against perceived anarchy. Disentangling the two strands, we can discern from the Convention's theology some looming dangers and some helpful ways of conceiving the struggle for Australia's soul.

The Convention was held in Old Parliament House from 2 to 13 February 1998. Its main task was to determine a republican model to be put to a referendum. It also reviewed the constitutional Preamble. The existing (1901) Preamble begins:

> Whereas the people of New South Wales, Victoria, South Australia, Queensland, and Tasmania, humbly relying on the blessing of Almighty God, have agreed to unite in one indissoluble Federal Commonwealth . . .

The Convention decided there should be a new Preamble, affixed before the old one, which would remain intact. Despite Professor George Winterton's repeated warnings that to have two Preambles, both referring to Almighty God, 'would look ridiculous',[1] the Convention decided that the new Preamble should also contain 'reference to "Almighty God"'.[2]

Some delegates thought God's constitutional position precarious. Archbishop Peter Hollingworth, then Anglican Archbishop of Brisbane, detected 'a move to delete the God reference', a sense that 'people want it out' and even the idea that 'the reference to God is offensive'.[3] Former Australian Democrat Senator and Republican Karin Sowada revealed later that she and other likeminded Christian delegates had been 'all united' on the clause, and poised to act in its defence:

> Alerted by a recent vote of the Constitutional Centenary Foundation to have this reference deleted, a number of us were conscious of a possible attempt to repeat this at the Convention. Some informal networking prior to the ConCon [Constitutional Convention] ensured that intelligence was shared so we were ready for the debate, and prepared with the numbers to work whatever committees were established to investigate the matter.[4]

And work them they did.

When a subgroup was formed to consider the so-called 'recognition clause',[5] its eight members included two Archbishops (Pell and Hollingworth, both still destined for still greater things—Pell as Cardinal, Hollingworth as Governor-General), a Bishop (John Hepworth, of the fringe Anglican Catholic breakaway church), a Lay Preacher (and former Liberal Senator, Baden Teague), and a member of the Christian Democrats (and former federal Liberal and parliamentary prayer group convenor, Alasdair Webster).[6] Webster, particularly, had a strong background in defending the monarchy as divinely ordained. Accompanying him to the Convention as an advisor was Richard Eason, whose book *Playing God: The roots of the Republican grab for ultimate power* (with a foreword by Sir Joh Bjelke-Petersen) argued that a republic would improperly usurp God's power.

But when you read the Convention's *Transcript of Proceedings*, this formidable group seemed to have little cause for concern. Whoever was advocating God's removal must have done so behind the scenes, as on the record, God's inclusion was unanimous. If there was a problem, it was that the 'recognition clause' is too narrow: speakers wanted the Preamble to embrace more religion, not less. Even before the subgroup considering the recognition clause made its report, delegates seized all kinds of pretexts to declare themselves for God.

Religious doubts were no barrier. Business leader Janet Holmes à Court confessed:

> As a Christian who cannot take the step of believing in God and therefore is not allowed to be a Christian, I do not have difficulty with the words 'on the blessing of Almighty God'.[7]

NSW magistrate and University of New England Chancellor Dr Pat O'Shane professed herself 'probably the most committed atheist in the chamber'. Nevertheless: 'I happen to respect the spiritual and religious beliefs of my fellow Australians. I personally do not have any objection to the words being retained'.[8] She took heart from comments Hollingworth had made on the practice of prayer in parliament. Prayer, he had said, 'should be recognised as something which all people of good faith can engage in, however they define their understanding of God—if they can'.[9] O'Shane took that to mean that 'the word "God" is a generic term', which made the clause 'unexceptional'. Thus reassured, she could 'endorse the proposal to retain those words in the preamble'.[10] Hollingworth then thanked O'Shane 'for your leadership on this matter because that is the kind of spirit I think we want to embrace'. He spelled out:

> The word 'God' is to be understood in the generic sense as every man, woman and child understands him/her to be according to their own particular experience. I think that probably covers the issue.[11]

He contended that 'the term "God" . . . in the Hebrew simply means "I am" or "I will be what I will be"',[12] and added:

> In the term God . . . you really could not get a more simple, basic description of us as a people and what we might become in our unfolding destiny.[13]

One might expect that this 'generic' theology, whose main referent seemed to be a vague nationalism, would have provoked controversy. No such thing. Self-described conservative evangelical Karin Sowada found 'keeping God in the Constitution' to be 'an expression of our dependence on God as creator and sustainer of all things'. That, of course, is a far cry from 'a description of us as a people and what we might become in our unfolding destiny', but the difference did not stop her endorsing Archbishop Hollingworth's 'well-chosen words'.[14] Baden Teague, who describes himself as evangelical but not conservative, also welcomed the 'generic' God even though, as he later clarified, 'by God, *I* mean the God worshipped in Australian churches'.[15] Others, without identifying themselves with any religious orientation, told the Convention that the 'generic' theology had quieted reservations they might otherwise have felt about a modern recognition clause.[16]

If delegates had a quibble, it was that 'God' did not go far enough. Janet Holmes à Court asked:

> I wonder . . . how Buddhists, Muslims, Aboriginal people and so on feel about having that. I do not want to take that

> [recognition clause] out, but is it possible that some extra phrase could go in which is more inclusive?[17]

By linking multicultural concerns to her own agnostic support for God early in the debate, she made interfaith sensitivity central. Any potential problem arose not from the lack of religious conviction, but from belief in some other kind of divinity.

Real Republican delegate Moira Rayner chaired one of the other Preamble-related subgroups. Its report to the Convention floor made an early pitch on the God question:

> We referred specifically . . . to the recognition of the spiritual wealth of people . . . you have all heard a number of statements of personal faith about this afternoon . . . for the vast majority of Australians, we have a spiritual commitment which we reflect in many different ways and which in its own wealth and diversity is part of our treasury of the nation.[18]

And so it went on.

The Convention's call was not for less preambular religion, but for more. No one wanted to expunge 'Almighty God', still less to abolish any kind of recognition clause, but some wanted to widen the clause's embrace.[19] In fact, the Convention's only sustained critique of God's inclusion came from Hollingworth himself. After raising, and rejecting, the objection about multicultural sensitivities, Hollingworth conceded:

> A small minority of non-believers believe—with some good reason, I concede, from past experience—that religion is a divisive force and they would want to remove the reference in the preamble and make Australia a strictly secular republic without any reference to the Divinity.[20]

However, he contended, the recognition clause, understood in the proper, 'generic' spirit, can 'unite all the citizen subjects of this nation'.[21]

In the end, the Resolutions Group proposed that a new Preamble should contain 'reference to "Almighty God"'. The Convention agreed without debate.[22] In the widely quoted quip attributed to Convention chair Barry Jones, 'God had a good convention'. For God, it was second time lucky.

At the 1890s Constitutional Conventions, the deity had had a much more difficult time. The recognition clause was hotly debated. While some delegates thought it was just what Australia needed to counteract cynicism, commercialism and moral decay,[23] others worried that its inclusion would open a back door to religious establishment, either by allowing future activist courts to make one religion official, or by less far-reaching measures such as making religious belief a qualification for holding public office. By the 1990s, the days when belief in a 'Supreme Being and a future state' was a necessary qualification for giving evidence in court (as it remained well into the nineteenth century in Australia)[24] or taking a seat in parliament (until 1888 in England)[25] and when only Anglican communicants could take university degrees, hold public offices or be legally married[26] had well and truly faded from public memory. The separation of church and state which so exercised the founders was assumed by the Canberra convention-goers as settled; no one suggested that 'recognising' God would lead to religiously discriminatory constitutional interpretations. Instead, debates suggested the recognition clause could reflect the nation's hopes or memories of faith, as in Holmes à Court's wistful self-description as 'a Christian who cannot take the step of believing in God and therefore is not allowed to be a Christian'. There were overtones of grief for lost certainties. In a modern version of the New Testament cry, 'Lord, I believe; help my unbelief',[27] some of 1998 enthusiasm for God might be paraphrased, 'I can no longer believe; I ask the nation to do that for me'. The recognition clause had become a collective statement whose virtue is the spiritual benefit it gives to individuals.

•

Debating a republic, we might expect the classical republican theme of the mutual independence of church and state to come to the fore. Not only did it not do so, but the 1998 Convention accepted, with apparent equanimity, a view which ran against at least three centuries of republican thought. The Hollingworth group's report successfully legitimated a hierarchical view of political authority with God at the top: 'the Divinity as the source of all power'. This belief was then incorporated into the wording of the successful motion. As Australians for a Constitutional Monarchy delegate Geoff Hourn put it, God was needed to keep elected representatives in their place:

> Obviously, many deities have graced the floors of this chamber. The key thing here is that the reference is to the 'Almighty God', and that is important to keep in mind.[28]

The point was picked up by Sowada's argument that the recognition clause expresses 'our dependence on God . . . as the one under whom all authority is established'. She argued:

> Keeping God in our Constitution is ultimately an expression of the fact that those who govern us are accountable for their actions to someone other than themselves.[29]

Sowada attended the Convention as an Australian Republican Movement delegate, which, together with her other political credential as a former Australian Democrat Senator, might be taken to indicate a strong commitment to popular sovereignty. In fact, as she revealed in a different forum, she regarded the choice of governmental system as less important than other factors. Noting that the Bible offers 'no particular support' for democracy, 'though the concept was well developed by the time of the New Testament', she concluded: 'It is impossible to find a basis to support one system of government over another anywhere in the Bible'. She acknowledged 'It can be argued that in our times, democratic systems of government are *the* most desirable from a Christian point of view', her rationale being 'they generally allow people wide religious freedoms, including the ability to openly and freely proclaim the gospel without fear of sanctions or death'. On the other hand, while democracy had benefits for evangelically minded Christians, what mattered most was that:

> the nature of good government, under whatever particular system, is rooted in the very character of God. God is fundamentally a God of order and peace, stability, fairness, compassion, mercy and justice—and the list could go on. For us as Christians, this is the litmus test. These qualities—humility, truth, loving justice and a desire to champion the destitute—these are the Biblical qualities of good leadership and government . . . We should support systems of government prepared to identify right and wrong, upholding those who do good and punishing those who do evil, without fear or favour.

Consequently, she was prepared to contemplate alternatives to democracy, given the right conditions.

> As Christians, how would we feel about a system of government where there was no parliament, no free elections, but where the country was ruled by a godly Christian monarch or dictator, the champion of truth, leading and yet serving the people with Christ-like humility, ruling justly and dedicated to obeying God?[30]

Sowada's picture might be attractive to a few Christians, but replacing democracy with theocracy would surely strike a chill into many other hearts. It is also not as Biblically uncontroversial as Sowada suggests. While the Bible does not endorse a particular form of government, it does have a consistently dubious view of human perfectibility: 'all have sinned, and all have fallen short of the glory of God' (Romans 3:23). Where would we find the ruler who could be trusted to keep a Christ-like humility once handed total power? The Bible inclines to Lord Acton's view about power's corrosive tendencies. Though the people of Israel eventually persuaded God, reluctantly, to let them have a king (1 Samuel 10–12), and the kings were divinely appointed (1 Samuel 15:1), they still had to be held in check. There was a special order of people, the prophets, whose job, like Nathan upbraiding David for the Bathsheba incident, was to speak the truth to power, however uncomfortable (2 Samuel 12: 1–23; Ezekiel 3:17–21; 2 Chronicles 36:11–15). Given the dangers of the role, it is not surprising that there were also charlatan prophets who, for a fee, would tell the powerful what they wanted to hear. Such complacency always led to trouble (Micah 3: 5–12). You can tell real prophets, who bring a reliable message from God, because they tell uncomfortable truths, often at considerable personal risk (Amos 7:10–17).

Whether or not they went as far as Sowada's willingness to entertain a virtuous Christian theocracy, some other speakers at the Constitutional Convention wanted God at the apex of the political structure, so as to keep politicians in check. Teague found that reason for including God to be 'very good, very Australian'. Like parliament's daily prayer, 'It's a way of saying this Parliament isn't the beginning and end of anything, we're part of the process'.[31] The feeling extends beyond the Convention, and republicanism. For example, according to Ross Cameron, the Liberal and monarchist[32] Prayer Breakfast enthusiast, 'it is good for politicians to accept that they are subordinate to a higher power'.[33]

The public justification is more instrumental than theological: civil life will go better if those at the top of the political structure do not see themselves as being the topmost link of the chain. It has a striking consequence. The claim that God is needed to provide something 'higher' than politicians implies that, without God, nothing would be.

It was a very 1990s concern. Not only did the argument about political hubris not crop up at the 1890s conventions, but the founders successfully resisted petitions from the public requesting more specifically political recognition phrases, such as 'acknowledging the Government of the World by Divine Providence' or acknowledging God 'as the Supreme Ruler of the Universe'. They did not need God to fill the gap at the top of the political structure: the system of government which they were in the process of establishing already had 'something higher' than politicians, the Crown.

A century later, political hubris was a serious concern. For monarchists and republicans alike, the Crown no longer did the job. That may tell us something about changes to perceptions of the parliament over the century. When Convention delegates, columnists and members and senators themselves gave political hubris as an argument for God's inclusion, they couched their worries as about 'politicians' (or an equivalent term such as 'our leaders'), implying a collection of individuals, rather than speaking collectively of 'the parliament'. The distrust seemed to be of individual egos rather than the more traditional liberal suspicion of top-heavy political institutions. Indeed, politician suspicion became a major theme of the republic referendum overall, as opponents of change tapped public distrust with the slogan, 'Say No to the Politicians' Republic!'

Modern Australia would seem to have lost a basic understanding of democracy. For democratic theory provides a secular version of 'something higher than politicians': political authority derives from the people.[34] Frighteningly, the democratic answer to political hubris was not raised in response to God's mooted inclusion in any discussion on the 1998 Convention floor or canvassed in the media by either supporters or opponents of God's inclusion. Indeed, Sowada reported that the Australian Republican Movement delegates, whom we might have expected to be particularly sensitive to potential compromises of popular sovereignty, 'took a straw poll' on the question of God's inclusion on the morning of the vote, and, despite some opposition, 'retention of the current wording referring to God's blessing was overwhelmingly supported . . . Many of us believed that it was important to acknowledge, as a nation, God's sovereignty over us'.[35]

The democratic, republican concept of 'the people' had been quietly swept aside in favour of 'the family', 'the individual' and the globalised world of religious and corporate evangelism. The ease with which 'the people' were forgotten marks another difference between Australia and America: for Americans, the republican ideal of 'the people' as the source of sovereignty is well developed, and written into the nation's institutions and practices at many levels (think of *The People v. Larry Flynt*)—in Australia, comparable prosecutions are brought by 'the Crown'). Consequently, American theocrats have to fight to bring back in a God scrupulously excluded from their Constitution and allowed into the Declaration of Independence in only the most carefully deist (or, as Hollingworth might have put it, 'generic') terms. In Australia, still a divinely ordained monarchy with the crown placed on the sovereign's head by the Archbishop of Canterbury, theocratic aspirations are often voiced as monarchist passion. Former Liberal leadership contender turned Christian Democrat Alasdair Webster told the Constitutional Convention that retaining the monarchy was essential because, at coronation:

> Our head of state accepts the Bible as 'the most valuable thing that this world affords'. He or she promises, to the utmost of their power, to maintain the laws of God and the true profession of the gospel. And, before any heir to the throne can get their hands on the sceptre, which is the symbol of kingly power, they must first accept the orb—a golden sphere surmounted by a cross—with the following words: 'Take this to remind you that the whole world is subject to the power and empire of Christ our redeemer'.

Webster anticipated controversy. 'Perhaps some of you are horrified that I dare to question the so-called will of the people. If you are, I venture to suggest that you have accepted the fallacy that democracy is the source of our freedom. In reality, nothing could be further from the truth.' Popular sovereignty was exactly the problem. In language reminiscent of the Family's suspicion of democracy as a manifestation of ungodly pride, Webster warned the Convention: 'In a republic, there is no legal authority higher than the will of the people', and the people's will, rather than God's will, 'determines what is right and wrong'.[36]

The 1990s arguments for God's retention in the Constitution are open to various interpretations. Those republicans who argue that Australian political consciousness has already abandoned the monarchy in all but name can take heart: the gut feeling that we need God to keep a lid on politicians' power suggests that the Crown's role as the top end of the line of political accountability has disappeared, except as God's representative. On the other hand, the Crown's fading from popular consciousness hardly yet amounts to a shift to a republican mindset.[37] Among those who saw God as the only thing between politicians and ultimate power were some of the country's most articulate and high-profile republicans: the very people one would expect to see politicians' power as kept in check by popular sovereignty. If confidence in the Crown had failed, it had not been replaced by the republican idea that sovereignty belongs to the people. Instead, for many, God was a (real or metaphorical) emergency stop-gap.

Many objections to the constitutional second coming could have been raised at the 1998 Convention. Delegates could have asked what place God has in the Constitution of a secular state. Even if recognition of God is relevant to the nation's life, it would have been reasonable to ask whether the Constitution is the place to do it. Believers might have found the 'generic' God too vague. Republicans might have feared that alluding to a divinely ordained political order threatened popular sovereignty. Reformers might have worried that tagging God to the Constitution improperly claims divine sanction for Australia's existing constitutional arrangements. Christians and Jews might have suspected that attaching the name of God to a human document strains the third commandment. Atheists might have felt their citizenship diminished by a religiously framed Constitution. Democrats might have scented a trap.

Instead, the public theology at the 1998 Constitutional Convention saw two Gods vying for recognition. What might be called the 'God of the constitutional gaps' tied divinity to hierarchical political arrangements, with God keeping politicians from the top layer. That God reasserted a more authoritarian and less democratic tradition, promising stability and inviolability. The God of the constitutional gaps may also have been filling a gap in Australians' national self-confidence. The seeming need for a God at the apex of our political structure—even a God many don't believe in—might have pointed to wider uncertainties. One such source of insecurity is the fact that democratic institutions often seem powerless to buffer citizens against the effects of globalisation.

In a world increasingly organised around competition, reliant on mobile and capricious international capital, national institutions weaken. Our sense of community and mutuality seem threatened. The Constitutional Convention's 'generic God' might have embodied a last hope for both order and community.

The second version of the 'generic God' expressed a hoped-for multicultural inclusivity, standing for 'who we are and what we might become', conceived in terms of another globalisation, one of tolerance and welcome. God symbolised a nation welcoming difference, yet bigger than its differences. That 'who we are and what we might become' took a religious (or quasi-religious) form was taken by delegates as an expression of goodwill from those who see themselves as the secular mainstream towards those to whom God still matters. Speaker after speaker specifically mentioned members of non-Christian faiths, arguing that recognising God in the revised Preamble would amount to a gesture of inclusion. The proposed generic God, embraced by atheist and believer alike, became a statement of unity and openness against the rise of 'Us and Them' politics. However, even this well-meaning formulation has dangers, as a seemingly forgotten line of especially religious argument has recognised.

First, the broadminded atheist embrace of other people's religion is uncomfortably close to the view we encountered in earlier chapters, that religion is a good thing for other people to have. As we saw, endorsing religious faith on other people's behalf (perhaps those more needy, less sophisticated or more at risk of moral lapse than ourselves) tends to mean, in practice, endorsing hierarchical, authoritarian forms of religion which will keep those who 'need' it in line. That was not the tone of the Convention debates, but instrumental views of religion ('I don't believe it myself, but I think it is a good thing for some other purpose') can easily slip into authoritarianism.

Second, identifying God with the nation potentially opens the way to the most destructive of nationalisms. If the nation's actions and aspirations are endowed with divine approval or cosmic significance, any contrary view (which, in practice, tends to mean any view other than that of whoever is in power at the time) is blasphemous. We have seen enough of the encroachment of theocratic ideologies in the American religious right, and their echoes in some Australian political rhetoric, to be extremely wary of any too-close association between God and nation. For the neoconservative side in the 'culture wars', God encourages freedom and enterprise for the 'chosen' and obedience to 'Biblical' law for everyone else. Their God rules through chosen leaders and male heads of households, sidelining other kinds of community associations, the welfare state and, ultimately, democracy.

The 1890s Constitutional Convention delegates by and large understood what many of their 1990s successors missed: deity is not something to trifle with. When it comes to including it in the Constitution, you can put it in, or you can take it out; but including it as a half-thought-through talisman of national something-or-other is asking for trouble. As I argued in chapter six, vague agnosticism, accepting religion for its instrumental uses but refusing to take it seriously, poses a surprising threat to Australian politics. As a nation, we could do with less accommodating, half-interested niceness on the faith front. We need more people who think seriously about religion, and are prepared to defend an opinion one way or another. Does that raise the spectre of religious extremism, even violence? As we shall see below, the American experience suggests that the risks are actually greater if religion is kept in the shadows. One result of officially excluding religion from public life is that its adherents feel increasingly alienated, and can eventually feel driven to increasingly extreme measures in order to be heard. Alternatively, religion can slip into power, scarcely noticed (here a prayer breakfast, there a lobby group; here a tweaking of the education system, there a diminution of legal protections for sinners). Once there, it assumes divine right, pushing other kinds of faith and non-faith to the margins.

•

God's easy run at the 1998 Constitutional Convention was facilitated by then Anglican Archbishop of Brisbane Peter Hollingworth's argument that God should be understood 'generically' as 'who we are and what we stand for as a nation'. Hollingworth's subsequent appointment by John Howard as Governor-General might be said to have brought the nation-endorsing 'generic' God to the highest levels. The controversy which almost immediately embroiled Hollingworth concentrated at first on his clerical status. Legal historian Helen Irving argued that, 'though permitted constitutionally (that is, legally)', Hollingworth's appointment was 'the most astonishing departure from convention'.[38] Irving justified her 'astonishment' by citing Section 116 of the Constitution. Section 116 prescribes that 'the Commonwealth shall not make any law for establishing any religion, or for imposing any religious observance, or for prohibiting the free exercise of any religion, and no religious test shall be required for any office or public trust under the Commonwealth'. The part that Irving found relevant is the prohibition of 'any religious test' for public office, but it is hard to see why. If, for example, a government were to decide that only Anglicans, or only Anglican clergy, could be Governor-General, that would surely violate Section 116. But, equally, saying that being an archbishop prevents someone being Governor-General would impose a religious test and thus violate Section 116. Arguably, Section 116 is exactly what makes it possible for a member of the clergy to hold office (like any other citizen), since it ensures that no slippage between clerical and state responsibilities can blur the church–state relationship. Also, the precedent is not as seamless as Irving suggested.

Hollingworth was not the first member of the clergy to hold vice-regal office in Australia. Don Dunstan appointed Churches of Christ Pastor Sir Douglas Nichols Governor of South Australia in 1976. Uniting Church minister and academic theologian Reverend Dr Davis McCaughey was governor of Victoria from 1986 until 1992. Among our near neighbours, Anglican Archbishop Sir Paul Reeves was Governor-General of New Zealand from 1984 until 1990. Clergy have also sat in both federal and State parliaments (in addition to NSW Legislative Councillors Reverend Fred Nile and Reverend Gordon Moyes, mentioned in previous chapters, Labor Member for Batman Reverend Brian Howe and Democrat Senator for Queensland Reverend John Woodley are recent examples).

Irving argued that Hollingworth's appointment 'proved to be an error' in which 'mixing church and state . . . had invited trouble on more than one front'. Yet the trouble which pursued Hollingworth was not specific to his clerical role. His sin was dealing inappropriately with child sexual abuse by others during his tenure as Archbishop of Brisbane. Similar controversy would have pursued—or at least, we must hope so—a Governor-General from any other walk of life found to have been similarly lenient.

In effect, Hollingworth was found guilty by public opinion of having been an ineffectual CEO, not of violating church–state separation.

At Hollingworth's appointment, and throughout his controversy-dogged tenure, his clerical status raised charges of religion–state blurring. In fact, Hollingworth's clerical status brought his religious role into focus, allowing transparency. Howard oversaw damage to religion–state separation, but not because he appointed an archbishop as Governor-General. The real damage, as shown in earlier chapters, came from departures like encouraging the discrediting of Indigenous religious beliefs so as to limit their interference with capitalist development, restricting churches' freedom to criticise government policy by binding them into silencing contracts and threatening to retain tax-exempt status only for those who leave government alone, handing over large components of taxpayer-funded welfare delivery to under-unionised, variably accountable and potentially inequitable church agencies, promoting conservative Christian schools and calling loudly for a return to 'values', and fostering semi-secret, unaccountable religious networks and 'faith-based diplomacy' within the government itself.

Once church scandal dragged Hollingworth from office, pundits applauded Howard's personally chosen, 'safe' replacement, former Western Australian Governor Major General Michael Jeffery. Yet Jeffery, appointed by a government which wants churches to keep out of politics, arguably brought church and state closer than the archbishop. Hollingworth announced at his appointment that he would cease preaching during his Yarralumla tenure; but Governor-General Jeffery has not been shy of holding up Jesus Christ as 'the greatest example of leadership who ever lived',[39] and even championing behind-the-scenes, semi-official, faith-based diplomacy which, as we saw in chapter ten, is associated with an international, theocratic movement that sees democracy as 'a manifestation of ungodly pride'. Australia's problem has been not too much visible religion in high places, but failing to recognise, justify and understand the religious currents that we have. We do Australia's soul no service by forcing religion out of visible public life into unanalysed undercurrents.

•

What to do with a deity? Fearing religious establishment, and knowing that state Gods can prove punitive, America's founders took pains to keep God to one side. They built on the growing tradition of English political theory which argued that, as John Locke put it in his 1689 *Letter Concerning Toleration*, 'the care of souls cannot belong to the magistrate', because giving civil authorities power to enforce belief ends in 'fire and faggot'.[40] God got a mention in the Declaration of Independence (in the carefully impersonal terms 'Creator' and 'Nature's God'), but deliberately not in the American Constitution, which instead enshrined religious freedom and prevented any federal religious establishment. Checking out the consequences in 1831, French political observer Alexis de Tocqueville reported that religion, though kept scrupulously from formal public recognition, should, paradoxically, be considered 'the first of [America's] political institutions' because it provided a guiding framework for individual citizens and, in a highly privatised form, was regarded by Americans as 'indispensable to the maintenance of republican institutions'.[41]

Later theorists of American liberalism, such as John Rawls, Ronald Dworkin and Robert Audi, took the founders' vision of church–state separation further in the direction of quarantining religion from public life. The result has been an intensifying tradition of court-imposed separation, with rulings that, for example, publicly funded nativity scenes can only be displayed on public land if their religious effect is diluted by a sufficient proportion of Santas and reindeer.[42] One consequence of such doctrinaire secularism, political theorist William Connolly argued, is that large numbers not only of the religiously committed, but also others whose fundamental beliefs are not easily separated from their lives as citizens, end up feeling marginalised and disenfranchised, sometimes to the point of violence.[43] The Oklahoma bombing, in Connolly's view, was just the extreme end of what happens when some people's deepest commitments are systematically excluded from nation-shaping decisions. On the other hand, incorporating religious views into public life in half-acknowledged, under-the-counter ways is no less dangerous. The backlash to the reindeer debates and the rigid separationism they have come to symbolise has produced a president announcing a global 'crusade' against 'evil'. Faith-based law raises the spectre of further exclusions, and holds out little hope of a tolerant, welcoming, generous society.

The problem is compounded in Australia by the fact that, as historian W.K. Hancock noted in 1930,[44] Australia has no distinctive political philosophy. More importantly, we have little in the way of shared philosophical traditions (whether home-grown or imported) for thinking about such matters as religion–state relations. Instead, religion–state relations have tended to be pragmatic, changing in response to short-term political goals. We have got by on a 'she'll be right' assumption that, particularly since the death of sectarianism in the 1960s and 70s, church–state issues could safely be left alone to sort themselves out. With that has gone the feeling that people, especially in public life, should be entitled to the privacy of whatever religious views they might hold. Candidates for office should not be held accountable for their faith, or required to explain any connections it might have to their politics.

No doubt many Australians would agree it should stay that way. However, when public figures begin to hint at faith-based politics, the public, which has to live with the politics if not the faith, can reasonably expect an explanation. When a prime minister lends his support, and taxpayers' money, to schools whose teachers are required to believe in the literal truth of every part of the Bible and that all non-Christians are condemned to eternal damnation, voters can reasonably expect to know which particular aspects of that agenda he endorses and in what ways it is being passed on to students. When a treasurer argues that interreligious tensions would be solved if everyone shared Christian values (a curious view in itself, given the history of wars between different Christian traditions!), or that social problems are best addressed by a return to the Ten Commandments, it seems time to question the presumption that such views are out of bounds for public questioning. When a health minister, elaborating the duties of a Christian politician, alludes to abortion as a national tragedy and invites Christians to build a groundswell against it, we need a conversation about the range of beliefs in our society, and how they might best accommodate one another. When a new party is launched, fielding candidates almost exclusively from a single denomination while declaring that it is not a Christian party, citizens can well ask what, in that case, a Christian party would be. In effect, such moves borrow a religious aura to baptise by association a whole political program, without the kind of explanation and accountability citizens normally expect of their leaders.

I am not for one moment suggesting that people should avoid grounding their political views in their religious faith, or that the religiously committed should stay clear of public life. As we have seen throughout this book, to many seriously religious people the much talked of border between 'spiritual' and 'political' matters is impossible to draw. Australia has benefited immeasurably from the many people who have been propelled into public life by their deep faith. But public displays of religiosity of the kinds that became increasingly prominent over the Howard's government's third term make it harder to sustain the view that public figures can politely be left to enjoy their faith in private. If politicians want to build their faith into their political personae, they owe us an explanation of where it fits. Otherwise, we risk drifting into an imitation of American presidential races where religious gestures are expected as a matter of course from all aspirants, while faith-based politics is treated as beyond discussion or critique.

Howard's assault on assumed separations, documented throughout this book, should end our philosophical innocence. With the repressive God of Howard conservatism rattling the back door of government policy while the Market God sits enthroned in treasury, we can no longer afford to leave religion–state questions to work themselves out, out of public view.

•

We can observe Australia's historic pattern of pragmatic church–state compromise acted out over the long term in the universities. Early in Australia's academic history, a degree of rapprochement existed between universities and religion. The University of Sydney, inaugurated in 1852, took in Presbyterian theological students under the *St Andrew's College Act 1867*[45] and offered its own post-graduate Bachelor of Divinity in the 1930s.[46] Thereafter, however, theological education was generally set up in church institutions and according to curricula determined by churches, and with academics paid out of church funds. As the state university system expanded, it remained chary of association with theological education; state sponsorship of theology (for example, on the German model) was seen as a dangerous lunge away from state secularism.

The 1980s and 1990s, however, saw a new generation of state universities throw open their corridors to theology schools. You can now take a degree in Christian theology at Flinders, Murdoch, Charles Sturt or Griffith Universities. In 1993, the Melbourne College of Divinity became affiliated with the University of Melbourne;[47] the Sydney College of Divinity and its member institutions have associations with the University of Western Sydney and Edith Cowan University, as well as continuing to support the teaching of higher degrees in theology at Sydney University and Charles Sturt. The explanation is not any sudden thirst for theological insight among university administrations but the Market God's increasing focus on 'industry links': church-run colleges have been able to sell themselves to universities as providers of vocational education for a ready-made market.

With the move into universities and also as a result of changing demographics, a substantial proportion of today's theology students, in contrast to past cohorts, do not go on to become clergy. That gives theological faculties an atmosphere broader than sharply vocational 'clergy training', and means that people familiar with the theological traditions central to dominant political and cultural institutions are available for work in many other areas. Hopefully, more theologically sophisticated media commentators would be able to seize a lot sooner on the inconsistencies and hypocrisies in any future Hindmarsh Island-style show trial. Hopefully, those formally trained in the history of theologians' teasing out of big questions will be less susceptible to the implicit and deniable racism lurking below the surface of seemingly bland talk about 'traditional values', and the smug self-justifications of 'prosperity gospel' theology in high places. By opening the door to serious theology, the Market God may have let in some of those best placed to help its unmasking.

However, Australian public life needs more than detailed, insiders' understanding of Christian theology. While theology has been on an upswing, the cross-cultural, multi-faith study of religion (as opposed to Christian theology) has been struggling in Australia. Student demand is strong, world events keep religion in focus. (At Victoria University, Wellington, where I teach, first year religious studies courses regularly draw up to two hundred students, many of them with no personal religious background but all with a drive to understand religion's place in the modern world.) While the University of Queensland (nine academic staff) and Sydney University (five academic staff) have comprehensive programs, smaller departments elsewhere battle on with limited resources, as at the University of New England and University of South Australia (two full-time academic staff each), or squeeze in religion as a component of other courses, such as sociology.

As we have seen, America is home to the fundamentalist right and a particular kind of anti-democratic religious politics; but it also has a rich tradition of liberal, democratic, republican thought about the issues raised by religious politics, enabling articulate resistance to the tide of theocracy. While church–state issues are fought acrimoniously in the courts, numerous degree programs in both religious studies and politics give detailed and respectful attention to religion–state relationships, religious freedom and the relationship between religion and politics. Not one Australian university department has the study of religion in Australian politics as a major departmental research focus. Only two—the University of Sydney and the Australian National University—offer an undergraduate elective on religion–politics intersections.

Religion is a potent ingredient in our postmodern national mix. Our highly secular political culture cannot continue to overlook its intricacies.

•

A common cry of the right is that politicians cannot make people nicer, and should not try. Howard protégé Tony Abbott argued, in a speech entitled 'The Ethical Responsibilities of a Christian Politician', that: 'It's easy to confuse the Christian calling of individuals with the public duty of governments. Love is a fine guide for individuals but folly in a government'. That is one more time Howard's team paralleled the American right: George W. Bush justified his 'faith-based' welfare programs with 'Governments cannot make people love one another. It's been the great false hope of the past. All you've got to do is pass a law and people will love one another. But love comes from a higher calling, a higher authority'.[48] But there is good evidence that governments can bring out people's better side. Here's an example.

In 1984, the *Sex Discrimination Act* outlawed sexual harassment in the workplace. At the time, it was highly controversial. Critics chorused that the Act was an unconscionable intrusion into private affairs, that workers would be at risk of prosecution for showing friendliness to a colleague, that human behaviour is too varied for legislative control and that, anyway, the force of law was a sledge-hammer applied to 'trivial' incidents. Within a short time of the Act's becoming law, such concerns were much harder to find. Careful wording and a successful public information campaign made clear that repeated, unwanted attention which insults or intimidates is very different from friendliness, and is far from trivial. Although sexual harassment still occurs, the culture of many workplaces has changed. Respectful relationships between men and women, bosses and subordinates are much more likely to be assumed. Howard government cuts to the Human Rights and Equal Opportunity Commission have meant that getting a sexual harassment hearing is both much harder and often prohibitively expensive, so this culture change may be vulnerable, but the Act showed that, with proper backup, legislation can change attitudes.

Studies of anti-racist education make a similar point. Generally speaking, anti-racist education which preaches tolerance does not work. Finding their views under attack, holders of racist opinions defend their position with increasing force, talking themselves into more entrenched racism. What changes attitudes is experiencing what it is like to live in non-racist ways, getting to know those people we might once have regarded as 'Them', and, importantly, working together to oppose racism.[49] Legislation which forces us to behave as though we are not racist has a good chance of fostering the reality. That is aside from big-picture moves like improving services and amenities, making up for economic disadvantage and so on. By legislating to bring out our best rather than our worst in our interactions, governments can make us nicer.

And they can make us nastier. By penalising some kinds of families and ruling some kinds of love second class, governments can encourage other families into frightened retreat. By sponsoring show trials to ridicule non-Christian beliefs, they can encourage us to see money as having the right to trample spiritual values. By draconian national security laws, and by immigration laws which put parts of our country beyond the rule of law, they can encourage us to fear and suspect our neighbours, to respond to racist dog whistles while keeping our motives hidden from ourselves, to see ever larger groups of our fellow-citizens, and of non-citizens who desperately need our help, as a menacing 'Them' trying to steal our wealth and safety. By dividing the unemployed, single parents and those with disabilities into deserving and undeserving, casting many as 'job snobs' and 'dole bludgers', they can persuade us to see poverty as failure by individuals, rather than a failure by us all.

Australia's democratic, egalitarian soul has sustained serious assaults from a government which encouraged our worst and endured 'small target' silence from an opposition that refused to bring out our best; but it is not destroyed. In 2000, hundreds of thousands in cities across Australia joined 'bridge walks' for Aboriginal reconciliation. In 2001, thousands joined Rural Australians for Refugees, wrote letters of welcome to refugees behind wire, paid visits, forged friendships, told stories. In 2003, Australians turned out in their hundred thousands to oppose an unprovoked and illegal war. Even as the 2004 Federal Budget delivered tax cuts for the rich, Australians lamented increasing inequality and consistently told pollsters they preferred social safety nets to tax cuts. Australians resist efforts to slice us into 'Us' and 'Them'. Howard might keep winning elections but, in between, he has not entirely had his way with Australia's soul.

Timeline of major events

26 July 1939	John Howard born
1946–51	John Howard attends Earlwood Primary School
1952–1956	John Howard attends Canterbury Boys' High School
1954	John Howard joins Liberal Party
1955	Lyall Howard (father) dies
1961	John Howard graduates LLB from Sydney University; appointed Sunday School Secretary, Earlwood Methodist Church
July 1962	John Howard admitted as a solicitor of the NSW Supreme Court; elected President of NSW Young Liberals
1963	John Howard joins Liberal Party State Executive

1965	John Howard joins Sydney solicitors' firm which became Truman, Nelson & Howard
4 April 1971	John Howard marries Janette Parker
18 May 1974	John Howard elected Member for Bennelong (Liberals in opposition)
13 December 1975	Coalition, under Malcolm Fraser, wins double dissolution election following 11 November dismissal of Whitlam Labor government
22 December 1975 –17 July 1977	John Howard is Minister for Business and Communications
17 July–20 December 1977	John Howard is Minister for Special Trade Negotiations
19 November 1977 –5 March 1983	John Howard is Treasurer (appointed following resignation of Phillip Lynch)
8 April 1982	John Howard elected Liberal deputy leader
5 March 1983	Labor Party, under Bob Hawke, wins double dissolution election; Andrew Peacock wins Liberal leadership
5 September 1985–May 1989	John Howard is Liberal leader (in opposition)
1986	Australia's first National Prayer Breakfast
July–August 1988	John Howard's comments about 'slowing' Asian immigration in the name of 'social cohesion' damage leadership
December 1988	*Future Directions* policy statement released
May 1989	Andrew Peacock resumes Liberal leadership
1990	John Hewson elected Liberal leader
1991	Paul Keating replaces Bob Hawke as Labor leader and prime minister

1992	High Court Mabo decision
1992	Lyons Forum formed
1993	John Hewson loses the 'unlosable' election, defeats John Howard (and others) in leadership contest, but his leadership is regarded as doomed
1994	John Hewson loses Liberal leadership to Alexander Downer; Peter Costello becomes deputy
30 January 1995	John Howard resumes Liberal leadership after Alexander Downer steps down; Peter Costello remains deputy
10 July 1995	Federal Aboriginal Affairs Minister Robert Tickner grants federal protection to Hindmarsh Island and Goolwa Channel area
May–November 1995	Hindmarsh Island Royal Commission
June–December 1995	Carmen Lawrence Royal Commission
2 March 1996	Coalition wins 94-seat landslide at the election
11 March 1996	John Howard sworn in as prime minister
February 1997	Australia's first National Student Leadership Forum on Faith and Values
April 1998	High Court Wik decision
3 October 1998	Coalition wins 'GST election'
8 August 1999	John Howard opens Oxford Falls Christian City Church
26 August 2001	*Palapa*'s passengers picked up by *Tampa*

11 September 2001	Terrorist attacks on New York and Washington
October 2001	'Children overboard' allegations surface, and are contested
10 November 2001	Coalition wins 'border protection' election
12 October 2002	Bali bombing
19 October 2002	John Howard opens Hillsong church complex in suburban Sydney
5 July 2003	John Howard announces he will lead Coalition into next election
August 2003	Lyons Forum re-formed
16 March 2004	Health Minister Tony Abbott speaks on 'The Ethical Responsibilities of a Christian Politician', raising the possibility of returning abortion to the federal political agenda
29 May 2004	Inaugural Australian National Day of Thanksgiving, sponsored by, among others, Catch the Fire Ministries, addressed by Treasurer Peter Costello
5 July 2004	Treasurer Peter Costello addresses 21 000 at Hillsong conference
September 2004	John Howard enthusiastically introduced at Perth Christian Life Centre as a 'Christian prime minister' (in contrast to opposition leader Mark Latham) at the launch of Liberal candidate Don Randall's campaign
8 October 2004	Howard government re-elected for a fourth term
2 November 2004	US President George Bush re-elected with increased Republican majorities in both houses

1 July 2005	Coalition gains full control of the Australian Senate; Family First Senator Steve Fielding sworn in

Notes

Chapter one Sunday morning at Earlwood Methodist

1 Undated church notice sheet, held in Uniting Church NSW Synod Archives. The sheet contains a preaching plan for the Sundays from August to November, the dates placing it in 1961.

2 Minutes of the Quarterly Meeting, 11 July 1960.

3 See David Marr, *The High Price of Heaven*, Sydney: Allen & Unwin, 1999, pp. 28–32; Tony Wright, 'Preacher Men', *Bulletin*, 29 August 2001; John Hewson, 'A Moving Picture of Hope', *Australian Financial Review*, 12 April 2002; Marcia Langton, 'Cost-Efficient, Triple-Documented Ethnic Cleansing', Address to the International Museums Conference, Melbourne, October 1998; Pru Goward, Australia Forum, ABC Radio National, 2 November 2003; Gerard Henderson, *A Howard Government?*, Pymble, NSW: HarperCollins, 1995; Ray Evans, 'For the Labourer is Worthy of his Hire', in Evans (ed.), *For the Labourer is Worthy of his Hire*, Proceedings of a Conference of the H.R. Nicholls Society at the Royal Parade Motor Inn, 3–5 April 1992; David Marr, Politics Seminar, Research School of Social Sciences, ANU, 6 August 2003; Anthony Albanese, Labor Member for Grayndler, 'John Howard could only be a Methodist!', interview with author, Parliament House, 28 June 1999.

4 Tony Priddle, letter to the editor, *Sydney Morning Herald*, 23–24 August 2003, p. 36.
5 ABC TV, 'What Our Leaders Believe', *Compass*, 20 September 1998.
6 See E.P. Thompson, *The Making of the English Working Class*, Harmondsworth: Penguin, 1968. See also Robert Featherstone Wearmouth, *Methodism and the Working Class Movements of England 1800–1850,* London: Epworth Press, 1937. For discussion see Graham Maddox, 'John Wesley and the spirit of capitalism', *Australian Religion Studies Review*, vol. 11, no. 2, 1998, pp. 85–97.
7 *Compass*, op. cit.
8 ibid.
9 See Paul Kelly, 'Security in Incumbency', *Weekend Australian*, 19–20 April 2003.
10 *70th Anniversary of Methodism in Earlwood*, printed by W.L. Farrell, Earlwood, 1948, p. 7.
11 *70th Anniversary of Methodism in Earlwood*, op. cit., p. 8; Minutes of the Circuit's Quarterly Meeting in July 1948 reported enrolments: 'Senior 27; Junior & Intermediate 121; Kindergarten 87; Total 235; Cradle Roll No Report; Young Worshippers League 26', Uniting Church NSW Synod Archives.
12 'Circuit News: Earlwood', *Methodist*, 14 November 1953, p. 12.
13 For example, the Methodist Young People's Department in Castlereagh Street, Sydney, offered weekly training classes for kindergarten level Sunday School teachers (see *Methodist*, 28 January 1950, p. 4); see also 'So you missed out?—But not quite: Here's what happened at the S.S. Superintendent's "living-in" conference arranged by the Y.P.D.', *Methodist*, 8 August 1953, p. 1.
14 'Young People's Dep't Scripture examinations', *Methodist*, 18 October 1952.
15 See Earlwood Circuit Directory, November 1961. His resignation is recorded in the minutes of the Earlwood Leaders' Meeting, 30 January 1963, Uniting Church NSW Synod Archives.
16 Whether churches can be understood as purveying political 'messages' is debated in Rodney Smith, 'Religion and electoral behaviour in Australia: The search for meaning', *Australian Religion Studies Review*, vol. 11, no. 2, 1998, pp. 17–37.
17 'Sunday School examinations', *Methodist*, 19 February 1955, p. 5.
18 'For Sunday Schools', *Methodist*, 16 May 1953.
19 'The Mission to the Nation: A progress report', *Methodist*, 29 January 1955, p. 7.
20 A.G. Manefield, 'The President speaks', *Methodist*, 5 February 1955, p. 3.
21 'The Mission to the Nation: A progress report', op. cit.

22 'Youth convention's message to Australia', *Methodist*, 19 February 1955, p. 4.
23 'Mission to Nation and critics', *Methodist*, 12 February 1955.
24 'Mission to the Nation: A progress report', *Methodist*, 19 November 1955, p. 7.
25 Minutes of the Quarterly Meeting, Earlwood Methodist Church, 10 October 1952.
26 Don Wright, *Alan Walker: Conscience of the nation*, Adelaide: OpenBook, 1997, p. 128.
27 ibid., p. 32.
28 Reverend A. Walker, 'Reconciliation for a divided world', *Methodist*, 10 October 1953, p. 1.
29 *Methodist*, 2 May 1953, cited in 'The Mission and politics', letter to the editor, *Methodist*, 22 May 1953, p. 12.
30 Quoted in 'The Mission to the Nation story', at <www.local.sa.uca.org.au/youth/ncyc>, 16 September 2003.
31 'You will approve! A new deal for part-Aboriginal children', *Methodist*, 10 December 1955, p. 1.
32 See for example Margaret Somerville, 'New children arrive', *Methodist*, 9 May 1953, p. 5.
33 See for example Jennifer Clark, 'Speaking out: Methodists on Yirrkala, 1963', paper presented to the Australian Association for the Study of Religions, Armidale, NSW, July 2002.
34 'Aborigines' Sunday', *Methodist*, 28 January 1950. In 1957, the National Aborigines' Day Observance Committee was established, the second Friday in July approved by the federal government as National Aborigines' Day, and National Aborigines' Sunday moved to the second Sunday in July. Rev. Dr A. Capell, 'Would You Like to be an Aborigine?', *Methodist*, 13 July 1963, p. 4.
35 Rev. Wesley S. Pidgeon, 'NADOC', *Methodist*, 9 July 1960, p. 7.
36 Rev. Dr A. Capell, 'Would You Like to be an Aborigine?', op. cit., p. 4. (Capitals in original.)
37 Senator John Woodley, interview with author, 11 August 1999.
38 Jennifer Clark, 'The soul of Australia: Using church newspapers to open up Australian history', *NLA News*, vol. 12, no. 6, March 2002.
39 'The terrible twins', *Methodist*, 19 March 1955, p. 6.
40 'Ten o'clock closing', *Methodist*, 5 February 1955, p. 3.
41 'The terrible twins', *Methodist*, op. cit.
42 'The church and the community: A weekly commentary', *Methodist*, 12 February 1955, p. 3.
43 G.L. Griffith, 'American diary', *Methodist*, 17 December 1955, p. 3.
44 'Child delinquency and the church', *Methodist*, 30 April 1955, p. 6.
45 'Design for depravity', *Methodist*, 17 September 1955, p. 3.

46 'The church and the community: A weekly commentary', *Methodist*, 28 May 1955, p. 3.
47 'Doorway to happiness: The home', *Methodist*, 10 September 1955, p. 1.
48 'RP', 'A woman's tremendous accomplishment', *Methodist*, 20 May 1950, p. 9.
49 'State aid for independent schools', *Methodist*, 9 December 1961, p. 4.
50 'The church and the community: A weekly commentary', *Methodist*, 7 May 1955, p. 3.
51 Neville Smith, 'Our world has moved', *Methodist*, 12 February 1955, p. 3. See also Gordon Dicker, '"Meet the Asians" and extend them the hand of friendship', *Methodist*, op. cit., p. 1.
52 Dr Cyril F. Garbett, 'Christianity and communism: Substance of the address given in the Sydney Town Hall by the Rt. Hon. the Archbishop of York', *Methodist*, 15 December 1951, pp. 1–3.
53 Rev. E.E.V. Collocott, 'Religion in the Soviet Union', *Methodist*, 4 July 1953, pp. 1–2, 5.
54 Rev. E.E.V. Collocott, 'Religion in China', *Methodist*, 12 December 1953, pp. 1–21.
55 See for example Allan D. Brand, 'The Christian church in communist countries', *Methodist*, 21 March 1953, p. 12; E.E.V. Collocott, 'Churches and the iron curtain', letter to the editor, *Methodist*, 18 August 1951. The editor regularly interpolated comments such as his caution appended to 'Churches Behind the Iron Curtain', *Methodist*, July 1951, p. 2, that communists' 'pronouncements may be smoother than butter, but war is in their hearts, and their pronouncements may be softer than oil, but they are really drawn swords—Ed.'
56 Rev. Clifford J. Wright, 'Methodist Bishop defends American democracy against McCarthyism', *Methodist*, 6 February 1954, p. 12. For detail see G. Bromley Oxnam, *I Protest*, Westport CT: Greenwood, 1954.
57 'The church and the community: A weekly commentary', *Methodist*, 14 May 1955, p. 3.
58 *Methodist*, 17 September 1955.
59 *Methodist*, 24 September 1955, p. 6.
60 Rev. Bertram R. Wyllie, 'The churches and world peace', *Methodist*, 15 August 1953, p. 1.
61 Rev. Bertram R. Wyllie, 'The World Peace Council and the World Council of Churches', *Methodist*, 29 August 1953, p. 1. See also Rev. Keith Dowding, 'The enemies of freedom', *Methodist*, 19 March 1955, p. 12; Alan Walker, 'The forbidden subject—peace!', *Methodist*, 7 June 1952, pp. 1, 7.
62 'The church and the community: A weekly commentary', *Methodist*, 14 May 1955, p. 3.

63 See for example 'South Africa—What of the church?', *Methodist*, 20 September 1952; 'The church and the community: A weekly commentary', *Methodist*, 30 April 1955, p. 3; 'Racial suspicion and hatred in South Africa', *Methodist*, 5 February 1955, p. 1; Herbert Tingsten, 'Stronghold of prejudice', *Methodist*, 1 October 1955, p. 6.
64 'The church and the community: A weekly commentary', *Methodist*, 30 April 1955, p. 3.
65 Rev. Bertram R. Wyllie, 'Is Australia fumbling its Asian opportunities?', *Methodist*, 7–14 May 1961, pp. 1, 3.
66 See, for example, 'The churches and refugees', editorial, *Methodist*, 21 March 1959.
67 'The church and the community: A weekly commentary', *Methodist*, 30 April 1955, p. 3.
68 'Child delinquency and the church', *Methodist*, 30 April 1955, p. 6.
69 'According to the President', *Methodist*, 17 December 1955, p. 3.
70 'According to the President', *Methodist*, 17 December 1955, p. 3.
71 Judith Brett, *Australian Liberals and the Moral Middle Class: From Alfred Deakin to John Howard*, Cambridge: Cambridge University Press, 2003, pp. 211–12.
72 Robert Howard, interview with author, Sydney, 4 November 2003.
73 Gerard Henderson, *A Howard Government? Inside the Coalition*, Pymble, NSW: HarperCollins, 1995.
74 Robert Howard, interview with author, op. cit.
75 Cited in Caroline Chung Simpson, '"Out of an obscure place": Japanese war brides and cultural pluralism in the 1950s', *Differences: A Journal of Feminist Cultural Studies*, vol. 10, no. 2, 1998.
76 Marian Mitchell, 'Our Tony', *Saturday Evening Post*, 7 July 1956, p. 30.
77 Interviews with author, Sydney, 31 October 2003.
78 Robert Howard, interview with author, op. cit.
79 Norma Hardy and Margaret Eyre, interview with author, 4 November 2004.

Chapter two Bypassing Lazarus

1 John Howard, interview with John Laws, Radio 2UE, 1 August 1988; interview with Paul Murphy, ABC Radio *PM*, 1 August 1988; Press Statement, 11 August 1988.
2 Among many such analyses, see Paul Kelly, *The End of Certainty*, Sydney: Allen & Unwin, 2nd edition, 1994, p. 428.
3 Occasionally, there have been gestures towards a greater role for the party organisation in policy; however, these have generally been

short-lived. See for example G. Starr, *The Liberal Party of Australia: A documentary history*, Richmond, Vic.: Drummond/Heinemann, 1980, pp. 278–80, 317–18; G. Starr, 'The Liberal Party of Australia', in G. Starr, K. Richmond and G. Maddox, *Political Parties in Australia*, Richmond, Vic.: Heinemann, 1978, pp. 57–66.

4 Graeme Starr, 'The Liberal Party of Australia' in *Political Parties in Australia*, op. cit., p. 43. The Nationals' policy is officially formed by the Federal Conference but in practice, given the exigencies of Coalition and the leeway afforded by party rules, it is as likely to be determined by the parliamentary party executive, often under pressure from the senior Coalition partner.

5 ibid., pp. 43–44. This Liberal Party characteristic has been heightened in recent years by the general trend toward executive dominance in Australian politics—see for example R. Macklin, 'For His Is the Power', *Canberra Times*, 18 March 2000.

6 Dean Jaensch, *The Liberals*, Sydney: Allen & Unwin, 1994, p. 150.

7 David Kemp, 'A Leader and a Philosophy', in H. Mayer (ed.), *Labor to Power: Australia's 1972 election*, Sydney: Angus and Robertson, 1973, p. 52.

8 ibid.

9 Ian Cook, 'From Menzies to Hewson: Two traditions of liberalism in the Liberal Party of Australia', in G. Stokes (ed.), *Australian Political Ideas*, Kensington, NSW: UNSW Press, 1994, pp. 169–70. The designations 'ameliorative' and 'individualistic' come from Peter Tiver, 'The Ideology of the Liberal Party: A Sketch and an Interpretation', *Politics* XI no. 2, 1976, pp. 156–64, 170.

10 Randall Stewart and Ian Ward, *Politics One*, South Melbourne: Macmillan, 1992, pp. 113, 115.

11 Dean Jaensch, *The Liberals*, op. cit., p. 150.

12 Andrew West, 'Balance Sheet Politics has No Place for Man of Ideals', *Sydney Morning Herald*, 17 October 1990, p. 4.

13 Marian Sawer, *The Ethical State: Social liberalism in Australia*, Melbourne: Melbourne University Press, 2004.

14 Australia, House of Representatives, *Debates*, 27 February 1995, p. 1019.

15 John Herron, interview with author, Parliament House, 11 August 1999.

16 Australia, *Senate*, Senator John Herron, 17 September 1990, p. 2418.

17 John Herron, interview, op. cit.

18 Jodie Brough, 'Newman's Plea a Blow to Anti-Euthanasia Forces', *Sydney Morning Herald*, 20 March 1997.

19 Jodie Brough, 'Why He's Dead Set Against Mercy Killing', *Sydney Morning Herald*, 17 March 1997.

20 Nikki Savva, 'The God Squad', *Age*, 2 April 1997.

21 Anne Davies, 'Severe Test for John Howard's Integrity', *Sydney Morning Herald*, 2 April 1997.
22 Rosemary Radford Ruether, *Christianity and the Making of the Modern Family*, Boston: Beacon, 2000, pp. 4–5, 156–80.
23 See for example *Australian Story,* ABC TV, 15 March 1997.
24 John Tierney, interview with author, Parliament House, 22 June 1999.
25 As stated on the CV faxed by his office, 13 November 2000.
26 Kevin Andrews, interview with author, Parliament House, 28 June 1999; see also for example M. Gordon, 'Holy Alliance: The Inside Story of Euthanasia's Demise', *Weekend Australian*, 29 March 1997.
27 Information supplied by Mr Forrest's office, 31 August 2000.
28 Interview, Parliament House, 24 June 1999.
29 ibid.
30 Chris Miles, interview with author, Parliament House, 30 June 1999; John Herron, interview with author, op. cit.
31 See for example John Woodley, 'Christians in the Lyons Den', a theological critique of the Forum which appeared in several church newspapers during 1997.
32 Nikki Savva, 'The God Squad', *Age*, 2 April 1997.
33 Chris Miles, interview with Matthew Abraham, ABC, 2CN, *Morning Show*, 10 November 1993.
34 Dean Jaensch, *The Liberals*, op. cit., p. 220.
35 ibid., p. 163.
36 ibid., p. 162.
37 On Hewson's position on government intervention in relation to social and economic questions, see Gerard Henderson, *Menzies' Child*, op. cit.
38 L. Taylor, 'Hewson Lashed Over Mardi Gras Support', *Australian*, 3 March 1994. See also Amanda Meade, et al., 'Libs Parade Ire at Hewson', *Sydney Morning Herald*, 4 March 1994.
39 Chris Miles, interview with author, op. cit.
40 Although the wording of the text takes the form of a letter, its presentation is more like a petition. The ABC received fourteen pages, each with a copy of the letter on parliamentary letterhead filling the top two-thirds and as many signatures as would fit filling the bottom third. The signatures on most pages appear roughly in the order of the chambers' seating plans. The signatures include those of all six Lyons Forum founders. The signatures on page four read, in order, John Howard, Tim Fischer, John Anderson, John Sharp, David Kemp, David Jull, Peter Costello, David Connolly. The text of each page reads:

Dear Mr Hill,
Having regard to the new arrangements negotiated with commercial television broadcasters regarding adult viewing hours we, Senators and

Members of the Australian Parliament, strongly believe that the present decision by the ABC to televise the Gay and Lesbian Mardi Gras for an hour at 8.30 Sunday night March 6th is inappropriate.

We recognise the great diversity of human activity that exists within the Australian community and that the ABC has a charter which provides for executive judgements to be made. However we strongly believe that this programming decision does not reflect what the overwhelming majority of Australian families would wish to watch on Sunday night at 8.30.

As representatives of millions of Australians it is our request that the ABC not broadcast the Mardi Gras as scheduled and a more suitable family programme be substituted.
Yours faithfully,

The text of the letter and list of signatories in alphabetical order were published in newspapers on 4 March 1994. Facsimile of original fourteen pages supplied by Roger Grant, Australian Broadcasting Corporation, 5 September 2000.

For a discussion of public reaction to the ABC broadcast see Ian Marsh, 'The 1994 Mardi Gras Telecast: Conflicting minorities and the judgement of public interests', *Australian Journal of Political Science*, vol. 30, no. 3, 1995, pp. 545–60.

41 Kathy Sullivan, interview with author, Parliament House, 28 June 1999.
42 ibid.
43 Margo Kingston, 'Hewson Lashes Conservatives', *Canberra Times*, 4 March 1994; see also Amanda Meade, et al., 'Libs Parade Ire at Hewson', *Sydney Morning Herald*, 4 March 1994.
44 Amanda Meade, et al., ibid.
45 Mary Easson, telephone interview with author, November 2000.
46 John Hewson, interview with John Laws, Radio 2UE, 3 March 1994.
47 Amanda Meade, et al., 'Libs Parade Ire at Hewson', op. cit.
48 Margo Kingston, 'Hewson Slates Howard Policy', op. cit.
49 ibid.
50 See for example Lyndall Curtis's recap of the previous week's stories on *PM*, ABC Radio National, 8 March 1994.
51 Mary Easson, telephone interview with author, op. cit.
52 See Kenneth Davidson, 'Which Families? Exposing the Lyons Forum', *Australian Rationalist*, 43, Autumn/Winter 1997, pp. 2–7. Davidson draws attention to the pattern in the Forum's 1995 manifesto *Empowering Australian Families* to present socially conservative views as being those of respondents' to the Forum's hearings, rather than as its own policy recommendations.

53 Kingston, 'Hewson Slates Howard Policy', op. cit.
54 John Hewson, interview with author, Sydney, 24 November 1999.
55 ibid.
56 Australia, *House of Representatives*, Debates, 28 February 1985, p. 431.
57 Alexander Downer, interview with author, Parliament House, 1 March 2000.

Chapter three The politics of death

1 Senate Legal and Constitutional Legislation Committee, Consideration of Legislation Referred to the Committee: Euthanasia Laws Bill 1996, March 1997, p. 7.
2 Australian Constitution, s. 122, 'Government of Territories'.
3 Australia, *House of Representatives*, Question without Notice: Euthanasia, 26 June 1996.
4 Australia, *Senate*, Senator Bob Collins, Third Reading Speech, 24 March 1997.
5 Australia, *House of Representatives*, Peter Costello, Second Reading Speech, 5 December 1996.
6 For a representative survey of media comment which interpreted the Bill as an expression of religious conservatism, see Margo Kingston, 'The Fight to Die', *Sydney Morning Herald*, 27 September 1996; Jodie Brough, 'Why He's Dead Set Against Mercy Killing', *Sydney Morning Herald*, 17 March 1997 and 'The Day Australians Found Their Voice', *Sydney Morning Herald*, 29 March 1997; Jeff Turner, 'Influence of the Lyons Forum in Senate Vote', *Advertiser*, 26 March 1997; Georgina Windsor and Dennis Shanahan, 'Stone Accuses Secret Forum', *Australian*, 26 March 1997.
7 Quoted in Jodie Brough, 'The Day Australians Found Their Voice', op. cit.
8 Ian Harris, et al. (eds), *House of Representatives Practice*, Canberra: Department of the House of Representatives, 2001, p. 553.
9 Australia, *House of Representatives*, Peter Reith, Second Reading Speech, 5 December 1996; *House of Representatives*, Trish Worth, Second Reading Speech, 6 November 1996.
10 Senator Bob Brown, Dissenting Report appended to Senate Legal and Constitutional Legislation Committee Consideration of Legislation Referred to the Committee: Euthanasia Laws Bill 1996, March 1997, section 2.3.

11 Australia, *House of Representatives*, Peter Costello, Second Reading Speech, 5 December 1996.
12 Australia, *House of Representatives*, Anthony Albanese, Second Reading Speech, 28 October 1996.
13 Australia, *Senate*, 21 August 1996.
14 Senator Kim Carr, interview with author, Parliament House, 30 June 1999.
15 Australia, *Senate*, Senator Bob Brown, 26 March 1997.
16 While in general supporters of the Bill gave their reasons for doing so as including their opposition to euthanasia, while those speaking against it argued in favour of voluntary euthanasia, there were exceptions, such as Senator Bob Collins, who declared his opposition to euthanasia while opposing the Bill as a violation of the Northern Territory's autonomy—see Australia, *Senate*, 25 March 1997.
17 Australia, *Senate*, Grant Chapman, 19 March 1997.
18 Australia, *Senate*, Paul Calvert, 19 March 1997.
19 Australia, *Senate*, Julian McGauran, 20 March 1997.
20 Australia, *Senate*, Barney Cooney, 18 March 1997.
21 Australia, *Senate*, Nick Sherry, 20 March 1997.
22 Australia, *Senate*, Michael Forshaw, 20 March 1997.
23 Australia, *Senate*, Meg Lees, 19 March 1997.
24 Australia, *Senate*, Sue Mackay, 19 March 1997.
25 Australia, *Senate*, Kate Lundy, 20 March 1997.
26 Tambling's status in the Uniting Church in Australia (UCA) is mentioned by Margo Kingston, 'The Fight to Die', op. cit. His position fits with that of other self-proclaimed members of the UCA such as Senator Lees, but not with that of Federal Parliament's only ordained member and the sole Democrat supporter of the Andrews Bill, UCA minister Reverend John Woodley. For a discussion of the theological foundations of the Uniting Church's tradition of reluctance to override personal autonomy on bioethical issues, see Andrew Dutney, 'Uniting Church Teaching on Abortion', *Australian Religion Studies Review*, 11(2), 1998, pp. 72–84 and, on euthanasia, Dutney, *Playing God: Ethic and faith,* Sydney: HarperCollins 2001, pp. 125–45 and Dutney, 'Christian Support for Voluntary Euthanasia', *Monash Bioethics Review*, 16(2), 1997, pp. 15–22. The Senate Legal and Constitutional Legislation Committee noted in a footnote that the Uniting Church's submission was 'less rigid and unequivocal' than those from other churches, but did not quote any of its arguments.
27 Australia, *Senate*, Grant Tambling, 19 March 1997.
28 Australia, *Senate*, Bruce Child, 20 March 1997.
29 Australia, *Senate*, Jocelyn Newman, 20 March 1997.

30 Rosemary Crowley, interview with author, Parliament House, 29 June 1999.
31 Australia, *Senate*, Rosemary Crowley, 18 March 1997.
32 Amanda Vanstone, interview with author, Parliament House, 10 August 1999.
33 Australia, *Senate*, Amanda Vanstone, 18 March 1997.
34 Australia, *Senate*, Bob Brown, 18 March 1997.
35 Australia, *Senate*, Brenda Gibbs, 18 March 1997.
36 Australia, *Senate*, Bruce Child, 20 March 1997.
37 Australia, *Senate*, Kim Carr, 20 March 1997.
38 Isaac Kramnick, et al., *The Godless Constitution: The case against religious correctness*, New York: W.W. Norton, 1996.
39 Kevin Andrews, interview with author, Parliament House, 28 June 1999.
40 Australia, *Senate*, Kate Lundy, op. cit.
41 Brough, 'The Day Australians Found their Voice', op. cit.
42 Michael Gordon, 'The holy alliance', *Weekend Australian*, 29–30 March 1997.
43 Australia, *Senate*, Chris Schacht, 20 March 1997.
44 The brochures are both entitled 'The Lyons Forum'. The version which calls the family 'God-ordained' lists an executive of Miles, Noel Hicks and Bradford. The other version has Kevin Andrews as secretary instead of Bradford, and an additional executive member, Elizabeth Grace.
45 Eric Abetz, interview with author, Parliament House, 24 June 1999. This view was put by a number of Lyons Forum members, including Senator Grant Chapman, Liberal Member for Macquarie Kerry Bartlett and Senator Alan Ferguson.
46 Chris Miles, interview with author, Parliament House, 30 June 1999.
47 Baden Teague, interview with author, College Park, SA, 2 July 1999.
48 John Tierney, interview with author, Parliament House, 22 June 1999.
49 Tim Fischer, interview with author, Parliament House, 24 August 1999.
50 Anthony Albanese, interview with author, Parliament House, 28 June 1999.
51 Ann Burlein, *Lift High the Cross: Where white supremacy and the religious right converge*, Durham: Duke University Press, 2001. On the American Christian Coalition, see William C. Martin, *With God on Our Side: The rise of the religious right in America*, New York: Broadway Books, 1996. Examples of exhortations to evangelical political activists to limit strategically their use of overtly theological language include Thomas C. Atwood, 'Through a Glass Darkly', *Policy Review* (Heritage Foundation), 54, 1990, pp. 34–55 and Charles

Colson, 'Don't Swing That Bible', *Citizen* (Focus on the Family), 5(4), 1991.

Chapter four Mothers and fathers

1. Camilla Nelson, *Perverse Acts*, Melbourne: Text Publishing, 1998. Nelson's allusion to the Lyons Forum was pointed out to me by Rodney Smith, who discusses *Perverse Acts* in relation to Australian politics in Rodney Smith, 'Imagining Australian Republics and Other Institutional Alternatives: Executives and parliaments in recent Australian literary fiction', *43rd Annual Conference of The Australasian Political Studies Association (APSA)*, Brisbane, Australia, 24–26 September 2001, paper online at <www.gu.edu.au/school/ppp/APSA2001/>.
2. Camilla Nelson, *Perverse Acts*, op. cit., pp. 219–20.
3. Margaret Attwood, *The Handmaid's Tale*, London: Virago, 1987.
4. Brian Loughnane, Tim Gartrell and Andrew Bartlett, interviews with Laurie Oakes, *Sunday*, Channel 9, 10 October 2004.
5. Glen Milne, 'Emboldened Howard set to reshape nation', *Sunday Telegraph*, 10 October 2004.
6. Chris Miles, interview with Catherine Job, ABC Radio National, *PM*, 28 September 1995.
7. Nikki Savva, 'The God Squad', *Age*, 2 April 1997; Bronwyn Pike, *A Lyons Share of Power: The influence of the religious right in contemporary Australian politics*, research paper, Melbourne: Evatt Centre, 1997.
8. 'X-rated out: NVE in', *Sydney Morning Herald* (Editorial), 10 June 1997.
9. Quoted in Paul Heinrichs, *Age*, 22 February 1997.
10. Nikki Savva, 'The God Squad', op. cit.
11. Kenneth Davidson, 'Which Families? Exposing the Lyons Forum', *Australian Rationalist*, 43, Autumn/Winter 1997, pp. 2–7.
12. Michael Gawenda, 'The Shadow Boxers of Morality and Policy', *Age*, 10 March 1994.
13. Adele Horin, 'Nominee for Social Post Gets PM Veto', *Age*, 11 May 1999.
14. David Marr, *The High Price of Heaven*, Sydney: Allen & Unwin, 1999, pp. 209–11.
15. For a more extensive list of examples of Howard's intervention to ensure appointment of those who support a conservative social agenda, see Mike Seccombe, 'Howard's Way', *Sydney Morning Herald*, 10 June

1999; Paola Totaro, 'PM Ousts Drug Advisers In Zero-Tolerance Stand', *Sydney Morning Herald*, 19 March 2001.

16 Pamela Williams, *The Victory: The inside story of the takeover of Australia*, Sydney: Allen & Unwin, 1997, p. 159. For discussion of the strategy as populism, see Marian Sawer and Barry Hindess (eds), *Us and Them: Anti-elitism in Australia*, Perth: API, 2004.

17 Eric Abetz, interview with author, Parliament House, 24 June 1999.

18 See press release, Office of the Attorney-General, 17 August 2000.

19 The fiat only applied to the Bishops' claim that the Victorian Act is not inconsistent with the *Sex Discrimination Act*. They were not allowed to put the other part of their proposed argument, namely, that the *Sex Discrimination Act*, although it was passed expressly to give effect to the CEDAW Convention, does not in fact implement the convention successfully. The Bishops had hoped to show that the *Sex Discrimination Act* was invalid legislation. If that argument had been successful, the matter of the *Sex Discrimination Act*'s inconsistency with the Victorian *Infertility Treatment Act* would of course have evaporated.

20 Charles Murray, 'The Time Has Come to Put a Stigma Back on Illegitimacy', *Wall Street Journal*, 29 October 1993.

21 Jodie Brough, 'No marriage, no child: Women face new ban', *Sydney Morning Herald*, 3 April 1997.

22 As well as his co-authored volume, *Social Capital: The individual, civil society and the state*, St Leonards, NSW: Centre for Independent Studies, 1997, Latham has written regularly for the CIS journal *Policy* and delivers occasional CIS lectures. For analysis of Latham's record on matters of gender, sexuality and race, see Carol Johnson, 'From the Suburbs: Mark Latham and the ideology of the ALP', paper presented to the Australasian Political Studies Conference, Hobart, September 2003, <www.utas.edu.au/government/APSA/Cjohnsonfinal.pdf>.

23 See Anne Summers, *The End of Equality: Work, babies and women's choices in 21st century Australia*, Sydney: Random House Australia, 2003, p. 246–7.

24 Eric Abetz, interview with author, Parliament House, 24 June 1999.

25 Pru Goward, 'Agenda', *Age*, 2 March 2003. For discussion see Jennifer Curtin, 'Representing the "Interests" of Women in the Paid Maternity Leave Debate', paper presented to the Australasian Political Studies Association Conference, Hobart, September 2003, <www.utas.edu.au/government/APSA/Jcurtinfinal.pdf>.

26 See Anne Summers, *The End of Equality*, op. cit.

27 Catherine Hakim, *Work-Lifestyle Choices in the 21st Century: Preference theory*, Oxford, UK: Oxford UP, 2000, pp. 84, 243.

28 See for example Susan McRae, 'Choice and constraints in mothers' employment careers', *British Journal of Sociology*, 54 (4), 2003, pp. 585–92.
29 Dennis Shanahan, 'PM Vetoes Maternity Leave Pay', *Weekend Australian*, 1 March 2003.
30 Anne Summers, *The End of Equality*, op. cit., p. 241.
31 Michael Pusey, *The Experience of Middle Australia: The dark side of economic reform*, Melbourne: Cambridge UP, 2003.
32 Catherine Hakim, 'Lifestyle Preferences as Determinants of Women's Differentiated Labor Market Careers', *Work and Occupations*, 29 (4), 2002, pp. 428–59, 442.
33 Catherine Hakim, *Work-Lifestyle Choices in the 21st Century*, op. cit., p. 93.
34 Catherine Hakim, 'A New Approach to Explaining Fertility Patterns: Preference Theory', *Population and Development Review*, 29 (3), 2003, pp. 349–74.
35 Anne Summers, *The End of Equality*, op. cit., pp. 148–53.
36 Elizabeth Hill, 'Government encourages women to work, but not too much else', *Sydney Morning Herald*, 17 May 2004.
37 Camilla Nelson, *Perverse Acts*, op. cit., p. 165.
38 John Howard, interview on *Sunday*, Channel 9, 2 March 2003.
39 Annabel Crabb, 'Overhaul divorce laws, MP urges', *Age*, 5 August 2002.
40 Malcom Turnbull, 'The Tyranny of Proximity: Australia in the 21st century', Vice Chancellor's Sesquicentenary Lecture Series, University of Sydney, 17 September 2002.
41 Malcolm Turnbull, 'Making the case for marriage', *Age*, 24 November 2003.
42 Tony Abbott, interview on *The Insiders*, ABC TV, 21 September 2003.
43 AAP, 'Howard Hits Out at Gay Marriage', *Age*, 5 August 2003.
44 John Howard, Question without Notice: Privilege, *House of Representatives*, 13 March 2002.
45 Linda Doherty, 'Hero or Villain: Heffernan divides Coalition', *Sydney Morning Herald*, 15 March 2002.
46 Jenny Hocking, 'Heffernan's Agenda Fits Howard's Plan', *Age*, 15 March 2002.
47 Cynthia Burack, 'Getting What "We" Deserve: Terrorism, tolerance, sexuality and the Christian right', *New Political Science*, 25 (3), 2003, pp. 329–49, at p. 347.
48 Michael Kirby, 'Justice Kirby's Statement', *Age*, 20 March 2002. That Kirby's mention of prayers was no mere rhetorical flourish is evident from his other statements about his own religious faith. In particular, see Michael Kirby, 'God and Me', Pitt Street Uniting Church, Sydney, 19 March 2004.

49 AAP, 'Latham Vows Compassionate Policies', *Sydney Morning Herald*, 6 December 2003.
50 John Herron, interview with author, Parliament House, 11 August 1999.
51 Alan Ferguson, interview with author, Parliament House, 29 November 1999.
52 Tony Abbott, interview *Sunday*, Channel 9, 14 March 2004.
53 Tony Abbott, 'The Ethical Responsibilities of a Christian Politician', Adelaide University Democratic Club, 16 March 2004.
54 Jason Koutsoukis, 'The Power of Prayer: Politicians who mix church and state', *Financial Review*, 22 January 2004.
55 Mike Seccombe, Aban Contractor and Mark Metherell, 'In God They Trust', *Sydney Morning Herald*, 12 April 2004.

Chapter five Secret politicians' business

1 Gerard Henderson, *A Howard Government?*, Sydney: HarperCollins, 1995, p. 26.
2 ibid., p. 28.
3 ibid., p. 27.
4 Liberal Party of Australia and National Party of Australia, *Future Directions: It's time for plain thinking*, Canberra: The Parties, 1988, pp. 89–90.
5 Geoffrey Blainey, *All for Australia*, North Ryde: Methuen Haynes, 1984.
6 Murray Goot, 'Public Opinion and the Public Opinion Polls' in Andrew Markus and M.C. Rickleffs (eds), *Surrender Australia? Essays in the study and uses of history*, Sydney: George Allen & Unwin, 1985, pp. 49–62.
7 Quoted in Andrew Theophanous, *Understanding Multiculturalism and Australian Identity*, Carlton South: Elikia Books, 1995, p. 113.
8 Paul Kelly, *The End of Certainty*, Sydney: Allen & Unwin, 2nd edition, 1994, p. 428.
9 Pamela Williams, *The Victory: The inside story of the takeover of Australia*, Sydney: Allen & Unwin, 1996, pp. 91–92, 100.
10 John Howard, *The Australia I Believe In: The values, directions and policy priorities of a Coalition government*, 1995, pp. 17–18.
11 Margaret Simons, *The Meeting of the Waters: The Hindmarsh Island affair*, Sydney: Hodder Headline, 2003.
12 Diane Bell, *Ngarrindjeri Wurruwarrin: A world that is, was and will be*, Melbourne: Spinifex, 1998.
13 Roger Sworder, *Mining, Metallurgy and the Meaning of Life*, Sydney: Quakers Hill Press, 1995.

14 Hugh Morgan, 'Landrights: A view', May 1984.
15 Tim Duncan, 'Western Mining's Messiahs of the New Right', *Bulletin*, 2 July 1985, pp. 67–70.
16 Hugh Morgan, 'Reflections on Coronation Hill', Adam Smith Club, 9 July 1991.
17 Hugh Morgan, Opening Address, Returned & Services League Victorian Branch, 78th Annual Conference, 30 June 1993.
18 Hugh Morgan, 'Mabo Reconsidered', Joe and Enid Lyons Memorial Lecture, Australian National University, 12 October 1992.
19 Tim Duncan and Anthony McAdam, 'New Right: Where it stands and what it means', *Bulletin*, 10 December 1985, pp. 38–45.
20 Ron Brunton, 'Blocking business: An anthropological assessment of the Hindmarsh Island dispute', Tasman Institute Occasional Paper B31, August 1995 and 'False culture syndrome', *IPA Backgrounder*, 8 (2), March 1996.
21 Margaret Simons, *The Meeting of the Waters*, op. cit., pp. 176–94.
22 ibid. pp. 64–67, 79.
23 ibid. pp. 103–109.
24 *Adelaide Review*, no. 137, April 1995, p. 15.
25 Andrew Robb, 'Lessons from the 1996 campaign', Address to the Sydney Institute, 1 May 1996, published in *The Sydney Papers*, 8 (2), 1996.
26 Transcript of the Carmen Lawrence Royal Commission, p. 2116.
27 Hendy Cowan, interview on ABC Radio News, 3 May 1995.
28 Roger Price, *House of Representatives*, 27 November 1995.
29 Richard Court, Western Australian *Legislative Assembly*, 25 May 1995.
30 *West Australian*, 22 November 1995.
31 For further discussion of McLachlan's role in the affair, see Margaret Simons, *The Meeting of the Waters*, op. cit.
32 John Howard, Press Release, 10 March 1995.
33 Margaret Simons, *The Meeting of the Waters*, op. cit., p. 286.
34 ibid., pp. 305–15.
35 Press Release from the office of Prime Minister Paul Keating, 21 May 1995.
36 Telephone interview between Michael Symons and Dale Baker, 1996. The information from Baker reported here accords with the account in Margaret Simons, *The Meeting of the Waters*, op. cit., p. 318. See also Michael Symons and Marion Maddox, 'Low Card From the Race Deck', *Age*, 15 February 1997.
37 Christopher Pearson, interview with Michael Symons and Marion Maddox, 1 July 1996.
38 For a close reading of Kenny's role in shaping the raw interview footage, see Marion Maddox, 'How Late Night Theology Sparked a

Royal Commission on Indigenous Australian Beliefs', *Sophia International Journal for Philosophical Theology Cross-Cultural Philosophy of Religion and Ethics*, 36 (2), 1997, pp. 111–35; and Margaret Simons, *The Meeting of the Waters*, op. cit., pp. 323–33.

39 John Howard, 'The Role of Government: A modern Liberal approach' (Headland Speech 1), Menzies Research Centre, 1995 National Lecture Series, 6 June 1995.

40 Michael Gordon, 'Howard's comfort zone', *Weekend Australian*, 17–18 June 1995, p. 25. Howard's simplification ignored several basic facts, including that the developers were in dire financial difficulties well before Tickner's ban. According to statements to the bankruptcy court, the developers' $15.5 million had fallen due on 17 May 1993, but (nearly one year later) no payments had been received and $1.6 million in interest had accrued.

41 Iris Stevens, *Report of the Hindmarsh Island Bridge Royal Commission*, Adelaide, 1995, p. 3.

42 Uniting Church in Australia, '"Rescind Decision to Hold Royal Commission" Say Uniting Church Groups', Media Release, 20 June 1995.

43 South Australian Council of Churches, 'Halt Royal Commission, Says Church Group', News Release, 27 June 1995.

44 Adelaide Diocesan Justice and Peace Commission, News Release, 19 June 1995.

45 Letters from Robert Lawson, Member Legislative Council, to Reverend Dean Brookes, 20 June 1995, and to Most Reverend Leonard Faulkner, 22 June 1995 (original emphasis).

46 Iris Stevens, *Report of the Hindmarsh Island Bridge Royal Commission*, op. cit., p. 246.

47 Robert Lawson, Member Legislative Council, letter to Most Reverend Leonard Faulkner, 22 June 1995, pp. 1–2. The question of how in any case one can determine whether a religious belief has been 'fabricated', and what such 'fabrication' means, see Marion Maddox, 'What is a "Fabrication"? The Political Status of Religious Belief', *Australian Religion Studies Review*, vol. 11, no. 1, 1998, pp. 5–17.

48 Iris Stevens, *Report of the Hindmarsh Island Bridge Royal Commission*, op. cit., p. 241.

49 *Advertiser*, 19 December 1995.

50 Anthony Albanese, *House of Representatives*, Hindmarsh Island Bridge Bill 1996, Second Reading, 6 November 1996, p. 6712.

51 Alexander Downer, interview with author, Parliament House, 1 March 2000.

52 Tony Abbott, interview with author, Parliament House, 24 June 1999.

53 Pamela Williams, *The Victory*, op. cit., p. 130.

54 Andrew Robb, 'Lessons from the 1996 Campaign', Address to the Sydney Institute, 1 May 1996, published in *The Sydney Papers*, 8 (2), 1996.
55 Deborah Jopson, 'Why Aborigines Now Fear the Worst', *Sydney Morning Herald*, 13 April 1996.
56 Lisa McLean, 'Assimilation Policies Still Have Relevance: Herron', *Australian*, 18 June 1996, p. 7.
57 *Australian*, 28–29 June 1996, pp. 6–7.

Chapter six Crossing the floor

1 In common with nominal Anglicans and Presbyterians, nominal Methodists disapproved of anti-Asian racism in the 50 per cent range. But regular attendance increased tolerance in another 22 per cent of Methodists, compared to an 18 per cent effect on Presbyterians, 7 per cent on Anglicans and 6 per cent on Catholics. Catholics are an anomaly in Mol's figures, with irregular attenders disapproving at a higher rate, 63 per cent, than the irregular attenders of other denominations, and the effect of regular churchgoing being more muted, producing 69 per cent disapproval. Hans Mol, *Religion in Australia*, Melbourne: Thomas Nelson, 1971, pp. 69–71.
2 Hans Mol, *The Faith of Australians*, Sydney: George Allen & Unwin, 1985, p. 159.
3 ibid., pp. 160–61.
4 Gordon Dicker, '"Meet the Asians" and extend them the hand of friendship', *Methodist*, 21 August 1954, p. 1.
5 Michael Phillips, 'The Politics and Theology of Aboriginal Reconciliation', PhD Thesis, University of Sydney, 2002, particularly chapter 3.
6 George Browning, interview by ABC TV *7.30 Report*, 20 November 1997.
7 Quoted in *Senate*, Answers to Questions Without Notice: Native Title, 26 November 1997.
8 New South Wales Council of Synod of the Uniting Church, Resolution 269/97S, February 1997.
9 Laurie Brereton, *House of Representatives*, Native Title Amendment Bill 1997: Second Reading, 2 October 1997. See also Kim Beazley, *House of Representatives*, Question Without Notice: Native Title, 25 November 1997.
10 Ron Boswell, interview by ABC TV *7.30 Report*, 20 November 1997.
11 Warren Entsch, interview by ABC TV *7.30 Report*, 20 November 1997.

12 John Howard, 'Churches and the Native Title Debate', Media Release, 20 November 1997.
13 For discussion of the American Christian right's use of this technique, see Ann Burlein, *Lift High the Cross: Where white supremacy and the Christian right converge*, Durham: Duke University Press 2002, pp. 146–49; Cynthia Burack, 'Getting What "We" Deserve: Terrorism, tolerance, sexuality and the Christian right', *New Political Science*, vol. 25, no. 3, September 2003, pp. 343–46.
14 John Howard, interview with Neil Mitchell, ABC Radio 3AW, 8 August 2003.
15 John Howard, *House of Representatives*, Questions Without Notice: Native Title, 20 November 1997.
16 Tim Fischer, *House of Representatives*, Questions Without Notice: Native Title, 25 November 1997.
17 Ann Burlein, *Lift High the Cross*, op. cit.; Cynthia Burack, 'Getting What "We" Deserve', op. cit.
18 Ann Burlein, *Lift High the Cross*, op. cit., pp. 103–06, 144–45.
19 John Howard, 'Transcript of the Prime Minister the Hon. John Howard MP Press Conference, Parliament House, Canberra', 7 November 1997, <www.pm.gov.au/news/interviews/1997/domcon.htm>.
20 ibid.
21 Alexander Downer, interview with author, Parliament House, 1 March 2000.
22 Paul Starick, 'Keep quiet on politics: PM's advice to church leaders', *Advertiser*, 16 February 2004.
23 ibid.; Michael Harvey, 'Howard warns church leaders', *Herald Sun*, 16 February 2004.
24 Alexander Downer, interview with author, op. cit.
25 Alexander Downer, 'Australian Politics and the Christian Church', Sir Thomas Playford Memorial Lecture, University of Adelaide, 27 August 2003.
26 Father Peter Gardiner, letter to the editor, *Advertiser*, 17 February 2004.
27 Rex Jory, 'Howard "Sermon" a Slap at Free Speech', *Advertiser*, 17 February 2004.
28 For example Richard McGregor, 'Crossing the Floor', *Weekend Australian*, 14–15 November 1998.
29 Brendan Nicholson, 'How the PM Nobbled the Bill', *Sunday Age*, 19 March 2000.
30 John Howard, interview by Tony Jones, ABC TV *Lateline*, 6 March 2000.
31 Brendan Nicholson, 'How the PM Nobbled the Bill', op. cit.
32 ibid.
33 Danna Vale, interview with author, Parliament House, 11 May 2000.

34 Margot Kingston, 'Political Lives: Marginal seat report, Hughes', *Sydney Morning Herald* Webdiary, 22 March 2001, <www.smh.com.au/articles/2003/11/21/1069027321297.html>.
35 Danna Vale, interview with author, op. cit.
36 Danna Vale, *House of Representatives*, 'Mandatory Sentencing Legislation: Suspension of Standing and Sessional Orders', 4 April 2000.
37 Danna Vale, interview with author, op. cit.
38 Chris Pyne, *House of Representatives*, 'Mandatory Sentencing Legislation', op. cit.
39 Stuart Rose, 'Is the term spirituality a word that everyone uses but nobody knows what anybody means by it?', *Journal of Contemporary Religion*, 16 (2), 2001, pp. 193–207; Grace Davie, *Religion in Britain Since 1945: Believing without belonging*, Oxford: Blackwell, 1994.
40 Mike Mawson, 'The spirit of religion: Why we should be more religious and less spiritual', paper presented at the 2004 conference of the Australian Association for the Study of Religions, Sydney, July 2004.
41 Gabrielle Chan, 'The high price of power', *Australian*, 23 January 2001.

Chapter seven People like that

1 For example, 'Having the Courage to Face Reality', *Daily Telegraph*, 6 August 2001; Mark Day, 'Tolerance Needs a Reality Check', *Daily Telegraph*, 8 August 2001; Will Temple, 'Gang Admits to Ethnic-Based Rape', *Daily Telegraph*, 11 August 2001; 'Commissioner Warns on Rapes', *Daily Telegraph*, 18 August 2001.
2 Alan Jones, Radio 2UE, 30 July 2001.
3 New South Wales Anti-Discrimination Board, *Race for the Headlines: Racism and media discourse* 2003, p. 58, at <www.lawlink.nsw.gov.au/adb.nsf/pages/raceheadlines>.
4 ibid., p. 60.
5 Ronald Wilson, response to questions following his paper, 'Reconciliation and Human Rights', Fulbright Symposium, University of Adelaide, 14–16 April 1998.
6 Hugh Mackay, *The Mackay Report*, 'Mind and mood', July 2001, pp. 30–31.
7 Quoted in David Marr and Marian Wilkinson, *Dark Victory*, Sydney: Allen & Unwin, 2003, p. 45.
8 ibid., pp. 45–46.
9 Suvendrini Perera, 'A Line in the Sea', *Race & Class*, 44 (2), 2002, pp. 23–39.

10 John Howard, interview on ABC Radio, *The World Today*, 28 August 2001.
11 David Marr and Marian Wilkinson, *Dark Victory*, op. cit., pp. 280–81.
12 Cited in ibid., pp. 189–90.
13 Tali Mendelberg, *The Race Card: Campaign strategy, implicit messages and the norm of equality*, Princeton: Princeton University Press, 2001, pp. 120, 126–27.
14 See for example Janet Albrechtson, 'Talking Race Not Racism', *Australian*, 17 July 2002.
15 Cited in David Marr and Marian Wilkinson, *Dark Victory*, op. cit., p. 279.
16 Anne Summers, *The End of Equality: Work, babies and women's choices in the 21st century Australia*, Sydney: Random House Australia, 2003, p. 107.
17 William Walker, 'Bush's Rhetoric Fuels Violence, Critics Charge: Influence of "war drum" words feared', *Toronto Star*, 19 September 2001.
18 ibid.
19 The phrase was most famously used in Bush's 28 January 2003 State of the Union address, repeated in numerous speeches since.
20 Katherine Shine, 'PM Outraged as Arson Destroys Mosque', *Sun Herald*, 23 September 2001.
21 Human Rights and Equal Opportunity Commission, 'Listen: National consultations on eliminating prejudice against Arab and Muslim Australians', Lakemba, 10 September 2003, <www.humanrights.gov.au> on 10 April 2004.
22 Stephen Hopper, interview by Tracy Bowden, ABC TV *7.30 Report*, 30 October 2002.
23 'Australia: Religious minorities—down and under', *Human Rights Feature* (publication of the Asia Pacific Human Rights Network and Human Rights Documentation Centre), 6 (2), 24–31 March 2003, <www.hrdc.net/sahrdc/hrfchr59/Issue2/Australia.htm> on 10 April 2004.
24 Morgan Poll Finding No. 3566, 'L–NP Jumps in Wake of Terrorist Attack in Bali', 8 November 2002.
25 Mark Riley, Matthew Moore and Paul Daley, 'ASIO Raids Justified, Claims PM', *Sydney Morning Herald*, 2 November 2002; see also 'Australia: Religious minorities—down and under', op. cit.
26 John Howard, interview by John Laws on Radio 2UE, 21 November 2002.
27 Malcolm Farr, 'Chairman John: Howard's revolt against "PC" titles', *Telegraph*, 4 March 1997.

28 Sex Discrimination Amendment (Teaching Profession) Bill 2004. For discussion see Kirsty Magarey, *Bills Digest*, 110, 2003–04, Information and Research Services, Department of Parliamentary Services, at <parlinfoweb.aph.gov.au/piweb/Repository/Legis/Billsdgs/W31C61.pdf> on 15 April 2004.
29 op. cit.
30 Orietta Guerrera and Andra Jackson, 'Minister Urges Watch on Islamic Schools', *Age*, 28 March 2003.
31 Matt McDonald, 'Be Alarmed, Be Very Alarmed: Fear, security and Australia's anti-terrorism kit', unpublished paper presented at Research School of Pacific and Asian Studies, Australian National University, 25 September 2003, p. 5.
32 See for example Jenny Hocking, 'Counter-Terrorism and the Criminalisation of Politics: Australia's new security powers of detention, proscription and control', *Australian Journal of Politics and History*, 49 (3), 2003, pp. 355–71.
33 Leadership profiles are under 'Resources' on the Forum's website at <www.nslf.org.au/>.
34 Peter Costello, 'Address National Student Leadership Forum, Parliament House, Canberra', 12 August 2003, at <www.treasurer.gov.au/tsr/content/speeches/2003/013.asp?pf=1> on 4 December 2003.
35 Editorial, 'Values learnt in schools', *Sydney Morning Herald*, 21 January 2004.
36 Mark Riley, 'Lesson for Latham in school debate', *Sydney Morning Herald*, 25 January 2004.
37 Linda Doherty, 'Class divide: Why parents are choosing private', *Sydney Morning Herald*, 24 January 2004.
38 John Howard, interview with Alan Jones, Radio 2GB, 28 January 2004, at <www.pm.gov.au/news/interviews/Interview659.html> on 21 February 2004.
39 See *Elk Grove Unified School District vs Newdow*, Supreme Court of the United States case no. 02–1624.
40 Mary Diebel, 'Ten Commandment Displays Contested Across the Nation', *Detroit News*, 27 August 2003.
41 The relevant case is *County of Allegheny et al. vs American Civil Liberties Union, Greater Pittsburgh Chapter*, Supreme Court of the United States 492 US 573, 3 July 1989.
42 William Connolly, *Why I Am Not A Secularist*, Minneapolis: University of Minnesota Press, 1999.
43 See for example Roland Robertson, *The Sociological Interpretation of Religion*, Oxford: Basil Blackwell, 1980, pp. 236–37.
44 Linda Doherty, 'Blow-out in private school aid', *Sydney Morning Herald*, 24 June 2003.

45 Kelly Burke, 'Giving children what parents can't—values', *Sydney Morning Herald*, 23 June 2003.
46 Linda Doherty, 'Class divide: Why parents are choosing private', *Sydney Morning Herald*, 24 January 2004. A more cynical view was put by Frank Moorehouse in a *Sydney Morning Herald* opinion piece, arguing that the main 'spiritual value' elite private schools teach, and 'all without having to utter a word', is a sense of superiority and automatic entitlement to privilege, see Frank Moorehouse, 'A sense of privilege poisons our schooling', *Sydney Morning Herald*, 7 April 2004.
47 John Howard, *House of Representatives*, 'Question Without Notice: Education: Funding', 12 August 2004.
48 Australian Association of Christian Schools, *Annual Report* 2002, p. 21.
49 Peter Crimmins, Executive Officer, AACS, telephone interview with author, 7 September 2004.
50 Christian Schools Australia, 'Our Statement of Faith', <www.christianschools.edu.au/Statement_Of_Faith.htm> on 8 September 2004.
51 Ephesians 5.22; Timothy 2:11–12.
52 Greg Roberts, 'Nationals Split Over Faulty First Deal', *Australian*, 8 October 2004.

Chapter eight Think tanks

1 David Barnett, 'Happy 30th, Mr Howard', *Australian*, 18 May 2004.
2 ibid.
3 Summaries of Howard's economic impact are provided, for example, in David Barnett and Pru Goward, *John Howard: Prime Minister*, Ringwood, Vic.: Viking, 1997; and Grattan's chapter on Howard in Michelle Grattan (ed.), *Australian Prime Ministers*, Frenchs Forest, NSW: New Holland, 2000.
4 On the social front, think of books such as David Marr and Marian Wilkinson, *Dark Victory*, op. cit.; Anne Summers, *The End of Equality*, op. cit.; and Robert Manne, *The Howard Years*, Melbourne: Black Inc., 2004.
5 See Judith Brett, 'The New Liberalism', in Robert Manne (ed.), *The Howard Years*, op. cit., pp. 74–93, especially pp. 86–87.
6 Cathy Greenfield and Peter Williams, 'Limiting Politics: Howardism, Media Rhetoric and National Cultural Commemorations', *Australian Journal of Political Science*, 38 (4), 2003, pp. 279–97.

7 William Martin, *With God On Our Side: The Rise of the Religious Right in America*, New York: Broadway Books, 1996, p. 221.
8 Dennis Fox, 'Using the Family to Advance Capitalism', at <www.dennisfox.net/papers/reagan-family.html> on 8 August 2003. On the Labour government's preference for 'families' over 'the family', see Steve Maharey (Minister for Social Development) Media Release, 'Government Wants the Best for all New Zealand Families', 4 December 2003, at <www.beehive.govt.nz/ViewDocument.cfm?DocumentID=18535> on 23 May 2004.
9 See for example Dennis Fox, 'Using the Family to Advance Capitalism', op. cit.
10 Quoted in Jonathan Mozzochi, et al., 'The New Right and the Christian Right', at <www.qrd.org/qrd/www/FTR/newright.html> on 27 November 2003.
11 Alan J. Day (ed.), *Think Tanks: An international directory*, New York: Longmans Current Affairs, 1993.
12 Philip Mendes, 'Australian Neoliberal Think Tanks and the Backlash Against the Welfare State', *Journal of Australian Political Economy*, 51, June 2003, pp. 29–56.
13 William Martin, *With God On Our Side*, op. cit.
14 See Leon Howell, *United Methodism @ Risk: A wake-up call*, Kingston, NY: Information Project for United Methodists, 2003, pp. 16–17.
15 Diane Knippers, 'Greeting from the President', at <www.ird-renew.org/Feedback/FeedbackList.cfm?c=1> on 25 September 2003.
16 Richard John Neuhaus, 'IRD Founding Document: Christianity and Democracy', at <www.ird-renew.org/Feedback/FeedbackList.cfm?c=11> on 25 September 2003.
17 See for example 'Karl Marx or Jesus Christ?', *Reader's Digest*, August 1982; 'Do You Know Where Your Church Dollars Go?', *Reader's Digest*, January 1983.
18 See their respective websites: 'UM Action', at <www.ird-renew.org/About/AboutMain.cfm>, 'Presbyterian Action for Faith and Freedom' at <www.ird-renew.org/Presbyterian/Presbyterianmain.cfm> and 'Episcopal Action', at <www.ird-renew.org/Episcopal/Episcopalmain.cfm>, all on 25 September 2003.
19 IRD, 'Episcopal Action', ibid.
20 IRD United Church Action Subdivision, at <www.ird-renew.org/About/AboutMain.cfm> on 24 May 2003.
21 Leon Howell, *United Methodism @ Risk*, op. cit. Recent examples include the numerous media releases from the IRD United Methodist Action Affiliated Confessing Movement, Renew Network and Good News representatives during the 2004 Methodist General Conference, particularly over the issue of gay and lesbian marriage: 'United

Methodists Become First Mainline Church Against Same Sex Marriage', Press Release, 3 May 2004, at <www.ird-renew.org/About/About.cfm?ID=873&c=43> on 24 May 2004; Rachel Zoll, 'Methodists Divided on Homosexuality Stand', *Boston Globe*, 6 May 2004; Ann Rodgers, 'Women's Division a Divisive Issue for United Methodists', *Pittsburgh Post-Gazette*, 5 May 2004.

22 Acton Institute, at <www.acton.org/policy> on 24 May 2003.

23 William Martin, *With God On Our Side,* op. cit., p. 212.

24 ibid., p. 216.

25 ibid., p. 217.

26 ibid., p. 325.

27 James Dobson and Gary Bauer, *Children at Risk*, Dallas: Word, 1990.

28 Martin op. cit., p. 307.

29 ibid.

30 Discussed in Katherine Yurica, *The New Messiahs*, at <www.yuricareport.com/Art%20Essays/The%20New%20Messiahs%20Excerpts.htm> on 23 May 2004.

31 William Martin, *With God On Our Side*, op. cit., p. 308.

32 ibid., p. 318.

33 ibid., p. 330.

34 Ken Baker, letter to the author, dated 30 May 1996.

35 For example Ron Brunton, 'The Significance of Shallow Traditions: The RAC on Aboriginal Interests in Kakadu', *Environmental Backgrounder*, 5, 15 May 1991; Ron Brunton, 'The False Culture Syndrome', *IPA Backgrounder*, 8 (2), March 1996.

36 Journalist Andrew Clark attributes the CIS's social policy push to a suggestion by right wing opinion columnist Padraic McGuinness. See Andrew Clark, 'In Their Own Image', *Australian Financial Review* (Magazine), 23 February 2001.

37 'History of CIS', at <www.cis.org.au/CISinfo/history.htm>; W. Da Silva, 'The New Social Focus', *Australian Financial Review (*Magazine), June 1996.

38 Geoffrey Brennan, with John K. Williams and W.R. Stent, *The Christian and the State*, CIS Occasional Papers 7, St Leonards, NSW: Centre for Independent Studies, 1983.

39 Anglican Church of Australia—Social Responsibility Commission, Catholic Commission for Justice and Peace, Australian Council of Churches and Uniting Church in Australia—Assembly Committee for Social Responsibility, *Changing Australia*, Blackburn, Vic.: Dove Communications, 1983.

40 Centre for Independent Studies, *Religion and the Free Society: Educating the Churches in the Principles and Processes of the Free Economy. Proposal for an Initial Program 1999–2001*, Section III.

41 ibid., Section I.
42 Available at <www.cis.org.au/> on 25 September 2003.
43 ibid.
44 Tasman Institute Ltd and Tasman Asia Pacific Pty Ltd, *Tasman Institute Annual Review*, November 1995, p. 2.
45 ibid.
46 ibid.
47 ibid., inside front cover.
48 See Bennelong Society, at <www.bennelong.com.au/pages/ben-aboutus.html> on 10 October 2003.
49 See Australian Council for Educational Standards, at <www.samuelgriffith.org.au/papers/html/volume11/v11app1.htm> on 10 October 2003.
50 See Galatians Group, *The Utopian Quest for Social Justice*, Proceedings of the Galatians Group Conference, August 1996, Armadale, VIC: The Galatians Group, 1996, pp. vii–ix.
51 Galatians 3:28.
52 Max Champion, 'Forword', *The Churches: Native to Australia or Alien Intruders?,* Proceedings of the Inaugural Conference of the Galatians Group, Clunies Ross Convention Centre, Melbourne, 15 and 16 August 1994, Holden Hill (SA): The Publisher, 1994, p. v.
53 See Galatians Group, *The Utopian Quest for Social Justice*, op. cit.
54 Peter McGauran, quoted in Nikki Savva, 'Mutterings Over a Modest Dinner', *Sun*, 18 October 1986, p. 6; see also Gary Sturgess, 'Move for a Body of Modest Members', *Bulletin*, 2 June 1981.
55 Sam Gregg, Address to the Society of Modest Members, Parliament House, Canberra, 15 February 1999.
56 Alan Wood, 'Captain gone from the bridge', *Australian*, 4 July 2000.
57 See William Martin, *With God On Our Side*, op. cit., pp. 332–35; and Linda Kintz, *Between Jesus and the Market: The emotions that matter in right wing America*, Duke University Press, 1997, especially chapters 6 and 7.
58 See Gerard Henderson, 'Wind of Change Ruffles Liberal Thinking', *Sydney Morning Herald*, 5 December 2000.
59 Peter Costello, interview by ABC Radio National, *Background Briefing*, 4 March 2001.
60 Peter Costello, Address to National Day of Thanksgiving Commemoration, Scots Church, Melbourne, 29 May 2004.
61 Justin Norrie, 'Costello heads to the Hills', *Age*, 6 July 2004.
62 Diana Bagnall, 'The New Believers', *Bulletin*, 11 April 2000.
63 Ken Coghill (ed.), *The New Right's Australian Fantasy*, Fitzroy: McPhee Gribble, 1986, pp. 23–24.

64 David Clarke, interview by ABC Ratio National, *The Religion Report*, 12 May 2004.
65 'In God they trust', *Sydney Morning Herald*, 12 April 2004.
66 ibid.
67 'Profit for Prophets', SBS TV *Insight*, 5 June 2003, viewable online at <www.sbs.com.au/insight/archive.php3?archive=1&artmon=6&arty=2003#>.
68 Bagnall op. cit.

Chapter nine Church, state and charity

1 John Howard, interview, Tweed Heads Civic Centre, 2 May 1995.
2 Louise Boylen, 'Churches Take on the Politicians', *Financial Review*, 18 December 1992.
3 See Don Watson, *Recollections of a Bleeding Heart: A portrait of Paul Keating PM*, Milsons Point, NSW: Random House, 2002, pp. 89–94.
4 Gerard Henderson, *Menzies' Child: The Liberal Party of Australia 1944–1994*, St Leonards, NSW: Allen & Unwin, 1994, p. 303.
5 Geoff Kitney, 'Libs' Attack on Church Just What PM Was Praying For', *Financial Review*, 13 October 1992.
6 Michelle Grattan, 'Keating Enters Fray in Church Battle Against Food Tax', *Age*, 12 October 1992.
7 Geoff Kitney, 'Libs' Attack on Church Just What PM Was Praying For', op. cit.
8 Moira Byrne, 'The Holy Lobby', unpublished honours thesis, Flinders Unversity, 1998, pp. 33–34.
9 See for example Don Aitkin, *Stability and Change in Australian Politics*, Canberra: Australian National University Press, 1982; Clive Bean, 'The Forgotten Cleavage? Religion and Politics in Australia', *Canadian Journal of Political Science*, vol. 32, no. 2, 1999, pp. 551–68; Hyam Gold, 'Religious Practice and Anti-Labor Partisanship: A class-based analysis', *Politics*, 14, 1979, pp. 47–54; David Kemp, *Society and Electoral Behaviour in Australia: A study of three*, St Lucia, QLD: University of Queensland Press, 1978; Hans Mol, *Religion in Australia*, Melbourne: Thomas Nelson, 1971 and *The Faith of Australians*, North Sydney: George Allen & Unwin, 1985; Ian McAllister, *Political Behaviour: Citizens, Parties and Elites in Australia*, Melbourne: Longman Cheshire, 1992, pp. 139–42; Tim Prenzler, 'The Influence of Religion in Australia', *The Australian Journal of Politics and History*, vol. 38, no. 2, 1992, pp. 274–88; Don Rawson, 'Australian Churches and Parties', paper presented to a seminar on Churches and Social Policy,

Research School of Social Sciences, Australian National University, December 1993. For an alternative explanatory framework, see Judith Brett, *Australian Liberals and the Modern Middle Class*, Melbourne: Melbourne University Press, 2003. For figures on party allegiance by religion in the 1996 election, and discussion, see Rodney Smith, *Australian Political Culture*, Frenchs Forest, NSW: Pearson Education 2001, pp. 264–77.

10 Rodney Smith, *Australian Political Culture*, op. cit, pp. 262–63.

11 J.D. Bollen, *Protestant Churches and Social Reform in New South Wales 1890–1910*, Carlton, VIC: Melbourne University Press, 1972, pp. 15–23.

12 Richard Ely, *Unto God and Caesar: Religious Issues in the Emerging Commonwealth 1891–1906*, Melbourne: Melbourne University Press, 1976, p. 5. The seeds of this stance were well-established in a number of Christian denominations.

13 Graham Maddox draws attention to John Wesley's advocacy of government responsibility to address the structural causes of unemployment and working-class poverty in the late eighteenth century in 'John Wesley and the Spirit of Capitalism', *Australian Religion Studies Review*, 11 (2) 1998, pp. 85–97; see also Graham Maddox (ed.), *The Political Writings of John Wesley*, Bristol: Thoemmes Press, 1998.

14 See for example John Howard, 'Fair Australia: Address to the Australian Council of Social Service' (Headland Speech 3), Sydney, 13 October 1995; Address to Benevolent Society's Sydney Leadership Dinner, Sydney Town Hall, 13 March 2001.

15 'Less cash for student de factos', *Advertiser*, 5 September 1997. See *Student and Youth Assistance (Sex Discrimination Amendment) Act 1997*.

16 Kirsten Lawson and Verona Burgess, 'Fahey Spares Govt Jobs Agency', *Canberra Times*, 10 February 2000.

17 John Howard, Launch of the Wesley Mission's Easter Appeal, Wesley Mission Centre, Sydney, 8 April 2004, at <www.pm.gov.au/news/speeches/speec784.html> on 23 April 2004.

18 Tony Abbott, interviewed by ABC TV *7.30 Report*, 7 January 2000.

19 Alan Cadman, *House of Representatives*, Appropriation Bill (No. 3) 1999–2000, Second Reading, 16 February 2000, p. 13561.

20 Peter Costello, 'Is Faith a Lost Cause?', address to Anglicare Lunch, WatersEdge, Pier One, Walsh Bay, Sydney, 27 June 2003.

21 Tony Abbott, 'Mutual Obligation and the Social Fabric', Bert Kelly Lecture to the Centre for Independent Studies, 3 August 2000.

22 Tony Abbott, 'The Moral Case for the Howard Government', Speech to Young Liberals, 23 January 2004.

23 Peter Costello, 'Is Faith a Lost Cause?', op. cit.

24 ibid.

25 ibid.

26 Peter Costello, interview with Sally Loane, Radio 2BL, 27 June 2003.
27 Alexander Downer, 'Australian Politics and the Christian Church', Sir Thomas Playford Memorial Lecture, University of Adelaide, 27 August 2003.
28 Alexander Downer, 'The Myth of Little Australia', speech to the National Press Club, 26 November 2003.
29 Quoted in David Marr and Marian Wilkinson, 'Howard, Beazley Lashed Over Race', *Sydney Morning Herald*, 8 November 2001.
30 Renee Barnes and Tim Clarke, 'Double Refugee Intake: Church Head', *Sydney Morning Herald*, 19 October 2003.
31 Paul Starick, 'Keep Quiet on Politics', *Advertiser*, 16 February 2004.
32 See Janet Albrechtsen, 'We're All Sinners to These Fanatics', *Australian*, 30 July 2003, p. 11; Andrew Bolt, 'Clerical Errors', *Herald Sun*, 1 September 2003, p. 19.
33 Rev. Dr William Ullathorne, *The Catholic Mission in Australia*, Sydney: A. Cohen, 1837.
34 Rev. Dr William Ullathorne, *The Horrors of Transportation*, Dublin: Richard Coyne, 1838.
35 Michael Hogan, *Australian Catholics: The social justice tradition*, North Blackburn, VIC: Collins Dove, 1993, p. 4. See also Dom Edward Cuthbert Butter, *The Life and Times of Bishop Ullathorne*, vol. 1, London, 1926, p. 104.
36 D.W.A. Baker, *Preacher, Politician, Patriot: A life of John Dunmore Lang*, Carlton South, VIC: Melbourne University Press, 1998, pp. 51, 54–56. See also John Dunmore Lang, *Transportation and Colonization*, London and Edinburgh: A.J. Valpy and Bell and Bradfute, 1837.
37 D.W.A. Baker, *Preacher, Politician, Patriot*, op. cit., p. 118.
38 ibid., p. 208.
39 See John Dunmore Lang, 'An Anatomical Lecture on the New Constitution', delivered at the Royal Australian Circus, Sydney, 17 January 1854, reproduced in David Headon and Elizabeth Perkins (eds), *Our First Republicans, John Dunmore Lang, Charles Harpur, Daniel Henry Deniehy: Selected writings 1840–1860*, Leichhardt, NSW: The Federation Press, 1998, pp. 47–54, at pp. 47–48.
40 John Dunmore Lang, *The Coming Event! Or, Freedom and Independence for the Seven United Provinces of Australia*, Sydney: John Sherriff, 1870, pp. 124–29.
41 ibid., p. 130 (italics in original).
42 D.W.A. Baker, *Preacher, Politician, Patriot*, op. cit.
43 Arnold Hunt, *This Side of Heaven: A history of Methodism in South Australia*, Adelaide: Lutheran Publishing House, 1985, p. 181.

44 Walter Phillips, *Defending 'A Christian Country': Churchmen and society in New South Wales in the 1880s and after*, St Lucia, QLD: University of Queensland Press, 1981.
45 Richard Ely, *Unto God and Caesar*, op. cit., pp. 7–8.
46 Joan Mansfield, 'The Social Gospel and the Church of England in New South Wales in the 1930s', *Journal of Religious History*, vol. 13, no. 4, 1985, pp. 411–33, at p. 413.
47 John Howard, Press Release, Leader of the Opposition, 21 February 1996.
48 see <unitingcarenswact.org.au/library/globalisation/MAIBSRDr.PDF> on 4 September 2003.
49 National Council of Churches in Australia, 'A Covenant for Employment: A position paper of the National Council of Churches in Australia', September 1999 at <www.ncca.org.au/departments/social_justice_network/documents_and_statements/Employment> on 3 September 2003. For detailed discussion of the principles guiding such ecumenical theological interventions, see Ann Wansborough, 'Speaking Together: A methodology for the National Council of Churches' contribution to public policy debate in Australia', unpublished PhD thesis, University of Sydney, 2000.
50 Michelle Grattan, 'Forced Work for Dole Immoral: Church', *Sydney Morning Herald*, 28 August 2000.
51 Tony Abbott, Media Release, 'Job Network 2 Boosts Regional Australia', 3 December 1999 and appended Key Points Fact Sheet.
52 Paul Osborne, 'Editing a Church Newspaper' in Robyn Douglas (ed.), *Directory of Christian Press*, Australasian Religious Press Association, 1999, pp. 8–10.
53 Tim Costello, *Tips From a Travelling Soul-Searcher*, St Leonards, NSW: Allen & Unwin, 1999, p. 77.
54 ibid.
55 ibid. Preece's account of WorkVentures is in Gordon Preece, *Changing Work Values: A Christian response*, Brunswick, Vic.: Acorn Press, 1995.
56 The allusion is to Matthew 6:41.
57 Peter Costello, speech to Salvation Army Red Shield Appeal Launch, Melbourne, 16 April 2002, at <www.treasurer.gov.au/tsr/content/speeches/2002/002.asp?pf=1> on 4 December 2003.
58 see <www.salvationarmy.org.uk/en/Library/publications/salvationist/2002/01–05/2002.01.05salvationist_05–01–2002_p4.xml.htm> on 4 December 2003.
59 Peter Costello, interview with Sally Loane, 2BL, 27 June 2003.
60 Jenness Gardener, Community and Public Sector Union, telephone interview with author, 19 May 2000.

61 Jim Pietrowski, Australian Services Union, personal communication with author. It is difficult to arrive at a precise percentage since, owing to the categories in which Australian Bureau of Statistics figures are recorded, the number of workers for church and charity organisations overall is not available. Moreover, the direct and indirect impact of volunteer workers in church and charity organisations is difficult to assess, given that volunteers are not eligible for union membership. Thus, Pietrowski calculated a unionisation rate of, at most, twenty per cent but cautioned that, for the reasons outlined, this is likely to be a substantial overestimate.

62 Tony Abbott, interview with ABC TV *7.30 Report*, 7 January 2000.

63 For example see 'Churches Blur Roles on Jobless Deal', *Canberra Times*, 8 January 2000.

64 Ray Cleary, interview with ABC Radio National, *Religion Report*, 24 March 1999.

65 ibid.

66 Charities Bill 2003. For comment see 'Democrats Remain Suspicious of Govt's Charities Definition', *The World Today*, ABC Radio, 30 July 2003; 'Charities Face Ban From Political Lobbying', ABC TV, *Lateline*, 31 July 2003.

67 Kenneth Davidson, 'The Insidious Silencing of Dissent', *Age*, 3 June 2004.

68 'The Greens Position . . . Shut Up or Shut Down! Charities Bill 2003—Affects Soup Kitchens to Environment Centres', at <www.bobbrown.org.au/300_campaigns_sub.php?&deptItemID=17> on 16 April 2004.

69 National Council of Churches of Australia, 'Submission by the Commission for Christian World Service, National Council of Churches in Australia, to the Board of Taxation regarding the Charities Bill 2003', September 2003, at <www.ncca.org.au/christianworldservice/at_work_in_australia/acfoa/charities_> on 17 April 2004.

70 IPA Media Release, August 2003.

71 <www.bobbrown.org.au/300_campaigns_sub.php?&deptItemID=17>.

72 Institute of Public Affairs, 'Submission to the Board of Taxation, *Draft Charities Bill 2003*', October 2003.

73 Peter Costello, 'Building Social Capital Requires Trust and Participation Among Individuals', address to the Sydney Institute, 16 July 2003. See also Peter Costello, 'The Spirit of the Volunteer', Inaugural Sir Henry Bolte Lecture, Caulfield Racecourse, Melbourne, 15 August 2001.

Chapter ten God under Howard

1 This form is still used in the Senate (see *Standing Orders and Other Orders of the Senate February 2000*, Senate Table Office, Canberra, 2000, p. 37). The House of Representatives uses a slightly edited form: 'Almighty God, we humbly beseech Thee to vouchsafe Thy blessing upon this Parliament. Direct and prosper our deliberations to the advancement of Thy glory, and the true welfare of the people of Australia.' (See *House of Representatives Standing and Sessional Orders As At 1 February 2000*, Department of the House of Representatives, Canberra, 2000, p. 14.) Both houses use the form of the Lord's Prayer from the *Book of Common Prayer* (1662).

2 Lisa Getter, 'Showing Faith in Discretion', *Los Angeles Times*, 27 September 2002.

3 See Norman Grubb, *Modern Viking: The story of Abraham Vereide, pioneer in Christian leadership*, Grand Rapids: Zondervan, 1961.

4 ibid.

5 Jeffrey Sharlet, 'Jesus Plus Nothing', *Harper's*, March 2003 available at *Harper's Online*, <www.harpers.org/JesusPlusNothing.html?pg=1>.

6 ibid.

7 Lisa Getter, 'Showing Faith in Discretion', op. cit.

8 Leslie Synn, 'Q&A with Jeffrey Sharlet', 21 March 2003, at <www.mediabistro.com/articles/cache/a46.asp> on 5 May 2004.

9 ibid.

10 Lisa Getter, 'Showing Faith in Discretion', op. cit.; Jeffrey Sharlet, 'Jesus Plus Nothing', op. cit. The allusion is to Matthew 6:1–4.

11 Lisa Getter, 'Showing Faith in Discretion', op. cit.

12 ibid. Jeffrey Sharlet, 'Jesus Plus Nothing', op. cit.

13 'Kenya Holds First National Prayer Breakfast', *Catholic World News*, 2 June 2003, at <www.cwnews.com/news/storytools.cfm?task=print&recnum=22705> on 19 May 2004.

14 'Bishop Mambo Organizes First Zambian National Prayer Breakfast', *Faith News Network*, 5 May 2004, at <www.faithnews.cc/articles.cfm?sid=4279> on 19 May 2004.

15 The description 'faith-based diplomacy' comes from former Family board member and head of the Washington-based International Centre for Religion and Diplomacy Douglas Johnson, cited in Lisa Getter, 'Showing Faith in Discretion', op. cit.

16 Jeffrey Sharlet, 'Jesus Plus Nothing', op. cit.

17 2 Samuel 12:1–18.

18 Jeffrey Sharlet, 'Jesus Plus Nothing', op. cit.

19 Jeffrey Sharlet, Interview with Guerrilla News Network, 'Meet the "Family": Undercover Among America's Secret Theocrats', at <www.guerrillanews.com/counter_intelligence/doc1760.html> on 5 May 2004.
20 Jeffrey Sharlet, 'Jesus Plus Nothing', op. cit.
21 Katherine Yurica, 'The Despoiling of America', *Yurica Report*, 11 February 2004, at <www.yuricareport.com/Dominionism/TheDespoilingOfAmerica.htm> on 13 May 2004.
22 Matthew 5:17–20.
23 Katherine Yurica, 'The Despoiling of America', op. cit.
24 *Constitution Reformation Act of 2004*, H.R. 3799, S 2082, February 2004.
25 Chuck Baldwin (conservative talk show host and former Florida Moral Majority leader), quoted in Katherine Yurica, 'New Dominionist Bill Limits the Supreme Court's Jurisdiction', 19 February 2004, at <www.yuricareport.com/Dominionism/ConstitutionRestorationAct.htm> on 13 May 2004.
26 James Heflin, 'Their Will Be Done: Creating a Theocracy in America', *Valley Advocate*, 25 March 2004, at <www.valleyadvocate.com/gbase/News/content?oid=oid: 59396> on 16 May 2004.
27 See Timothy D. Terrell, 'An Ally For Change', *Chalcedon Report*, 23 October 2002.
28 See J. Esmond Birnie, 'Testing the Foundation of Theonomy and Reconstruction', *Scottish Bulletin of Evangelical Theology*, 15, 1997, pp. 8–26; Glen Peoples, 'Theonomy Defended: A Response to J. Esmond Birnie', *Theonomy Online*, at <theonomy.orcon.net.nz/Birnie.html> on 19 May 2004.
29 William Martin, *With God On Our Side,* op. cit., p. 354.
30 ibid.
31 See for example Rob Boston, *The Most Dangerous Man in America? Pat Robertson and the Rise of the Christian Coalition*, Amherst, NY: Prometheus, 1996; Frederick Clarkson, *Eternal Hostility: The struggle between democracy and theocracy*, Monroe, ME: Common Courage, 1977; Sara Diamond, *Roads to Dominion: Rightwing movements and political power in the US*, New York: Guilford Press, 1995; Shadia B. Drury, *Terror and Civilisation: Christian politics and the Western psyche*, New York: Palgrave Macmillan, 2004.
32 Andrew Buncombe, 'Thou shalt be like Bush', *New Zealand Herald*, 1 May 2004.
33 The quotation is from Bush's remarks at a church service commemorating the 11 September victims and is recorded, among other sources, in the PBS documentary *The Jesus Factor*, screened in the USA in May 2004.

34 Rick Perlstein, 'The Jesus landing pad: Bush White House checked with rapture Christians before latest Israel move', *Village Voice*, 18 May 2004.
35 Antonin Scalia, 'God's Justice and Ours', *First Things* 123, May 2002, pp. 17–21, at <www.firstthings.com/ftisshes/ft0205/articles/scalia.html> on 16 May 2004.
36 George Monbiot, 'US Christian fundamentalists are driving Bush's Middle East policy', *Guardian*, 20 April 2003.
37 Ray Evans, 'Gnosticism and the High Court of Australia' in Max Champion (ed.), *Surrendered Values: The challenge for church and society*, Proceedings of the Galatians Group Conference, August 1998, Armadale, VIC: The Galatians Group, 1998, pp. 27–45. A version also appeared in *Quadrant*, 40 (6), 1999, pp. 20–26.
38 ibid., p. 34.
39 See for example Ray Evans, 'Social Justice and Millennarianism' in *The Utopian Quest for Social Justice*, Proceedings of the Galatians Group Conference, August 1996, Armadale, VIC: The Galatians Group, 1996, pp. 151–58.
40 Gil Duthie, *I Had 50,000 Bosses: Memoirs of a Labor Backbencher, 1946–1975*, Sydney: Angus and Robertson, 1984, p. 243.
41 At <www.pcf.org.au/pcf/> on 18 April 2001.
42 Diana Bagnall, 'The New Believers', *Bulletin*, 11 April 2000.
43 ibid.
44 Luke 12:33–34.
45 Luke 19:24–25.
46 Matthew 6:24–34.
47 See <www.orangebaptistchurch.org.au/Sermons/Incarnational%20 Ministry.htm> on 4 June 2004.
48 Robert Griffith, 'Leadership in Our Nation', Sermon preached in Orange Baptist Church, NSW, 30 September 2001 at <www.orangebaptistchurch.org.au/Sermons/LeadershipinourNation.htm> on 4 June 2004.
49 See <http: //www.robertgriffith.net/about_robert.asp> on 4 June 2004.
50 Robert Griffith, 'Campaign update' email, quoted in Alan Ramsey, 'Blue ribbon said "In with best show"', *Sydney Morning Herald*, 17 September 2004.
51 Griffith, 'Leadership in Our Nation', op. cit.
52 'National Prayer Breakfast', *Family World News*, December 2003, at <www.pastornet.au/fwn/2003/dec/art15.html>; 'The Superintendent Writes', 9 November 2003, at <www.wesleymission.org/ministry/superwrites/031109.asp> on 24 May 2004.

53 Ramon Williams, 'Governor General Launches National Day of Thanksgiving', *Australian Christian Channel*, at <www.acctv.com.au/articledetail.asp?id=2607> on 19 May 2004.
54 Gordon Moyes, 'Superintendent Writes', 29 February 2004, at <www.wesleymissio.org.ministry/superwrites/040229.asp>. The Australian proposal mirrors the 53-year-old American National Day of Prayer, devoted to nationalistic prayers for 'our troops, our leaders and our nation', held on the first Thursday each May—see <www.nationaldayofprayer.org/campaign> on 7 May 2004.
55 Bruce Baird, *House of Representatives*, Adjournment: Korea: Visit, 1 June 2000.
56 Address by His Excellency Major General Michael Jeffery AC CVO MC Governor-General of the Commonwealth of Australia on the occasion of an afternoon tea for Asia Pacific Leaders who attended the National Prayer Breakfast, 3 November 2003.
57 Luke McIlveen, 'MPs Paid To Go On Holy Missions', *Australian*, 14 April 2003.
58 See 1 Corinthians 16:22.
59 Fred Nile, 'An Inspiring Korean Experience', *Family World News*, September 2001, at <www.pastornet.net.au/fwn/2001/sep/art01.html> on 24 May 2004.
60 Robert Griffith, 'Christian Leadership in our Nation', op. cit.
61 Kevin Rudd, interview with author, Parliament House, 15 February 2000.
62 ibid.
63 Danna Vale, interview with author, Parliament House, 11 May 2000.
64 Harry Quick, interview with author, Parliament House, 15 February 2000.
65 Karin Sowada, interview with author, Sydney University, 21 July 1999.
66 Jeffrey Sharlet, 'Jesus Plus Nothing', op. cit.; Lisa Getter, 'Showing Faith in Discretion', op. cit.
67 Form letter signed 'Dr Brendan Nelson MP, Federal member for Bradfield, on behalf of the Parliamentary Hosts', 23 February 1998.
68 Lisa Getter, 'Showing Faith in Discretion', op. cit.
69 ibid.
70 For example, publicity materials for the 1998 Forum list 42 Parliamentary Hosts: 27 Liberal, 4 National, 3 Democrat and 8 ALP.
71 See Brendan Nelson, *House of Representatives*, 'Adjournment: National Student Leadership Forum on Faith and Values', 11 December 1996.
72 Promotional blurb for Cameron's address to the Gymea Baptist Church Men's Breakfast, 29 April 2001, at <www.gymeabaptist.org.au/mens_brekky.htm> on 9 May 2004.

73 Jock Cameron, interview with author, Parliament House, 6 December 1999.

74 According to acknowledgements by Major General Michael Jeffery, Address to the National Prayer Breakfast. Full text in 'Governor General addresses National Prayer Breakfast', *Insights Magazine*, 4 November 2003 at <nsw.uca.org.au/news/2003/gg-prayer-breakfast-_04–11–03.htm> on 12 August 2003.

75 Ross Cameron, interview with author, Parliament House, 11 August 1999. Latham describes himself as an agnostic—see 'Latham Vows Compassionate Policies', *Age*, 6 December 2003; Paul Daley, 'The Making of Mark Latham', *Bulletin*, 12 May 2004; Gay Alcorn, Malcolm Schmidtke and Liz Minchin, 'Apocalypse Now? The Westie Who Wants the Lodge', *Age*, 13 March 2004.

76 Michael Duffy, *Latham and Abbott*, Sydney: Random House Australia, 2004, pp. 271, 357.

77 Ross Cameron, interview with the author, op. cit.

78 Ross Cameron, *House of Representatives,* Adjournment: National Student Leadership Forum on Faith and Values, 2 April 1998, p. 2430.

79 See Brij V. Lal, 'Rabuka: No Other Way' (Review), *The Journal of Pacific History,* vol. 35, no. 3, December 2000, p. 319.

80 Jock Cameron, interview with author, Parliament House, 6 December 1999.

81 Leslie Synn, 'Q&A with Jeffrey Sharlet', 21 March 2003, at <www.mediabistro.com/artic.es/cache/a46.asp> on 5 May 2004. On the continuing push for Fiji to embrace theocracy, see for example 'Religious Groups Uneasy Over Call For Christian State in Fiji', Radio Australia News, 21 August 2003, at <www.abc.net.au/ra/newstories/RANewsStories_929229.htm> on 16 May 2004.

82 The reference is to Paul's instruction to itinerant Christian missionaries to earn their keep rather than sponge off their hosts.

83 Ross Cameron, interview with author, op. cit.

84 Amos 2:6–16.

85 Matthew 6:24.

86 Matthew 21:12–17.

87 Karl Polanyi, *The Great Transformation*, New York: Beacon Books, 1957 [1944], p. 130.

88 ibid., p. 133.

89 ibid., p. 135.

90 Harvey Cox, 'The Market as God: Living in the New Dispensation', *Atlantic Monthly,* 283 (3), March 1999.

91 Karl Marx, 'Contribution to the Critique of Hegel's Philosophy of Right' in *K. Marx and F. Engels on Religion*, Moscow: Foreign Languages Publishing House, 1955 [1844], p. 41.

92 Michael Symons, 'Australian Public Holidays and the Disenchantment of the Calendar' in Anthony Corones, et al., *Food in Festivity: Proceedings of the fourth symposium of Australian gastronomy*, Sydney, October 1988, p. 151.
93 Quoted in Judith Brett, *Age*, 24 September 1996.
94 Department of Employment, Workplace Relations and Small Business, Issues Paper, Regulatory Review of the *Affirmative Action (Equal Opportunity for Women) Act 1986*, March 1998.
95 Steven Ciobo, First Speech to Parliament, 13 February 2002.
96 *Compass*, op. cit.
97 See Helen Irving, 'A True Conservative?' in Robert Manne (ed.), *The Howard Years*, Melbourne: Black Inc., 2004, pp. 94–118; David Marr and Marian Wilkinson, *Dark Victory*, op. cit., pp. 102–28, 144–46.

Epilogue

1 *Constitutional Convention (2nd to 13th February 1998) Transcript of Proceedings*, p. 796. For more detailed discussion of the preamble debate, see chapter two of Marion Maddox, *For God and Country: Religious dynamics in Australian federal politics*, Canberra: Department of the Parliamentary Library, 2001.
2 ibid. The recommendations for the Preamble that survived were: introductory language in the form 'We the people of Australia'; reference to the origins of the Constitution, and acknowledgement that the commonwealth has evolved into an independent, democratic and sovereign nation under the Crown; recognition of our federal system of representative democracy and responsible government; affirmation of the rule of law; acknowledgement of the original occupancy and custodianship of Australia by Aboriginal peoples and Torres Strait Islanders; recognition of Australia's cultural diversity; affirmation of respect for our unique land and the environment; reference to the people of Australia having agreed to re-constitute our system of government as a republic; and concluding language to the effect that '[We the people of Australia] asserting our sovereignty, commit ourselves to this Constitution'. Three additional points were recommended for consideration by Parliament: affirmation of the equality of all people before the law; recognition of gender equality; and recognition that Aboriginal people and Torres Strait Islanders have continuing rights by virtue of their status as Australia's Indigenous peoples. See Resolutions B 1–10, C 1, 2 and 4, D 2 and 3, Minutes of Day 8, Constitutional Convention, Old Parliament House, 2–13 February 1998, at <www.

dpmc.gov.au/convention/report2/minutes8.htm>. The Convention also passed two restraints on a new Preamble: 'the Preamble should state that it not be used to interpret the other provisions of the Constitution'; and 'care should be taken to draft the Preamble in such a way that it does not have implications for the interpretation of the Constitution'.

3 ibid., p. 426.

4 Karin Sowada, 'One Christian's View of the Convention', *Southern Cross*, vol. 4, no. 2, March 1998, p. 17.

5 The existing phrase, 'humbly relying on the blessing of Almighty God', is known as the recognition clause, following the nineteenth century constitutional conventions' debates as to whether God should be 'invoked' or only 'recognised'.

6 Other members of the subgroup were Mr Adam Johnston, Ms Dannalee Bell and Ms Lucinda Bell, who was note-taker.

7 *Constitutional Convention (2nd to 13th February 1998) Transcript of Proceedings*, p. 425.

8 ibid., p. 425.

9 ibid., p. 427.

10 ibid., p. 429.

11 ibid., p. 527.

12 ibid. (The reference is to Exodus 3:14.)

13 ibid.

14 *Constitutional Convention*, *Transcript of Proceedings*, op. cit., pp. 480–81.

15 Baden Teague, interview with author, College Park, South Australia, June 1999.

16 For example, Marguerite Scott, Constitutional Convention Transcript of Proceedings, op. cit., p. 477.

17 ibid., p. 425.

18 ibid., p. 435.

19 Other speeches making this point include Tasmanian Greens Leader Christine Milne, ibid., p. 429.

20 ibid., p. 426.

21 ibid.

22 ibid., p. 799.

23 For discussion see Richard Ely, *Unto God and Caesar*, op. cit.

24 A. Castles, *An Australian Legal History*, Sydney: The Law Book Company, 1982, pp. 532–34; J. Maloney, *An Architect of Freedom: John Hubert Plunkett in New South Wales 1832–1869*, Canberra: Australian National University Press, 1973, pp. 135–36.

25 W. Holdsworth, *A History of English Law*, vol. viii (2nd edition), London: Methuen, 1937, p. 411.

26 See Douglas Pike, *Paradise of Dissent: South Australia 1829–1857*, London: Longmans; Green & Co., 1957, pp. 20–21.
27 Mark 9:24
28 *Constitutional Convention, Transcript of Proceedings*, op. cit., p. 428.
29 ibid., pp. 480–81.
30 Karin Sowada, 'Defining a Role for the Church in Australian Political Life', Lecture 4, Halifax–Portal Lectures 2002, <www.aceir.cathcomm.org/aceir/Halifax-Portal/2002_4.shtml>.
31 Baden Teague, interview with author, College Park, South Australia, 2 July 1999.
32 Confirmed by telephone call to his office, 15 February 2000.
33 Ross Cameron, interview with author, Parliament House, 11 August 1999.
34 The democratic argument need not, of course, be atheistic; it just says that the nature of political power is a question of a different order from theological debate. Observers since at least the early nineteenth-century visit of Alexis de Tocqueville have pointed out that American republicanism has historically been underpinned by religion. See Alexis de Tocqueville, *Democracy in America* (2 vols), New York: Alfred A. Knopf, 1953 [v. 1 1835, v. 2 1840].
35 Karin Sowada, 'God and the Republic', <www.anglicanmedia.com.au/old/cul/sowada.htm>.
36 Alasdair Webster, *Constitutional Convention Transcript of Proceedings*, op. cit., 5 February 1998, p. 200.
37 As argued, for example, by Mark McKenna, *The Captive Republic: A history of republicanism in Australia 1788–1996*, Cambridge: Cambridge University Press, 1996, pp. 256–59; Malcolm Turnbull, *The Reluctant Republic*, Port Melbourne, VIC: William Heinemann, 1993, pp. 6–7; Kate Carnell, 'A Test of Maturity' in John Uhr (ed.), *The Case for Yes*, Leichhardt, NSW: The Federation Press, 1999, pp. 13–14; Amanda Vanstone, 'The People's Debate', in John Uhr (ed.), *The Case for Yes*, op. cit., p. 29.
38 Helen Irving, 'A True Conservative?' in Robert Manne (ed.), *The Howard Years*, op. cit., pp. 108–109.
39 'Speech by His Excellency Major General Michael Jeffery, AC CVO MC (Ret'd), Governor-General of the Commonwealth of Australia, at a Western Australian Newspaper Leadership Events Program "Leadership Matters" Breakfast, Hyatt Regency Hotel, Perth, February 2004', at <www.gg.gov.au/speeches>.
40 John Locke, *Two Treatises of Government and A Letter Concerning Toleration*, edited and with an introduction by Ian Shapiro, Yale University Press, 2003.
41 Alexis de Tocqueville, *Democracy in America*, op. cit., pp. 305–306.

42 *Lemon vs Kurtzman* 406 US 602 (1971); *County of Allegheny vs American Civil Liberties Union* 493 US 573 (1989).

43 William E. Connolly, *Why I Am Not A Secularist*, Minneapolis: University of Minnesota Press, 1999.

44 W.K. Hancock, *Australia*, London: Ernest Benn, 1930.

45 Geoffrey Barnes and Chris Ridings, 'The Founding of United Theological College, New South Wales', Part 2, *Church Heritage*, 10 (3), 1998, p. 151.

46 'Universities' qv in A. Chisolm (ed.), *The Australian Encyclopaedia in Ten Volumes*, Sydney: The Grollier Society of Australia.

47 Melbourne College of Divinity, *Manual for BD, DipTheol, DipLS*, Kew, Vic.: Melbourne College of Divinity, 1996–1997, p. i.

48 Quoted in 'The Jesus Factor', PBS *Frontline*, screened in the USA and Canada in early May 2004. Transcript at <www.pbs.org/wgbh/pages/frontline/shows/jesus/etc/script.html>.

49 For a sample of such debates, see Lawrence Stenhouse, Gajendra Verma, Robert Wild and Jon Nixon, *Teaching About Race Relations: Problems and effects*, London: Routledge and Kegan Paul, 1982; Louise Derman-Sparks and Carol Brunson Phillips, *Teaching/Learning Anti-Racism: A developmental approach*, New York: Teacher's College Press, 1997.

Index